AIDA Europe Research Series on Insurance Law and Regulation

Volume 15

The AIDA Europe Research Series on Insurance Law and Regulation is the first book series of its kind and area of specialization. It comprises volumes on topics researched and written with an international, comparative or European perspective.

The regulatory response to the financial crisis in 2008 has pushed towards the adoption of transnational principles and rules also in the field of insurance by encouraging the convergence of national regulations to common regulatory framework. The need for a common legal language emerges to fully understand the process of transnational convergence in place and its impact on national legislation. On the other hand, persisting national peculiarities must be examined in the light of the transnational convergence of rules and concepts. Moreover, new risks, business practices and customers' issues are emerging worldwide, so requiring increasingly global responses.

The scope of the series is to bring together academics, practitioners and policy makers in order to exchange views and approaches to the topics concerned, which are based on the new transnational dimension of insurance law, business and regulation. All contributions are peer reviewed.

Helmut Heiss • Martin Lorenzon
Ann-Catherine Nabholz • Marta Ostrowska
Editors

Insurance Ombudsman Schemes

A Comparative Analysis

Springer

Editors
Helmut Heiss
University of Zurich
Zürich, Switzerland

Ann-Catherine Nabholz
Head of Process Management
Ombudsman of Private Insurance
and of Suva
Zürich, Switzerland

Martin Lorenzon
Ombudsman of Private Insurance
and of Suva
Zürich, Switzerland

Marta Ostrowska
University of Zurich
Zürich, Switzerland

ISSN 2662-1770 ISSN 2662-1789 (electronic)
AIDA Europe Research Series on Insurance Law and Regulation
ISBN 978-3-032-01499-3 ISBN 978-3-032-01500-6 (eBook)
https://doi.org/10.1007/978-3-032-01500-6

This Springer imprint is published by the registered company Springer Nature Switzerland AG
The registered company address is: Gewerbestrasse 11, 6330 Cham, Switzerland

Contents

Part I Generalities

1 Introduction ... 3
Helmut Heiss
1.1 Personal Preliminary Remarks ... 3
1.2 The Topic ... 5
1.3 The Concept: Comparative Law ... 7
1.4 Outlook ... 9
Annex: Questionnaire ... 9
References ... 14

2 Law-based Ombudsman Schemes ... 15
Jaana Norio
2.1 Introduction ... 15
2.2 Where It All Started: Protection of Individuals Against Public Authorities ... 17
2.3 Specific Ombudsman Schemes ... 22
2.4 General Features and Distinctions ... 46
Legal Sources ... 49
Documents ... 52
References ... 52

3 On Union Law Concerning Alternative Dispute Resolution Methods with Regard to Insurance Disputes ... 53
Jens Gal
3.1 Introduction ... 53
3.2 ADR Directive ... 54
3.3 ODR Regulation ... 59
3.4 IDD ... 61
3.5 Solvency II System ... 62
3.6 EIOPA Regulation ... 63
3.7 Varia ... 64

3.8 Conclusion ... 68
Legal Sources ... 69
Documents ... 70
References ... 71

Part II Comparative Analysis

4 Insurance Ombudsman Schemes ... 75
Marta Ostrowska
4.1 Introduction ... 75
4.2 Institutional Framework of the Ombudsman Schemes ... 78
4.3 Insurance Ombudsman Jurisdiction ... 89
4.4 Procedure: The Art of Dispute Resolution ... 93
4.5 Market Trends and Practical Observations ... 102
4.6 Beyond the Numbers: What Insurance Ombudsman Complaints Reveal About Market Dynamics ... 103
4.7 Measuring Effectiveness of Insurance Ombudsman Schemes ... 105
4.8 Consumer Awareness and Accessibility of Insurance Ombudsman Schemes ... 108
4.9 Conclusive Remarks: A Reflection on the Evolution and Future of Insurance Ombudsman Schemes ... 108

Part III Country Reports

5 Belgium ... 113
Laurent de Barsy
5.1 Institutional Framework ... 113
5.2 Insurance Ombudsman Jurisdiction ... 118
5.3 Procedure ... 119
5.4 Statistical Data ... 124
5.5 Insurance Ombudsman Practice ... 124
5.6 Accessibility and Accountability ... 126
Legal Sources ... 126

6 Croatia ... 129
Loris Belanić and Hrvoje Pauković
6.1 Institutional Framework ... 129
6.2 Insurance Ombudsman Jurisdiction ... 137
6.3 The Procedure ... 140
6.4 Statistical Data ... 149
6.5 Insurance Ombudsman Practice ... 150
6.6 Accessibility and Accountability of the Ombudsman Scheme ... 156
6.7 Conclusion ... 157
Legal Sources ... 158
References ... 159

7 **Finland** 161
Anu Koskenvuo
7.1 Introduction 161
7.2 Insurance Ombudsman Jurisdiction 169
7.3 Procedure 170
7.4 Statistical Data 179
7.5 Insurance Ombudsman Practice 179
7.6 Other 181
Legal Sources 182
Documents 182
References 182

8 **France** 183
Arnaud Chneiweiss
8.1 Institutional Framework 183
8.2 Insurance Ombudsman Jurisdiction 189
8.3 Procedure 192
8.4 Statistical Data 197
8.5 Insurance Ombudsman Practice 199
8.6 Other 201
Legal Sources 203

9 **Germany** 205
Wilhelm Schluckebier and Constantin Graf von Rex
9.1 Institutional Framework 205
9.2 Insurance Ombudsman Jurisdiction 212
9.3 Procedure 214
9.4 Statistical Data 218
9.5 Insurance Ombudsman Practice 219
9.6 Accessibility and Accountability 221
Legal Sources 222
Documents 223
Reference 223

10 **Ireland** 225
Sadhbh Kurzawska
10.1 Institutional Framework 225
10.2 Jurisdiction 237
10.3 Procedure 243
10.4 Statistical Data 255
10.5 Insurance Ombudsman Practice 259
10.6 Other 264
Legal Sources 268
Documents 268

11 Netherlands 271
Eveline Ruinaard and Colinda Guijt
11.1 Institutional Framework 271
11.2 Procedure 282
11.3 Statistical Data 295
11.4 Complaints About Insurance 296
11.5 Other 298
Legal Sources 300
Literature 301

12 Poland 303
Michał Ożóg, Paweł Rokosz, and Karolina Mendecka
12.1 Introduction 303
12.2 Historical Development 304
12.3 The Insurance Ombudsman in Poland 304
12.4 The Polish Financial Ombudsman: A New Quality of Consumer Protection 306
12.5 Statutory Position of the Financial Ombudsman Service 308
12.6 Competences of the Financial Ombudsperson: General Remarks 311
12.7 The Financial Ombudsman's Intervention Measures 317
12.8 Complaints Handling Process and Requests for Out-of-Court Dispute Resolution 319
12.9 Summary 330
References 331

13 Spanish System 333
Juan Bataller Grau
13.1 Introduction 333
13.2 Legal System 334
13.3 The Insurer's Complaints Service and Ombudsperson 340
13.4 Claims Before the Claims Service of the DGSFP 343
13.5 The Proposed Independent Authority 347
13.6 Conclusion: A Critique of the Spanish System 350
References 351

14 Switzerland 355
Martin Lorenzon and Ann-Catherine Nabholz
14.1 Institutional Framework 355
14.2 Insurance Ombudsman Jurisdiction 363
14.3 Procedure 366
14.4 Statistical Data 376
14.5 Insurance Ombudsman Practice 377
14.6 Accessibility and Accountability 379
References 380

Part I
Generalities

Chapter 1
Introduction

Helmut Heiss

1.1 Personal Preliminary Remarks

43 years ago, from 7 to 9 October 1982 to be precise, a joint German-Austrian conference on the subject of "Legal Protection in Private Insurance Matters: Civil Court - Supervisory Authority - Ombudsman?"[1] was held at the University of Innsbruck under the direction of *Fritz Reichert-Facilides*.[2] *Oscar Schürch*, the private insurance ombudsman in Zurich at the time, gave a lecture on his experiences.[3] Another presentation was devoted to a comparative overview of the insurance ombudsman in European countries.[4] It was particularly striking that a private insurance ombudsman had existed as an alternative form of dispute resolution in Zurich since 1972, which was lacking in both Austria and Germany and, it must be said quite clearly from today's perspective, was also vehemently rejected by the insurance industry at the time.

In initiating this conference, Reichert-Facilides took an important step towards the academic study of a phenomenon that had previously received too little

[1] See Reichert-Facilides (1984).

[2] *24 October 1929 - †23 October 2003 (see https://www.ius.uzh.ch/de/staff/professorships/alphabetical/heiss/projects/peicl/whoweare/fritzreichert-facilides.html. Accessed 16 Apr 2025); Full Professor of Law at the University of Innsbruck (1970–1998).

[3] Schürch in Reichert-Facilides (1984), p. 98.

[4] Burger, Der Versicherungsombudsmann in europäischen Staaten - eine vergleichende Übersicht, in Reichert-Facilides (1984), p. 56 ff.

H. Heiss (✉)
University of Zurich, Zürich, Switzerland
e-mail: helmut.heiss@ius.uzh.ch

H. Heiss et al. (eds.), *Insurance Ombudsman Schemes*, AIDA Europe Research Series on Insurance Law and Regulation 15,
https://doi.org/10.1007/978-3-032-01500-6_1

attention, at least in German-speaking countries: the "ombudsman". The idea was so inspiring that shortly afterwards Reichert-Facilides and his colleagues in Innsbruck initially created an informal "European Ombudsman Academy", which was institutionalised in 1988 in the form of an association as the "European Ombudsman Institute". The website[5] of this still highly active institute bears witness to the visionary act of its founding fathers. The ombudsman has demonstrated its role as a key institute for ensuring a fair balance of interests between parties across a wide variety of sectors, in particular in public administration and the private sector.

The author of this introduction began his academic career in September 1985 as a doctoral researcher and assistant at Fritz Reichert-Facilides' Chair. Since the materials for the conference had only just been published (1984) and the founding work for the later European Ombudsman Institute was in full swing, he also came into contact with the topic of the insurance ombudsman. He was fascinated by the topic and later on always dealt with it in his lectures on private insurance law at the Universities of Greifswald (1999–2004), Mannheim (2004–2007) and Zurich (since 2007). It was particularly fortunate that after moving to the University of Zurich, contact was also established with the Ombudsman for Private Insurance and SUVA,[6] Mr *Martin Lorenzon*.[7] The author of these lines would like to take this opportunity to thank Mr *Lorenzon* most sincerely for taking on the task of teaching students about the Swiss experience with the ombudsman system as part of the lecture on private insurance law.

These personal observations also explain the genesis of this volume: the idea for it was born out of contact with the Swiss insurance ombudsman. The fact that this project could be realised in cooperation with the Zurich insurance ombudsman *Martin Lorenzon* is particularly pleasing, not least because the Zurich ombudsman's office had previously been involved in the conference at the University of Innsbruck in 1982. No less important is the fact that two co-editors and co-authors, *Marta Ostrowska*[8] and *Ann-Catherine Nabholz*,[9] have given the project decisive impetus both academically and organisationally.

The joint project of this volume thus represents an ideal joint venture between academia and practice, on a topic that cannot be adequately explored without the involvement of practitioners and which, from an academic perspective, is urgently waiting to be addressed. The integration of this project into the work of the Insurance Law Special Interest Group (Insurance Law SIG) of the European Law Institute in Vienna[10] therefore seems particularly fortunate, as does the participation of the

---

[5] www.eoi.at. Accessed 16 Apr 2025.

[6] Schweizerische Unfallversicherungsanstalt, the Swiss Social Accident Insurance Institution.

[7] See https://versicherungsombudsman.ch/ueber-uns/. Accessed 16 Apr 2025.

[8] Dr. iur., postdoctoral researcher and lecturer, secretary-general of the PRICL project, Law Faculty, University of Zurich, www.ius.uzh.ch/en/staff/professorships/alphabetical/heiss/team/martaostrowska.html. Accessed 16 Apr 2025.

[9] Dr. phil.I, Head of Process Management, Ombudsman for private insurance and SUVA.

[10] For this SIG and the "Insurance Ombudsman Schemes" project, see www.europeanlawinstitute.eu/hubs-sigs/sigs/insurance-law-sig/. Accessed 16 Apr 2025.

ombudsman's offices from nine countries via the Swiss ombudsman, *Martin Lorenzon*. Their reports provide the "live soundtrack", so to speak, of the ombudsman system in the reporting countries.

The four members of the editorial team would like to thank the authors of this volume in particular. They undertook the task of answering an extensive and highly detailed questionnaire in the form of country reports, thereby creating the basis for the comparative law report contributed by *Marta Ostrowska*. The editors are no less grateful to the authors of the special reports on historical and EU law aspects of the subject and on the ongoing efforts to create an insurance ombudsman in Spain. These reports round off and complete the comparative view of the country reports.

We would also like to thank the European Chapter of AIDA[11] and the Chairperson of its Scientific Committee, *Pierpaolo Marano*,[12] for including this volume in the "AIDA Europe Research Series on Insurance Law and Regulation".[13] As a result, this work is gaining visibility in academia and practice, especially internationally.

It would be a great pleasure if this volume were to be well received by the readership and thus contribute to the dissemination of the ombudsman idea. It would be even more gratifying if this work were to inspire other authors to take a closer look at the insurance ombudsman.

1.2 The Topic

The topicality of the subject of "legal protection in private insurance matters" is unbroken and the figure of the insurance ombudsman is still an insufficiently researched institution. The occurrence of an insured event marks the beginning of a particularly vulnerable phase of the contractual relationship for the insured person. The direct consequences of an insured event occurring, which can range from the death of loved ones and disability to existentially threatening loss of assets, weigh heavily on the shoulders of the insured person. At the same time, the occurrence of an insured event marks the moment of truth for the insurance cover and the loyalty of the insurance company. Gaps in cover and the insurance company's reluctance to settle claims increase the vulnerability of the insured person. In contrast, strong insurance cover and loyal behaviour on the part of the insurance company can reduce or even contain vulnerability. If differences of opinion and therefore problems arise during this vulnerable phase, effective legal protection for the insured is of crucial importance. The insurance supervisory authorities are generally unable to provide this, as they are not usually appointed to pursue claims from individual policyholders. In principle, the civil courts are called upon to do so. However, their proceedings are usually formal, lengthy and costly. While insurance companies also

[11] Association Internationale de Droit des Assurances/The International Insurance Law Association.

[12] Prof. Dr., Milan, for details see https://aidainsurance.org/people/pierpaolo-marano. Accessed 16 Apr 2025.

[13] See www.springer.com/series/16331. Accessed 16 Apr 2025.

have staying power in court proceedings, time and money play an eminent role for policyholders. In this respect, the need for an informal, quick and inexpensive or even free procedure is obvious, especially in insurance matters. This applies in particular to consumer insurance.[14]

It is therefore not surprising that ombudsman schemes have been created in numerous countries that are exclusively or at least also responsible for insurance matters. This applies not only to the European legal systems examined in this volume, but worldwide. In contrast, it is surprising that these systems of alternative dispute resolution in insurance matters have not received much attention from legal scholars. When *Judith P. Summer*'s dissertation on "Insurance Law and the Financial Ombudsman Service" was published in 2010, the author justified her choice of topic as follows: "This book was inspired through frustrating years as a solicitor advising clients about insurance claims going before the Financial Ombudsman Service without any text book guidance or discussion being available".[15] And in a special Foreword to this work, *Walter Merricks*, Chief Ombudsman 1999–2009 says: "This pioneering book breaks new ground. It represents the first serious attempt to analyze the work of the Financial Ombudsman Service, and it does so by putting it in the context of insurance law".[16] This finding contrasts drastically with the real significance of the Ombudsman Service: "The Ombudsman Service has become, by virtue of the cost-free consumer access, *de facto* almost the exclusive forum for adjudication of insurance disputes".[17] The conclusion is therefore not surprising: "It is therefore all the more important that legal researchers and commentators take serious note of the ombudsman jurisdiction".[18]

Little has changed in this regard since the publication of the aforementioned work. Ombudsman schemes in matters relating to insurance only occasionally receive in-depth academic attention, such as in the volume "Alternative Dispute Resolution Systems Regarding Private Insurance" published in 2014 by *Samim Unan* on behalf of the Turkish Chapter of AIDA.[19] There are also a few monographs, such as the aforementioned doctoral thesis by *Judith P. Summer* and another by *Thomas v. Hippel* from 2000, which also offers a legal comparison.[20] There is therefore reason to revisit the topic and give it new impetus through a comparative analysis.

[14] On the importance of ombudsman schemes in consumer insurance already Heiss, General Report, in: Heiss (2012), p. 7, #.

[15] Summer (2010), p. vii (Preface).

[16] Merricks, Foreword, in: Summer (2010), p. v.

[17] Merricks, Foreword, in: Summer (2010), p. v.

[18] Merricks, Foreword, in: Summer (2010), p. v.

[19] AIDA Turkey, Alternative Dispute Resolution Systems Regarding Private Insurance, Istanbul 2014.

[20] von Hippel (2000).

1.3 The Concept: Comparative Law

1.3.1 Working Method: Questionnaire—Country and Special Reports—Comparative Law Report

This volume aims to deal with the topic of the insurance ombudsman from a comparative law perspective. To this end, it makes use of a traditional comparative law working method. The editors have drawn up a questionnaire which is intended to guarantee, as far as possible, a uniform structure and comparable content of the individual country reports.[21] To a certain extent, the questionnaire also helps to ensure that the terminology used is as uniform as possible, unless national patterns of terminology have made it necessary to deviate. The questionnaire included six sections covering areas such as institutional framework, jurisdictional scope, funding mechanisms, procedural rules and operational practices. It combines both general and detailed questions to ensure a nuanced understanding of each jurisdiction's specific scheme while maintaining comparability. To guarantee consistency, rapporteurs were asked to focus specifically on the insurance sector, even if their ombudsman offices handled a broader range of financial services.

The country reports on nine national ombudsman schemes in Europe fulfil a dual function. On the one hand, they provide information on the respective national ombudsman scheme. Secondly, they provide the basis for the comparative law report that builds on them. They therefore serve both as a practical report and as the basis for a scientific comparison. The same applies to the special reports on historical and EU law issues relating to the ombudsman scheme and on Spain's efforts to create an insurance ombudsman.

The comparative law report highlights the similarities and differences between the national ombudsman schemes. It also repeatedly comments on the functionality of the different systems. However, the comparative law report largely refrains from evaluating the different systems as "better" or "worse". Each reader may make such an assessment for themselves, but it can only be scientifically justified if a uniform and consistent assessment criterion is applied. For example, if the ombudsman scheme were based on the enforcement of rights in favour of the consumer, ombudsman offices with decision-making powers would prove to be superior. However, the opposite would be the case if the focus were primarily on mediation and arbitration between consumers and insurance companies. In this case, the ombudsman model, which acts as a mediator rather than a decision-maker in disputes, would be preferred.

[21] The questionnaire is printed as an appendix to this introduction.

1.3.2 The European Focus and the Choice of Jurisdictions Represented in the Analysis

This comparative law book draws on nine country reports covering nine European jurisdictions: Belgium, Croatia, Finland, France, Germany, Ireland, the Netherlands, Poland, and Switzerland. Each country has a well-established insurance ombudsman scheme, which allowed the study to be structured around a unified questionnaire, simplifying the comparison process.

The study is geographically focused on Europe to limit variations and ensure comparability. European countries have a relatively long history of consumer protection, comparable cultural, legal and economic background, and a regulatory environment that is largely harmonised by EU membership (with Switzerland as a notable exception) or regional cooperation through bodies, such as FIN-NET or a European network of ADR entities. This shared foundation allows for meaningful comparison, while still allowing for an exploration of differences in how insurance ombudsman schemes are implemented.

The selection of jurisdictions reflects those that represent various regions of Europe and have agreed to participate in the study. The Roman legal systems are well-represented by the reports from France, Belgium, and the Netherlands. The Germanic legal tradition is covered through the reports from Germany and Switzerland. Finland exemplifies the Nordic legal systems, while Croatia and Poland represent Central and Eastern Europe. Finally, beyond continental Europe, the Irish report introduces a common law perspective.

1.3.3 Limitations

Yet, despite its comprehensive approach, this analysis is not without its limitations. First, the reliance on structured questionnaires means that the data's accuracy depends on the thoroughness and interpretation of the rapporteurs. Variations in how questions were understood or answered could have led to inconsistencies, and in some cases, key questions were left unanswered, limiting direct comparison.

Second, the study encountered challenges due to differences in legal terminology and concepts across jurisdictions. Terms used in one legal system may not have an exact equivalent in another, and even seemingly identical terms can carry different implications depending on their regulatory context.

Third, the study was limited to jurisdictions that agreed to participate, meaning it excludes potentially informative examples from non-participating countries. As a result, the country reports are best understood as case studies rather than definite regional models and any attempt to extrapolate broader regional trends from these findings should be met with caution.

Lastly, while the study provides a detailed look at legal and procedural frameworks, it does not fully address consumer satisfaction or the real-world effectiveness of these schemes. Future research could complement this analysis by incorporating more empirical approach.

1.4 Outlook

The findings of this comparative study have practical implications beyond academic curiosity. For countries without an insurance ombudsman scheme, the report may offer a blueprint for creating an effective dispute resolution body based on tested models. For those already with existing ombudsman institutions, the analysis may serve as a benchmarking tool, helping policymakers and regulators to assess, refine, and enhance their current systems by adopting best practices observed in other countries.

Although this study focuses primarily on institutional design and procedures, it also raises questions that warrant further exploration. For instance: How do various procedural frameworks affect consumer satisfaction and insurer compliance? To what degree does ombudsman activity influence market behavior and regulatory reforms? By addressing these questions, future research could shed light on the broader effects of these schemes on consumer protection and insurance market dynamics.

Annex: Questionnaire

1. Institutional Framework		
Please describe the legal nature and the institutional framework of the Insurance Ombudsman office. You may consider the following questions as guidance in drafting your report.		
1.1	Establishment	
	1.1.1	When was the Insurance Ombudsman scheme established? What is/was the background of establishing the scheme?
	1.1.2	Is the Insurance Ombudsman scheme established by law or voluntarily (e.g., by industry)?
	1.1.3	If the Insurance Ombudsman is established by law, please indicate the regulatory framework for its activity.
	1.1.4	If the Insurance Ombudsman is established voluntarily, please specify by whom and whether it is subject to standards laid down by law and/or overseen by the financial regulator?

(continued)

(continued)

1. Institutional Framework		
1.2	Governance model	
	1.2.1	Is there a governance body to oversee the operations of the Insurance Ombudsman scheme (a board/a council)? If so, please describe its composition and appointment of its members.
1.3	Coverage	
	1.3.1	Is the Insurance Ombudsman scheme exclusively for the insurance sector or does it cover different financial sectors? If so, which sectors?
1.4	Insurance business covered	
	1.4.1	Are insurance businesses[22] under an obligation to participate in the Insurance Ombudsman scheme?
	1.4.2	If so, is that by law, as a condition of a regulatory license or a result of membership of an industry association?
1.5	Appointment of the Ombudsperson	
	1.5.1	Who can be appointed as Insurance Ombudsman? What requirements must a candidate for the Insurance Ombudsman meet?
	1.5.2	How is the Insurance Ombudsman appointed and on what terms?
	1.5.3	What is the term of office and is the term subject to renewal?
	1.5.4	Is it possible to remove the Insurance Ombudsman early? If so, under which circumstances and who may take such a decision?
1.6	Funding	
	1.6.1	How is the Insurance Ombudsman budget raised?
	1.6.2	Is the Insurance Ombudsman funded by the state (out of taxation) or by a financial regulator (out of its budget)?
	1.6.3	Are the complaints free of charge?
	1.6.4	Is the Insurance Ombudsman funded by the industry? If so, on what terms? If the Insurance Ombudsman is funded by case fees payable by the insurance businesses, are there any "free" cases per year offered to the insurance businesses?
1.7	Insurance Ombudsman functions	
	1.7.1	What are the main functions of the Insurance Ombudsman?
	1.7.2	Does the Insurance Ombudsman play any role in educating customers with regard to their financial capabilities?
	1.7.3	Does the Insurance Ombudsman assist the early resolution of cases by insurance businesses through e.g., publishing details of the Insurance Ombudsman's approach to common disputes, giving advice to complainants and financial services businesses on its approach, helping train insurers etc.?
1.8	Insurance Ombudsman Office	
	1.8.1	What is the Insurance Ombudsman's staff structure?
	1.8.2	How many investigators (case analysts) does the Insurance Ombudsman office employ? How many of them have legal education background?
	1.8.3	Are the Insurance Ombudsman office's employees required to undertake ongoing training to develop their skills and knowledge?

(continued)

[22] 'Insurance business' is insurance company, insurance agent and insurance broker.

(continued)

2. Insurance Ombudsman Jurisdiction		
Please describe the Insurance Ombudsman's jurisdictional scope. You may consider the following questions as guidance in drafting your report.		
2.1	Substantive scope	
	2.1.1	How is the Insurance Ombudsman substantial scope of jurisdiction defined?
	2.1.2	Which activities are covered by the Insurance Ombudsman scheme?
	2.1.3	Is the Insurance Ombudsman's role limited to disputes based on existing contracts or does it extend to commercial decisions (such as the acceptance of the risk, pricing of the premium, discrimination etc.)?
	2.1.4	Is the Insurance Ombudsman entitled to handle enquiries as well as disputes?
	2.1.5	Is there a minimum amount for claims that can be referred to the Insurance Ombudsman?
2.2	Personal scope	
	2.2.1	Who can file a complaint? Are small businesses considered consumers? Does the Insurance Ombudsman accept complaints from prospective customers as well?
	2.2.2	Which insurance businesses are covered by the Insurance Ombudsman scheme?
2.3	Territorial scope	
	2.3.1	How is the territorial jurisdiction of the Insurance Ombudsman determined? Does the Insurance Ombudsman's jurisdiction depend on the place where the activity complained about was performed, the habitual residence of a complainant or another factor?
2.4	Time limits	
	2.4.1.	Is there a time limit within which complaints must be made to the Insurance Ombudsman?

3. Procedure		
Please describe the main characteristics of the complaint handling process. You may consider the following questions as guidance in drafting your report.		
3.1	Regulatory framework	
	3.1.1	What are the applicable procedural rules?
	3.1.2	Are the procedural rules set by law or by the Insurance Ombudsman?
3.2	Complaint and enquiry handling process	
	3.2.1	Please describe the steps of the complaint handling process. Does it involve conciliation/mediation? How and by whom are cases decided?
	3.2.2	Is the complaint handling an informal or formal process?
	3.2.3	May the Insurance Ombudsman initiate a proceeding ex officio?
	3.2.4	Are consumers allowed to jointly submit their complaints to the Insurance Ombudsman (collective proceedings)? If so, what are the requirements?
	3.2.5	How are the complaints received?
	3.2.6	Does submission of a complaint to the Insurance Ombudsman interrupt the limitation period for bringing a claim to court?
	3.2.7	Please describe the enquiry handling process, if one exists.

(continued)

(continued)

3. Procedure		
3.3	Admissible complaints	
	3.3.1	Is there a definition of a complaint? What are the requirements for a complaint to be considered admissible?
	3.3.2	Are consumers required to take their complaint to the insurance business first? If so, are there rules (and time limits) for complaint-handling by insurance business? Please specify.
	3.3.3	Is there a minimum amount for which claims can be referred to the Insurance Ombudsman?
	3.3.4	May the Insurance Ombudsman dismiss the complaint without considering its merits (early dismissal)? If so, when?
3.4	Obtaining information and collecting evidence	
	3.4.1	How does the Insurance Ombudsman collect the information and evidence necessary to decide a case?
	3.4.2	Does the Insurance Ombudsman have power to require information and documents relevant to decide a case? If so, from whom and/or on what terms?
	3.4.3	Is the insurance business obliged to provide information upon the Insurance Ombudsman's request? If so, what are the consequences of failing to comply?
	3.4.4	Does the Insurance Ombudsman's request override any duty of confidentiality that insurance businesses owe to any third party?
3.5	Outcome of the process	
	3.5.1.	What is the outcome of the complaint and/or enquiry handling process? Does the Insurance Ombudsman issue a decision/recommendation/opinion, etc.? Please specify. If the outcome is a decision issued by the Insurance Ombudsman, please see Sect. 3.6 below. Otherwise, please describe the nature and the main characteristics of the relevant outcome. You may consider the questions from Sects. 3.6 and 3.7 as guidance in drafting your report.
3.6	Insurance Ombudsman decision	
	3.6.1	What type of decisions are made by the Insurance Ombudsman?
	3.6.2	Are decisions by the Insurance Ombudsman non-binding, binding on the insurance business or binding on both parties? If decisions are binding, are they binding automatically? What are the consequences of not complying with a decision?
	3.6.3	Is the decision of the Insurance Ombudsman based on a strict law or on fairness (equity)? What should the Insurance Ombudsman take into account when deciding a case (but not be bound by)?
	3.6.4	How does the Insurance Ombudsman determine the law applicable in cross-border complaints? Will the Insurance Ombudsman decide on a complaint subject to foreign law?
	3.6.5	What are the Insurance Ombudsman's individual redress powers?
	3.6.6	Is there a maximum amount that the Insurance Ombudsman can award?
	3.6.7	Is the Insurance Ombudsman's decision final?
	3.6.8	Is the Insurance Ombudsman's decision enforceable by the courts?
	3.6.9	Is the Insurance Ombudsman decision published? Are the names of both parties or the insurance business published?
3.7	Oversight by courts	
	3.7.1	Can the decision of the Insurance Ombudsman be appealed against in court by either or both parties?
	3.7.2	Is the Insurance Ombudsman scheme subject to judicial review by courts?

(continued)

(continued)

4. Statistical Data	
Please describe the work of the Insurance Ombudsman using the relevant statistical data. You may consider the following questions as guidance in drafting your report.	
4.1	How many complaints are received per year? How many of them were declined?
4.2	What is the average time taken to resolve disputes?
4.3	How many complaints are resolved per year?
4.4	What is the ratio of complaints resolved in favour of the complainant per year?
4.5	What is the ratio of complaints resolved in favour of the insurance business per year?
4.6	Are the Insurance Ombudsman's decisions/recommendations usually complied with / followed by the parties? Is there any statistical data?

5. Insurance Ombudsman practice		
Please describe the main observations about insurance market, consumer protection and effectiveness of the Insurance Ombudsman scheme that result from the Insurance Ombudsman's practice over the last (few) year(s). You may consider the following questions as guidance in drafting your report.		
5.1	Market trends	
	5.1.1	Which insurance product and/or service is complained about most often and why?
	5.1.2	Which area(s) of insurance business presents the highest risk to consumer protection?
	5.1.3	What is the approach taken by insurance businesses towards the Insurance Ombudsman?
5.2	Limitations	
	5.2.1	Are there any limitations resulting from the legal and/or institutional framework of the Insurance Ombudsman that hinder the effective functioning of the scheme?
	5.2.2	How do you assess consumers' financial awareness and literacy? Does it improve over time? If so, how?
5.3	*De lege ferenda* postulates	
	5.3.1	What changes would you suggest, if any, in order to improve the effectiveness of the existing scheme?

6. Other		
Please describe other relevant aspects which are not covered by Chapters I–V. You may consider the following questions as guidance in drafting your report.		
6.1	Accessibility	
	6.1.1	How do consumers know about, and find, the Insurance Ombudsman?
	6.1.2	Are there any barriers to accessing the Insurance Ombudsman?
	6.1.3	Is the insurer obliged to provide the customer with information about the Insurance Ombudsman and the option of involving the Insurance Ombudsman?
	6.1.4	Does the Insurance Ombudsman have a website and/or social media? If so, please provide a link to the website/social media platform.

(continued)

(continued)

6. Other		
6.2	Accountability	
	6.2.1	Does the Insurance Ombudsman report on its work? If so, how often and to whom?
	6.2.2	What information does the Insurance Ombudsman publish (disclose)?
	6.2.3	Is the Insurance Ombudsman scheme budget subject to a consultation and/or an approval procedure? If so, please describe the procedure.

References

Heiss (ed) (2012) Insurance Contract Law between Business Law and Consumer Protection, Zurich, p 7

Reichert-Facilides (ed) (1984) Rechtsschutz in Privatversicherungssachen: Civil Court - Supervisory Authority - Ombudsman? Vienna

Summer (2010) Insurance Law and the Financial Ombudsman Service, London

von Hippel (2000) Der Ombudsmann im Bank- und Versicherungswesen: eine rechtsdogmatische und -vergleichende Untersuchung, Tübingen

Chapter 2
Law-based Ombudsman Schemes

The Finnish Experience

Jaana Norio

2.1 Introduction

"Ombudsman" is a historical Swedish word that has been in use for many centuries. According to the Dictionary of the Swedish Academy (*Svenska Akademiens ordbok*), "ombudsman" could be defined as a person assigned to represent one or several other natural or legal persons, especially in a legal or economic context. However, the dictionary also mentions that the term could be used for an official who, in their capacity as a representative of the King or Parliament, supervises compliance with laws and regulations.[1]

Dating back to 1809, the use of the word ombudsman to refer to ombudsman schemes originated in Sweden, where the first ombudsman scheme (*justitieombudsman*) was created, followed by Finland (1920), Denmark (1955), and Norway (1962). The common core of the role of these kinds of public ombudsman schemes can be described as "the protection of citizens against violations of their rights, abuse of powers, error, negligence, unfair decisions, and maladministration by the public administration and by public servants".[2]

However, the present ombudsman schemes are not only about protecting citizens against public authorities and other persons performing public tasks. On the contrary, ombudsman schemes are increasingly being established for a given

[1] Svenska Akademiens ordbok.

[2] Letto-Vanamo (2017), p. 237.

J. Norio (✉)
University of Helsinki, Faculty of Law, Helsinki, Finland
e-mail: jaana.norio@helsinki.fi

H. Heiss et al. (eds.), *Insurance Ombudsman Schemes*, AIDA Europe Research Series on Insurance Law and Regulation 15,
https://doi.org/10.1007/978-3-032-01500-6_2

functional area or matter or for a specific group of people, without the idea of a confrontation between the citizen and a public authority and thus of the citizen's need for protection against the public authority. The relationship in question may well be between two private parties (such as a consumer and a business), or it may depend on the individual case as to whether protection will be provided against a public authority, a private entity or a private entity performing public duties.

The term "ombudsman" is used in different contexts, and so "ombudsman scheme" can also have many meanings.[3] In this chapter, the term "ombudsman scheme" refers to an independent authority established by law, whose field of activity covers the whole country. This excludes municipal or regional ombudsman schemes established by law,[4] as well as ombudsman schemes set up, for example, by private organisations, specific industries or companies.[5] "Ombudsman" could mean both an official (and a person) and a function. However, throughout this chapter ombudsman refers to an authority, a scheme or the institution, not to a person holding a position of a certain Ombudsman.

Common features of the ombudsman schemes discussed in this chapter are independence, impartiality and autonomy. Independence means that the Ombudsman is free from external pressure, and is not subject to political influence or manipulation, in particular, by the executive branch. Thus, an Ombudsman should not be part of a ministry or other authority in the sense that a minister or official could influence the Ombudsman's decisions or actions.

In other respects, there may be notable differences between ombudsman schemes. For example, the background of the ombudsman scheme can be entirely national or based on international examples, influence or requirements. An ombudsman scheme sometimes exists for a rather limited purpose, while at other times, the scope of a scheme is quite large. An important distinction is whether the jurisdiction and tasks of an Ombudsman are at a general level or at an individual level. The extent to which different ombudsman schemes have obligations based on constitutional provisions, EU legislation or international treaties also varies.

The purpose of the ombudsman scheme could include, for example, supervision, protection, prevention or promotion. The aim of supervision could be to detect and address grievances, to identify development targets and to take them forward. The Ombudsman's tools could include monitoring, inspections, and formal and informal ways of obtaining information. Protection could refer to individual cases and some form of access to justice approach. An important question is whether the Ombudsman resolves disputes or assists an individual in legal conflicts, or whether the Ombudsman resolves complaints without directly affecting the individual's legal

---

[3] See e.g. Beqiraj et al. (2018), pp. 5–6, 11–13.

[4] A Finnish example are patient ombudspersons (*potilasasiavastaava, patientombud*) and social services ombudspersons (*sosiaaliasiavastaava, socialombud*). Clients who consider themselves to have been mistreated by health care or social welfare services, or who need advice on their rights, can consult a patient ombudsperson or a social services ombudsperson respectively.

[5] A Finnish example is the Finnish Financial Ombudsman Bureau (*Vakuutus- ja rahoitusneuvonta, FINE*).

position. Prevention could include, for example, binding decisions prohibiting certain behaviour or practices, or the drafting of guidelines for good practices. Promotion could include monitoring, gathering and sharing information, taking initiatives, to name just a few modes of operation.[6]

As the ombudsman schemes referred to in this chapter can be viewed from different perspectives, the extent to which the schemes appear similar or different might also depend on the perspective. Namely, one could emphasize the importance of the Ombudsman for oversight of legality, see the Ombudsman as a means of access to justice, or even pay attention to the role of the Ombudsman in norm giving.[7]

This chapter examines ombudsman schemes as defined above from a Finnish perspective. Even though the Ombudsman Institution does not have its origin in Finland, but in Sweden, Finland has a rather long and varied ombudsman history. The intention is not to provide a detailed or exhaustive description of these various schemes. The idea is to give an overall picture of the different ombudsman schemes, mainly based on the legislation and government proposals,[8] and then, based on this national material, to give one conceivable answer to the questions: Where do these kinds of schemes come from? What is their nature and function? What are the similarities and differences between the different schemes?

2.2 Where It All Started: Protection of Individuals Against Public Authorities

The oldest ombudsman scheme in Finland is the Parliamentary Ombudsman (in Finnish *eduskunnan oikeusasiamies*, in Swedish *riksdagens justitieombudsman*),[9] based on the model of the Swedish *justitieombudsman*, the world's oldest ombudsman in the modern sense, from 1809.[10] When Finland became an independent

[6] See e.g. Koulu (2022), pp. 13–17.

[7] See e.g. Beqiraj et al. (2018), pp. 5–6; Koulu (2022), pp. 15–17; Letto-Vanamo (2017), p. 237.

[8] In Finland, there are two official languages, namely Finnish and Swedish. Therefore, legislation and government proposals (*hallituksen esitys* in Finnish, *regeringens proposition* in Swedish) are available in both Finnish and Swedish. In this chapter, the titles of different ombudsmen are provided in both Finnish and Swedish below. As Finnish is the first language of the vast majority of the Finnish people, the titles of different acts and decrees are given only in Finnish and references are made to the Finnish versions of government proposals with their page numbers. However, the Swedish versions can be found using the numbers given of the legislation and government proposals, see https://www.finlex.fi/fi/. Accessed 16 Apr 2025. A selection of English translations of Finnish legislation is available in https://www.finlex.fi/en/laki/kaannokset/. Accessed 16 Apr 2025.

[9] For information in English, see the website of the Parliamentary Ombudsman: https://www.oikeus-asiamies.fi/en/eoa. Accessed 16 Apr 2025.

[10] Husa and Jyränki (2023), p. 405; Letto-Vanamo (2017), p. 237.

country in 1917,[11] the new Constitution Act[12] established not only the Parliamentary Ombudsman but also the Chancellor of Justice (*valtioneuvoston oikeuskansleri, justitiekanslern i statsrådet*),[13] both supreme overseers of legality. It could be debated whether the Chancellor of Justice possesses the qualities of an Ombudsman Scheme. In any case, it is not possible to understand the Finnish system of oversight of legality without knowledge of both the Parliamentary Ombudsman and the Chancellor of Justice and their relationship to each other. For this reason, this chapter also deals with the Chancellor of Justice.

The Chancellor of Justice is a transformation of the post of the Procurator, which had been attached to the Senate.[14] The main task of the Chancellor of Justice was to supervise authorities and civil servants to ensure that they obeyed the law and fulfilled their duties so that no one was oppressed in their legal rights. The Parliamentary Ombudsman, chosen by Parliament in accordance with the original idea of an Ombudsman, was to supervise compliance with the law in the activities of the courts and other authorities.[15]

One could reasonably ask why a system with two parallel supreme overseers of legality with rather similar jurisdictions was created. Clearly, the reasons were political. The Procurator was a high-ranking, relatively independent supervisor of both authorities, the Government and the Governor-General—the highest-ranking official in Finland during the period when Finland was an autonomous Grand Duchy of Russia (1809–1917). However, there was dissatisfaction with the Procurator during the years before and soon after Finland became independent. The Procurator was seen as a trusted figure of the Government. As a counterweight, a Parliamentary Ombudsman who enjoyed the trust of Parliament was considered necessary.[16]

The first years of the Parliamentary Ombudsman were rather modest, and in 1932, the Government even proposed to Parliament that the position of the Ombudsman be abolished. However, Parliament did not accept this proposal. Since then, the necessity of the Parliamentary Ombudsman has not been questioned.[17] On the contrary, the Parliamentary Ombudsman has become a respected institution alongside the Chancellor of Justice.

The purpose of both the Parliamentary Ombudsman and the Chancellor of Justice is to protect persons against unlawfulness in the exercise of official authority. Originally, therefore, the subject of the Parliamentary Ombudsman's supervision were public authorities and officials. In 1991, the Constitution was amended (Act 1221/1990) to include public sector employees and other persons performing public

---

[11] Finland was a province of the Kingdom of Sweden for more than 600 years until 1809, and an autonomous Grand Duchy of Russia during the period 1809–1917.

[12] Suomen Hallitusmuoto (94/1919).

[13] For information in English, see the website of the Chancellor of Justice: https://oikeuskansleri.fi/en/frontpage. Accessed 16 Apr 2025.

[14] Husa and Jyränki (2023), p. 405.

[15] The Constitution Act, §§ 46, 49, Letto-Vanamo (2017), p. 237.

[16] Hidén (1970), p. 11; Hidén (1973), pp. 30–32; Husa and Jyränki (2023), p. 405.

[17] Hidén (1973), pp. 32–33.

duties. The reason for these amendments was to clarify that the task of both the Chancellor of Justice and the Parliamentary Ombudsman is to supervise that those performing public tasks comply with the law and fulfil their obligations, and that it is irrelevant in which organisational form and by which officials or employees the public duties are performed. Therefore, private entities are also subject to supervision to the extent that they perform public duties.[18] These entities can include, for example, providers of health services, child protection institutions, nursing homes and pension insurance companies. Thus, the privatisation of public tasks increases the number of private sector operators supervised by the two supreme overseers of legality.[19]

Pursuant to § 69 of the current Constitution of Finland,[20] attached to the Government, there is a Chancellor of Justice and a Deputy Chancellor of Justice. They are appointed by the President of the Republic.[21] The Chancellor of Justice supervises the lawfulness of the official acts of the Government and the President of the Republic. The Chancellor of Justice is also tasked with ensuring the observance of the law and the fulfilment of obligations by the courts of law, other authorities, civil servants, public employees and other persons when they are performing a public task. In the performance of their duties, the Chancellor of Justice monitors the upholding of basic rights and liberties and human rights. In addition, the Chancellor of Justice, upon request, provides the President, the Government and the Ministries with information and opinions on legal matters. The Chancellor of Justice submits an annual report to Parliament and the Government on its activities and observations on how the law has been obeyed.[22]

The Parliamentary Ombudsman and two Deputy Ombudsmen are elected by Parliament for a four-year term. Thus, unlike the Chancellor, the Ombudsman is not an official with a permanent position. The Parliamentary Ombudsman is tasked with ensuring that the courts of law, other authorities and civil servants, public employees and other persons, when the latter are performing a public task, obey the law and fulfil their obligations. In the performance of their duties, the Parliamentary Ombudsman shall monitor the upholding of basic rights, liberties and human rights. The Parliamentary Ombudsman submits an annual report to Parliament on its work, including observations on the state of the administration of justice and on any shortcomings in legislation.[23]

---

[18] Hallituksen esitys Eduskunnalle eräiden valtioneuvoston oikeuskansleria ja eduskunnan hyphenationalternatives oi-keus-asiamiestä koskevien säännösten muuttamista koskevaksi lainsäädännöksi 72/1990 vp, pp. 13–15.

[19] Tuori and Kotkas (2023), pp. 840–841, see also Lehtimaja (2000).

[20] Suomen perustuslaki (731/1999).

[21] In addition, the President appoints for a maximum of five years a deputy to the Deputy Chancellor of Justice, who will perform his duties when the Deputy Chancellor of Justice is unable to do so.

[22] Constitution of Finland, § 108. For more details about the tasks of the Chancellor of Justice, see the Act on the Chancellor of Justice (*laki valtioneuvoston oikeuskanslerista* (193/2000)).

[23] Constitution of Finland, §§ 38, 109. Some of the Parliamentary Ombudsman's special duties also derive from UN conventions and resolutions. The Ombudsman is part of the National Human

Throughout history, at the Constitution level, the jurisdictions of the Chancellor of Justice and the Parliamentary Ombudsman as the supreme overseers of legality have been and are still not quite equal, but rather similar.

In terms of workload, the most significant form of overseeing the legality of the performance of public tasks for both overseers is to investigate the complaints these overseers receive.[24] In 2023, the Parliamentary Ombudsman received a total of 7124 complaints. The largest number of complaints concerned social welfare with 1136, the police with 855, health care with 803 and criminal sanctions with 591 complaints.[25] The Chancellor of Justice dealt with 1268 complaints.[26]

It is important to note that it is even possible to make a complaint concerning an issue which is not one's own. The overseers can also investigate a matter at their own initiative. The Parliamentary Ombudsman and the Chancellor of Justice will not investigate the same matter at the same time, nor will they reinvestigate a matter on which the other overseer of legality has already issued a decision.[27]

Another mode of operation of the supreme overseers of legality are inspections.[28] The Chancellor of Justice can inspect authorities, institutions and other bodies. The Chancellor of Justice also reviews penalty judgments. The Parliamentary Ombudsman likewise conducts on-site investigations in public offices and institutions. The Parliamentary Ombudsman has a special duty to make regular inspection visits to prisons and other institutions, such as psychiatric hospitals, where persons can be confined against their will. Other places visited are units of the Defence Forces and the Border Guard.[29]

If the overseers of legality detect illegal procedures or the neglect of duties, they can take various measures, depending on the case. These measures include prosecution for breach of official duty, a reprimand, an expression of an opinion and a

Rights Institution of Finland (*Suomen kansallinen ihmisoikeusinstituutio, Nationella hyphenation människo-rättsinstitutionen*) as set forth in the so-called UN Paris Principles (A/RES/48/134) together with the Human Rights Centre (*Ihmisoikeuskeskus, Människorättscentret*) established in 2012 and its Delegation. The Parliamentary Ombudsman is also appointed as the National Preventive Mechanism (NPM) under the Optional Protocol to the UN Convention against Torture and other Cruel, Inhuman or Degrading Treatment or Punishment. In addition, the tasks set out under art. 33(2) of the Convention on the Rights of Persons with Disabilities of 2006 legally fall within the competence of the Ombudsman and the Human Rights Centre and its Delegation. See Parliamentary Ombudsman of Finland: Summary of the Annual Report 2022 (2023), pp. 27, 46–107. For detailed information about the tasks of the Parliamentary Ombudsman, see the Act on the Parliamentary Ombudsman (*laki eduskunnan oikeusasiamiehestä* (197/2002)).

[24] Hallituksen esitys eduskunnalle laiksi valtioneuvoston oikeuskanslerin ja eduskunnan hyphenation oikeus-asiamiehen tehtävien jaosta 179/2021 vp, pp. 9, 11.

[25] Parliamentary Ombudsman of Finland: Summary of the annual report 2023 (2024), p. 37.

[26] Valtioneuvoston oikeuskanslerin tilastot vuodelta 2023 (2024), p. 5.

[27] Parliamentary Ombudsman of Finland: The Ombudsman and the Chancellor of Justice. https://www.oikeusasiamies.fi/en/the-ombudsman-and-the-chancellor-of-justice-. Accessed 16 Apr 2025.

[28] In 2023, 83 inspections were conducted by the Parliamentary Ombudsman, Parliamentary Ombudsman of Finland: Summary of the annual report 2023 (2024), p. 43.

[29] Act on the Chancellor of Justice, § 3, Act on the Parliamentary Ombudsman, § 5.

recommendation. They can also act so that an error or grievance is corrected. However, it is important to note that the overseers of legality do not have the power to alter a decision made by the supervised. Naturally, if a complaint concerns, for example, a procedure or a circumstance, the decision of the overseer may lead to the matter being corrected and, the complainant receiving legal protection. However, complaints are not a form of appeal, so if a person is dissatisfied with an authority's decision, they must file an appeal. Neither of the supreme overseers of legality has the task of assisting individuals, for example, in an appeals procedure.

Neither the Chancellor of Justice nor the Parliamentary Ombudsman has the jurisdiction to create legal rules, but they can both contribute to legislation by making suggestions for improvements or additions to the legislation.[30]

Over the decades, there has been a certain division of labour between these actors, based either on regulations or on practices formed in operation. A new Act on the division of duties between the Chancellor of Justice and the Parliamentary Ombudsman[31] entered into force in 2022. The competence of the supreme overseers of legality to supervise the authorities and private parties performing public tasks has remained unchanged. The Act only reformed the division of duties to correspond both to the special tasks laid down in the legislation and to the specialisation that has been established on the basis of international treaties or in practice. The aim of the reform was to reduce the problems caused by overlapping duties, to improve the quality and effectiveness of legal oversight, and to support the uniformity and consistency of the decision-making practice. Thus, it is still possible to file a complaint to both supervisors in the same way as before, although complaints are mainly transferred between the supervisors according to their division of labour.[32]

According to the new division of labour, the Parliamentary Ombudsman oversees more extensively the upholding of fundamental and human rights at the individual level and, in particular, the upholding of the rights and treatment of vulnerable persons. This includes matters relating to the rights of the individual in social and health care and social insurance, as well as the oversight of the rights of children, elderly persons and disabled persons. As a rule, the Parliamentary Ombudsman will also primarily oversee matters concerning pre-trial investigation authorities and security authorities.[33]

The Chancellor of Justice's oversight of legality is now directed at examining structural issues related to the upholding of fundamental, human and other rights in the development of public administration. This also includes matters that would otherwise have been the focus of the Parliamentary Ombudsman under the new Act.

[30] Act on the Chancellor of Justice, § 7, Act on the Parliamentary Ombudsman, § 11.

[31] Laki valtioneuvoston oikeuskanslerin ja eduskunnan oikeusasiamiehen tehtävien jaosta (330/2022).

[32] Hallituksen esitys eduskunnalle laiksi valtioneuvoston oikeuskanslerin ja eduskunnan hyphenation oikeus-asiamiehen tehtävien jaosta 179/2021 vp, pp. 1, 28–31.

[33] Act on the division of duties between the Chancellor of Justice and the Parliamentary Ombudsman, § 3, Hallituksen esitys eduskunnalle laiksi valtioneuvoston oikeuskanslerin ja eduskunnan hyphenationalternatives oi-keus-asiamiehen tehtävien jaosta 179/2021 vp, pp. 33–36.

The Chancellor of Justice has also concentrated oversight over matters relating to the development of automatic administrative systems, the organisation of anti-corruption activities, as well as public procurement, competitive tendering and state subsidies.[34]

It should be emphasised once again that the competence of the supreme overseers of legality to supervise public authorities and private parties performing public tasks has not been changed by this new Act and is rather uniform. However, under the Act, the Parliamentary Ombudsman and the Chancellor of Justice primarily transfer cases between themselves based on which authority is responsible for handling them under the new Act. In practice, most of the matters covered by the delegation procedure concern the matters designated to be handled by the Parliamentary Ombudsman and are delegated from the Office of the Chancellor of Justice to the Office of the Ombudsman.

To conclude, both these supreme overseers of legality can be seen as protectors of citizens against the state and other public authorities. Although this is true at a general level, it is important to bear in mind that the protection is not provided for against the actions of public authorities *per se* but in relation to the performance of public duties. Therefore, not all actions of the public authorities fall under the jurisdiction of the supreme overseers of legality, and conversely, some actions of non-authorities do.

2.3 Specific Ombudsman Schemes

Although the Parliamentary Ombudsman and the Chancellor of Justice may focus their work for a certain period of time, their jurisdiction is general. The other common feature of these two actors is that their jurisdiction is linked only to the performance of public tasks. Therefore, every now and then, the question arises as to whether there is a need for a specific ombudsman for a particular group of people or for a certain topic. And if so, what should be the relationship between the specific and the general ombudsman schemes.

In addition to the so-called supreme legality supervisors, i.e. the aforementioned Parliamentary Ombudsman and the Chancellor of Justice, various ombudsman schemes have been founded in Finland to ensure the legal protection of individuals. Six of them can be categorised as autonomous and independent special ombudsman schemes for fundamental and human rights issues, namely the Ombudsman for Equality, for Non-Discrimination, for Children, for Older People, for Data Protection and for Intelligence.[35]

[34] Act on the division of duties between the Chancellor of Justice and the Parliamentary Ombudsman, § 2, Hallituksen esitys eduskunnalle laiksi valtioneuvoston oikeuskanslerin ja eduskunnan hyphenaitonalternatives oi-keus-asiamiehen tehtävien jaosta 179/2021 vp, pp. 31–33.

[35] See Hallituksen esitys eduskunnalle laiksi lapsiasiavaltuutetusta 163/2004 vp, p. 5, Hallituksen esitys eduskunnalle laiksi vanhusasiavaltuutetusta 82/2021 vp, p. 12.

In addition to these ombudsman schemes, there are a number of other ombudsman schemes whose common denominator—if any—seems to be the idea of protection against a private party.

2.3.1 *Equality and Non-Discrimination*

2.3.1.1 Ombudsman for Equality

In Finland, the Act on Equality between Women and Men (Equality Act)[36] entered into force in 1987. By then, special legislation on equality between men and women already existed in all other Nordic countries: Iceland (1976), Denmark (1978), Norway (1979) and Sweden (1980).[37]

The purpose of the Finnish Act is to prevent discrimination based on gender, to promote equality between women and men, and to improve the status of women, particularly in working life. From 2015 onwards, the aims of the Act also include the prevention of discrimination on the basis of gender identity or gender expression. The scope of the Act is not limited to working life and labour relations but is general. However, the Act is not applicable to relationships between family members, other private relationships, or activities associated with religious practice.[38]

When the Equality Act was drafted, the idea was that the main focus of the monitoring of compliance with the law would be on advice and guidance. Special authorities were deemed necessary to ensure expertise in equality issues and uniform application of the law. There was no authority that could take over equality issues, and mere general supervision of legality was not enough. Therefore, a new authority was considered necessary. In other Nordic countries, board-type institutions had been established to monitor the implementation of equality laws, and the Norwegian and Swedish systems included an Ombudsman, too. In Finland, it was not considered appropriate to entrust one authority with both an advisory role and the making of binding decisions in individual cases.[39] Therefore, both an ombudsman scheme and a tribunal were founded, namely the Ombudsman for Equality (*tasa-arvovaltuutettu, jämställdhetsombudsman*)[40] and the Equality Tribunal (*tasa-arvolautakunta, jämställdhetsnämnd*), which is now the Non-Discrimination and Equality Tribunal (*yhdenvertaisuus- ja tasa-arvolautakunta, diskriminerings- och*

---

[36] Laki naisten ja miesten välisestä tasa-arvosta (609/1986).

[37] Hallituksen esitys Eduskunnalle naisten ja miesten välistä tasa-arvoa koskevaksi lainsäädännöksi 57/1985 vp, p. 5.

[38] Equality Act, §§ 1–2. The Act was amended by Act 1329/2014.

[39] Hallituksen esitys Eduskunnalle naisten ja miesten välistä tasa-arvoa koskevaksi lainsäädännöksi 57/1985 vp, pp. 5, 9–10.

[40] For information in English, see the website of the Ombudsman for Equality. https://tasa-arvo.fi/en/front-page. Accessed 16 Apr 2025.

jämställdhetsnämnd).[41] They monitor compliance with the Equality Act both in private activities and in public administration and in business. Since public authorities are also overseen, it could be argued that this supervision can, in a sense, also be considered to be part of the general oversight of legality.[42] The Ombudsman for Equality's main responsibility is to supervise, whereas the Tribunal makes decisions in individual cases.[43]

The Ombudsman for Equality is an authority appointed by the Government, with each term lasting a maximum of five years. It is located under the administrative branch of the Ministry of Justice. It is expressly stated in the law that the Ombudsman for Equality is autonomous and independent in their activities.[44]

The Ombudsman for Equality's main duty is to supervise compliance with the Equality Act: to monitor compliance with the Equality Act, particularly its prohibitions on discrimination; to promote the implementation of the intention of the Equality Act by means of initiatives, advice and guidance; to provide information on the equality legislation and its application; to monitor the implementation of equality between women and men in different sectors of society; and to take action to promote reconciliation in matters concerning discrimination as referred to in the Equality Act.[45] In addition to national co-operation with other authorities, the Ombudsman for Equality also actively cooperates with both Nordic and European authorities on issues of equality and non-discrimination.[46]

Thus, the Ombudsman for Equality's responsibilities consist of both promoting equality and combating discrimination, and the Ombudsman acts at both a general and an individual level. From the very beginning, the intention has been that the main focus of the Ombudsman for Equality's guiding and advisory activities would be on monitoring compliance with the law.[47] If the Ombudsman for Equality notices that the obligations of the Equality Act are not being observed, or that the regulations of the Act are being violated, the Ombudsman must seek to prevent this by providing guidance and advice. The Ombudsman also has the right to place an unlawful matter before the National Non-Discrimination and Equality Tribunal, which in turn has the power to prohibit the unlawful procedure.[48]

For anyone who suspects that they have been the target of the discrimination referred to in the Equality Act, the Ombudsman for Equality also has important

---

[41] For information in English, see the website of the present Non-Discrimination and Equality Tribunal. https://yvtltk.fi/en/index.html. Accessed 16 Apr 2025.

[42] Koulu (2022), p. 51.

[43] Hallituksen esitys Eduskunnalle naisten ja miesten välistä tasa-arvoa koskevaksi lainsäädännöksi 57/1985 vp, s. 10.

[44] Act on the Ombudsman for Equality (*laki tasa-arvovaltuutetusta* (1328/2014)), § 1.

[45] Act on the Ombudsman for Equality, § 2.

[46] For more information, see Ombudsman for Equality: International activity. https://tasa-arvo.fi/en/international-activity. Accessed 16 Apr 2025.

[47] Hallituksen esitys Eduskunnalle naisten ja miesten välistä tasa-arvoa koskevaksi lainsäädännöksi 57/1985 vp, p. 27.

[48] Equality Act, §§ 20–21.

tasks. Firstly, such a person can ask the Ombudsman for instructions and advice on the matter. The Ombudsman may take measures to reconcile a matter of discrimination referred to in the Equality Act. This kind of proposal is not binding, but on application, the Non-Discrimination and Equality Tribunal can confirm it.[49] The Ombudsman can also, if necessary, assist a person in legal proceedings concerning the payment of compensation, provided that the Ombudsman considers the matter to be of significant importance in terms of the application of the Equality Act.[50]

The Ombudsman for Equality's task is to issue statements on whether the Equality Act has been violated in an individual case. A significant proportion of the statements relate to discrimination in working life. The main purpose of these statements is to help the person who suspects a case of discrimination to assess whether the Equality Act has possibly been violated and whether there is reason to take legal or other follow-up action in the matter. If the person decides to take the case to court, the Ombudsman's statements will not bind the court.[51]

The Ombudsman for Equality reports to the Government every year on the work they undertake. In addition, the Ombudsman for Equality submits a report to Parliament on the state of gender equality every four years. The Ombudsman for Equality can issue a report together with the Non-Discrimination Ombudsman.[52]

2.3.1.2 Non-Discrimination Ombudsman

The history of the Non-Discrimination Ombudsman is different from that of other Finnish Ombudsman schemes. In fact, this ombudsman scheme could be seen as the result of the evolution that took place concerning the concept of non-discrimination, in which international legislation and treaties were also essential.

The first Ombudsman Scheme in this field was the Ombudsman for Aliens (*ulkomaalaisvaltuutettu, utlänningsombudsman*) whose task was to work to secure the status of foreigners in Finland and to promote cooperation between foreigners, different authorities and different organisations. The Ombudsman for Aliens was attached to the Ministry of Social Affairs and Health, where an official with tasks of a similar kind had been working since 1984. The Ombudsman was to act on a general level, namely with initiatives, advice and instructions to promote the securing of the status of foreigners in cooperation with other authorities and organisations; to provide general information on the status of foreigners and legislation concerning foreigners; to participate in the production of information material aimed at foreigners; and to monitor the conditions and status of foreigners in various areas of social life. At an individual level, the Ombudsman had certain tasks in relation to asylum

[49] Equality Act, §§ 19–20.

[50] Act on the Ombudsman for Equality, § 3, Ombudsman for Equality: Monitoring the Equality Act. https://tasa-arvo.fi/en/monitoring-the-equality-act. Accessed 16 Apr 2025.

[51] Nieminen (2018), p. 440.

[52] Act on the Ombudsman for Equality, § 5.

and deportation issues. In addition, the Ombudsman could help a foreigner in securing their rights and, if necessary, provide legal aid if they considered the matter very important in terms of the foreigner's legal protection. If the Ombudsman found that a foreigner had been discriminated against, they were supposed to give advice and instructions to ensure that the discrimination would not continue or repeat itself.[53]

The jurisdiction of the Ombudsman for Aliens covered only foreigners, not persons belonging to national minorities. However, racism and ethnic discrimination were problems in Finland and abroad, and attention was also paid to this type of discrimination in the EU and the UN.[54] In 2001, the Ombudsman for Aliens was replaced by the Ombudsman for Minorities (*vähemmistövaltuutettu*, better hyphenations *minoritets-ombuds-man*) with the aim of preventing ethnic discrimination, promoting good ethnic relations, protecting the status and rights of ethnic minorities and foreigners as well as monitoring the principle of ethnic non-discrimination. The Ombudsman for Minorities was, in contrast to the Ombudsman for Aliens, located within the Ministry of Employment. The means of the new Ombudsman for Minorities resembled those of the previous Ombudsman for Aliens, including the possibility to help individuals subjected to ethnic discrimination in securing their rights and, if necessary, in getting them legal aid if the Ombudsman for Minorities considered the matter very important in terms of the prevention of ethnic discrimination.[55] It was explicitly mentioned that the jurisdiction of the Parliamentary Ombudsman and the Chancellor of Justice remained unchanged, that is, ethnic discrimination still fell into their jurisdiction, too.[56] In 2004, when the EU Non-Discrimination Directives (2000/43/EC and 2000/78/EC)[57] were being implemented, the first Finnish Non-Discrimination Act[58] was drafted and also the position of the Ombudsman for Minorities was strengthened.[59]

In 2014, a new Non-Discrimination Act was drafted with the aim of promoting equality and preventing discrimination, as well as enhancing the protection provided for by law to those who have been discriminated against. The prohibition of discrimination is defined as follows: no one shall be discriminated against on the grounds of age, origin, nationality, language, religion, belief, opinion, political

---

[53] Act on the Ombudsman for Aliens (*laki ulkomaalaisvaltuutetusta* (446/1991)), Hallituksen esitys Eduskunnalle laiksi ulkomaalaisvaltuutetusta 169/1990 vp, p. 1.

[54] Hallituksen esitys Eduskunnalle syrjintäasiain valtuutettua koskevaksi lainsäädännöksi 39/2001 vp, pp. 1, 6–8.

[55] Act on the Ombudsman for Minorities (*laki vähemmistövaltuutetusta* (660/2001)), §§ 1–4.

[56] Hallituksen esitys Eduskunnalle syrjintäasiain valtuutettua koskevaksi lainsäädännöksi 39/2001 vp, pp. 9, 17–18.

[57] Council Directive 2000/43/EC of 29 June 2000 implementing the principle of equal treatment between persons irrespective of racial or ethnic origin and Council Directive 2000/78/EC of 27 November 2000 establishing a general framework for equal treatment in employment and occupation [2000] OJ L180/22.

[58] Yhdenvertaisuuslaki (1325/2014).

[59] Hallituksen esitys Eduskunnalle laiksi yhdenvertaisuuden turvaamisesta sekä eräiden siihen liittyvien lakien muuttamisesta 44/2003 vp, pp. 1, 29, 56–59.

activity, trade union activity, family relationships, state of health, disability, sexual orientation or other personal characteristics.[60] It should be noted that gender is not included in this list, as the separate Equality Act is still in force and is supervised by the Ombudsman for Equality.[61] According to the Non-Discrimination Act, discrimination is prohibited regardless of whether it is based on a fact or an assumption about the person concerned personally or about another person. In addition to direct and indirect discrimination, harassment, denial of reasonable accommodation and an instruction or order to discriminate constitute discrimination as referred to in this Act. The Act applies to both public and private activities, but not to activities pertaining to private or family life or the practise of religion.[62]

It was considered that the existing ombudsman schemes were no longer sufficient and different alternatives were presented: additional specific ombudsman schemes, combining some of the existing ombudsman schemes or broadening the jurisdiction of the Ombudsman for Minorities. The latter alternative was chosen; combining different ombudsman schemes was not considered feasible as each of them applied different substantive legislation.[63] Thus, the Ombudsman for Minorities was replaced by the Non-Discrimination Ombudsman (*yhdenvertaisuusvaltuutettu, diskrimineringsombudsman*),[64] an authority appointed by the Government, with each term lasting a maximum of five years, located in the administrative sector of the Ministry of Justice.[65]

The duties and rights of the Non-Discrimination Ombudsman are mainly provided for in the Non-Discrimination Act and the Act on the Non-Discrimination Ombudsman.[66] The task of the Non-Discrimination Ombudsman is to promote equality and to prevent discrimination. In addition, the Ombudsman acts as the national reporter on human trafficking and violence against women. The Ombudsman also has tasks similar to those of the Ombudsman for Aliens: the Ombudsman works towards improving the rights and status of foreign nationals and supervises the removal of foreign nationals from the country.[67] Despite the rather general title, the Non-Discrimination Ombudsman monitors compliance with the Non-Discrimination Act only outside the workplace, and there are separate labour protection officials

[60] Non-Discrimination Act, §§ 1, 8.

[61] According to the Constitution of Finland (731/1999), § 6, everyone is equal before the law. No one shall, without an acceptable reason, be treated differently from other persons on the grounds of sex, age, origin, language, religion, conviction, opinion, health, disability or other reason that concerns their person.

[62] Non-Discrimination Act, §§ 2, 8.

[63] Hallituksen esitys eduskunnalle yhdenvertaisuuslaiksi ja eräiksi siihen liittyviksi laeiksi 19/2014 vp, p. 36.

[64] For information in English, see the website of the Non-Discrimination Ombudsman. https://yhdenvertaisuusvaltuutettu.fi/en/front-page. Accessed 16 Apr 2025.

[65] Act on the Non-Discrimination Ombudsman, § 1.

[66] Laki yhdenvertaisuusvaltuutetusta (1326/2014).

[67] Act on the Non-Discrimination Ombudsman, § 1, Hallituksen esitys eduskunnalle yhdenvertaisuuslaiksi ja eräiksi siihen liittyviksi laeiksi 19/2014 vp, p. 95.

who monitor compliance with the Act in the workplace. There is thus a clear distinction between the jurisdiction of the Non-Discrimination Ombudsman and that of the Ombudsman for Equality, a solution that has also been criticised.[68]

The tasks of the Non-Discrimination Ombudsman are fulfilled, for example, by preparing and commissioning surveys, publishing reports and taking initiatives; giving advice and statements; promoting information, education and training; participating in European and international cooperation; and monitoring phenomena related to human trafficking and issues related to violence against women and domestic violence. If it is necessary to ensure compliance with the Non-Discrimination Act, inspections may be carried out.[69]

The Non-Discrimination Ombudsman does not resolve disputes at an individual level; for this purpose, there is an impartial and independent judicial body called the Non-Discrimination and Equality Tribunal (*yhtenvertaisuus- ja tasa-arvolautakunta*, *diskriminerings- och jämställdhetsnämnden*). However, the Non-Discrimination Ombudsman may take steps to achieve reconciliation and assist a victim of discrimination, or a possible victim of human trafficking, in securing their rights or, if necessary, in obtaining legal aid for this purpose.[70] Although there is no requirement for the matter to be of general importance, in practice this is usually required to receive assistance in court proceedings.[71]

The Non-Discrimination Ombudsman submits an annual report on its activities to the Government and a report on the realisation of Non-Discrimination to Parliament every four years.[72]

2.3.2 *Data Protection and Intelligence*

2.3.2.1 The Data Protection Ombudsman

The Finnish Data Protection Ombudsman (*tietosuojavaltuutettu, dataombudsman*) originates from 1987. At that time, the Data Protection Ombudsman was an authority appointed by the President, with each term lasting a maximum of five years.[73] The Data Protection Ombudsman's tasks were based on the Act on Personal Data Files,[74] the predecessor of the national Data Protection Act. An authority was con-

[68] See Kortteinen (2019), pp. 290–291.

[69] Act on the Non-Discrimination Ombudsman, §§ 3, 6.

[70] Act on the Non-Discrimination Ombudsman, § 7. The same applies also to a victim of countermeasures, that is, to someone who is subject to negative consequences because of having complained or taken action to ensure equality.

[71] Kiiskinen (2019), p. 295.

[72] Act on the Non-Discrimination Ombudsman, § 8.

[73] Act on the Data Protection Board and the Data Protection Ombudsman (*laki tietosuojalautakunnasta ja tietosuojavaltuutetusta* (474/1987)), § 6.

[74] Henkilörekisterilaki (471/1987).

sidered necessary to safeguard the aims of this new legislation. An ombudsman scheme was considered necessary in order to ensure the independence, which was needed, as experiences gained in other countries demonstrated. It would obviously be unthinkable, for example, that one department of a Ministry would supervise the activities of other units in the same administrative branch in terms of data protection.[75] The Data Protection Ombudsman's tasks included monitoring, supervision and providing guidance concerning the establishment of personal data files and the use and disclosure of information contained therein. The Ombudsman thus had a preventive role and was supposed to act on their own initiative. In addition, those who detected or suspected violations of the law could report them to the Ombudsman. If an illegal procedure was detected, the Ombudsman was to act to correct it, primarily by providing guidance and advice.[76] Over the decades, the Data Protection Ombudsman's tasks developed.[77]

Nowadays, the Data Protection Ombudsman[78] is an authority appointed by the Government, with each term lasting a maximum of five years. It is located under the administrative branch of the Ministry of Justice. It is expressly stated in the Data Protection Act[79] that the Data Protection Ombudsman is autonomous and independent in their activities. There are also at least two Deputy Data Protection Ombudspersons.[80]

The Data Protection Ombudsman acts as the independent national public supervisory authority mentioned in art. 51 of the General Data Protection Regulation (GDPR),[81] and is responsible for monitoring the application of the Regulation in order to protect the fundamental rights and freedoms of natural persons with regard to processing and to facilitate the free flow of personal data within the Union. In addition, the Ombudsman has general jurisdiction in data protection matters, partly based on EU legislation and partly based on national legislation, such as the Data Protection Act. Even before the entry into force of the GDPR, the international requirements for a data protection supervisor were laid down in the Council of Europe's Convention for the Protection of Individuals with regard to Automatic

[75] Hallituksen esitys Eduskunnalle henkilörekisterilaiksi ja siihen liittyviksi laeiksi 49/1986 vp, p. 17.

[76] Act on Personal Data Files, §§ 29, 34.

[77] See e.g. Hallituksen esitys eduskunnalle EU:n yleistä tietosuoja-asetusta täydentäväksi lainsäädännöksi 9/2018 vp, pp. 8–15.

[78] For information in English, see the website of the Data Protection Ombudsman. https://tietosuoja.fi/en/home. Accessed 16 Apr 2025.

[79] Tietosuojalaki (1050/2018).

[80] Data Protection Act, §§ 8–9, 11, Hallituksen esitys eduskunnalle EU:n yleistä tietosuoja-asetusta täydentäväksi lainsäädännöksi 9/2018 vp, p. 93.

[81] Regulation (EU) 2016/679 of the European Parliament and of the Council of 27 April 2016 on the protection of natural persons with regard to the processing of personal data and on the free movement of such data, and repealing Directive 95/46/EC (General Data Protection Regulation) [2016] OJ L119/1.

Processing of Personal Data[82]—which, for Finland, entered into force in 1992—as well as by the EU Data Protection Directive.[83]

As for the competence, tasks and powers of the Data Protection Ombudsman, the Finnish Data Protection Act includes references to arts. 55–59 of the GDPR. In addition, the Ombudsman has some other tasks and powers, too.[84] In line with art. 57, the tasks of the Ombudsman include, *inter alia*, monitoring and enforcing the application of the GDPR; promoting awareness and providing information at both the individual and the more general level; advising Parliament, the Government, and other institutions and bodies on legislative and administrative measures relating to the protection of the rights and freedoms of natural persons with regard to processing; handling complaints lodged by a data subject, or by a body, organisation or association in accordance with art. 80, and, where appropriate, investigating the subject matter of the complaint and informing the complainant of the progress and the outcome of the investigation within a reasonable period, in particular where further investigation or coordination with another supervisory authority is necessary. The Data Protection Ombudsman is also a qualified entity allowed to bring representative actions in line with the EU Representative Actions Directive.[85]

In connection with the Office of the Ombudsman, there is an Expert Board, appointed by the Government for terms of three years. The task of the Expert Board is to issue, upon request of the Data Protection Ombudsman, opinions on significant questions related to the application of the legislation governing the processing of personal data.[86]

From the point of view of the registered person, the right to file a complaint with the Data Protection Ombudsman is noteworthy, and the right is not limited to situations where the art. 77 GDPR is applicable.[87] The Data Protection Ombudsman can, for example, give advice or instructions in such a case and, depending on the nature of the case, even issue an appealable administrative decision.[88] The power to issue such decisions, which has its background in the EU law, is not in line with the powers of other Finnish ombudsman institutions.

It is the Sanctions Board, not the Data Protection Ombudsman, that is tasked with imposing the administrative fines mentioned in art. 83 GDPR. This Board

[82] CETS No. 108.

[83] Directive 95/46/EC of the European Parliament and of the Council of 24 October 1995 on the protection of individuals with regard to the processing of personal data and on the free movement of such data [1995] OJ L281/31.

[84] Data Protection Act, § 14.

[85] Directive (EU) 2020/1828 of the European Parliament and of the Council of 25 November 2020 on representative actions for the protection of the collective interests of consumers and repealing Directive 2009/22/EC [2020] OJ L409/1.

[86] Data Protection Act, §§ 12, 17.

[87] Data Protection Act, § 21.

[88] Hallituksen esitys eduskunnalle EU:n yleistä tietosuoja-asefusta täydentäväksi lainsäädännöksi 9/2018 vp, p. 103.

consists of the Data Protection Ombudsman and the Deputy Data Protection Ombudspersons.[89]

In line with art. 59 GDPR, the Ombudsman prepares an annual report on its activities, which is submitted to Parliament and the Government and is also made available to the public.[90]

As regards the relation between the different ombudsman schemes, it is expressly set out in the Finnish Data Protection Act that the Data Protection Ombudsman does not supervise the activities of the Chancellor of Justice and the Parliamentary Ombudsman.[91]

2.3.2.2 The Intelligence Ombudsman

In the late 2010s, new legislation was drafted in relation to both civilian and military intelligence. In this context, it was also necessary to organise the supervision of intelligence activities. This supervision can be divided into internal and external supervision, as well as legality and parliamentary supervision. At that time, there was no special external legality supervisor responsible for intelligence activities; instead, legality supervisors performed the relevant tasks in addition to their other duties. Therefore, it was considered that the proposed new intelligence powers afforded to the authorities required the organisation of an effective and independent legality supervision. In addition, other aspects, such as international human rights treaties, European Union legislation and general limitations on fundamental rights were mentioned as reasons for an effective supervision.[92]

It was for the purpose of external legality supervision that a new ombudsman scheme was considered to be the right solution. The Intelligence Ombudsman (*tiedusteluvalvontavaltuutettu, underrättelsetillsynsombudsman*)[93] is an authority appointed by the Government for terms of five years each. It is expressly stated in the Intelligence Oversight Act[94] that the Intelligence Ombudsman is autonomous and independent in conducting their activities. Originally, it was attached to the office of the Data Protection Ombudsman.[95] This organisational solution aimed only at achieving administrative synergies and did not limit the status, tasks or powers of the Data Protection Ombudsman. When drafting the new law, it was emphasised that the tasks and powers of the Intelligence Ombudsman do not limit the tasks or supervisory authority of other special ombudsman schemes or the supreme over-

[89] Data Protection Act, § 24.

[90] Data Protection Act, § 14.

[91] Data Protection Act, § 14.

[92] Hallituksen esitys eduskunnalle laiksi tiedustelutoiminnan valvonnasta ja laiksi valtion virkamieslain 7 §:n muuttamisesta 199/2017 vp, p. 32.

[93] For information in English, see the website of the Intelligence Ombudsman. https://tiedusteluvalvonta.fi/en/home. Accessed 16 Apr 2025.

[94] Laki tiedustelutoiminnan valvonnasta (121/2019).

[95] Intelligence Oversight Act, §§ 5–6.

seers of legality.[96] As of 2025, the Intelligence Ombudsman is one of the ombudsman schemes located in the Agency for Special Authorities in the Judicial Administration (*Oikeushallinnon viranomaiset -virasto, ämbetsverket Specialmyndigheterna inom justitieförvaltningen*).

Publicity is important as a means of controlling the public authorities. Therefore, also in terms of supervision, intelligence is quite unique due to its secrecy. The Intelligence Ombudsman is tasked with supervising the legality of intelligence gathering methods and the use of intelligence, as well as the legality of other intelligence operations conducted by the Finnish Security and Intelligence Service and the military intelligence authorities. The Intelligence Ombudsman is also tasked with supervising the upholding of fundamental and human rights in intelligence activities; promoting the realisation of legal protection and adherence to related best practices in intelligence activities; and monitoring and assessing the functioning of the legislation in the Intelligence Ombudsman's purview and proposing improvements where necessary.[97]

It is of crucial importance that, regardless of the regulations concerning the maintenance of secrecy, the Intelligence Ombudsman is entitled to obtain from authorities and other bodies with public administration duties the information and reports necessary for the performance of its oversight duties. The Intelligence Ombudsman may also conduct inspections on the premises of authorities and other bodies with public administration duties in order to supervise the legality of intelligence activities. In connection with such inspections, the Intelligence Ombudsman has the right to access all the premises and information systems necessary for the supervision of the authority or body.[98]

The Intelligence Ombudsman seeks to ensure the legality of intelligence activities, primarily by informing the subject of supervision of its opinion on lawful procedure, good governance or the promotion of fundamental and human rights. If the Intelligence Ombudsman finds that the subject of supervision has violated the law in its intelligence activities, an admonition can be given or, ultimately, an order issued to suspend or terminate the use of the intelligence gathering method. The Intelligence Ombudsman may also refer the matter to the pre-trial investigation authority.[99]

It is always an important issue to determine the extent to which an ombudsman acts at an individual level. However, it is precisely in cases of violations of intelligence legislation that the victim needs the help of an authority. Anyone who considers that their rights have been infringed in the course of intelligence activities, or that such operations have otherwise violated the law, can file a written complaint to the Intelligence Ombudsman in matters falling under its supervisory powers. The

[96] Hallituksen esitys eduskunnalle laiksi tiedustelutoiminnan valvonnasta ja laiksi valtion virkamieslain 7 §:n muuttamisesta 199/2017 vp, p. 37.

[97] Intelligence Oversight Act, § 7; Intelligence Ombudsman: Brochure 2024. https://tiedusteluvalvonta.fi/en/home. Accessed 16 Apr 2025.

[98] Intelligence Oversight Act, §§ 8, 10.

[99] Intelligence Oversight Act, §§ 15–18.

Ombudsman will then take the necessary measures to safeguard the legality of intelligence activities, the upholding of basic and human rights or the provision of judicial relief.[100] Such a complaint does not constitute an appeal or extraordinary appeal, but it is an additional way of getting legal protection. The main features of this complaint correspond to what is stated in relation to complaints to the Parliamentary Ombudsman or the Chancellor of Justice.[101]

A person subjected to intelligence gathering, or who suspects that they have been subjected to intelligence gathering, can ask the Intelligence Ombudsman to investigate the lawfulness of the use of such methods.[102]

The Intelligence Ombudsman will issue a written decision on the complaint or investigation request, which will be delivered to the complainant or person who made the investigation request. This decision is not subject to appeal.[103]

The tasks of the Intelligence Ombudsman form part of the external legality supervision. The Intelligence Ombudsman is responsible for the legal oversight of intelligence activities, whereas the Data Protection Ombudsman supervises the intelligence authorities' record-keeping and other processing of personal data. The Parliamentary Ombudsman and the Chancellor of Justice are also involved, as the former supervises the operative dimension of intelligence activities, and the latter supervises these activities at the strategic level.[104] The tasks and powers of the Intelligence Ombudsman do not limit those of the Data Protection Ombudsman, of any other special Ombudsman or of the Parliamentary Ombudsman or the Chancellor of Justice.[105] This model, which is based on cooperation between different ombudsman schemes, enables supervision to be undertaken from several legal perspectives and the cost-effective use of special expertise.[106]

The Intelligence Ombudsman reports annually on its activities to Parliament, the Parliamentary Ombudsman, and the Government.[107]

---

[100] Intelligence Oversight Act, § 11.

[101] Hallituksen esitys eduskunnalle laiksi tiedustelutoiminnan valvonnasta ja laiksi valtion virkamieslain 7 §:n muuttamisesta 199/2017 vp, p. 54.

[102] Intelligence Oversight Act, § 12.

[103] Hallituksen esitys eduskunnalle laiksi tiedustelutoiminnan valvonnasta ja laiksi valtion virkamieslain 7 §:n muuttamisesta 199/2017 vp, pp. 54, 57.

[104] Hallituksen esitys eduskunnalle laiksi tiedustelutoiminnan valvonnasta ja laiksi valtion virkamieslain 7 §:n muuttamisesta 199/2017 vp, p. 37, Intelligence Ombudsman: Oversight of Intelligence. https://tiedusteluvalvonta.fi/en/home. Accessed 16 Apr 2025.

[105] Hallituksen esitys eduskunnalle laiksi tiedustelutoiminnan valvonnasta ja laiksi valtion virkamieslain 7 §:n muuttamisesta 199/2017 vp, p. 37. In addition to these Ombudsman offices, the Intelligence Oversight Committee is responsible for parliamentary oversight, see Intelligence Oversight Act, §§ 2–4.

[106] Intelligence Ombudsman: Oversight of Intelligence. https://tiedusteluvalvonta.fi/en/oversight-of-intelligence. Accessed 16 Apr 2025.

[107] Intelligence Oversight Act, § 19.

2.3.3 *Protection Against Private Actors*

In addition to the ombudsman schemes discussed above, there are some private sector ombudsman schemes, which seem to be based on a similar idea as the original Swedish Ombudsman Institution, namely that of two parties, one of whom requires protection against the other. The idea behind these schemes is that there is an unbalanced contractual relationship between two parties.

2.3.3.1 The Consumer Ombudsman

In the 1970s, special consumer protection legislation was drafted in the Nordic countries and new authorities for consumer matters were founded. The solutions were not identical. In Finland, the special consumer protection norms were included in just one act, the Consumer Protection Act.[108] At the time the Finnish legislation was being prepared, Sweden, Norway, and Denmark each had established a new Consumer Ombudsman to supervise consumer matters.[109] Thus, it is no wonder that Finland also introduced its own Consumer Ombudsman (*kuluttaja-asiamies, konsumentombudsman*).[110]

In the light of later ombudsman schemes, one could suppose that the Consumer Ombudsman would have become the only new authority. Yet, this was not the case. Municipal (now state) authorities were established to provide advice to consumers, both at a general level and in individual cases and even to help a consumer and a trader to reach an amicable settlement in a dispute. The Consumer Disputes Board (now called *kuluttajariitalautakunta, konsumenttvistenämnden*) was founded to handle complaints and make non-binding recommendations. A new Market Court (now *markkinaoikeus, marknadsdomstolen*) was founded to preclude unlawful procedures by traders.[111]

It was concluded that the effectiveness of consumer protection depended decisively on the authorities receiving information about deficiencies that have occurred in practice and being able to intervene quickly. Therefore, it was necessary to have an authority whose main task is to supervise the procedure followed in the marketing and trade of consumer goods, and the Consumer Ombudsman was established as such an authority.[112] From the very beginning, the main task of the Consumer Ombudsman was, and still is, the supervision of marketing and contract terms.[113]

---

[108] Kuluttajansuojalaki (38/1978).

[109] See e.g. Hallituksen esitys Eduskunnalle kuluttajansuojalainsäädännöksi 8/1977 vp, pp. 8–10.

[110] For information in English, see the website of the Finnish Competition and Consumer Authority, Consumer Affairs. https://www.kkv.fi/en/consumer-affairs/. Accessed 16 Apr 2025.

[111] See e.g. Hallituksen esitys Eduskunnalle kuluttajansuojalainsäädännöksi 8/1977 vp, pp. 1–2, 10–11, 57–73.

[112] Hallituksen esitys Eduskunnalle kuluttajansuojalainsäädännöksi 8/1977 vp, p. 62.

[113] Nowadays Consumer Protection Act, Chapter 2 § 20 and Chapter 3 § 4.

However, the amount of legislation both at a national and EU level has of course increased enormously.

In practice—and in fact without any norms about it—the Consumer Ombudsman's proactive work has become very important. It includes, for example, the issuing of several guidelines on marketing and the negotiations with various industry associations regarding their standard contract terms. To some extent, the Ombudsman also gives advice to traders on their future marketing.[114]

As for the supervision of marketing and contract terms, the Consumer Ombudsman makes its own observations, but the information received, for example from consumers, competing traders, the aforementioned consumer advisors and other authorities, is also very important. If the Consumer Ombudsman detects infringements of law, the first step is to negotiate with the trader. This kind of procedure often results in the submission of a written commitment by the trader with a promise not to continue or repeat the illegal procedure.[115] In the event that this commitment is not maintained, the Consumer Ombudsman can issue an injunction against the continuance or repetition of the behaviour if the matter is not significant. If the matter is of significance, then it is the Market Court that issues such an injunction on the Consumer Ombudsman's initiative.[116]

The Consumer Ombudsman mainly acts at a general level. Nevertheless, assisting an individual consumer with their case has also always been possible, provided that it is important for the application of the law and in the general interest of consumers or where a trader does not comply with a decision issued by the Consumer Dispute Board, which in accordance with art. 20(2) of the EU ADR Directive[117] nowadays also includes other ADR bodies.[118] The Consumer Ombudsman also has the possibility to use a group action (public action) and representative action.[119] It is also possible for the Ombudsman to file a group complaint to the Consumer Disputes Board.[120]

As regards the administrative organisation of the Consumer Ombudsman's position, there was initially an ombudsperson with an office of their own.[121] Over the decades, there have been different organisational structures. At present, the Consumer Ombudsman is located in the Finnish Competition and Consumer Agency

[114] Viitanen (2024), pp. 1138–1139.

[115] Viitanen (2024), p. 1139.

[116] Consumer Protection Act, Chapter 2 §§ 16–17, Chapter 3 §§ 2–3.

[117] Directive 2013/11/EU of the European Parliament and of the Council of 21 May 2013 on alternative dispute resolution for consumer disputes and amending Regulation (EC) No 2006/2004 and Directive 2009/22/EC [2013] OJ L165/63.

[118] Act on the Competition and Consumer Authority (*laki Kilpailu- ja kuluttajaviras-tos-ta* (661/2012)), § 13.

[119] Directive (EU) 2020/1828 of the European Parliament and of the Council of 25 November 2020 on representative actions for the protection of the collective interests of consumers and repealing Directive 2009/22/EC [2020] OJ L409/1.

[120] Act on the Competition and Consumer Authority, §§ 14–15.

[121] Act on the Consumer Ombudsman (*laki kuluttaja-asiamiehestä* (40/1978)), § 3.

(*kilpailu- ja kuluttajavirasto, konkurrens- och konsumentverket*) as the head of consumer matters, which seems a bit unusual given the requirement of independence and autonomy of an ombudsman. However, it is expressly provided in the law that the supervisory activities of the Agency must be organised in such a way that the independence and autonomy of the Consumer Ombudsman in the performance of its supervisory duties are secured.[122]

The field of consumer protection also provides an interesting example of the interplay between a law-based ombudsman scheme and a private ombudsman system: already in 1971—i.e. years before the creation of the Consumer Ombudsman scheme—the Consumers Insurance Agency (*Kuluttajien vakuutustoimisto, Konsumenternas Försäkringsbyrå*) and the Insurance Complaints Board (*Vakuutuslautakunta, Försäkringsnämnden*) were established.[123] These later developed into the Finnish Financial Ombudsman Service (FINE) (*Finanssialan sopimuspohjainen asiakasorganisaatio (FINE), Finansbranschens avtalsbaserade kundorganisation (FINE)*)[124] in various stages. FINE is neither law-based nor financed with public funds. Rather, it was established through an agreement between the authorities and the private sector.[125] At the moment, the contracting parties are the Finnish Competition and Consumer Authority (*Kilpailu- ja kuluttajavirasto, Konkurrens- och konsumentverket*), the Financial Supervisory Authority (*finanssivalvonta, finansinspektionen*) and Finance Finland (FFI) (*Finanssiala ry*). There is an even closer connection between the Consumer Ombudsman and FINE: a member is appointed to FINE's Supervisory Board by the Finnish Competition and Consumer Authority, and that member is usually the Consumer Ombudsman.[126]

The FINE organisation includes both the Finnish Financial Ombudsman Bureau, which serves as the Bureau of the organisation, and three complaints boards, namely the Insurance Complaints Board, the Banking Complaints Board, and the Investment Complaints Board.[127] It is clear that a private organisation does not have supervisory powers. Despite being financed by the Finance Finland, an association of financial sector actors, FINE is not a self-regulatory body, either. According to art. 1 of its Regulations (in force since 1 January 2021):

> [t]he purpose of FINE is to promote the interests of customers and enhance their trust in the financial operations, to improve financial literacy among the consumers and otherwise develop the everyday practices in the financial sector in line with sound development principles. [...] FINE's core operations include its advisory, information and dispute resolution services. However, FINE does not provide investment advice, nor does it perform individual product or service comparisons.

---

[122] Act on the Competition and Consumer Authority, § 4.

[123] Saario (2001), pp. 259–260.

[124] For information in English, see the website of the FINE. https://www.fine.fi/en/front-page.html. Assessed 16 Apr 2025.

[125] Saario (2001); Luukkonen (2011), pp. 9–10.

[126] Regulations of the Finnish Financial Ombudsman Bureau (FINE) (2021), Art. 2, Annual Reports of FINE 2009– (in Finnish).

[127] Regulations of the Finnish Financial Ombudsman Bureau (FINE) (2021), Art. 1.

When comparing the Consumer Ombudsman with FINE it can be noted that the former focuses on the collective level and, to some extent, traders even on individual level, but only rarely assists individual consumers. In contrast, FINE concentrates on the customers; FINE shares information at a general level and, most importantly, also at the individual level. Thus, these two actors complement each other. When the consumer authority system is viewed as a whole, FINE's tasks overlap with those of state consumer advisory services, and the tasks of the Insurance and Banking Complaint Boards overlap with the tasks of the Consumer Complaint Board. As far as these ADR bodies are concerned, the question of whether there is a need for both a public and a private board has been discussed. In 2015, a working group set up by the Ministry of Justice argued that it is important to maintain a uniform decision-making practice in all fields of consumer law. Therefore, the Consumer Disputes Board's scope of jurisdiction should not be reduced, and the consumers' freedom to choose between two different complaint boards—Consumer Disputes Board and Insurance Complaint Board—was also considered important.[128] In 2024, however, the Rapporteur's Report on the development needs in the activities of the Consumer Disputes Board suggested that any overlap with the activities of the public Consumer Disputes Board and the private Finnish Financial Ombudsman Bureau FINE and its Boards should be eliminated by limiting the public Consumer Disputes Board's scope of jurisdiction.[129]

2.3.3.2 Food Market Ombudsman

In 2019, a new Food Market Act[130] came into force. The Act applies to contracts and practices between traders concerning trade in agricultural and food products. The provisions of this Act on the terms and conditions of contracts also apply to contractual practices (§ 1). The aim of the Food Market Act is to improve the functioning of the food market and to safeguard the position of disadvantaged operators in the food supply chain. Originally, the aim was to ensure that contracts for the sale of agricultural products would be in written form and have a certain minimum content.[131] More precise requirements for the content of the contracts were added later, based on the EU Unfair Trading Practices Directive.[132] Another aim of the Act is to

[128] Kuluttajariitojen vaihtoehtoinen riidanratkaisu (2015), pp. 36–37.

[129] Kuluttajariitalautakunnan toiminnan kehittämistarpeet (2024), p. 93.

[130] Elintarvikemarkkinalaki (1121/2018).

[131] Hallituksen esitys elintarvikemarkkinalaiksi ja laiksi oikeudenkäynnistä markkinaoikeudessa annetun lain 1 luvun 6 §:n ja 5 luvun 2 §:n muuttamisesta 121/2018 vp, p. 1.

[132] Directive (EU) 2019/633 of the European Parliament and of the Council of 17 April 2019 on unfair trading practices in business-to-business relationships in the agricultural and food supply chain [2019] OJ L111/59.

prohibit the use of unfair contract terms, practices contrary to good business practice and procedures that are otherwise inappropriate for the other party.[133]

When the Food Market Act was drafted, the need for a special authority was brought up as no special official procedure for solving problems in food supply chain existed. At that time, an ombudsman scheme already existed in some EU countries, at least in France, Great Britain and Slovenia. As the relationship between the parties in the food supply chain and in consumer contracts are typically considered to be unbalanced, and as contracts are an important object of supervision, it is no wonder that the Consumer Ombudsman was taken as a model for establishing the jurisdiction and tasks of the new ombudsman scheme.[134]

The Food Market Ombudsman (*elintarvikemarkkinavaltuutettu, livsmedelsmarknads-ombudsman*)[135] is an authority appointed by the Government, with each term lasting a maximum of five years. It is located under the administrative branch of the Ministry of Agriculture and Forestry. For practical reasons, the Food Market Ombudsman is situated at the Finnish Food Authority, but it is expressly stated in the law that the Ombudsman is autonomous and independent in their activities.[136]

The role of the Food Market Ombudsman is to improve the functioning of the food market, to monitor the market and to prevent practices that violate good business practices. The Ombudsman can issue recommendations, opinions and proposals relating to the functioning of the food supply chain. There is an interesting obligation for the Ombudsman to cooperate with the self-regulatory body of the food chain, namely the Board of Trading Practices in the Food Supply Chain (*Elintarvikeketjun kauppatapalautakunta, Nämnden för handelskutym inom livsmedels-kedjan*): in order to avoid overlaps and conflicts, the Ombudsman must request an opinion from the self-regulatory body before issuing a recommendation. Even at an individual level, the Ombudsman can inform and advise actors in the field on good business practices. The Ombudsman must, in particular, act in matters that are of considerable importance in terms of the functioning of the food chain or where considerable problems can be assumed to occur most frequently.[137]

In its supervisory capacity, the Food Market Ombudsman monitors the contractual terms and practices used in the food supply chain and the implementation of good business practices. If the Food Market Ombudsman suspects a violation of

---

[133] Hallituksen esitys elintarvikemarkkinalaiksi ja laiksi oikeudenkäynnistä markkinaoikeudessa annetun lain 1 luvun 6 §:n ja 5 luvun 2 §:n muuttamisesta 121/2018 vp, p. 1.

[134] Hallituksen esitys elintarvikemarkkinalaiksi ja laiksi oikeudenkäynnistä markkinaoikeudessa annetun lain 1 luvun 6 §:n ja 5 luvun 2 §:n muuttamisesta 121/2018 vp, pp. 20–26, 33.

[135] For information in English, see the website of the Food Market Ombudsman. https://www.ruokavirasto.fi/en/food-market-ombudsman/food-market-ombudsman/. Accessed 16 Apr 2025.

[136] Food Market Act, §§ 5–6, Hallituksen esitys elintarvikemarkkinalaiksi ja laiksi oikeudenkäynnistä markkinaoikeudessa annetun lain 1 luvun 6 §:n ja 5 luvun 2 §:n muuttamisesta 121/2018 vp, pp. 36–37.

[137] Food Market Act, § 5, Hallituksen esitys elintarvikemarkkinalaiksi ja laiksi oikeudenkäynnistä markkinaoikeudessa annetun lain 1 luvun 6 §:n ja 5 luvun 2 §:n muuttamisesta 121/2018 vp, pp. 54–55. The Board is an independent and impartial self-regulatory body, operating in connection with the Finland Chamber of Commerce (*Keskuskauppakamari, Centralhandelskammaren*).

those regulations related to its supervisory authority, it must attempt to induce the trader to voluntarily stop the illegal activity through negotiations. If necessary, the Food Market Ombudsman can assist the parties by investigating the matter and trying to promote an amicable settlement of the matter.[138]

In terms of judicial relief, a case regarding the violation of certain specific provisions of the Food Market Act that falls under the supervision of the Food Market Ombudsman can be referred to the Ombudsman for consideration. Depending on the case, the initiator may be, for example, the contracting party; an actor to whom the contractual term applies or whose activities it may negatively affect; a registered association operating to promote the interests of entrepreneurs, or the supplier of the goods. If a case involving the violation of a provision that falls under the supervision of the Food Market Ombudsman has not been brought to their attention, the Food Market Ombudsman must take it up of its own accord. The Food Market Ombudsman can give an admonition, a public warning, or impose a prohibition on the buyer from continuing or renewing the procedure. These are binding decisions, not mere recommendations. It is even possible to impose a penalty fee, which is levied by the Market Court on the proposal of the Food Market Ombudsman. In addition, in the event that the Food Market Ombudsman does not have the power to make a decision independently, the Market Court issues such a decision on the initiative of the Ombudsman.[139]

2.3.3.3 The Cooperation Ombudsman

The need for an ombudsman scheme to supervise compliance with legislative acts on cooperation within undertakings—that is, cooperation between employers and employees—was not based on the need for an entirely new type of supervision. The problem was that the existing supervision was located in the Ministry of Economic Affairs and Employment, in addition to the legislative process. Therefore, the supervision was not considered autonomous and independent, in the way that legality supervision should be according to the principles of the Constitution.[140]

For this reason, the Act on the Cooperation Ombudsman[141] established a new supervisory body. The Cooperation Ombudsman (*yhteistoiminta-asiamies, samarbetsombudsman*)[142] is an authority appointed by the Government, with each term lasting a maximum of five years. It has so far been located under the administrative branch of the Ministry of Economic Affairs and Employment, but since 1 January 2025, it is now located within the Agency for Special Authorities in Judicial

[138] Food Market Act, § 9.

[139] Food Market Act, §§ 8, 10, 11, 11 a, 12, 12 a.

[140] Hallituksen esitys Eduskunnalle laiksi yhteistoiminta-asiamiehestä ja eräiksi siihen liittyviksi laeiksi 177/2009 vp, pp. 1, 10, 12.

[141] Laki yhteistoiminta-asiamiehestä (216/2010).

[142] For information in English, see the website of the Cooperation Ombudsman. https://yt-asiamies.fi/en/frontpage. Accessed 16 Apr 2025.

Administration. It is expressly stated in the law that the Cooperation Ombudsman is autonomous in their activities.[143]

The task of the Cooperation Ombudsman is to supervise compliance with certain legislative acts on cooperation within undertakings, employee involvement and personnel funds, and the implementation of the objectives of these Acts.[144] In addition, the Cooperation Ombudsman is tasked with, for example, providing advice on the application of these acts and with undertaking initiatives and issuing instructions to promote and improve cooperation between employers and employees and the fulfilment of other personnel representation systems, and with supervising over the activities and administration of personnel funds to ensure that these comply with the Act on Personnel Funds and the by-laws of the fund.[145]

When the Cooperation Ombudsman was established, the individual level of its tasks was emphasised, namely the task of giving instructions and advice in individual cases. This kind of service, offered by the authority as the primary means of supervision, was considered significant for both companies, their personnel and personnel representatives.[146]

In line with many other ombudsman schemes, the Cooperation Ombudsman has the right to obtain the information and documents necessary for supervision, and also to carry out inspections to the extent required by the supervision duty. However, if it is evident that an employer is violating the Act on the Cooperation Ombudsman or other laws mentioned above, or regulations or orders issued pursuant to them, or is continuing or renewing an illegal procedure, the Ombudsman must issue a written request to correct the illegal procedure or prevent its renewal. In certain cases, the Ombudsman has also the power to order an employer or a company to fulfil its duties under penalty of a fine. In potentially criminal cases, the Cooperation Ombudsman is required to report the matter to the police for a preliminary investigation.[147]

The Cooperation Ombudsman has issued several non-binding instructions on various topics. Furthermore, the Ombudsman can, of course, take initiatives concerning legislation.

[143] Act on the Cooperation Ombudsman, § 1.

[144] Act on Co-operation within Undertakings (*yhteistoimintalaki* (1333/2021)), Act on Co-operation within Finnish and Community-wide Groups of Undertakings (*laki yhteistoiminnasta suomalaisis-sa ja yhteisönlaajuisissa yritysryhmissä* (335/2007)), Act on Employee Involvement in European Companies and European Cooperative Societies as well as on Employer Obligations and Employee Involvement in Cross-Border Restructuring of Companies (*laki henkilöstöedustuksesta eurooppayhtiössä ja eurooppaosuuskunnassa sekä työnantajavelvoitteista ja henkilöstöedustuksesta rajat ylittävissä yritysjärjestelyissä* (758/2004)), Act on Personnel Funds (*henkilöstörahastolaki* (934/2010)).

[145] Act on the Cooperation Ombudsman, §§ 1–2.

[146] Hallituksen esitys Eduskunnalle laiksi yhteistoiminta-asiamiehestä ja eräiksi siihen liittyviksi laeiksi 177/2009 vp, pp. 1, 11.

[147] Act on the Cooperation Ombudsman, §§ 6–8.

2.3.4 Bankruptcy Ombudsman

It is characteristic of the idea of ombudsman schemes that a particular group of people is 'protected' against a particular group of actors, for example citizens against public authorities or consumers against traders. The Bankruptcy Ombudsman appears to deviate from this pattern as its tasks do not seem to be based on such a clearly defined two-party relationship in this sense.

In the 1990s, the need for a special control system for bankruptcies was justified, among other things, on the basis that, despite the social and economic impact of bankruptcies, there was no actual supervision by the authorities. Furthermore, the need for an official body with the responsibility for the development of procedures connected with the administration of bankruptcy estates or bankruptcies in general was mentioned. Although both the tax administration and the labour administration had been active in bankruptcies relating to the public interest, their activity was based on their status as creditors. Supervision by creditors or by the Finnish Bar Association over its members was considered insufficient. In order to guarantee a high level of expertise and uniform application practice, it was considered important to concentrate the conduct of supervision in one authority. In Sweden, a special authority, *tillsynsmyndighet*, had been supervising bankruptcies since 1980.[148]

Thus, in 1995, the Act on the Supervision of the Administration of Bankruptcy Estates[149] was enacted, according to which the task of the Bankruptcy Ombudsman (*konkurssiasiamies*, *konkursombudsman*)[150] is to supervise the administration of bankruptcy estates. The Bankruptcy Ombudsman is appointed by the Government. It is located under the administrative branch of the Ministry of Justice.[151] According to the Government proposal, the Ombudsman is impartial in their supervision activities.[152]

The Bankruptcy Ombudsman's supervisory role includes the following tasks: monitoring the operation of bankruptcy estates and promoting and developing proper bankruptcy estate management practices through initiatives, advice and instructions; supervising that bankruptcy estates are managed in accordance with the law and proper bankruptcy estate management practices and that the administrators of the bankruptcy estates properly perform their duties; taking care, if necessary, of auditing the debtor's accounts and activities; taking the necessary measures

---

148 Hallituksen esitys Eduskunnalle laeiksi konkurssipesien hallinnon valvonnasta sekä konkurssisäännön muuttamisesta 249/1994 vp, pp. 5–7.

149 Laki konkurssi-pesien hallinnon valvonnasta (109/1995).

150 See the website of the Bankruptcy Ombudsman. https://www.konkurssiasiamies.fi/. Accessed 16 Apr 2025.

151 Act on the Supervision of the Administration of Bankruptcy Estates, § 1, Decree on the Supervision of the Administration of Bankruptcy Estates (*asetus konkurssipesien hallinnon valvonnasta* (111/1995)), § 3.

152 Hallituksen esitys Eduskunnalle laeiksi konkurssipesien hallinnon valvonnasta sekä konkurssisäännön muuttamisesta 249/1994 vp, p. 11.

to deal with negligence, abuse or other matters requiring correction; and taking care of the public receivership of bankruptcy estates.[153]

Thus, the Bankruptcy Ombudsman's supervisory tasks include both the administration of the bankruptcy estate and the debtors.[154] In fulfilling this task, the right to obtain information and to conduct inspections is vital. Should the Bankruptcy Ombudsman find that the estate has been administered inappropriately, it can inform the administrator and the creditors of the findings, and this may be sufficient to resolve the issue. In the event that it is not, the Bankruptcy Ombudsman does not have a right to order the administrator to act in a certain way or to instruct the meeting of creditors to make or to refrain from making a certain kind of decision. The Bankruptcy Ombudsman can, however, inform the proper authorities about its view. The Ombudsman has the right to turn to the court to compel administrators who have neglected their duties to fulfil their duties by means of coercion, or to apply for the administrators' dismissal from their duties.

In their role of promoting and developing proper bankruptcy estate management practices, the Bankruptcy Ombudsman may also give instructions and take initiatives concerning legislation. The Advisory Board for Bankruptcy Affairs (*konkurssiasiain neuvottelukunta, delegation för konkursärenden*), which assists the Bankruptcy Ombudsman, plays a central role in developing proper bankruptcy estate management.[155] The Board has namely taken as its primary task the preparation of written guidance concerning the proper practice of administering a bankruptcy estate. Since the Bankruptcy Ombudsman has a general duty to give advice and instructions concerning the administration of bankruptcy estates, it is possible for courts, administrators of bankruptcy estates, creditors, debtors, and other parties involved in bankruptcies to turn to the Ombudsman to get an opinion on a matter concerning bankruptcy proceedings or administering bankruptcy estates.[156]

The Bankruptcy Ombudsman's tasks do not include resolving complaints, but it is, of course, possible to take into account information received about possible problems in a certain bankruptcy estate. Generally, the Bankruptcy Ombudsman does not provide legal assistance in individual cases, either.[157] However, it is possible for the Bankruptcy Ombudsman to assist a bankruptcy debtor, a creditor or a bankruptcy administrator in a bankruptcy case or in a lawsuit related to a such case, provided that the matter is of general importance.[158]

[153] Act on the Supervision of the Administration of Bankruptcy Estates, § 1.

[154] The Ombudsman has also the duty to supervise the restructuring proceedings of companies, see Act on the Supervision of the Administration of Bankruptcy Estates, §§ 9–11.

[155] Decree on the Supervision of the Administration of Bankruptcy Estates, § 7.

[156] The website of the Bankruptcy Ombudsman. https://www.konkurssiasiamies.fi/. Accessed 16 Apr 2025.

[157] Hallituksen esitys Eduskunnalle laeiksi konkurssipesien hallinnon valvonnasta sekä konkurssisäännön muuttamisesta 249/1994 vp, p. 14.

[158] Act on the Supervision of the Administration of Bankruptcy Estates, § 6.

2.3.5 *Promoting Ombudsman Schemes*

In all the ombudsman schemes mentioned earlier in this chapter, supervisory and, broadly speaking, access-to-justice-related responsibilities are included. In addition, however, there are the Ombudsman for Children and the Ombudsman for Older People, who do not act at the individual level. Their tasks could be characterised as promoting the position of children and older people, respectively, at a general level. Despite these specific jurisdictions, these ombudsman schemes also belong to the group of special ombudsman schemes for fundamental and human rights issues.[159]

The individual protection of children and older people by ombudsman schemes is provided by the supreme overseers of legality, in practice by the Parliamentary Ombudsman. In addition, issues concerning older people in particular could also belong to the jurisdiction of the Non-Discriminatory Ombudsman.

2.3.5.1 Ombudsman for Children

As early as the 1980s, a private organisation[160] had an Ombudsman for Children, whose main task was to provide legal advice, but who also worked on producing legislative projects. During the 1990s, however, the Finnish Parliament discussed the possibility of establishing a law-based Ombudsman for Children. Pressure to establish an independent body responsible for children's issues in Finland primarily came from the UN Committee on the Rights of the Child and, at a general international level, from the Council of Europe. Examples of an ombudsman scheme were provided by other Nordic countries: Norway was the first in the world to have an Ombudsman for Children (1981), followed by Sweden (1993) and Iceland (1995).[161]

There were two options for the role of the Ombudsman: to concentrate on influencing social policy and legislation at a general level or to focus on protecting the interests and rights of individual children in various problem situations. Based on international experience, it was pointed out that it would be difficult to combine these two tasks, as they would require different modes of operation. Therefore, a model was chosen according to which the tasks of the Parliamentary Ombudsman would remain unchanged as far as children were concerned, and the tasks of the Ombudsman for Children would not overlap with those of the Parliamentary Ombudsman; they would instead be complementary. Thus, the new Ombudsman

[159] See Hallituksen esitys eduskunnalle laiksi lapsiasiavaltuutetusta 163/2004 vp, p. 5, Hallituksen esitys eduskunnalle laiksi vanhusasiavaltuutetusta 82/2021 vp, p. 12.

[160] The Mannerheim League for Child Welfare (*Mannerheimin Lastensuojeluliitto – Mannerheims Barnskyddsförbund*). The task was terminated in 2004. See Hallituksen esitys eduskunnalle laiksi lapsiasiavaltuutetusta 163/2004 vp, p. 5.

[161] Hallituksen esitys eduskunnalle laiksi lapsiasiavaltuutetusta 163/2004 vp, pp. 1–2, 5–7.

would operate at a general level and proactively, whereas the Parliamentary Ombudsman would continue with mainly *ex post* individual case supervision.[162]

The Ombudsman for Children (*lapsiasiavaltuutettu, barnombudsman*)[163] was founded by the Act on the Ombudsman for Children,[164] which came into force in 2005. The Ombudsman for Children is an authority appointed by the Government, with each term lasting a maximum of five years. Originally, it was located under the administrative branch of the Ministry of Social and Health but was later transferred to that of the Ministry of Justice. It is expressly stated in the law that the Ombudsman is autonomous and independent in their activities.[165]

The mission of the Ombudsman for Children is to ensure that children's status and rights are taken into account in legislation and social decision-making. Its task is to promote the realisation of children's interests and rights in cooperation with other authorities, organisations and other similar actors in their field. In so doing, the Ombudsman for Children shall, for example, assess the realisation of children's interests and rights, monitor the living conditions of children and young people, monitor legislation and social decision-making and evaluate their effects on children's well-being. Through initiatives, advice and instructions, the Ombudsman for Children works to develop social decision-making in matters concerning children and to advance the fulfilment of children's interests in society. Additional responsibilities include conveying information, developing forms of cooperation between different actors, and promoting the implementation of the UN Convention on the Rights of the Child. The Ombudsman for Children is required to report annually to the Government and to Parliament once every four years.[166]

2.3.5.2 Ombudsman for Older People

The idea of an Ombudsman for Older People emerged as early as 2006 and later resurfaced. Unlike in the case of children, no national private ombudsman existed, although this kind of activity was regionally piloted from 2007 to 2010 and was found to be both successful and necessary. The growing number of older people as well as the large range of issues related to older people were arguments in favour of a new ombudsman scheme. However, when the law proposal was finally drafted, it was also claimed that the tasks intended for the Ombudsman for Older People were already undertaken by existing authorities. The risk was also raised that the creation of a new authority could lead to a fragmentation of fundamental and human rights

[162] Hallituksen esitys eduskunnalle laiksi lapsiasiavaltuutetusta 163/2004 vp, pp. 8–9.

[163] For information in English, see the website of the Ombudsman for Children. https://lapsiasia.fi/en/front-page. Accessed 16 Apr 2025.

[164] Laki lapsiasiavaltuutetusta (1221/2004).

[165] Act on the Ombudsman for Children, § 1.

[166] Act on the Ombudsman for Children, §§ 1–3.

actors. Some considered that there was no need for a new body if it did not have the power to handle complaints or carry out supervision.[167]

As with the Ombudsman for Children, a model was chosen according to which the tasks of the Parliamentary Ombudsman would remain unchanged, and the tasks of the Ombudsman for Older People would not overlap but complement those of the Parliamentary Ombudsman. However, the situation was different from the Ombudsman for Children in the sense that there now also existed the Non-Discrimination Ombudsman supervising compliance with the Non-Discrimination Act and preventing age-based discrimination.[168]

The Nordic example was Norway, where the Act on Ombudsman for Older People came into force in 2020. In other parts of Europe, at least Malta, Northern Ireland and Wales already had their ombudsman schemes in place, by the time the Finnish Act on the Ombudsman for Older People[169] was passed in 2021.[170] The Ombudsman for Older People (*vanhusasiavaltuutettu, äldreombudsman*)[171] is an authority appointed by the Government, with each term lasting a maximum of five years. Initially, the Ombudsman affiliated with the Non-Discrimination Ombudsman's office, operating as an independent unit while sharing certain premises and administrative services. However, starting in 2025, they function within the administrative branch of the Ministry of Justice. It is expressly stated in the Act that the Ombudsman for Older People is autonomous and independent in their activities.[172]

The Ombudsman's mission is to promote the status and rights of older people.[173] Its main task is to exert societal influence on the status and rights of the elderly and to bring the elderly's perspective and matters concerning the elderly to the fore in social discussions and decision-making. Thus, in line with the Ombudsman for Children, the Ombudsman for Older People only acts at a general level and does not deal with individual complaints or other issues.[174]

The Ombudsman for Older People fulfils their duties by: monitoring and assessing the position of the elderly and the realisation of their rights; monitoring legislation and decision-making in society and assessing its impact on the elderly; taking initiatives, expressing opinions and participating in social discussions; drawing up and commissioning surveys and commission reports; promoting the provision of information; disseminating information on the elderly; and promoting cooperation

---

[167] Hallituksen esitys eduskunnalle laiksi vanhusasiavaltuutetusta 82/2021 vp, pp. 3, 15, 25.

[168] Hallituksen esitys eduskunnalle laiksi vanhusasiavaltuutetusta 82/2021 vp, p. 16.

[169] Laki vanhusasiavaltuutetusta (753/2021).

[170] Hallituksen esitys eduskunnalle laiksi vanhusasiavaltuutetusta 82/2021 vp, pp. 23–24.

[171] For information in English, see the website of the Ombudsman for Older People. https://vanhusasia.fi/en/front-page. Accessed 16 Apr 2025.

[172] Act on the Ombudsman for Older People, §§ 1–2.

[173] Act on the Ombudsman for Older People, § 1.

[174] Hallituksen esitys eduskunnalle laiksi vanhusasiavaltuutetusta 82/2021 vp, pp. 1, 16.

between actors dealing with issues related to older people and actors representing the older people.[175]

The activities of the Ombudsman for Older People are not restricted to a specific age group, as older people are understood to be a broad-ranged group, and their diversity is also taken into account.[176]

The Ombudsman for Older People provides the Government with an annual report on its activities and submits a report to Parliament every four years on the status of older people and the fulfilment of their rights.[177]

2.4 General Features and Distinctions

The following is a summary of the general features and distinctions of the Finnish ombudsman schemes, the oldest of which date back to 1920 and the new era that began with the Consumer Ombudsman in 1978. Even as a national summary, it gives an idea of what such schemes are all about.

What seems to be characteristic of most of the ombudsman schemes is the idea of protecting a certain group of people against a certain group of actors, for example citizens against public authorities or consumers against traders. Only the Bankruptcy Ombudsman and the Ombudsmen for Children and for Older People do not quite seem to adhere to this pattern. This ‘protection against’ feature may also be seen as the distinguishing factor between ombudsman schemes and other types of supervisory authorities that supervise a particular branch (e.g. financial markets) or activity (e.g. competition) more generally and from multiple viewpoints. This certainly does not mean that the latter authorities do not also pay attention to the interests of those in need of protection, such as consumers or, more generally, customers.

With regard to the independence of an ombudsman scheme, which was taken as a criterion in this chapter, the ombudsman offices are usually located under the administrative branch of a ministry, in most cases the Ministry of Justice. This is considered to be “independent”, and the independence and autonomy of each Ombudsman is usually even expressly mentioned in the respective Act. Ombudspersons are appointed at a high level, usually by the Government, not by a Ministry. As of 1 January 2025, the following ombudsman schemes, together with some other authorities, are located in the Agency for Special Authorities in Judicial Administration (*Oikeushallinnon viranomaiset -virasto, ämbetsverket Specialmyndigheterna inom justitieförvaltningen*): Ombudsman for Equality, Non-Discrimination Ombudsman, Data Protection Ombudsman, Ombudsman for Intelligence, Bankruptcy Ombudsman, Ombudsman for Children and Ombudsman

[175] Act on the Ombudsman for Older People, § 3.

[176] Ombudsman for Older People: Duties and authority of the Ombudsman for older people. https://vanhusasia.fi/en/duties-and-authority-of-the-ombudsman-for-the-older-people. Accessed 16 Apr 2025.

[177] Act on the Ombudsman for Older People, § 5.

for Older People. The Agency is under the administrative branch of the Ministry of Justice. This is just an administrative change that does not affect the jurisdictions or tasks of these authorities or their independence and autonomy. Nevertheless, it was mentioned in the Government proposal that this reform improves the independence of the authorities included in the new authority at the level of principle, as the authorities have now been moved further away from the politically led ministry.[178]

Where do the ombudsman schemes come from? The idea of protecting citizens against all kinds of errors, omissions and abuses by the public administration and by public servants seems to be embedded in the concept of rule of law. It was easy for Finland to find the ombudsman model used by its neighbour in Sweden. As far as ombudsman schemes other than the Parliamentary Ombudsman and the Chancellor of Justice are concerned, however, it seems to be typical for some new legislation to be drafted, following which an ombudsman scheme is considered necessary for supervisory purposes. There have often been one or more Nordic examples of an ombudsman scheme for a similar purpose, but sometimes the examples come from elsewhere. However, it should be kept in mind that choosing an ombudsman model is one thing and defining the jurisdiction and tasks is another. Therefore, similar titles do not necessarily translate into similar jurisdictions and tasks.

Ombudsman schemes seem to be permanent in the sense that once established they are not abolished. However, especially when such a scheme is closely linked to a specific act or other piece of legislation, the tasks of the ombudsman evolve in line with the amendments concerning that act or piece of legislation. It is also worth noting that different new tasks and obligations, for example based on EU law or international treaties, are often incorporated into the existing ombudsman schemes. The evolution of the Ombudsman for Aliens to the Ombudsman for Minorities and then to the Non-Discriminatory Ombudsman is the only case where the mere evolution of tasks within one ombudsman scheme was not sufficient.

Furthermore, ombudsman schemes seem to be an independent phenomenon, not just an intermediate step from, for example, a privately based ombudsman scheme to a massive supervisory authority. There is only one example of such a development, namely the Competition Ombudsman (*kilpailuasiamies, konkurrensombudsman*). In the 1970s, this kind of ombudsman scheme was considered necessary in order to enhance the negotiation procedure on which the elimination of the harmful effects of competition restrictions was at that time based.[179] The Competition Ombudsman was to act as a supervisor of the public interest in matters relating to the promotion of economic competition. Its task was to make proposals to the Competition Council (*kilpailuneuvosto, konkurrensrådet*) to eliminate the harmful effects of competition restrictions. The Competition Ombudsman also had to monitor the prevailing conditions of competition in economic life and to take initiatives to promote the acceptance of economic competition from a general point of view.

[178] Hallituksen esitys eduskunnalle laiksi Oikeushallinnon erityisviranomaiset -virastosta ja siihen liittyviksi laeiksi 31/2023 vp, p. 6.

[179] Hallituksen esitys Eduskunnalle laiksi taloudellisen kilpailun edistämisestä 212/1972 vp, p. 1.

The Competition Ombudsman had to primarily deal with restrictions on competition that were of considerable importance to consumers, that affected the competitive relations of an entire business sector or that made it considerably more complicated or impossible for an entrepreneur to do business.[180] However, when the competition legislation was significantly reformed in the 1980s, there was no longer room for an ombudsman scheme; instead, a whole new competition authority (*kilpailuvirasto, konkurrensverket*) with a central position in the application of the new law on restrictions of competition and in supervision was deemed necessary. Thus, the human resources of the Competition Ombudsman's office were incorporated into the new authority and the position of this Ombudsman was abolished.[181]

It is possible to categorise the ombudsman schemes in a number of ways, for instance as follows. First, there are the supreme overseers of legality, namely the Chancellor of Justice and the Parliamentary Ombudsman. The following six specific ombudsman schemes are usually regarded as ombudsman schemes for fundamental and human rights, namely Ombudsman for Equality, Non-Discrimination, Data Protection, Intelligence, Children, and Older People.[182] Although fundamental and human rights are of course linked to the Constitution and therefore seem to be somehow related to something 'public', these specific ombudsman schemes, with the exception of the Intelligence Ombudsman, do not exist for the specific purpose of protecting citizens against public authorities. Their jurisdiction is based on a specific field, and it varies on a case-by-case basis as to whether the "target" of the respective Ombudsman's actions is a public authority or someone else. For example, both the Ombudsman for Equality and the Non-Discrimination Ombudsman also deal with issues concerning public authorities, and one could argue that in doing so they are involved in general legality supervision.[183]

A typical feature of these ombudsman schemes is that the jurisdictions of existing ombudsman schemes have not been affected by the jurisdiction of a new ombudsman scheme, and therefore more than one Ombudsman may deal with similar issues, such as those concerning older people, from different angles.

In this chapter, three ombudsman schemes have been categorised under the heading 'Protection against private actors'. The unifying feature of these schemes seems to be a clearly unbalanced relationship: consumers versus traders, producers versus traders and employees versus employers. By far the most important of these ombudsman schemes is the Consumer Ombudsman, in a sense a private-sector counterpart to the supreme overseers of legality.

Almost every Ombudsman has supervisory tasks. In contrast to supervisory authorities, the supervision is not based on the regular reporting duties of those subject to the supervision, but on monitoring, case-by-case inspections or requests

[180] Act on the Competition Ombudsman (*laki kilpailuasiamiehestä* (424/1973)), § 2, Decree on the Competition Ombudsman (*asetus kilpailuasiamiehestä* (475/1973)), §§ 1–2.

[181] Hallituksen esitys Eduskunnalle laiksi kilpailunrajoituksista 148/1987 vp, pp. 11–12, Act on the Competition Authority (*laki kilpailuvirastosta* (711/1988)).

[182] For example, Hallituksen esitys eduskunnalle laiksi vanhusasiavaltuutetusta 82/2021 vp, p. 12.

[183] Koulu (2022), p. 51.

for information, or special inspections of certain branches, say of prisons or child welfare institutions by the Parliamentary Ombudsman. Some Ombudsmen have the power to issue an injunction against the continuance or repetition of certain illegal behaviour, while in some cases the Ombudsman can take the initiative for such a decision. The Ombudsmen do not have the power to enact binding rules. However, because non-binding guidelines not only provide guidance but also express the respective Ombudsman's understanding of the line between permitted and prohibited actions, such guidelines are rather important. Ombudsmen may also be active in proposing new legislation.

For the supreme overseers of legality, dealing with individual complaints is a central part of their tasks. The outcome of a complaint is a decision on whether the use of public authority was appropriate in the case in question, not a decision that alters the legal position of the complainant or anyone else. It may be surprising, however, that ombudsman schemes act at a general level more often than at an individual level. As far as specific ombudsman schemes are concerned, the powers to resolve disputes, or even to assist an individual in any way in resolving a dispute, are rather limited. Moreover, a requirement for the provision of such assistance is usually that there is not only an individual but also a more general interest involved in the case.

Legal Sources

Act on the Competition Authority (*laki kilpailuvirastosta* (711/1988))

Act on the Competition Ombudsman (*laki kilpailuasiamiehestä* (424/1973))

Act on Co-operation within Finnish and Community-wide Groups of Undertakings (*laki yhteistoiminnasta suomalaisissa ja yhteisönlaajuisissa yritysryhmissä* (335/2007))

Act on Co-operation within Undertakings (*yhteistoimintalaki* (1333/2021))

Act on the Data Protection Board and the Data Protection Ombudsman (*laki tietosuojalautakunnasta ja tietosuojavaltuutetusta* (474/1987))

Act on Employee Involvement in European Companies and European Cooperative Societies as well as on Employer Obligations and Employee Involvement in Cross-Border Restructuring of Companies (*laki henkilöstöedustuksesta eurooppayhtiössä ja eurooppaosuuskunnassa sekä työnantajavelvoitteista ja henkilöstöedustuksesta rajat ylittävissä yritysjärjestelyissä* (758/2004))

Act on Equality between Women and Men (Equality Act) (*laki naisten ja miesten välisestä tasa-arvosta* (609/1986))

Act on Personal Data Files (*henkilörekisterilaki* (471/1987))

Act on Personnel Funds (*henkilöstörahastolaki* (934/2010))

Act on the Chancellor of Justice (*laki valtioneuvoston oikeuskanslerista* (193/2000))

Act on the Competition and Consumer Authority (*laki Kilpailu- ja kuluttajavirastos-ta* (661/2012))

Act on the Consumer Ombudsman (*laki kuluttaja-asiamiehestä* (40/1978))

Act on the Cooperation Ombudsman (*laki yhteistoiminta-asiamiehestä* (216/2010))
Act on the division of duties between the Chancellor of Justice and the Parliamentary Ombudsman (*laki valtioneuvoston oikeuskanslerin ja eduskunnan oikeusasiamiehen tehtävien jaosta* (330/2022))
Act on the Non-Discrimination Ombudsman (*laki yhdenvertaisuusvaltuutetusta* (1326/2014))
Act on the Ombudsman for Aliens (*laki ulkomaalaisvaltuutetusta* (446/1991))
Act on the Ombudsman for Children (*laki lapsiasiavaltuutetusta* (1221/2004))
Act on the Ombudsman for Equality (*laki tasa-arvovaltuutetusta* (1328/2014))
Act on the Ombudsman for Minorities (*laki vähemmistövaltuutetusta* (660/2001))
Act on the Ombudsman for Older People (*laki vanhusasiavaltuutetusta* (753/2021))
Act on the Parliamentary Ombudsman (*laki eduskunnan oikeusasiamiehestä* (197/2002))
Act on the Supervision of the Administration of Bankruptcy Estates (*laki konkurssipesien hallinnon valvonnasta* (109/1995))
Constitution Act (*Suomen Hallitusmuoto* (94/1919))
Constitution of Finland (*Suomen perustuslaki* (731/1999))
Consumer Protection Act (*kuluttajansuojalaki* (38/1978))
Convention on the Rights of Persons with Disabilities of 2006
Council Directive 2000/43/EC of 29 June 2000 implementing the principle of equal treatment between persons irrespective of racial or ethnic origin and Council Directive 2000/78/EC of 27 November 2000 establishing a general framework for equal treatment in employment and occupation [2000] OJ L180/22
Council of Europe Convention for the Protection of Individuals with Regard to Automatic Processing of Personal Data. Council of Europe Treaty Series 108, Council of Europe, 1981
Data Protection Act (*tietosuojalaki* (1050/2018))
Decree on the Competition Ombudsman (*asetus kilpailuasiamiehestä* (475/1973))
Decree on the Supervision of the Administration of Bankruptcy Estates (*asetus konkurssipesien hallinnon valvonnasta* (111/1995))
Directive (EU) 2019/633 of the European Parliament and of the Council of 17 April 2019 on unfair trading practices in business-to-business relationships in the agricultural and food supply chain [2019] OJ L111/59
Directive (EU) 2020/1828 of the European Parliament and of the Council of 25 November 2020 on representative actions for the protection of the collective interests of consumers and repealing Directive 2009/22/EC [2020] OJ L409/1
Directive 2013/11/EU of the European Parliament and of the Council of 21 May 2013 on alternative dispute resolution for consumer disputes and amending Regulation (EC) No 2006/2004 and Directive 2009/22/EC [2013] OJ L165/63
Directive 95/46/EC of the European Parliament and of the Council of 24 October 1995 on the protection of individuals with regard to the processing of personal data and on the free movement of such data [1995] OJ L281/31
Equality Act, see Act on Equality between Women and Men
Food Market Act (*elintarvikemarkkinalaki* (1121/2018))

Hallituksen esitys Eduskunnalle eräiden valtioneuvoston oikeuskansleria ja eduskunnan oikeusasiamiestä koskevien säännösten muuttamista koskevaksi lainsäädännöksi 72/1990 vp
Hallituksen esitys eduskunnalle EU:n yleistä tietosuoja-asetusta täydentäväksi lainsäädännöksi 9/2018 vp
Hallituksen esitys Eduskunnalle henkilörekisterilaiksi ja siihen liittyviksi laeiksi 49/1986 vp
Hallituksen esitys Eduskunnalle kuluttajansuojalainsäädännöksi 8/1977 vp
Hallituksen esitys Eduskunnalle laeiksi konkurssipesien hallinnon valvonnasta sekä konkurssisäännön muuttamisesta 249/1994 vp
Hallituksen esitys Eduskunnalle laiksi kilpailunrajoituksista 148/1987 vp
Hallituksen esitys eduskunnalle laiksi lapsiasiavaltuutetusta 163/2004 vp
Hallituksen esitys eduskunnalle laiksi Oikeushallinnon erityisviranomaiset -virastosta ja siihen liittyviksi laeiksi 31/2023 vp
Hallituksen esitys Eduskunnalle laiksi taloudellisen kilpailun edistämisestä 212/1972 vp
Hallituksen esitys eduskunnalle laiksi tiedustelutoiminnan valvonnasta ja laiksi valtion virkamieslain 7 §:n muuttamisesta 199/2017 vp
Hallituksen esitys Eduskunnalle laiksi ulkomaalaisvaltuutetusta 169/1990 vp
Hallituksen esitys eduskunnalle laiksi valtioneuvoston oikeuskanslerin ja eduskunnan oikeusasiamiehen tehtävien jaosta 179/2021 vp
Hallituksen esitys eduskunnalle laiksi vanhusasiavaltuutetusta 82/2021 vp
Hallituksen esitys Eduskunnalle laiksi yhdenvertaisuuden turvaamisesta sekä eräiden siihen liittyvien lakien muuttamisesta 44/2003 vp
Hallituksen esitys Eduskunnalle laiksi yhteistoiminta-asiamiehestä ja eräiksi siihen liittyviksi laeiksi 177/2009 vp
Hallituksen esitys Eduskunnalle naisten ja miesten välistä tasa-arvoa koskevaksi lainsäädännöksi 57/1985 vp
Hallituksen esitys Eduskunnalle syrjintäasiain valtuutettua koskevaksi lainsäädännöksi 39/2001 vp
Hallituksen esitys eduskunnalle yhdenvertaisuuslaiksi ja eräiksi siihen liittyviksi laeiksi 19/2014 vp
Hallituksen esitys elintarvikemarkkinalaiksi ja laiksi oikeudenkäynnistä markkinaoikeudessa annetun lain 1 luvun 6 §:n ja 5 luvun 2 §:n muuttamisesta 121/2018 vp
Intelligence Oversight Act (*laki tiedustelutoiminnan valvonnasta* (121/2019))
Non-Discrimination Act (*yhdenvertaisuuslaki* (1325/2014))
Optional Protocol to the UN Convention against Torture and other Cruel, Inhuman or Degrading Treatment or Punishment
Regulation (EU) 2016/679 of the European Parliament and of the Council of 27 April 2016 on the protection of natural persons with regard to the processing of personal data and on the free movement of such data, and repealing Directive 95/46/EC (General Data Protection Regulation) [2016] OJ L119/1
Regulations of the Finnish Financial Ombudsman Bureau (FINE). Available at https://www.fine.fi/en/about-us/regulations-and-code-of-conduct.html

UN Paris Principles – Principles relating to the Status of National Institutions (The Paris Principles) (Resolution A/RES/48/134), adopted on 20 December 1993

Documents

FINE: Annual Reports 2009– (in Finnish). Available at: https://www.fine.fi/tietoa-finesta/vuosikertomukset.html
Parliamentary Ombudsman of Finland: Summary of the Annual Report 2022 (2023). Available at: https://www.oikeusasiamies.fi/en/toimintakertomukset1
Parliamentary Ombudsman of Finland: Summary of the Annual Report 2023 (2024). Available at: https://www.oikeusasiamies.fi/en/toimintakertomukset1
Valtioneuvoston oikeus-kans-le-ri tilastot vuodelta 2023 (2024). https://oikeuskansleri.fi/vuosikertomukset-ja-tilastot

References

Beqiraj J, Garahan S, Shuttleworth K (October 2018) Ombudsman schemes and effective access to justice: a study of international practices and trends. International Bar Association. https://www.ibanet.org/document?id=Ombudsman-report-2018
Hidén M (1970) Eduskunnan oikeusasiamies. Suomalaisen Lakimiesyhdistyksen julkaisuja A-sarja N:o 90, Helsinki
Hidén M (1973) The Ombudsman in Finland: the first fifty years. Institute of Governmental Studies, University of California, Berkeley
Husa J, Jyränki A (2023) Valtiosääntöoikeus, 3rd edn. Kauppakamari, Helsinki
Kiiskinen H (2019) Valvonta: 19 § Yhdenvertaisuusvaltuutetun tehtävät ja toimivalta. In: Anttila O, Ojanen T (eds) Yhdenvertaisuuslaki kommentein. Alma Talent, Helsinki, pp 293–302
Kortteinen J (2019) Valvonta: 18 § Valvontaviranomaiset. In: Anttila O, Ojanen T (eds) Yhdenvertaisuuslaki kommentein. Alma Talent, Helsinki, pp 289–292
Koulu R (2022) Julkiset asiamiehet oikeuksiin pääsyn tukena. Comi, Helsinki
Kuluttajariitalautakunnan toiminnan kehittämistarpeet. Selvityshenkilön raportti. Oikeusministeriön julkaisuja, Selvityksiä ja ohjeita 2024:4. Available at: http://urn.fi/URN:ISBN:978-952-400-999-7
Kuluttajariitojen vaihtoehtoinen riidanratkaisu. Oikeusministeriö, Mietintöjä ja lausuntoja 25/2015. Available at: http://urn.fi/URN:ISBN:978-952-259-434-1
Lehtimaja L (2000) Privatisering ur laglighetsövervakningens synvinkel. JFT 136:587–596
Letto-Vanamo P (2017) Access to justice – a concept with many meanings. JFT 153:233–241
Luukkonen I (2011) Esipuhe. In: Sisula-Tulokas L, Luukkonen I, Sirén E, Raulos V (eds) Vakuutus- ja rahoitusneuvonta 40 vuotta. Vakuutus- ja rahoitusneuvonta, Helsinki, pp 9–12
Nieminen K (2018) 2. Tasa-arvo sukupuolten välillä. In: Koskinen S et al (eds) Työoikeus, 5th edn. Alma Talent, Helsinki, pp 377–442
Saario M (2001) Kolme vuosikymmentä kuluttajan asialla. In: Sisula-Tulokas L, Luukkonen I, Saario M (eds) Kuluttajien vakuutustoimisto ja Vakuutuslautakunta 30 vuotta. Kuluttajien vakuutustoimisto & Vakuutuslautakunta, Helsinki, pp 257–281
Svenska Akademiens ordbok. https://svenska.se/saob/?id=O_0569-0162.59Tt&pz=7
Tuori K, Kotkas T (2023) Sosiaalioikeus, 6th edn. Alma Talent, Helsinki
Viitanen K (2024) Kuluttajaoikeuden pääpiirteet. In: Villa S et al Yritysoikeus. Alma Insights, Helsinki, pp 1129–1162

Chapter 3
On Union Law Concerning Alternative Dispute Resolution Methods with Regard to Insurance Disputes

ADR Specific Requirements of the ADR Directive, ODR Regulation, IDD, Solvency II et al.

Jens Gal

3.1 Introduction

The most cataclysmic contribution of Union law to the proliferation of alternative dispute resolution methods within the insurance sector—at least from a German perspective[1]—was, quite surprisingly, probably the European Commission's recommendation to all Member States to establish a dispute resolution system, such as especially an ombudsman system, (in the banking sector) in 1990.[2] Whilst the numerous (also insurance) ombudsman systems created subsequently—which have been covered amply in the country reports presented in this book—will often leave little necessity for further ADR mechanisms, the European Union saw fit to patch any potential gap in consumer protection. It did so by providing additional methods by which consumers may seek redress against actors within the insurance industry and establishing quality standards. Despite lingering doubts regarding whether the

[1] Gal (2014), p. 11 on the reasons for which the German insurance industry was motivated by the Commission's recommendation to set up an ombudsman procedure; incorrect in this respect, Rott (2018), p. 121, who believes that banking and insurance ombudsman schemes were established by the industries due to Union law constraints.

[2] Commission (1990), cf. esp. the sixth principle in the annex. Despite being limited to the banking sector, this recommendation immediately spread to the insurance sector.

J. Gal (✉)
Regional Court of Frankfurt am Main and Institut für Versicherungsrecht, Goethe University, Frankfurt, Germany
e-mail: gal@jur.uni-frankfurt.de

H. Heiss et al. (eds.), *Insurance Ombudsman Schemes*, AIDA Europe Research Series on Insurance Law and Regulation 15,
https://doi.org/10.1007/978-3-032-01500-6_3

created patchwork of alternative venues, where policyholders may lodge complaints, optimally furthers consumer protection, the European Union is at least consistent in its approach: where an insurance-related problem involves a consumer (sensu stricto), there must be available an effective means of alternative dispute resolution.

This chapter will present and describe the ADR mechanisms as provided for, called for or specified by the ADR Directive, the ODR Regulation, the IDD, the Solvency II System and also other instruments of Union law. It remains to be seen whether this combination of provisions truly increases the level of protection or only serves to uphold consumer protection *en principe* by at the same time creating undue costs which ultimately and all too often will be borne by either the consumer (through increased prices) or the taxpayer.

3.2 ADR Directive

Whilst many Member States or their respective insurance industries had put into place an ombudsman procedure available for all insureds—sometimes irrespective of whether or not they are consumers—well before the turn of the century, this was not the case for all Member States and certainly not for all consumer disputes within other sectors. The EU set out to remedy this perceived lack[3] by introducing the ADR Directive[4] pursuant to art. 114 TFEU.[5] Whilst a need for harmonisation in respect of consumer disputes in insurance matters may be doubted, considering the fact that there are (almost) no consumers who will seek insurance cover cross-border,[6] the ADR Directive was generally very much called for, given the ever increasing tendency of consumers to contract with providers (or in terms of the ADR Directive: traders) seated in other Member States in almost all other economic sectors.

[3] The Commission had previously tried to further consumer protection by means of recommendations: Commission (1998); *id.* (2001); with regard to the EU's *acquis communautaire* in relation to out-of-court dispute resolution in consumer matters at this point, see, among others, Isermann and Berlin (2012); for a comprehensive overview, Micklitz and Rott (2023), paras. 760 et seqq.

[4] Directive 2013/11/EU of the European Parliament and of the Council of 21 May 2013 on alternative dispute resolution for consumer disputes and amending Regulation (EC) No 2006/2004 and Directive 2009/22/EC (Directive on consumer ADR) [2013] OJ L165/63.

[5] Recital 1 ADR Directive.

[6] Cf. Basedow (2000), p. 17; Heiss (2016), para. 14. To reiterate, as recently as 2007, the share of gross premiums which insurers seated in the Union collected by making use of their freedom of service and (*nota bene*) freedom of establishing a branch amounted to a measly 4% of all gross premiums, see Commission (2014), p. 9; see also Loacker (2009), p. 289 (esp. fn. 9 with further references). There are, however, some exceptions, for example automotive hull and third-party liability insurance for a rental car contracted by a consumer from home for a holiday.

3.2.1 *Requirement Concerning the Establishment of an ADR Mechanism*

The ADR Directive is intended to fulfil three main objectives:[7] firstly, it is designed to broaden the availability of ADR mechanisms for all types of domestic[8] and cross-border disputes covered by the Directive; secondly, it is intended to harmonise minimum quality standards that apply to consumer ADR procedures; and, thirdly, it is meant to increase consumers' and traders' awareness of the existence of such procedures. In order to realise these objectives, Member States are obligated to take certain actions.

With regard to the most pertinent provisions of the ADR Directive, Member States are required under art. 5(1) of the ADR Directive to facilitate access by European consumers to ADR procedures as well as to ensure that disputes covered by the Directive involving a trader established on their respective territories can be submitted to an ADR entity which complies with the requirements set out. Since insurance disputes, at least those involving consumer insurance, clearly fall within the scope of art. 2(1) of the ADR Directive in connection with the definitions provided in art. 4 of the ADR Directive, Member States were thenceforth under a legal obligation to ensure the existence of an ADR procedure, be it an ombudsman procedure or a comparable mechanism.

Member States were enabled to fulfil their obligation to ensure a nationwide system of ADR entities "by building on existing properly functioning ADR entities and adjusting their scope of application, if needed, or by providing for the creation of new ADR entities".[9] Based on the positive experience with the existing ombudsman procedures for insurance disputes, many Member States opted to "legalise" those mechanisms, rather than create alternative venues for consumer complaints (at least for this sector, and at least for the traders who acceded to this scheme). This was not always merely by choice, since a functioning provider of an ADR mechanism, set up in accordance with the Directive, had a legal right to be included in the list of recognised ADR entities to be drawn up by the competent body in accordance with art. 20(2) of the ADR Directive.[10]

[7] See Recital 7 ADR Directive.

[8] There remains doubt about how the Union may introduce legislation to govern ADR mechanisms for purely national consumer disputes under art. 114 TFEU; cf. critically, for instance, Meller-Hannich et al. (2014), pp. 15 et seq.; Micklitz and Rott (2023), paras. 765.

[9] Recital 24 ADR Directive.

[10] Cf. Recital 15 ADR Directive; see also Hirsch (2013), p. 2090, who correctly points out that, when in doubt, an ADR entity might petition the national courts to decide on the question of whether it is in line with the ADR Directive and, thus, must be admitted to the list of recognised ADR entities.

3.2.2 *Qualitative Requirements Attaching to the ADR Mechanism and Entity*

In order to become and remain a recognised (sectoral) ADR entity, all ombudsman schemes are required to notify the competent authority within their Member State and to explain that their set-up and procedure is in line with the minimum requirements of the Directive.[11] Within most Member States this was but a pure formality, since the existing insurance ombudsman systems far exceeded any such requirements and continue to do so.[12] It may nevertheless be helpful to point out the most salient requirement an ADR mechanism for insurance disputes needs to fulfil.

Pursuant to art. 6(1) of the ADR Directive, the natural persons in charge of ADR—i.e. in insurance, the ombudsperson—must possess the necessary expertise, and shall be independent and impartial, with independence being paramount. In this respect, the question arises as to whether, in addition to the personal independence of the ombudsperson, the institutional independence of the ADR entity is also required.[13] It can be deduced from art. 6(4) of the ADR Directive that the persons entrusted with ADR may be employed or remunerated by the professional association concerned, as long as independence is guaranteed *via* additional organisational and accompanying measures, such as in particular a separate budget of a sufficient amount. An ADR entity that is organisationally and financially supported by a trade association—which is the case for many ombudsman schemes—therefore meets the requirements of the Directive if its independence is guaranteed accordingly. To further promote the acceptance of the ombudsperson's decisions, measures should be put into place to ensure that the ADR body is objectively recognised as legally independent by external actors. This can be achieved, for example, by establishing the ADR support organisation as an independent registered association, which may provide for an autonomous body[14] that is not under control of the traders and that decides on the competences, the rights and obligations of the ombudsperson, the rules of procedure, and the budget.

Art. 5(4) of the ADR Directive contains a list of circumstances under which access to the instituted ADR procedure may be limited under procedural rules. Access may be refused, for example, in relation to complaints that are already pending before another ADR entity or a court, are frivolous or vexatious, exceed or fall below a pre-defined amount in dispute,[15] are time-barred according to the predefined time limit—which, however, must meet certain criteria—, or seriously

[11] See arts. 19 et seq. ADR Directive.

[12] Cf. country reports YYY above.

[13] This question is raised, among others, by Hirsch (2013), p. 2091; also enquiring in this direction, Meller-Hannich et al. (2014), p. 18.

[14] Cf., for example, Gal (2014), pp. 16 et seq. *et passim*, where the supervisory board of the German *Versicherungsombusmann e.V.* is discussed.

[15] Recital 25 ADR Directive: "When providing for a monetary threshold, Member States should always take into account that the real value of a dispute may vary among Member States and,

impair the effective operation of the ADR entity, for example because it is "too complex and would therefore be better resolved in court".[16] Hence, any ombudsman entity should review its specific barriers to access in light of this provision and, in case of doubt, should seek clarification from the national "competent authority" within the meaning of art. 18 of the ADR Directive, since non-compliance might endanger the entity's acceptance as a competent ADR provider under art. 20(2) of the ADR Directive. Furthermore art. 5(7) of the ADR Directive allows for complaints made against traders in a specific economic sector to be limited to members of the relevant organisation or association (as is the case with many insurance ombudsman systems).[17]

It is not stated in the ADR Directive which powers the ADR entity should be granted to resolve disputes. It may be authorised to make a proposal for conciliation, to suggest a goodwill settlement, to mediate a settlement, to propose a solution or to impose such a solution.[18] In practice, as highlighted above in the national reports, ombudspersons are entrusted with rather varying powers. These can range from mediation and conciliation to non-binding recommendations and binding decisions. In this regard, it is recognised in art. 2(4) of the ADR Directive that it is for the Member States to determine whether ADR entities should be granted the power to impose solutions. Pursuant to art. 10(2) of the ADR Directive, however, a solution can only be imposed on the parties if they were informed in advance about a binding decision being a possible outcome and they expressly accepted this.[19] Thus, while the ADR Directive does not prevent the establishment of ADR procedures which provide for decisions to be binding on the consumer, it seems that such a procedural framework is not without its deficits, since it might cause consumers to shy away from making use of an alternative dispute resolution mechanism, to which they are not accustomed, out of fear of being deprived of their usual legal remedies.[20]

Under ADR Directive, fees may be levied, yet no reference is made on their extent. Since the ADR mechanism is to be created in order to strengthen consumer

---

consequently, setting a disproportionately high threshold in one Member State could impair access to ADR procedures for consumers from other Member States."

[16] Recital 25 ADR Directive.

[17] In such a case, however, Member States need to provide for a "catch-all"-ADR mechanism that applies to the sectoral traders that are not members of the customary sectoral ADR entity, see Cortés (2016), p. 17 (fn. 21 with further references); in Germany, for example, this would be the *Universalschlichtungsstelle des Bundes*. This, of course, creates considerable problems since such a universal ADR entity would not necessarily possess the expertise to handle sector specific disputes, which would mean that by not acceding to a special ombudsman scheme a trader would deprive its customers of access to a better functioning ADR system.

[18] Recital 21 ADR Directive.

[19] The company's consent is irrelevant if a Member State enacts legislation that requires decisions of the ADR entity to be binding on the trader, or such consent is inferred from the fact that the trader made a self-commitment by seeking membership of the sponsoring association which in the rules of procedure provides for a decision to be binding on the trader; cf. Hirsch (2013), p. 2092.

[20] Therefore, most insurance ombudsman procedures are, generally, free of charge and non-binding on the consumer; see, for example, country reports YYY.

protection, it can be argued that any fee imposed must be of such a modest amount in comparison to potential court fees so as to motivate consumers to enter into ADR.

All too often only a quick decision is a good decision, a dictum even more appropriate to ADR, since timeliness is regarded as one of its main advantages over court procedures.[21] Hence, under art. 8(e) of the ADR Directive, there is a maximum time limit of 90 days for the ADR "decision", with the period starting upon receipt of the complete complaint file.[22] Furthermore, where a decision is not binding at least on the claimant, art. 12(1) of the ADR Directive requires that parties "are not subsequently prevented from initiating judicial proceedings in relation to that dispute as a result of the expiry of limitation or prescription periods during the ADR procedure". Every Member State must, therefore, create provisions under which limitation periods are suspended during the pending or ongoing ADR proceedings.

The ADR Directive also contains a wealth of provisions governing obligations relating to publication, information, transparency, data protection, notification, reporting, and cooperation that are to apply to entrusted ADR entities, and also to the traders (see art. 13 of the ADR Directive), as well as control and supervisory rules applicable to the competent bodies.[23] Any ombudsman entity would be well advised to pay heed to the implementation law applicable and to take into account the provisions of the ADR Directive.

3.2.3 *Reform*

Whilst ombudsman procedures in the insurance sector have rendered admirable results throughout the Union, they may have remained lacklustre in some Member States, and ADR procedures have left much to be desired in other commercial sectors. This prompted the EU to consider a more inclusive approach. To this end, the European Commission recently launched several surveys—including a public consultation on the need to amend the ADR Directive which closed in 2022[24]—and (co-)organised several events addressing the topic.[25] In October 2023, the Commission published its proposal on the amendment of the ADR Directive.[26] For

[21] Cf. Gal (2024a), paras. 31 et seqq. (with a view to arbitration).

[22] Recital 40 ADR Directive clarifies that the relevant moment is the time at which the complaint file with all relevant documents is made available, with the request for the documents necessary for the handling of the appeal as well as the statements (and, if applicable, replies) of the parties being excluded from the calculation of the time limit.

[23] See for an overview, for example, Meller-Hannich et al. (2014), pp. 25 et seqq.; Cortés (2016), pp. 17 et seqq.

[24] See European Commission, Consumer protection law – cross-border enforcement. https://ec.europa.eu/info/law/better-regulation/have-your-say/initiatives/13430-Functioning-of-cross-border-consumer-law-enforcement-in-the-EU/public-consultation_en. Accessed 16 Apr 2025.

[25] For more details, cf. Biard (2022), p. 181.

[26] Commission (2023).

present purposes, it seems superfluous or rather premature to comment on all of the changes proposed. Nevertheless, it should be pointed out that ADR sponsoring associations, ombudsman entities and insurers would be well advised to keep themselves in the loop: change is on the horizon.

3.3 ODR Regulation

The ADR Directive is supplemented by the Online Dispute Resolution Regulation (hereinafter ODR Regulation),[27] which is intended, in particular, to remove the obstacles that attach to disputes arising from cross-border consumer transactions, but applies to any disputes arising from online sales or service contracts between a consumer residing in the Union and a trader established therein,[28] by enabling disputes to be settled entirely by electronic means. Since consumers will seldom seek cross-border insurance cover,[29] the ODR Regulation has no noteworthy effect regarding its prime objective in the realm of insurance, yet remains applicable to purely national disputes.

In implementing the ODR Regulation, the Commission has created an electronic platform on which consumers (and traders[30]) can submit their complaints using an electronic form. All (online) traders to which the ODR Regulation applies are obliged under art. 14(1) of the ODR Regulation to provide an easily accessible link to the Commission's platform for online dispute resolution[31] on their website and to provide information set out art. 14(2) of the ODR Regulation. Said platform is an interactive website that is free to use for the parties involved, however, its use requires certain identification methods and apps,[32] which might in itself serve to dissuade some consumers from making use of the platform. The platform is intended to function as a central contact point that either grants the parties a forum to resolve their dispute bilaterally or proposes one or more (presumably competent) ADR entities and forwards the complaint to the ADR entity on which the parties have agreed.

[27] Regulation (EU) 524/2013 of the European Parliament and of the Council of 21 May 2013 on online dispute resolution for consumer disputes and amending Regulation (EC) No 2006/2004 and Directive 2009/22/EC (Regulation on consumer ODR) [2013] OJ L165/1.

[28] Recitals 10 and 11 ODR Regulation. Contrary to Micklitz and Rott (2023), para. 768, there exist no exceptions for contracts concluded online regarding services to be performed offline; cf. Recital 15.

[29] See n. 7 above.

[30] Traders may only lodge a claim on the ODR platform if it regards a dispute with a consumer hailing from a Member State that allows for this, i.e., Belgium, Germany, Luxembourg, and Poland.

[31] Available at https://www.ec.europa.eu/consumers/odr. Accessed 16 Apr 2025.

[32] See disclaimer on the ODR platform: "Dear user, for security reasons all commission IT services will have to implement multi-factor authentication (MFA). This means that as of 01 November you would need to use your phone (MFA by SMS), your smartphone (EU Login App, available from Google Play and App store) or a security key (Yubikey, Fido2key, U2F, etc)". Accessed 02 Feb 2024).

If the ADR entity in question levies a fee, the ODR platform informs the parties of these costs in advance.

Pursuant to art. 7(1) of the ODR Regulation, Member States must designate ODR contact points in which at least two ODR advisors are active. These ODR contact points can be public authorities, but Member States may—and are encouraged to—also assign this function to their respective centre in the ECC-Net.[33] The ODR advisors are required under art. 7(2) of the ODR Regulation to perform certain tasks, such as informing the parties about the advantages and disadvantages of the available ADR procedures and pointing the consumer towards other means of redress, especially if the trader does not agree to the alternative dispute resolution, while always making clear to consumers that they are under no obligation to make use of any of the ADR mechanisms on offer and remain free to directly petition the courts.[34] If the parties agree on an ADR entity, this entity will inform them of the terms of the procedure. A decision should normally be issued within 30 days.

Despite the considerable costs incurred in the establishment and operation of the ODR platform, the ODR contact points and the ODR network to be established, the ODR system has had rather modest success—which is presumably one of the main reasons why the Commission sees a need for reform.[35] The lack of any practical relevance of the ODR system probably hinges on the fact that traders are not obliged to participate in ADR proceedings and therefore will all too often not agree on submitting a dispute to an ADR entity. This, however, seems utterly irrelevant for consumer insurance disputes. Since such disputes rarely exhibit a cross-border aspect, consumers are in no need to contact a middleman, as they will almost invariably directly address their complaint to the competent national ombudsperson, whose contact must be provided by the insurer (or insurance intermediary) with the required information material.[36]

[33] See YYY below.

[34] For purely internal online consumer disputes, which will almost invariably be the case for consumer insurance disputes, the Member States are free to refrain from grant their ODR contact points with the powers and duties of art. 7(2) of the ODR Regulation; cf. art. 7(3) et seq. of the ODR Regulation.

[35] See YYY above.

[36] Since the insurance sector is rigorously supervised, in contrast to other sectors contracting with consumers, it can be expected that the vast majority of consumers will receive this information and will additionally be informed of the option of ADR by insurers if a dispute arises.

3.4 IDD

The Insurance Distribution Directive (hereinafter IDD)[37] is intended to strengthen and consolidate the provisions of the previous Insurance Mediation Directive[38] (hereinafter IMD)[39] and to that end also requires the establishment of adequate ADR procedures for the settlement of disputes between customers and insurance distributors. Pursuant to art. 2(1)(8) IDD, insurance distributor is to be understood in the broadest manner possible, i.e. including insurance intermediaries, ancillary insurance intermediaries and insurance undertakings.

Under art. 14 IDD, on the one hand, Member States are required to force insurers (and potentially other insurance distributors) to set up an internal complaints mechanism open to "customers and other interested parties, especially consumer associations,"[40] in order to lodge complaints about insurance and reinsurance distributors, which must at minimum receive answers to their complaint. Whilst this internal complaints function seems crucial to bolster consumer protection, it does not amount to an ADR procedure.

On the other hand, and more importantly in the context of the present chapter, Member States are required under art. 15(1) IDD to

> ensure that adequate and effective, impartial and independent out-of-court complaint and redress procedures for the settlement of disputes between customers and insurance distributors concerning the rights and obligations arising under this Directive are established in accordance with the relevant Union legislative acts and national law, using existing bodies where appropriate.

This provision did not change the situation for insurers; it did, however, have an impact on disputes involving insurance intermediaries.[41] Where disputes arose between consumers and the latter in the past, Member States were previously only required to "promote" such ADR procedures under art. 11 IMD, not to "establish" them. Insofar art. 15(1) IDD led to the closure of a relevant gap in the protection provided, while allowing Member States to empower already existing insurance ombudsman systems to also deal with these additional disputes. There is, however, no need to submit the ADR mechanism designed for insurance intermediaries to the same principles as those applied to the mechanism provided in the ADR Directive for disputes involving insurers. In this regard, there is no reference in the IDD to the principles set out in the ADR Directive; rather, the ADR procedure must "only" be

---

[37] Directive (EU) 2016/97 of the European Parliament and of the Council of 20 January 2016 on insurance distribution (recast) [2016] OJ L26/19.

[38] Directive 2002/92/EC of the European Parliament and of the Council of 9 December 2002 on insurance mediation [2003] OJ L9/3.

[39] Castle (2019), pp. 97 et seqq.; Hofmann et al. (2018), pp. 740 et seqq.; Bernardino (2015), p. 7; Montemaggiori (2021), p. 336 with further references.

[40] Cf., e.g., Bähr in Kaulbach et al. (2019), § 51 VAG para. 10 with regard to problems relating to the interpretation and transposition of art. 14 IDD.

[41] Cf. Montemaggiori (2021), pp. 336 et seq.

"adequate and effective, impartial and independent".[42] Since the ADR Directive is based on the same understanding of the qualities necessary of an ADR mechanism,[43] there are nevertheless good reasons to assert that the ADR mechanism to be provided under the IDD, in general, should be devised to meet the standards of the ADR Directive, even if a national legislature may choose to not extend certain qualities—such as the power of the ombudsperson to take binding decisions in respect of the trader—to disputes relating to insurance intermediaries.[44]

3.5 Solvency II System

Pursuant to the second paragraph of art. 183(1) and art. 185(3)(l) of Solvency II Directive,[45] the insurer shall inform the policyholder of

> the arrangements for handling complaints [of policyholders, lives assureds or beneficiaries] concerning contracts including, where appropriate, the existence of a complaints body, without prejudice to the right of the policy holder to take legal proceedings.

The Solvency II System, thus, implies that any insurer licensed within the EU must at a minimum establish an internal complaints function, which it must also make known to its policyholders prior to contract conclusion.[46]

Whilst such an internal mechanism cannot be regarded as ADR, the institution of such a mechanism will at the very least aid to weed out obviously unlawful decisions made by the claims handling division of an insurer, help consumers to understand their respective insurer's decision as well as aid them in assessing the likelihood of success of any potential claim. Furthermore, insurers are obliged by said provisions to inform the consumer of (other) ADR venues, if they are available—under the national law transposing the provisions of the ADR Directive, the ODR Regulation or the IDD—whilst pointing out that it is possible to make such a "complaint" without prejudice to the right of the policyholder to lodge a claim before court. If, however, the applicable ombudsman procedure allows for decisions that are also binding on consumers, rather than only on insurers (or insurance intermediaries), the information provided should also make clear that the option to

42 The first sentence of art. 15(1) IDD; cf. also Montemaggiori (2021), pp. 337 et seq.

43 See YYY above.

44 Such is the case, for example, in YYY; see YYY[country reports] above/below.

45 Directive 2009/138/EC of the European Parliament and of the Council of 25 November 2009 on the taking-up and pursuit of the business of Insurance and Reinsurance (Solvency II) (recast) [2009] OJ L335/1.

46 This rule, apparently, seemed so obvious that the Union abstained from dedicating even one measly recital to the question of complaints handling. This is rather problematic, since it remains unclear whether insurers are permitted to forgo an internal complaints mechanism if they provide for an external ADR mechanism; see Sasserath-Alberti and Hartig (2012), pp. 531 et seq. who is very critical.

petition the ombudsperson might under certain conditions, or to a certain extent, limit the legal right to sue.

Rather surprisingly, the Solvency II Directive remains silent on complaints submitted to national supervisory authorities. Whilst the absence of an explicit rule should not be understood to forbid the national supervisory authority to hear such complaints,[47] there is no rule obliging them to do so—unless a Member State has chosen to empower its supervisory authority to act as the competent "ADR entity" of the legal instruments described previously. At least some Member States, sometimes due to constitutional constraints, have chosen to grant their supervisory authorities such powers.[48]

3.6 EIOPA Regulation

Whilst the European Insurance and Occupational Pensions Authority (EIOPA) is mostly "the supervisor of supervisors",[49] it has in recent years, nevertheless, assumed some powers to "hear" consumer complaints and certainly saw fit to have its say on such complaints at national level.

While EIOPA is entrusted with extensive powers regarding consumer protection—see in particular art. 9 of the EIOPA Regulation[50]—, it is not empowered to receive complaints by consumers against insurers and other traders such as intermediaries. Yet, consumers may make a complaint to EIOPA regarding a perceived breach of Union law by an insurance supervisory authority of a Member State. In such a procedure, however, the consumer is not a complainant in the true sense of the term, but rather a "reporting person".[51] It seems that appeals by consumers against decisions of EIOPA under art. 60 of the EIOPA Regulation are only possible in very limited circumstances since it is difficult to imagine a situation in which a

[47] Since the Solvency II Directive is for the most part a minimum harmonisation directive; see Gal (2021), para. 29 for more details.

[48] With regard to Germany, cf. s. 4b of the Act Establishing the Federal Financial Supervisory Authority (*Finanzdienstleistungsaufsichtsgesetz*, hereinafter FinDAG); in Germany, the complaints mechanism to the German Federal Financial Supervisory Authority (hereinafter BaFin) is a specialised means to grant the fundamental right enshrined in art. 17 of the German Constitution (*Grundgesetz*) to petition public authorities; cf. Hilgenstock in Dreher (2024), § 4b FinDAG para. 1; BaFin, however, does not adjudicate a dispute, instead it only uses the information provided by the consumer to establish if the insurer in question is in breach of its supervisory duties; cf. Diehl in Höra and Schubach (2022), § 38 paras. 118 et seqq.

[49] Gal (2024b), art. 2 EIOPA-VO para. 8.

[50] Regulation (EU) 1094/2010 of the European Parliament and of the Council of 24 November 2010 establishing a European Supervisory Authority (European Insurance and Occupational Pensions Authority), amending Decision No 716/2009/EC and repealing Commission Decision 2009/79/EC [2010] OJ L331/48.

[51] See the detailed discussion in Gal (2024b), art. 17 EIOPA-VO paras. 12 and 20 as well as *ibid.* art. 17a EIOPA-VO paras. 1 et seqq.

decision is directly addressed to consumers or affects them directly and individually.[52]

EIOPA has, nevertheless, attempted to harmonise complaints handling *via* soft-law instruments, i.e. by issuing the Complaints-Handling Guidelines.[53] These Guidelines issued under the powers set out in art. 16 of the EIOPA Regulation are not directly applicable to insurers; they only address the supervisory authorities, which have, however, for the most part chosen to adhere[54] to these Guidelines.[55] The standards for the internal complaints-handling by insurers under the Solvency II System are set out in the Guidelines and certain aspects of insurance ADR are also addressed. Firstly, according to Guideline 4 para. 13, it is the task of supervisory authorities to ensure that insurance undertakings provide the competent national authorities or ombudsman service with information on complaints and complaints-handling. Secondly, the supervisory authority should ensure that insurance undertakings provide clear, accurate and up-to-date information about the complaints-handling process, including the availability of an ombudsman or alternative dispute resolution (ADR) scheme.[56] Finally, supervisory authorities are required under Guideline 7 para. 16(d) to ensure that if an insurance undertaking takes a final decision that does not fully satisfy the complainant's demand, it will provide, inter alia, information on the option of submitting a complaint to an ombudsman service, alternative dispute entity, national competent authority and so on.

3.7 Varia

While the provisions of Union law discussed above set out the most important minimum requirements to which insurance ADR must adhere, many other legal instruments of the EU at least allude to ADR in the insurance sector. The most important of these will be discussed *en passant*—without claiming to give an exhaustive account.

---

[52] Cf. Gal (2024b) art. 60 EIOPA-VO para. 26, providing greater detail; the same is true of the right to petition the Commission under art. 60a of the EIOPA Regulation, cf. *ibid.* art. 60a EIOPA-VO paras. 4 et seq.

[53] EIOPA (2012).

[54] Adherence will usually mean that the Guidelines are transposed into a national soft-law instrument addressed to the insurance undertakings; for example, see BaFin, Circular 3/2013 (VA), which remains applicable even after the German supervisory authority passed its "catch-all" MaGo Circular; see BaFin, Circular 2/2017 (VA), para. 10.

[55] Guidelines issued by EIOPA (the Guidelines on Complaints-Handling are no exception) will almost without fault receive a "comply" or "intend to comply" response from the national supervisory authorities; see Gal (2024b), art. 16 EIOPA-VO para. 64, providing much more detail.

[56] See Guideline 6 para. 15(c)(ii) EIOPA (2012); it is to be understood that such information should also be provided on the respective insurer's homepage.

3.7.1 *ECC-Net*

Well before starting to harmonise consumer ADR, the Union and the European (Economic) Community respectively attempted to enhance the protection afforded to consumers making use of their Four Freedoms in regard of cross-border contracts for goods or services by establishing networks between national ADR entities *via* soft-law initiatives.

Without detailing the establishment of the Network of Euroguichets in 1992 and of the Network for the extra-judicial settlement of consumer disputes (EEJ-Net) in 2001,[57] it should be noted that the European Commission established the European Consumer Centres Network (ECC-Net) by merging the aforementioned networks with a view to efficiently providing consumers with information about their rights within the internal market and providing free assistance to consumers facing problems in enforcing their rights.[58]

The ECC-Net is a consumer information and assistance structure with contact points ("clearing houses") in each Member State.[59] The aim of ECC-Net is to provide consumers with information on their rights and obligations regarding cross-border disputes.[60] A consumer will submit the claim to its national contact point, e.g. the ECC Poland; the latter will liaise with the contact point in the Member State in which the trader is seated, e.g. the ECC Germany, to reach an amicable solution, or direct the consumer to the available ADR entities.[61]

Due to the existence of the FIN-Net, the ECC-Net plays but a reduced (albeit enduring[62]) role in handling insurance disputes and will assist consumer-policyholders to contact the relevant insurance ADR entity. The ECC-Net is, however, rather active in publishing policy papers which might also be given consideration by insurance ombudspersons.

3.7.2 *FIN-Net*

Beginning in 2001, the European Commission started to promote the creation of the Network for Financial Services (FIN-Net) among ADR entities active in the banking, financial and insurance sectors within the Member States, in order to connect

[57] See Council Resolution of 25 May 2000 on a Community-wide network of national bodies for the extra-judicial settlement of consumer disputes [2000] OJ C155/1.

[58] Danzeisen et al. (2020), pp. 10 et seq.

[59] Montemaggiori (2021), p. 335; for a good overview, see Danzeisen et al. (2020).

[60] Art. 1(2) ECC-Net (2014) Vademecum.

[61] Cf. arts. 3 et seqq. ECC-Net (2014) Vademecum.

[62] For the most part, the ECC-Net is important to insurance disputes, since the respective ECC of the Member States will often be named as the ODR contact points, see YYY above.

such national competent bodies which are “duty-bound” to comply with the requirements of the Recommendation 98/257/EC.[63]

FIN-Net presently comprises of 62 ADR entities in 30 countries (in Member States, Iceland, Liechtenstein and Norway). The collaboration is currently based on a Memorandum of Understanding[64] (MoU) that not only provides for network members, but also for temporary members (for which recognition is pending) and affiliated ADR entities (which operate in countries where the ADR Directive does not apply, e.g. in Switzerland).

Without going into too much detail on the duties of cooperation, the MoU basically obliges members to set up their procedure in a manner that adheres to both the ADR Directive and the additional standards set out by the MoU.

3.7.3 Mediation Directive

In view of the existence of insurance ombudsman systems and the acceptance that these procedures have gained, insurers are rather reserved in making use of mediation procedures to defuse conflicts with insureds.[65] In this respect, the Mediation Directive[66] and the respective implementing legislation passed by the Member States have had little to no relevance in the insurance sector.

3.7.4 PEPP Regulation

The PEPP Regulation[67] obliges the providers and distributors of pan-European pension products to establish an internal complaints-handling mechanism, yet, under art. 50(4) they are also obliged to provide customers with the contact of at least one ADR body that is competent to deal with disputes concerning PEPP customers’ rights and obligations.

Member States are under no duty to establish a distinctive ADR entity and procedure. Pursuant to art. 51(1) of the PEPP Regulation, the procedure must be in line with the requirements laid down in the ADR Directive and, where possible, the

---

[63] Commission (1998).

[64] FIN-Net (2016). FIN-Net is, hence, a public-private structure which is based on each national ombudsman services’s decisions to accede to FIN-Net by also underwriting its MoU.

[65] For an extensive overview of insurance mediation in Germany, and especially mediation clauses sometimes used in consumer litigation insurance, see e.g. Wendt in Klowait and Gläßer (2018), part 3 ch. J paras. 8 et seqq.

[66] Directive 2008/52/EC of the European Parliament and of the Council of 21 May 2008 on certain aspects of mediation in civil and commercial matters [2008] OJ L136/3.

[67] Regulation (EU) 2019/1238 of the European Parliament and of the Council of 20 June 2019 on a pan-European Personal Pension Product (PEPP) [2019] OJ L198/1.

remit of ADR bodies established thereunder shall be extended to also include dealing with PEPP disputes. In this respect, it seems desirable that insurance ombudspersons also assume "jurisdiction" over those disputes. This might, however, create problems for any ADR entities that only offer their services to resolve disputes involving their member undertakings.

3.7.5 PRIPPs Regulation

In contrast, the PRIIPs Regulation[68] remains less transparent regarding ADR procedures. Under art. 19(a) and (b) of the PRIIPs Regulation, manufacturers, sellers and advisors of or on PRIIPs (packaged retail and insurance-based investment products) are required to set up an effective internal complaints mechanism for retail investors.

In art. 19(c) of the PRIIPs Regulation, it is declared that there must be an effective redress procedure available to retail investors in the event of cross-border disputes. Since the Regulation is otherwise silent, it may safely be assumed that the procedure must align with the ADR Directive, and the remit of already existing ombudsman schemes may be broadened to also include disputes concerning PRIIPs.

3.7.6 PRICL

The importance that the Union attaches to ombudsman procedures can also be inferred from art. 1:302 of the Principles of European Insurance Contract Law (PEICL). It is stated in this provision that a choice in favour of the application of the PEICL to the insurance contract cannot lead to a consumer being deprived of its options to submit a dispute to an ADR entity.

While it is currently—despite the initial intention[69]—not possible to choose the PEICL exclusively as the law applicable in lieu of the autonomous national insurance contract laws of the Member States, the PEICL highlight that they would not hinder recourse to any out-of-court redress mechanism available.

This rule seems especially important since many ombudsman procedures refuse to handle disputes which are based on foreign law.[70] In this regard, art. 1:302 PEICL also serves to point out that the PEICL, if they were to be put in force in the whole

[68] Regulation (EU) 1286/2014 of the European Parliament and of the Council of 26 November 2014 on key information documents for packaged retail and insurance-based investment products (PRIIPs) [2014] OJ L3521.

[69] Heiss (2016), para. I 34 et seqq. with further references; Gal (2009), p. 191.

[70] See art. 1:302 C4 PEICL, also providing several examples of insurance ombudsman procedural rules.

Union in the future, would not constitute a foreign but common law and disputes should thus be handled by any ombudsperson, otherwise competent.[71]

If ever Union law should allow for the PEICL to be selected as the applicable law to (cross-border) insurance contracts—which is to be hoped for, but remains uncertain for the time being—any ombudsperson would have to build up the expertise to also settle disputes under insurance contracts governed by the PEICL.

3.8 Conclusion

Without underplaying certain deficits of some insurance ombudsman procedures in certain Member States, the national reports presented in this book, for the most part, paint a picture of unmitigated success. If there is any economic sector that has taken seriously the need to establish an impartial, independent, transparent, efficient, and fair ADR procedure, it has been the insurance industry, despite all too often being maligned as rampantly consumer unfriendly.

Existing insurance ombudsman schemes have been successful in practice, and hopefully by paying heed to the aforementioned Union law, yet time, tide, and the EU wait for no man or ADR mechanism. A reform of the ADR Directive, and presumably all of the supplementary legal instruments, seems imminent and can be expected to bring about change that is anything but incremental. Since the Commission regards the variation among different sectoral ADR mechanisms to at least be problematic,[72] it is to be feared that insurance ombudsman procedures will be held hostage by the deficits within other economic sectors. It remains to be seen whether the ADR system in the Union will keep its character of minimum harmonisation or will move more into the direction of full harmonisation. Hope remains that the EU will keep in mind that a consumer complaint cannot be equated with a consumer complaint, creating the necessity for sector-specific ADR mechanisms. An ombudsperson cannot be expected to have the same level of expertise in dealing with complaints concerning different sectors, such as telecommunication contracts, the delivery of building materials and the mediation of insurance contracts. Hitherto, the ADR Directive—and the supplementary legal instruments—have been based on a minimum harmonisation approach, giving ample regard to the fact that ADR schemes already existed in many Member States and were strongly shaped by national or sectorial contexts,[73] and therefore the models diverged significantly across Europe.[74] While this approach towards harmonisation may have led to ADR procedures in certain sectors in some Member States remaining unsatisfactory, it

[71] Art. 1:302 C4 PEICL.

[72] Commission (2023), p. 1 where the Commission states that it wishes to maintain the minimum harmonisation approach but nevertheless highlights its shortcomings.

[73] This holds especially true for the insurance sector, keeping in mind that insurance contract law has for the most part remained autonomous law of the Member States; cf. Weber-Rey (2006).

[74] Biard (2022), p. 182.

has also enabled the Member States, traders and interest groups to best tailor ADR mechanisms to specific sectoral needs. A switch now to an approach of full-harmonisation would be akin to throwing out the baby with the bathwater This is especially true where the consumer insurance sector is concerned, which for the most part continues to be a purely national market governed by national law and shaped by country-specific general conditions of insurance.

While it, thus, seems obvious that the present book will need to be revised in the not-so-distant future, *nil desperandum*, insurance ombudsman procedures can be expected to adapt to new regulatory requirements with ease as they have done in the past. Ombudsman procedures will continue to facilitate consumer protection and at the same time, improve the image of insurance by aiding consumers to better understand their insurers' decisions.

Legal Sources

Directive (EU) 2016/97 of the European Parliament and of the Council of 20 January 2016 on insurance distribution (recast), in OJ L 26 of 02.02.2016, pp. 19 et seqq. https://eur-lex.europa.eu/legal-content/EN/TXT/HTML/?uri=CELEX:32013L0011

Directive 2002/92/EC of the European Parliament and of the Council of 9 December 2002 on insurance mediation [2003] OJ L9/3. https://eur-lex.europa.eu/legal-content/EN/TXT/?uri=CELEX:32002L0092

Directive 2008/52/EC of the European Parliament and of the Council of 21 May 2008 on certain aspects of mediation in civil and commercial matters [2008] OJ L136/3. https://eur-lex.europa.eu/legal-content/EN/TXT/HTML/?uri=CELEX:32008L0052

Directive 2009/138/EC of the European Parliament and of the Council of 25 November 2009 on the taking-up and pursuit of the business of Insurance and Reinsurance (Solvency II) (recast) [2009] OJ L335/1. https://eur-lex.europa.eu/legal-content/EN/TXT/HTML/?uri=CELEX:32009L0138

Directive 2013/11/EU of the European Parliament and of the Council of 21 May 2013 on alternative dispute resolution for consumer disputes and amending Regulation (EC) No 2006/2004 and Directive 2009/22/EC (Directive on consumer ADR) [2013] OJ L165/63. https://eur-lex.europa.eu/legal-content/EN/TXT/HTML/?uri=CELEX:32013L0011

Gesetz über die Bundesanstalt für Finanzdienstleistungsaufsicht (Finanzdienstleistungsaufsichtsgesetz – FinDAG), in BGBl. 2002, p. I-1310. English translation https://www.bafin.de/SharedDocs/Veroeffentlichungen/EN/Aufsichtsrecht/Gesetz/findag_aktuell_en.html

Regulation (EU) 1094/2010 of the European Parliament and of the Council of 24 November 2010 establishing a European Supervisory Authority (European Insurance and Occupational Pensions Authority), amending Decision No 716/2009/EC and repealing Commission Decision 2009/79/EC [2010] OJ

L331/48. https://eur-lex.europa.eu/legal-content/EN/ALL/?uri=CELEX:32010R1094

Regulation (EU) 1286/2014 of the European Parliament and of the Council of 26 November 2014 on key information documents for packaged retail and insurance-based investment products (PRIIPs) [2014] OJ L352/1. https://eur-lex.europa.eu/legal-content/EN/TXT/HTML/?uri=CELEX:32013L0011

Regulation (EU) 2019/1238 of the European Parliament and of the Council of 20 June 2019 on a pan-European Personal Pension Product (PEPP) [2019] OJ L1981. https://eur-lex.europa.eu/legal-content/EN/TXT/HTML/?uri=CELEX:32019R1238

Regulation (EU) 524/2013 of the European Parliament and of the Council of 21 May 2013 on online dispute resolution for consumer disputes and amending Regulation (EC) No 2006/2004 and Directive 2009/22/EC (Regulation on consumer ODR) [2013] OJ L1651. https://eur-lex.europa.eu/legal-content/EN/TXT/HTML/?uri=CELEX:32013R0524

Documents

BaFin, Circular 2/2017 (VA) – Minimum Requirements under Supervisory Law on the System of Governance of Insurance Undertakings (*Mindestanforderungen an die Geschäftsorganisation von Versicherungsunternehmen* [MaGo]). https://www.bafin.de/SharedDocs/Veroeffentlichungen/EN/Rundschreiben/2017/rs_1702_mago_va_en.html

BaFin, Circular 3/2013 (VA) – Minimum requirements for complaints-handling by insurance undertakings (*Mindestanforderungen an die Beschwerdebearbeitung durch Versicherungsunternehmen* – Reference n° VA 43 – I 2512 – 2013/0007). https://www.bafin.de/SharedDocs/Veroeffentlichungen/EN/Rundschreiben/rs_1303_beschwerdebearbeitung_va_en.html

Commission (1990) – Commission Recommendation 90/109/EEC of 14 February 1990 on the transparency of banking conditions relating to cross-border financial transactions [1990] OJ L67/39. https://eur-lex.europa.eu/legal-content/EN/TXT/HTML/?uri=CELEX:31990H0109

Commission (1998) – Commission Recommendation 98/257/EC of 30 March 1998 on the principles applicable to the bodies responsible for out-of-court settlement of consumer disputes [1998] OJ L115/31. https://eur-lex.europa.eu/legal-content/EN/TXT/HTML/?uri=CELEX:31998H0257

Commission (2001) – Commission Recommendation of 4 April 2001 on the principles for out-of-court bodies involved in the consensual resolution of consumer disputes [2001] OJ L109/56. https://eur-lex.europa.eu/legal-content/EN/TXT/HTML/?uri=CELEX:32001H0310&qid=1689515652783

Commission (2002) – Commission, 'Green Paper on alternative dispute resolution in civil and commercial law' COM (2002) 196 final. https://eur-lex.europa.eu/legal-content/EN/TXT/HTML/?uri=CELEX:52002DC0196

Commission (2014) Final Report of the Commission Expert Group on European Insurance Contract Law. https://commission.europa.eu/document/download/f6e132ce-1d2f-418d-97b0-34f9e8e58bb2_en?filename=final_report_en.pdf&prefLang=pl

Commission (2023) – Commission, 'Proposal for a Directive of the European Parliament and of the Council amending Directive 2013/11/EU on alternative dispute resolution for consumer disputes, as well as Directives (EU) 2015/2302, (EU) 2019/2161 and (EU) 2020/1828'. COM (2023) 649 final. https://eur-lex.europa.eu/legal-content/EN/TXT/PDF/?uri=CELEX:52023PC0649

Council (2000) – Council Resolution of 25 May 2000 on a Community-wide network of national bodies for the extra-judicial settlement of consumer disputes [2000] OJ C155/1. https://eur-lex.europa.eu/legal-content/EN/TXT/HTML/?uri=CELEX:32000Y0606(01)

EIOPA (2012) Guidelines on Complaints Handling by Insurance Undertakings (EIOPA-BoS-12/069). https://www.eiopa.europa.eu/system/files/2019-03/guidelines_on_complaints-handling_by_insurance_undertakings_eiopa-bos-12069_.pdf

European Consumer Centres' Network (ECC-Net) (2014) Vademecum. https://commission.europa.eu/system/files/2023-01/ECC%20Net%20vademecum%20revision%20FINAL.pdf

FIN-Net (2016) Memorandum of Understanding on a Cross-Border Out-of-Court Complaints Network for Financial Services. https://finance.ec.europa.eu/document/download/7b30f574-0413-4620-a970-f7bf67813b9c_en?filename=memorandum-of-understanding_en.pdf

References

Basedow J (2000) Die Gesetzgebung zum Versicherungsvertrag zwischen europäischer Integration und Verbraucherpolitik. In: Reichert-Facilides F, Schnyder A (eds) Versicherungsrecht in Europa. Helbing und Lichterhahn, Basel et al

Bernardino G (2015) Insurance distribution in a challenging environment. Speech at the Annual Meeting of the European Federation of Insurance Intermediaries (BIPAR). https://www.eiopa.europa.eu/system/files/2019-08/2015-06-05-bipar-meeting.pdf

Biard A (2022) Consumer ADR/ODR in Europe—a wind of change. J Eur Consum Mark Law 2022:181

Castle H (2019) ADR and insurance-based investment products. In: Marano P, Rokas I (eds) Distribution of insurance-based investment products: the EU regulation and the liabilities. Springer, Cham

Cortés P (2016) The new landscape of consumer redress: The European Directive on consumer alternative dispute resolution and the regulation on online dispute resolution. In: *id.* (ed) The new regulatory framework for consumer dispute resolution. Oxford University Press, Oxford

Danzeisen I, Synanidi M, Valentine D, Zeindlmeier N (eds) (2020) 15 Years of ECC-Net. ECC Germany, Kehl. https://commission.europa.eu/system/files/2021-01/ecc_net_anniversary_report_2020-_15_years_of_ecc_net.pdf

Dreher M (ed) (2024) Versicherungsaufsichtsgesetz, 14th edn. C.H. Beck, Munich

Gal J (2009) Entwurf des Common Frame of Reference für Versicherungsverträge. Versicherungsvertragsrecht 2009:190
Gal J (2014) The German Insurance Ombudsman System. In: Ünan (ed) Alternative dispute resolution systems regarding private insurance. Sigorta Hukuku Türk Derneği (AIDA Turkey), Istanbul
Gal J (2021) Introduction D ("Insurance Supervisory Law"). In: Bruck E, Möller H (eds) Versicherungsvertragsgesetz, 10th edn. De Gruyter, Berlin et al
Gal J (2024a) Schiedsgerichtsbarkeit und Versicherung. In: Langheid T, Wandt M (eds) Münchener Kommentar zum VVG, 3rd edn. C.H. Beck, Munich
Gal J (2024b) Commentary on all articles of the EIOPA Regulation. In: Dreher M (ed) Versicherungsaufsichtsgesetz, 14th edn. C.H. Beck, Munich
Heiss H (2016) Introduction. In: Basedow J, Birds J, Clarke M, Cousy H, Heiss H, Loacker L (eds) Principles of European Insurance Contract Law (PEICL), 2nd expanded edn. Otto Schmidt, Cologne
Hirsch G (2013) Außergerichtliche Beilegung von Verbraucherstreitigkeiten – ein alternativer Zugang zum Recht entsteht. Neue Juristische Wochenschrift 2013:2088
Hofmann A, Neumann JK, Pooser D (2018) Plea for uniform regulation and challenges of implementing the new IDD. Geneva Pap Risk Insur 43:740–769
Höra K, Schubach A (eds) (2022) Münchener Anwaltshandbuch Versicherungsrecht, 5th edn. C.H. Beck, Munich
Isermann E, Berlin C (2012) Außergerichtliche Streitbeilegung in Verbraucherangelegenheiten – Bestandsaufnahme und Maßnahmenpaket der EU für 2014/2015. Verbraucher und Recht 2012:47
Kaulbach D, Bähr G, Pohlmann P (eds) (2019) Versicherungsaufsichtsgesetz, 6th edn. C.H. Beck, Munich
Klowait J, Gläßer U (eds) (2018) Mediationsgesetz, 2nd edn. C.H. Beck, Munich
Loacker L (2009) Insurance soft law? Versicherungsvertragsrecht 2009:289
Meller-Hannich C, Höland A, Krausbeck E (2014) "ADR" und "ODR": Kreationen der europäischen Rechtspolitik. Eine kritische Würdigung. Zeitschrift für Europäisches Privatrecht 2014:8
Micklitz H-W, Rott P (2023) Verbraucherschutz. In: Dauses M, Ludwigs M (eds) Handbuch des EU-Wirtschaftsrechts. Loose-leaf collection (last updated April 2023). C.H. Beck, Munich
Montemaggiori F (2021) Considering the IDD within the EU legal framework on ADR systems. In: Marano P, Noussia K (eds) Insurance distribution directive—a legal analysis. Springer, Cham
Rott P (2018) Consumer ADR in Germany. J Eur Consum Mark Law (EuZML) 2018:121
Sasserath-Alberti N, Hartig H (2012) EIOPA-Verordnung: Rechtliche Herausforderungen für die Praxis. Versicherungsrecht 2012:524
Weber-Rey D (2006) Harmonisation of European Insurance Contract Law. In: Vogenauer S, Weatherill S (eds) The harmonisation of European contract law. Hart Publishing, Oxford

Part II
Comparative Analysis

Chapter 4
Insurance Ombudsman Schemes

A Comparative Analysis

Marta Ostrowska

4.1 Introduction

Insurance plays a fundamental role in modern society, providing financial security and contributing to economic stability. Yet, when disputes arise between policyholders and insurers, the system's reliability is put to the test. Consumers expect a resolution process that is fair, accessible and efficient. However, traditional litigation is often slow, expensive and impractical for many policyholders, creating a gap in effective dispute resolution.

To bridge this gap, insurance ombudsman schemes have emerged as an alternative dispute resolution mechanism. These independent bodies offer a streamlined, consumer-friendly approach, resolving disputes more efficiently than the courts while maintaining fairness and impartiality.

The purpose of this comparative analysis is to dissect the structure and functioning of insurance ombudsman schemes across Europe to identify key elements that contribute to their success or present challenges. By analysing different models, the research aims to provide insights for policymakers, regulators, and industry stakeholders, highlighting best practices and essential design features that contribute to an effective ombudsman system.

Thanks to Diego Fanuli for his help with the preliminary analysis of the country reports.

M. Ostrowska (✉)
University of Zurich, Zürich, Switzerland
e-mail: marta.ostrowska@ius.uzh.ch

H. Heiss et al. (eds.), *Insurance Ombudsman Schemes*, AIDA Europe Research Series on Insurance Law and Regulation 15,
https://doi.org/10.1007/978-3-032-01500-6_4

4.1.1 Why This Comparative Review Matters

This importance of this comparative review extends beyond academic inquiry; its findings have tangible policy and market implications. For jurisdictions without an insurance ombudsman scheme, the analysis may offer a roadmap—an evidence-based guide to designing a functional system from scratch. For those with existing schemes, it may serve as a benchmarking tool, identifying strengths, weaknesses and areas for refinement.

Beyond the institutional design, the analysis of different schemes also encourages broader questions. For example, does a consumer-friendly ombudsman improve insurer behaviour, or does it encourage frivolous complaints? How do procedural choices impact compliance and trust? Can these schemes meaningfully influence broader market regulation?

Understanding these dynamics is not just a theoretical exercise; it is fundamental to building stronger consumer protection mechanisms and more resilient insurance markets.

4.1.2 The European Focus: Why These Jurisdictions?

This comparative analysis is based on reports regarding insurance ombudsman schemes across nine European jurisdictions: Belgium, Croatia, Finland, France, Germany, Ireland, the Netherlands,[1] Poland and Switzerland.[2] The selection of these countries was not incidental. Each represents a distinct legal and regulatory tradition, providing a diverse yet comparable foundation for analysis.

Europe presents a particularly relevant setting for this comparative analysis. Consumer protection frameworks are well established, legal and economic systems share common foundations, and regulatory harmonisation—driven by EU directives and institutions such as FIN-NET—creates an environment conducive to comparative analysis. Even Switzerland, which operates outside EU jurisdiction,[3] offers an instructive contrast as a non-harmonised system with its own established ombudsman model.

The jurisdictions covered in this comparative analysis reflect a balance of different legal traditions. The civil law framework is well represented through the Roman legal systems of France, Belgium, and the Netherlands, as well as the Germanic traditions of

[1] The Netherlands does not have a traditional ombudsman institution, but it has established the *Klachteninstituut Financiële Dienstverlening (Kifid)* as an alternative dispute resolution mechanism for financial services.

[2] The comparative analysis does not include the Spanish report. At the time of the study, Spain had not yet established an insurance ombudsman scheme, although significant legal developments were underway to introduce a similar alternative dispute resolution system for insurance services. These circumstances prevented the Spanish rapporteur from following the questionnaire, making it impossible to meaningfully compare the jurisdiction with others.

[3] Although not an EU Member State, Switzerland is a FIN-NET affiliate.

Germany and Switzerland. Finland introduces a Nordic perspective, while Croatia and Poland provide insight into Central and Eastern European regulatory approaches. Ireland, as the only common law jurisdiction in the sample, adds further diversity to the analysis.

By bringing together these varied perspectives, this comparative analysis provides a nuanced view of how insurance ombudsman schemes function in different legal and regulatory environments. At the same time, the European context ensures that the comparison remains meaningful, given the region's shared commitment to consumer protection and regulatory coherence.

4.1.3 Methodology

To ensure a systematic comparison, the comparative analysis is based on data collected through a structured questionnaire covering key elements of each ombudsman scheme: institutional design, jurisdiction, funding, procedures and operational practices. Rapporteurs were instructed to focus specifically on the insurance sector, even when broader financial services were covered by their ombudsman offices.

4.1.4 Caveats and Limitations

While this comparative review offers a comprehensive examination of insurance ombudsman schemes, it has its limitations. Firstly, the findings are only as strong as the data collected. The reliability of the findings is inherently tied to the accuracy and completeness of the data collected through structured questionnaires. The interpretation of questions by rapporteurs may have varied, and differences in legal terminology across jurisdictions could have influenced responses, leading to potential inconsistencies. In some cases, incomplete answers limited direct comparisons.

Secondly, the selection of jurisdictions was contingent on voluntary participation, which means that the comparative review does not provide an exhaustive overview of every European insurance ombudsman scheme. The absence of certain (valuable) jurisdictions may result in gaps, making the findings more reflective of the participating countries rather than the basis of a definitive regional model.

Thirdly, while the study focuses on legal and procedural frameworks, it does not fully address the real-world effectiveness of these ombudsman schemes. Consumer satisfaction, the practical enforcement of decisions and the broader impact on market behaviour remain outside the scope of this analysis. A more empirical approach, incorporating qualitative assessments and consumer feedback, would be necessary to complement this institutional perspective.

Despite these limitations, the comparative review provides valuable insights into the design and operation of insurance ombudsman schemes across Europe. The findings serve as a foundation for further research and as a resource for policymakers and industry stakeholders seeking to refine existing mechanisms or establish new ones.

4.2 Institutional Framework of the Ombudsman Schemes

Ombudsman schemes were first created in Sweden in the nineteenth century and then expanded in the second half of the twentieth century, primarily in advanced economies with stable democracies and a strong tradition of consumer protection—notably Denmark, Finland and Norway.[4] These models gradually spread across Europe, adapting to the distinct constitutional, legal, cultural and economic contexts of each jurisdiction. Initially, ombudsman schemes were broad in scope, designed to shield citizens from administrative abuse by public authorities in general. It was only as economies developed and market complexities grew that the necessity for consumer protection against private companies became evident and prompted the formation of sector-specific ombudsman frameworks. This progression, from general oversight to specialised financial and insurance-focused mechanisms, reflects a clear top-down evolution, as described in the country reports.

4.2.1 The Evolution

The findings reveal that the establishment of the ombudsman schemes was shaped by a mix of consumer protection imperatives, regulatory harmonisation and industry efforts to enhance transparency and trust.

The core objective of these schemes is to respond to a fundamental challenge of our era: **how to protect individuals** in a world in which financial markets are moving ever faster, products are becoming more intricate, and the balance of knowledge is tilted in favour of large financial institutions. Consumers' reluctance to litigate low-value disputes,[5] costly, and time-consuming court proceedings,[6] the growing complexity of financial products and the resulting increased information asymmetry[7] are repeatedly mentioned in the national reports as the main problems faced by financial services consumers.

Beyond consumer protection, many schemes were established to **improve the public image of the insurance sector and rebuild trust** after criticisms concerning perceived unfair practices or lack of transparency. For instance, Belgium's ombudsman was created specifically to address the negative public perception of insurers and prevent disputes from escalating.

It is also highlighted in the reports that the creation of the schemes was not solely a national affair. The **European Union played a pivotal role**, shaping the development of such schemes through legislative frameworks such as the ADR Directive

---

[4] See Chap. 2 Norio, J., Law-based Ombudsman Schemes. The Finnish experience.

[5] Poland, Switzerland, Sect. 14.1.1.

[6] Croatia, Sect. 6.1.

[7] Poland, Sect. 12.3, Switzerland.

and the ODR Regulation.[8] These laws were introduced as part of a broader effort to create a single, harmonised market, thereby enabling disputes to be resolved efficiently across borders.

However, despite the common rationale behind setting up the ombudsman institutions, the ways in which they were established vary. **The schemes were created either through legislation or voluntarily** by a financial services industry association. The latter was the case in the majority of the jurisdictions analysed,[9] with the respective insurance industry founding the scheme. In some cases, such as in Finland and the Netherlands, however, the story took a unique turn. Such schemes were co-created together with consumer associations (the Netherlands) or public authorities (Finland), suggesting a subtle interplay of voluntary action and societal pressure and that the establishment of the respective scheme arose in response to expectations from public (consumers) and/or the state (government). Interestingly, some of these schemes that began as industry-led initiatives later gained formal legal recognition under national insurance legislation. This trend is evident in countries like Belgium, Germany and the Netherlands. Although the respondents do not specify the reasons for such a transition, it may be due to advantages that legally recognised schemes have over voluntary ones, such as greater credibility in the eyes of consumers and enhanced authority to compel cooperation from financial services businesses.

In contrast, in jurisdictions such as Ireland and Poland, the ombudsman schemes were established directly by virtue of legislation, reflecting a more centralised approach towards resolving the same challenges.

4.2.2 Coverage: Ombudsman Scheme for Financial Services or Insurance Only?

The top-down development of ombudsman schemes resulted in the creation of sector-specific frameworks, such as financial ombudsman schemes. Of the jurisdictions analysed, some have a financial ombudsman scheme that covers the entire financial sector (Finland, Ireland, the Netherlands, Poland), while others have more specialised schemes focused on insurance market only (Belgium,

[8] Directive 2013/11/EU of the European Parliament and of the Council of 21 May 2013 on alternative dispute resolution for consumer disputes and amending Regulation (EC) No 2006/2004 and Directive 2009/22/EC (Directive on consumer ADR) [2013] OJ L165/63 and Regulation (EU) 524/2013 of the European Parliament and of the Council of 21 May 2013 on online dispute resolution for consumer disputes and amending Regulation (EC) No 2006/2004 and Directive 2009/22/EC (Regulation on consumer ODR) [2013] OJ L165/1. See more on this in Chap. 3, Gal, J., On Union Law Concerning Alternative Dispute Resolution Methods with Regard to Insurance Disputes.

[9] Belgium, Sect. 5.1.1, Croatia, Sect. 6.1.1, Finland, Sect. 7.1.1, Germany, Sect. 9.1.1, the Netherlands, Sect. 11.1.1, Switzerland, Sect. 14.1.1..

Croatia, France, Germany, Switzerland). A country's decision to adopt either a specialised insurance ombudsman scheme or a financial ombudsman scheme with a broader scope may reflect the size of its financial market and/or its distinct regulatory, economic and cultural background.

In countries with a smaller financial market or in which the financial services are less diverse, a single financial ombudsman scheme is usually often sufficient to manage the volume and variety of disputes effectively. In this regard, Finland, Ireland and the Netherlands are exemplars. In larger and more diverse markets, such as France and Germany, separate schemes—such as an insurance ombudsman scheme—can provide more targeted and effective oversight, especially in sectors that see a higher volume of complaints or have specific consumer concerns. Belgium and Switzerland, despite their small geographical size, have mature and diverse financial markets. This, coupled with a relatively high level of financial literacy among their respective population and the public's expectation of specialised, expert handling of their disputes, may explain their decision to implement an insurance-specific ombudsman scheme.

In contrast to the aforementioned trends, Poland provides an interesting example of a jurisdiction in which the long-established insurance-specific ombudsman scheme was transformed into a general financial ombudsman scheme not too long ago. This shift was driven by the absence of a dedicated ombudsman for non-insurance related financial services and a growing need to ensure equal consumer protection across the financial sector. The origins of Poland's insurance ombudsman scheme, rooted in a response to insurer bankruptcies, may indicate a reactive legislative approach, which evolves in response to pressing market failures, rather than proactive long-term planning.

4.2.3 Insurance Business Covered

The choice between a financial ombudsman and an insurance-specific ombudsman scheme is closely tied to a fundamental question: who is subject to the scheme?

In some jurisdictions, insurance businesses are legally obliged to participate in the ombudsman scheme as a condition of conducting business.[10] **Mandatory participation** is a natural consequence in jurisdictions in which an ombudsman scheme was established directly by virtue of legislation (Ireland and Poland). However, the same obligation was also implemented in Belgium[11] and the

[10] The obligation to participate in the scheme is tied to the regulatory licencing process.

[11] The obligation of Belgian insurers to cooperate with the scheme stems from the Belgian Insurance Act, which defines the scope of the ombudsman scheme's services as covering any complaint related to the execution of an insurance contract governed by Belgian law. See Belgium, Sect. 5.1.3.

Netherlands,[12] where each respective scheme was created as part of a joint initiative undertaken by the industry and consumer association. In this case, mandatory participation most likely reflects consumer demands.

Other jurisdictions adopt a more **mixed approach**, blending voluntary participation with institutional obligations. In countries such as Croatia,[13] Finland[14] and France,[15] participation in the scheme is tied to membership of an industry association. This creates a system in which participation is technically voluntary but practically unavoidable—joining the association automatically brings insurers under the scheme's jurisdiction. One potential advantage of such de facto mandatory participation is that it reduces barriers to accessing the scheme, which may also strengthen trust among consumers.

Switzerland represents an example at the far end of the spectrum: a **system based purely on voluntary participation**. In this case, as the ombudsman scheme is an industry-led initiative, the decision to participate lies entirely with insurers. However, providing for such freedom comes at a cost. If an insurance company does not opt in, the ombudsman has no authority to handle complaints against it.

These different approaches indicate the following pattern: where the level of trust in the industry is high—whether on the part of consumers and/or governments—there is less reliance on legal enforcement. Instead, the system operates on the assumption that insurers, motivated by reputational concerns and societal expectations, will join the scheme voluntarily. The Swiss scheme exemplifies this trend: there is no coercion, yet many insurers participate. The underlying assumption is simple: freedom works well when there is a strong foundation of trust. In contrast, where the level of trust is lower, laws must be passed to ensure compliance. The variety of approaches taken—from the mandatory systems implemented in Belgium, Ireland and Poland to the voluntary framework used in Switzerland—reflects not just legal preferences but also cultural attitudes toward accountability and the balance between regulation and freedom.

---

[12] In the Netherlands the obligation to cooperate stems from the Financial Supervision Act (see The Netherlands, Sect. 11.1.1).

[13] Insurance companies that are members of the Croatian Insurance Bureau (HUO) are automatically subject to the scheme's jurisdiction. See Croatia, Sect. 6.1.3.

[14] The Finnish Financial Intermediaries (FFI) association entails automatic participation in the ombudsman scheme. See Finland, Sect. 7.1.3.

[15] The French Insurance Federation's members voluntarily agreed to participate in *La Médiation de l'Assurance*. See France, Sect. 8.1.4.

4.2.4 Appointment of the Ombudsperson

The nature of an ombudsman scheme—whether broad in scope or specific to insurance—directly influences another element of the institutional framework: who appoints the ombudsperson? The appointment process is not merely an administrative formality. It is a critical element of the structure because behind the technicalities of selection and terms of appointment lies the question of trust: who should decide who mediates between consumers and powerful industries, and how is their impartiality ensured?

The analysis of the country reports reveals a spectrum of practices, ranging from **government-led appointments** to **industry-controlled selections**. In some jurisdictions,[16] the **government** plays a direct and decisive role in appointing the ombudsperson. The appointment by the relevant ministry follows either an open competition (Ireland) or a recommendation by another government official (Poland).

Other jurisdictions delegate the selection and appointment process to **industry bodies**, often pointing to their professional expertise. Where this is the case, the appointing power belongs to the management and/or governing body of the ombudsman scheme[17] or of the industry association.[18] The appointed candidate is either recommended by another internal body or selected directly from all of the applicants.

This diversity in appointment processes may indicate differing priorities: some jurisdictions emphasise public accountability and credibility through government-led appointments, while others prioritise industry expertise.

An important aspect of the selection process is the set of personal qualities and professional qualifications required of candidates for the position of ombudsperson. The array of requirements varies among the schemes, which may reflect different emphases on independence and expertise. Educational and professional qualifications are mentioned in all of the reports analysed. These include a university degree (either in general or in a specific field, e.g. law) and/or specialised knowledge and experience in insurance and/or in resolving consumer disputes (either by specifying the minimum years of experience in financial markets or specific qualifications or skills). Furthermore, the country reports mention a variety of other requirements such as good reputation,[19] knowledge of official languages spoken in the country of the office,[20] a clear criminal record,[21] citizenship

[16] Ireland, Sect. 10.1.5, Poland, Sect. 12.5.

[17] Governing Board in Belgium, Sect. 5.1.4, General Assembly of the ombudsman scheme in Germany, Sect. 9.1.5, Foundation Board in Switzerland, Sect. 14.1.5.

[18] Management Board of the Croatian Insurance Bureau in Croatia, Sect. 6.1.5.

[19] Belgium, Sect. 5.1.4, Switzerland, Sect. 14.1.5.

[20] Belgium, Sect. 5.1.4, Switzerland, Sect. 14.1.5.

[21] Croatia, Sect. 6.1.5, Poland, Sect. 12.5.

of the country of the office[22] and leadership qualities.[23] In Germany, candidates must not have had full-time employment with an insurance company for at least three years prior to their appointment.[24] This rule adds yet another layer of protection, ensuring that those entrusted with oversight remain free from industry influence.

In addition to the appointment procedure, an ombudsperson's independence and impartiality are also reinforced by the **employment/service terms**, of which the term of office, the possibility of reappointment and early removal are the key aspects that affect independence.

In most jurisdictions analysed, the ombudsperson is appointed for a **fixed term** (3 years,[25] 4 years,[26] 5 years[27]), with the exception of Belgium and Switzerland.[28] The Swiss ombudsman scheme does not specify any term of office, i.e. the appointment is not limited in time and, therefore, no rules on renewal exist.

Where the ombudsperson's term of office is fixed, it is also **renewable**. Interestingly, the schemes differ as to how the term limits are set. For instance, in Germany and Poland, the law allows for only one reappointment and in the Netherlands, the limit is defined by age, i.e. the appointed official may be reappointed until they reach the age of 74.[29]

While the length and renewability of the term of office may contribute to independence, the likely clearest indication of independence lies in the conditions for removal. Regardless of whether the term of office is fixed or not, most of the country reports mention that the ombudsperson **cannot be removed** from office (although this is not absolute). This is reflected in the very strict grounds provided for dismissal (e.g. health incapacity (Ireland, Poland), misconduct or gross violations of duty (Croatia, Germany, Poland, Switzerland)) and procedural safeguards against arbitrary dismissal (e.g. high thresholds, such as two-thirds majority votes (Germany) or case-specific reviews by governing boards (France, Switzerland)). The authority to dismiss is granted to the body empowered to appoint the ombudsperson. In government-led models, the authority to dismiss is held by the government or its representatives,[30] while in industry-led models, it lies with governance bodies within the organisation or association.[31]

---

[22] Poland, Sect. 12.5.

[23] Switzerland, Sect. 14.1.5.

[24] Germany, Sect. 9.1.5.

[25] Croatia, Sect. 6.1.5, Finland, Sect. 7.1.4, France, Sect. 8.1.5.

[26] Poland, Sect. 12.5.

[27] Germany, Sect. 9.1.5, Ireland, Sect. 10.1.5, the Netherlands, Sect. 11.1.5.

[28] Belgium, Sect. 5.1.4, Switzerland, Sect. 14.1.5.

[29] The Dutch system is, in fact, more nuanced and accounts for the health and mental capacity of arbitrators serving on Kifid's financial disputes tribunal who reach the age of 70. In such cases, reappointment remains an option, but the term of office is reduced from five years to one year. See the Netherlands, Sect. 11.1.5.

[30] Ireland, Sect. 10.1.5, Poland, Sect. 12.5.

[31] Croatia, Sect. 6.1.5, Germany, Sect. 9.1.5, Switzerland, Sect. 14.1.5.

Overall, the jurisdictions analysed seem to operate on the assumption that the combination of longer and renewable terms of office with strict rules governing early removal is more effective in supporting the independence and impartiality of the office. This is because it has greater potential to reduce political and industry pressures (for example, enabling unpopular but fair decisions without worrying about employment security and supporting the development and implementation of long-term strategies) and encourage public trust and credibility.

4.2.5 Funding

Just as the appointment process may safeguard independence, so too may the funding model—an essential factor in determining whether the ombudsman can function without external pressures. Who pays for the ombudsman scheme, and how does this affect its impartiality?

Country reports reveal that most jurisdictions analysed rely on a **full industry funding model,**[32] placing the main financial burden on the industry. Insurance businesses finance the ombudsman office through a range of different levies, including levies tied to market share[33] or complaint volume,[34] flat-rate fees[35] and case fees.[36] **Ireland** stands out with a **hybrid model,** blending industry contributions with public funding, though government support is strictly reserved for pension-related cases—meaning insurance-related disputes remain industry-funded, as in other countries.

Importantly, in none of the jurisdictions analysed is the ombudsman's budget financed by consumers. **Filing a complaint is free of charge**, which reinforces the mission of ombudsman schemes to provide an impartial, consumer-friendly dispute resolution system and fosters accessibility to its services. However, two exceptions exist: fees may be levied for the submission of an appeal[37] or for out-of-court dispute resolution[38] in select cases.

When designing the ombudsman scheme's budget, the represented jurisdictions seem to follow straightforward economic rationale: those who create the disputes should pay to resolve them. This aligns with the classic "polluter pays" principle—since insurance businesses generate the complaints, it is only natural that they bear the financial burden of the dispute resolution system. Shifting this cost onto consumers, whether through taxation or service fees, would either create barriers to access, undermining the very purpose of the scheme, or force those

[32] Belgium, Sect. 5.1.5, Croatia, Sect. 6.1.6, France, Sect. 8.1.6, Finland, Sect. 7.1.5, Germany, Sect. 9.1.6, the Netherlands, Sect. 11.1.6, Poland, Sect. 12.5, Switzerland, Sect. 14.1.6.

[33] Belgium, Sect. 5.1.5, Germany, Sect. 9.1.6, the Netherlands, Sect. 11.1.6, Switzerland, Sect. 14.1.6.

[34] Belgium, Sect. 5.1.5, France, Sect. 8.1.6.

[35] France, Sect. 8.1.6., Switzerland, Sect. 14.1.6.

[36] Finland, Sect. 7.1.5, Germany, Sect. 9.1.6.

[37] The Netherlands, Sect. 11.1.6.

[38] Poland, Sect. 12.8.2.2.

who never file a complaint to subsidise the system, raising questions of fairness. At first glance, the industry-funded model seems both rational and fair. Yet, it entails an inherent paradox: can an ombudsman scheme truly remain impartial when it is financially dependent on the very industry it is responsible for overseeing? The risk is that the ombudsperson will become too well-acquainted with the industry and will shape policies and decisions in ways that subtly favour insurers. This is precisely why robust institutional safeguards, such as the appointment process and terms of office discussed above, are essential for mitigating this risk and for ensuring that an ombudsman scheme remains an impartial guardian of consumer rights, rather than becoming a mere extension of the industry.

4.2.6 Insurance Ombudsman Functions

Insurance ombudsman schemes provide a dispute resolution mechanism, but they rarely do only that. Across the represented jurisdictions, their functions extend well beyond settling conflicts between consumers and insurers. Most ombudsman schemes **shape consumer awareness**, **influence industry practices**, and, in some cases, even **impact regulatory policy**.

At its core, the ombudsperson's primary role is to **handle complaints and resolve disputes between consumers and insurance businesses** through, among other things, alternative dispute resolution (ADR) mechanisms. This may include mediation, arbitration or informal negotiation. The specifics vary by jurisdiction, but the underlying idea remains the same: providing an accessible, out-of-court mechanism that helps avoid litigation. Details regarding the procedure are discussed in Sect. 4.4 below.

In addition to resolving disputes, many ombudsman offices play an **informational role, ensuring that consumers understand their rights and the remedies available**. This function operates at two levels. At an individual level, the ombudsperson explains procedures to complainants, helping them navigate their specific cases. At a systemic level, they disseminate knowledge about insurance products, complaint procedures and market practices, contributing—whether explicitly or implicitly—to the **financial literacy** of the public.[39] Interestingly, some schemes formalise financial education as part of the ombudsperson's mandate.[40] However, there is not yet enough data available to assess whether such an explicit legal mandate leads to greater effectiveness compared to other schemes that educate consumers without a formal mandate.

Beyond these functions, several ombudsman offices aim to **improve overall market practices**. This function manifests in two forms. Firstly, the ombudsperson

[39] Croatia, Sect. 6.1.7, Finland, Sect. 7.1.6.1, Ireland, Sect. 10.1.7, the Netherlands, Sect. 11.1.7.2, Poland, Sect. 12.3.

[40] Finland, Sect. 7.1.6.1, Poland, Sect. 12.6.

promotes better practices by actively **engaging with insurance businesses**. For instance, the Croatian ombudsperson sends non-binding recommendations to insurers in cases of recurring violations. In Germany, Ireland and Switzerland, anonymised complaint data is shared with insurers to provide feedback on the most frequent issues. In Ireland and the Netherlands a more interactive approach is taken by holding regular meetings with consumer representatives, insurance businesses and supervisory authorities to discuss recent developments in its complaints-handling activities.

Secondly, beyond direct industry engagement, some ombudspersons wield **influence over financial regulations**, offering insights to policymakers and providing guidance on legislative reforms.[41] France provides a striking example: the French ombudsperson has successfully influenced contract clarity and policyholder rights by bringing problematic contract clauses to the attention of lawmakers and the market. This function is not merely reactive—it has the potential to actively reshape the law.

A by-product of these informative and influencing functions is **dispute prevention**. Many ombudsman offices mitigate future conflicts simply by publishing the reports on the most frequent violations and/or types of complaints,[42] case-studies[43] and a selection of anonymised ombudsman's decisions,[44] along with the fines imposed on the basis of such decisions.[45] In Switzerland, this preventive function is taken a step further: consumers are encouraged to resolve issues with the insurer at an early stage via a dedicated helpline, which provides advice before disputes escalate.

Finally, while training consumers and industry professionals is not a formal duty in any of the schemes analysed, many ombudsman offices occasionally conduct lectures and workshops when invited by external organisations. This suggests that while education is usually not part of their official mandate, it is often seen as an essential component of improving market functioning.

Although the insurance ombudsperson is a mediator, in many jurisdictions, the role is extended to include **consumer guidance**,[46] **industry oversight**[47] and **regulatory influence.**[48] The differences in balancing these functions may depend on the resources available—some focus purely on mediation, while others actively shape market behaviour and regulation.

---

[41] Belgium, Sect. 5.1.6, Croatia, section , Ireland, Sect. 10.1.7.2, Poland, Sect. 12.6.

[42] Croatia, Sect. 6.1.7, the Netherlands, Sect. 11.1.7.3.

[43] Ireland, Switzerland, Sect. 14.1.7.

[44] Germany, Sect. 9.1.7, Ireland.

[45] Ireland, Poland, Sect. 12.6.

[46] Examples: Finland—preparing comparisons of financial products, Sect. 7.1.6.1; Ireland—publishing accessible information in relation to how to make a complaint, Sect. 10.1.7.

[47] The Croatian ombudsperson assesses whether insurers comply with ethical standards rather than just legal obligations, Sect. 6.1.7.

[48] Examples: Belgium—parliamentary questions and recommendations in the Ombudsman annual report, Sect. 5.1.6; Finland—contributing to the preparation of the financial sector legislation, Sect. 7.1.6.1; Ireland—providing advice in relation to any proposals for legislation upon the request of the Minister, Sect. 10.1.7; Poland—providing guidance on legislative reforms, Sect. 12.6.

4.2.7 Insurance Ombudsman Office

The effectiveness of an insurance ombudsman scheme hinges on two critical factors: the competence of the ombudsperson and the expertise of the staff. Yet, competence alone is not enough. To ensure effectiveness and independence, the ombudsman office must be staffed with sufficient personnel to handle the case volume and market demands. An understaffed ombudsman office, no matter how skilled, risks delays that may lead to frustration and, eventually, undermine its credibility and public trust.

At first glance, the size (i.e. the number of the employees) of ombudsman offices seem to reflect the size of the jurisdiction, the size and maturity of the financial (insurance) market, the case volume, and/or whether the ombudsman scheme covers the insurance sector exclusively or the financial sector more broadly. While France has the biggest office[49] among the schemes analysed that cover the insurance sector exclusively, Ireland leads[50] among those covering multiple financial sectors. Switzerland, in contrast, stands out as both the smallest office and the only one with a decentralized model, with regional branches serving the country's linguistic communities. This structure is not accidental—it ensures equal access for all customers, regardless of language.

The backbone of these offices is the team of case analysts, who are responsible for handling enquiries and complaints. Many jurisdictions emphasise legal training as a key qualification for these roles, ensuring that decisions are rooted in expert knowledge of insurance law. Continuous professional development is also common, with staff regularly attending training programmes to stay updated on legal and regulatory changes.

Although the data from the country reports is insufficient to identify a clear trend, it is worth noting that French ombudsman scheme appears to be highly specialised, enabling more in-depth case analysis. With a relatively high number of staff members, the French office organizes its employees into distinct departments, each specialising in different types of insurance products.

These differences arise from variations in the volume of complaints and the resources available. While some offices operate with large teams of specialised legal experts, others function with minimal personnel. Yet, regardless of these disparities, the end goal is the same: ensuring that they operate in an independent, fair and effective manner. Whether they achieve this goal depends not just on the office structure and qualifications, but also on how well they can sustain their operations under changing constraints.

---

[49] The French Insurance Ombudsman scheme employs 80 employees, Sect. 8.1.8.

[50] The Irish Financial Services and Pensions Ombudsman office employs 93 employees, Sect. 10.1.8.1.

4.2.8 Accountability and Transparency

Accountability is a fundamental requirement of any institution that claims to protect consumers. An insurance ombudsman office holds a powerful position as an intermediary between insurance providers and the public, resolving disputes that can significantly impact people's lives. Without proper accountability, it risks becoming an obscure institution, or detached from those it serves.

What supports accountability at its core is transparency. An effective insurance ombudsman scheme must not operate in secrecy; it must instead provide clear information about its jurisdiction, procedures and decision-making processes—preferably on its website and through other appropriate channels. The reporting practices of the ombudsman offices across the jurisdictions analysed indicate variations in terms of frequency, recipients and the extent of public disclosure.

Annual reporting is a universal standard across all of the jurisdictions. However, in some countries, such as Croatia[51] and Germany,[52] the ombudsman offices provide additional interim reports, offering semi-annual updates or specific activity reports. In the Netherlands, an efficiency review is conducted every four years, for which an assessment report must be provided. **The recipients of these reports** also vary. In Belgium reports are directed toward legislators and political decision-makers. In Croatia, the reports are submitted to the governing bodies of the ombudsman scheme, but they are also made available to insurers and the national supervisory authority. By contrast, reporting is extended to the media and the public in Germany. A mixed approach is taken in Ireland, the Netherlands and Switzerland, with reporting to both regulatory bodies and the public.

Another important element closely tied to the accountability of any ombudsman scheme is its **budget** and the way it is managed. A structured budget approval process requires an ombudsman office to justify its financial needs and spending plans. This transparency of resource allocation prevents misuse of funds and thus strengthens trust in the institution. In Finland and Germany, budget decisions are made through multiple layers of internal governance, including executive committees and supervisory boards. A similar approach is taken in Ireland, with budget approvals linked to the strategic plan overseen by the Financial Services and Pensions Ombudsman Council. Ministerial approval is mandated in the Netherlands and this ensures a direct governmental role in financial oversight. In France and Switzerland, foundation boards or general assemblies of institutional

[51] The Croatian Ombudsman office submits a semi-annual brief report on their activities to the Council of the Insurance Ombudsman Service. See Croatia, Sect. 6.6.2.

[52] The German Ombudsman office submits an annual activity report on its activities of the previous year. See Germany, Sect. 9.6.2.

members are relied on to approve budgets, reflecting a more industry-driven governance structure.

4.3 Insurance Ombudsman Jurisdiction

The jurisdiction of an insurance ombudsman scheme refers to the scope of authority within which an ombudsman office can handle complaints, resolve disputes and provide remedies relating to insurance matters. However, this is not merely a technical question of legal authority; it also defines the boundaries of consumer protection in the insurance sector. Who can complain? About what? Against whom? When does an ombudsperson have the power to intervene, and when must disputes be taken elsewhere?

The country reports reveal a variety of approaches; nevertheless, the following pattern emerges: most ombudsman schemes cover disputes between consumers and insurance businesses arising under an insurance contract, provided the dispute falls within the scope of the jurisdiction's law and the complaint is filed within the prescribed time limit. These limitations are designed in this way to balance access to justice with the practical constraints of an out-of-court system.

4.3.1 Substantive Scope: What Counts as a Dispute?

At the heart of an ombudsman scheme's authority lies the substantive scope of jurisdiction—the types of disputes it can address. While some ombudsman schemes refer to disputes arising from the **conduct of financial service providers**[53] or define **parties to the dispute**,[54] most schemes take a **contract-based approach**, limiting disputes specifically to issues arising under an insurance contract. Yet, this approach, while straightforward, may also leave unintended gaps.

Insurance products today are not what they used to be. They increasingly resemble investment vehicles, hybrid financial products or even risk-sharing schemes that do not fit neatly into traditional legal categories. Therefore, defining the scope too narrowly may leave certain contracts outside of the ombudsman scheme's reach. This issue is evident in Germany, where the ombudsman scheme's jurisdiction is limited to complaints relating to an insurance contract, or "a contract that has a close economic connection with an insurance contract".[55] Such phrasing grants the ombudsperson interpretational discretion, which may work in favour of consumer protection.

[53] Ireland, Sect. 10.2.1, Poland, Sect. 12.6.

[54] The Netherlands, Sect. 11.1.3.

[55] Germany, Sect. 9.2.1.

Another crucial consideration is whether the financial value of a claim should influence the ombudsman's jurisdiction. In most jurisdictions, the **value of the claim made under the insurance contract is irrelevant**, hence, even disputes involving symbolic amounts can be brought before the ombudsperson. However, a break from this norm is presented in Germany and the Netherlands, where an upper limit of EUR 100,000 and EUR 1,000,000 respectively is imposed. In Germany, disputes of a value exceeding this threshold must be adjudicated in court and are therefore beyond the jurisdiction of the German insurance ombudsman scheme, whereas the scheme in the Netherlands will handle such complaints partially, i.e. only up to the limit; any excess must be pursued separately in court. This raises a valid question: should ombudsman schemes handle high-value disputes, or should such cases automatically be taken to court? The answer has implications for the accessibility and the efficiency of both judicial and extrajudicial dispute resolution mechanisms.

While financial limits rarely create boundaries, there are other exclusions that substantially affect the scope of jurisdiction. Most jurisdictions **exclude complaints related to social insurance (pensions, health, unemployment)**[56] **and those related to insurers' commercial decisions**[57]—such as risk acceptance, premium pricing or underwriting practices. The rationale is that these issues reflect business strategy rather than contractual disputes, making them unsuitable for intervention by an ombudsman office. However, this distinction may not always be clear-cut—what happens when pricing policies lead to systemic consumer complaints?

Not all ombudsman schemes strictly limit themselves to handling disputes. Some extend their role by responding to **general enquiries**[58] and providing guidance before a dispute formally arises. In Switzerland, for instance, the ombudsperson does not simply resolve cases but also provides second opinions on insurers' decisions, helping consumers assess whether they even have a valid complaint. While this practice increases accessibility and prevents unnecessary disputes, it also requires significant resources, making it a luxury that not all ombudsman schemes can afford.

Finally, in defining what counts as admissible disputes, closer attention must be paid to the insurance provider as not all insurance businesses necessarily fall within the ombudsman's jurisdiction. Most schemes include **licenced insurers and intermediaries operating within their jurisdiction**, but some impose additional requirements. For instance, it is common to require insurance providers (either by law or the scheme's internal policy) to be members of the scheme or insurance industry association[59] or to have a specific agreement with the scheme.[60]

---

[56] Germany, Sect. 9.2.1, the Netherlands, Sect. 11.1.3.

[57] Finland, Sect. 7.2.1, France, Sect. 8.2.1.3, Germany, Sect. 9.2.1, Ireland, Sect. 10.2.1, Switzerland, Sect. 14.2.1.

[58] Finland, Sect. 7.2.1, Switzerland, Sect. 14.2.1.

[59] Croatia, Sect. 6.2.3, Germany, Sect. 9.2.3, the Netherlands, Sect. 11.1.3, Switzerland, Sect. 14.2.2.

[60] Finland, Sect. 7.2.2.

4.3.2 Personal Scope: Who Gets to Complain?

A second critical dimension of jurisdiction is who has standing to file a complaint. At first glance, this may seem straightforward: consumers who feel wronged by their insurance providers should be able to seek redress. Generally, the ombudsman schemes stand by this belief and offer a broad, inclusive approach—allowing policyholders, insureds, beneficiaries and even third parties with a legitimate interest in the insurance contract to file complaints.[61] However, there may be exceptions under which some complainants are excluded—either to streamline resources, preserve fairness or, in some cases, simply as an unintended consequence of legal definitions.

In Switzerland, for example, complainants who have legal representation are excluded. The logic in this case is: it is not the ombudsman scheme's role to to take over the tasks of legal protection insurers, whose services have already been paid for through the insured person's premium. More broadly, this restriction leads to a shift in the ombudsman scheme's role from being a universal dispute resolution body to a protector of the weakest parties in the insurance relationship. Yet it raises a question: does having a lawyer truly eliminate the need for an ombudsman scheme? Or does it merely create a two-tier system in which only the legally unrepresented benefit from this consumer protection mechanism?

The exclusions may also result from the way the concept of **'consumer'** is defined and understood. The EU Member States adhere to the definition of 'consumer' set forth in key EU consumer protection directives[62] and that is consistent with the definition of consumer in the ADR Directive.[63] According to this definition **small businesses** are not considered to be consumers and may therefore fall outside of the ombudsman scheme's jurisdiction. Interestingly, however, the represented schemes extend the definition of consumer and explicitly allow small businesses[64] to file complaints. In France, this is taken a step further by extending the ombudsman scheme's protection to medium-sized businesses and even local authorities.

[61] For instance, injured parties with non-contractual claims against insurers (Belgium, Sect. 5.2.2, Croatia, Sect. 6.2.2, Finland, Sect. 7.2.1, Switzerland) or a legal personal representative of a consumer who has died (Ireland, Sect. 10.2.2).

[62] Directive 2011/83/EU of the European Parliament and of the Council of 25 October 2011 on consumer rights, amending Council Directive 93/13/EEC and Directive 1999/44/EC of the European Parliament and of the Council and repealing Council Directive 85/577/EEC and Directive 97/7/EC of the European Parliament and of the Council [2011] OJ L304/64 and Directive 2005/29/EC of the European Parliament and of the Council of 11 May 2005 concerning unfair business-to-consumer commercial practices in the internal market and amending Council Directive 84/450/EEC, Directives 97/7/EC, 98/27/EC and 2002/65/EC of the European Parliament and of the Council and Regulation (EC) No 2006/2004 of the European Parliament and of the Council ('Unfair Commercial Practices Directive') [2005] OJ L149/22.

[63] Pursuant to Art. 4(1)(a) of the ADR Directive, 'consumer' means any natural person who is acting for purposes which are outside his trade, business, craft or profession.

[64] However, what constitutes a small business differs across jurisdictions. Countries usually define small businesses by setting a turnover limit (see e.g. Ireland, Sect. 10.2.2).

The rationale behind such extension is clear: if the ombudsman scheme's mission is to protect the weaker party, then why stop at individual consumers? Small and medium-sized businesses can be just as vulnerable as individuals when dealing with large insurance companies.

Finally, Ireland offers yet another perspective on how to understand the ombudsman scheme's mission and expands its jurisdiction even further. The Irish ombudsman scheme does not just deal with contractual disputes—it also reviews complaints about the conduct of financial service providers. This means that even **prospective consumers**—people who have merely been offered or denied a financial service—can file complaints. This is a rather radical departure from the norm. Most ombudsman schemes provide for intervention only after a contract has been formed; in Ireland, intervention is permitted before the contract is formed. This practice accentuates the fact that market conduct matters. Where an insurer engages in deceptive or unfair practices before a contract is signed, the consumer still deserves protection.

4.3.3 Territorial Scope: Where Does Jurisdiction Stop?

Rather than being defined directly by territorial connecting factors (e.g. residence of a complainant, headquarters of the insurance provider), the scope of the services provided by ombudsman schemes is determined by **the law applicable to the dispute**.[65] For EU Member States, this means that insurance services provided by insurers licenced in other EU Member States (operating under the freedom of services principle) may also be subject to the local ombudsman scheme.[66]

4.3.4 Time Limits: When Is It Too Late to Complain?

Access to the ombudsman is not unlimited in time. While some schemes adhere to **general limitation periods set by contract law**,[67] others set specific time limits. For instance, in France, a complaint must be submitted within two months of first expressing dissatisfaction in writing for it to be considered. In the Netherlands, complainants have three months from receipt of the insurer's final decision but this period is extended to up to one year if the insurer fails to inform the consumer of their right to complain. The time limit in Ireland differs depending on the type of a financial service a complaint relates to. For long-term financial services, a compliant must be made within six years from the date of the conduct complained of, or

[65] Belgium, Sect. 5.2.3, France, Sect. 8.2.3, Germany, Sect. 9.2.3, Ireland, Sect. 10.2.3.1, the Netherlands, Sect. 11.1.3, Switzerland, Sect. 14.2.3.

[66] See e.g. Ireland, Sect. 10.2.3.

[67] Belgium, Sect. 5.2.4, Finland, Sect. 7.2.2, Germany, Sect. 9.2.4, Switzerland, Sect. 14.2.4.

within three years of when the complainant knew (or should have known) about the conduct—whichever period is the last to expire. In some cases, the Ombudsman may allow more time if there are good reasons and it would be fair to do so. For financial services other than long-term, a compliant must be made within six years from the date of the conduct complained of.[68]

Each approach reflects a trade-off between efficiency and fairness. A shorter time limit ensures that complaints are fresh and manageable, but it also risks excluding consumers who take longer to realise their rights. A longer time limit provides greater access but can overburden an ombudsman office with old disputes.

4.4 Procedure: The Art of Dispute Resolution

Insurance is built on trust that claims will be paid, contracts will be honoured and disputes will be handled fairly. Yet, when disagreements arise between consumers and insurance providers, how those disputes are resolved is just as important as the outcome itself. The design of the insurance ombudsman scheme's procedure determines whether consumers experience a fair, transparent and accessible process or feel trapped in yet another bureaucratic maze.

A well-structured ombudsman procedure is aimed at levelling the playing field between consumers and insurers, ensuring that the former—who often lack legal expertise and financial resources—can successfully challenge decisions without the burden of expensive litigation. Although each of the analysed country reports presents its own unique way of proceeding with complaints and resolving disputes, each design choice—whether insurers must respond to complaints first, whether mediation is encouraged or whether rulings are binding or advisory—reflects a balance struck between consumer protection and efficiency. Some ombudsman schemes prioritise speed and informality, aiming to resolve cases quickly through negotiation. Others emphasise detailed investigations and legal consistency, ensuring that similar complaints lead to similar outcomes.

Regardless of the nuances, what is common among all the jurisdictions represented is that the ombudsman scheme is not the first stop. Rather, it is the last resort. Insurance businesses bear the primary responsibility for handling complaints, not only because the complaint arises from their conduct or the insurance contract they offered, but also because they have the data and the resources to resolve issues quickly. In theory, this encourages insurers to treat complaints fairly to avoid escalation. In practice, however, consumers often face delays, denials and bureaucratic hurdles, which makes the ombudsman institution a crucial safeguard. To prevent complaints from being disregarded or mishandled, insurers must follow strict procedural requirements. They are required to establish a clear and accessible complaints process, ensuring that policyholders know where and how to file a complaint.

[68] See Section 51 of the Irish Financial Services and Pensions Ombudsman Act 2017.

A designated officer must oversee complaints handling, guaranteeing accountability within the company. Additionally, insurers must adhere to specific response deadlines,[69] providing sufficient time for a thorough review but not so long that it causes frustration. Once a decision is reached, it must be communicated in writing, explaining the outcome and informing the consumer of their right to escalate the complaint if they remain dissatisfied. Only when an insurer fails to respond or provides a resolution that is unsatisfactory to the consumer does the ombudsman mechanism take hold, offering an independent review of the dispute.[70]

Insurance ombudsman schemes across jurisdictions **operate on a reactive basis, i.e. they can only initiate proceedings upon receiving a complaint.** Most of the jurisdictions represented do not grant the ombudsman institution the power to act *ex officio*—i.e. to initiate investigations or proceedings independently, without a formal complaint. This limitation is closely tied to the semi-formal and voluntary nature of ombudsman procedures, which are designed to offer an alternative to litigation rather than enable the institution to serve as a regulatory watchdog. An important exception is the Polish ombudsperson, who is uniquely empowered to act both *ex officio* and *ad instantiam partis*.[71]

The method of receiving complaints varies from highly digitalised systems (online via the ombudsman scheme's website and complaint form or email)[72] to traditional mail[73] and in-person support where complaints may be filed orally.[74] Typically, the ombudsman schemes use multi-channel approaches, permitting verbal, written or electronic filings. This is to increase the efficiency through the automated digital systems while also ensuring accessibility for vulnerable consumers through personalised support.

In principle, insurance ombudsman schemes do not allow **collective complaints**, i.e. consumers must submit complaints individually rather than as a group. However, some jurisdictions have developed **alternative mechanisms to address systemic issues** affecting multiple consumers. For instance, Finland's Complaints Board can issue preliminary rulings when it anticipates that it will receive multiple complaints on the same legal issue, providing guidance to consumers and insurers while suspending related cases until a ruling is made. A notable exception comes from

[69] For example, 30 days in Finland, Sect. 7.3.3, 2 months in France, Sect. 8.3.3.2, 40 days in Ireland, Sect. 10.3.3.

[70] The Belgium Ombudsman scheme represents here an exception and does not require a consumer to file a complaint with an insurer first, Sect. 5.3.2.1.1.

[71] Art. 24(1) of Act of 5 August 2015 on the Handling of Complaints by Financial Market Entities and the Financial Ombudsman (*Ustawa z dnia 5 sierpnia 2015 r. o rozpatrywaniu reklamacji przez podmioty rynku finansowego i o Rzeczniku Finansowym*) Journal of Laws 2019, item 2279, as amended (hereinafter the RF Act).

[72] Belgium, Sect. 5.3.2.5, Croatia, Sect. 6.3.2.5, Finland, Sect. 7.3.2.2.1, France, Sect. 8.3.2, Ireland, Sect. 10.3.2.1, the Netherlands, Sect. 11.2.2.1, Poland, Sect. 12.8.1, Switzerland, Sect. 14.3.2.5.

[73] Croatia, Sect. 6.3.2.5, Ireland, Poland, Sect. 12.8.1.

[74] Germany, Sect. 9.3.2, Ireland, Poland, Sect. 12.8.2.

Switzerland, where the ombudsman institution has occasionally engaged in collective interventions. During the COVID-19 pandemic, amicable settlements were successfully negotiated under the Swiss ombudsman scheme for thousands of businesses that had been denied compensation under epidemic insurance policies. While this approach remains exceptional and issue-specific, it demonstrates that the use of collective redress mechanisms is possible and can emerge in response to pressing consumer issues. A potential shift toward recognising collective claims may already be on the horizon, considering that the Belgian ombudsman scheme has initiated discussions with the Belgian Financial Services and Markets Authority to formalise a process for grouping cases.

4.4.1 Admissibility and Initial Assessment

Before a complaint is reviewed, it is assessed whether it falls within an ombudsman scheme's jurisdiction. During this initial stage of assessment, complaints are evaluated against the admissibility criteria. It is also often assessed whether mediation/conciliation is a viable option before escalating the case to a formal investigation.[75]

Although the **admissibility criteria for complaints** may vary across jurisdictions, there are typically two common requirements: the complaint must fall within the scope of the ombudsman's jurisdiction (see Sect. 4.3 above) and consumers must have attempted to resolve the issue with the insurer first.

If a complaint fails to meet these procedural requirements, an **ombudsman office may dismiss complaints without reviewing these on their merits.** Besides the procedural essentials, different additional criteria are applied. For instance, the complaint will be dismissed immediately if it is outrageous or has a significant impact on the ombudsman's office operations; the dispute does not involve a monetary or other financial interest, or it is unfounded or motivated by a wish to cause intentional harm. Furthermore, it is underscored in many of the country reports that the scheme will not handle a complaint that has already been brought before the courts and tribunals or similar alternative dispute resolution body,[76] nor if the complaint has been definitively resolved through an agreement reached between the consumer and insurance provider. These additional criteria serve to maintain efficiency on the part of the ombudsman office and prevent the scheme from being unnecessarily burdened, ensuring that resources are allocated to cases with genuine merit.

Admission of a complaint to the proceedings before the ombudsperson usually has an important legal consequence. As the example of most of the jurisdictions analysed shows, **submitting a complaint to the ombudsman scheme typically**

---

[75] See e.g. Finland, Sect. 7.3.2.2.1, and Ireland, Sect. 10.3.2.1.

[76] Belgium, Sect. 5.3.2.1.1, Finland, Sect. 7.3.3, Ireland, Switzerland.

interrupts the limitation period, effectively pausing the time frame within which a consumer can initiate legal action. This suspension lasts for the duration of the ombudsman proceedings and resumes only after the ombudsperson has issued their decision.[77] This approach ensures that consumers do not lose their right to bring a case to court while seeking an out-of-court resolution. In contrast, jurisdictions such as Croatia and Switzerland **do not recognise ombudsman proceedings as grounds for interrupting or suspending limitation periods.** In these systems, consumers must monitor the legal time limits applicable while their complaint is being reviewed. The Swiss ombudsman service explicitly advises complainants to take proactive measures, such as obtaining a waiver of the limitation period from the insurer or initiating legal proceedings if a time limit is nearing expiration.

This divergence may highlight an important procedural trade-off—jurisdictions that suspend limitation periods offer stronger consumer protection, preventing complainants from being disadvantaged by lengthy ombudsman processes. However, in systems where limitation periods continue running, consumers are required to be more vigilant about their legal rights, ensuring that they do not unintentionally forfeit their ability to litigate.

4.4.2 Evidence Collection and Case Assessment

Once a complaint is deemed admissible, the ombudsman office conducts **fact-finding and a legal assessment**. Across jurisdictions, the process of collecting evidence varies, reflecting different procedural philosophies but also the ombudsperson's authority.

This matter links to a more fundamental question for any dispute resolution system: **who must prove their case?**

Croatia and Switzerland represent jurisdictions that adopt a **quasi-judicial approach**, where **the primary burden of proof rests on the consumer.** The complainant must submit all relevant documents and prove their case, though the ombudsman office may request additional information if needed. The Netherlands also follows a judicial model, adopting civil court evidentiary rules—whoever makes a claim must prove it, unless fairness dictates otherwise. This tilts the balance toward legal formalism, making evidence collection less consumer-friendly but potentially more rigorous.

Other jurisdictions emphasise **consumer accessibility**, placing minimal burden on complainants and **requiring insurers to supply all relevant documentation**.[78] However, the effectiveness of this practice is ultimately dependent on the ombudsman scheme's ability to compel cooperation. In this regard, the contrast between

[77] See e.g. Belgium, Sect. 5.3.2.1.3.

[78] Belgium, Sect. 5.3.2.1.2, Finland, Sect. 7.3.4., Ireland, Sect. 10.3.4 Poland, Sect. 12.8.1.

different approaches is striking. Some schemes have clear enforcement mechanisms, ensuring that insurers comply or face tangible consequences: in Belgium and in the Netherlands, if an insurer does not respond or provides incomplete information, the ombudsman office may alert the market authority.[79] In Poland, if the insurer does not provide the documents or information requested, the ombudsperson may impose a monetary penalty of up to PLN 1 million.[80] Other schemes rely solely on soft pressure and informal persuasion, leaving little recourse when an insurer refuses to cooperate.[81]

There are also powerful ombudsman schemes, equipped with **investigatory powers** rivalling those of courts, capable of hearing the parties,[82] summoning evidence, asking for expert opinions[83] and even conducting on-site inspections.[84]

The manner in which evidence is gathered and assessed affects not only the efficiency but also the legitimacy of an ombudsman scheme. A more interventionist ombudsman scheme may be better at addressing power imbalances but risks slowing down the process. A more passive ombudsman scheme may ensure efficiency but, at the same time, may disadvantage consumers who lack the resources to build a strong case.

4.4.3 *The Role of Mediation*

Evidence collection is only one part of the equation. The manner in which a dispute is resolved is just as important as how it is investigated. It can be argued that formal adjudication provides certainty, but it may be slow, rigid or even adversarial. Mediation, by contrast, offers a different path—one that prioritises dialogue over conflict and flexibility over legal formality. It plays a crucial role in reducing case backlogs and maintaining insurer-consumer relationships. Rather than imposing a ruling from above, mediation allows parties to craft their own solutions, tailored to their specific needs. It is hoped that this approach fosters greater satisfaction and voluntary compliance, as people may be more inclined to accept an outcome they helped shape. Yet, while all ombudsman schemes seek to resolve disputes amicably, the extent to which mediation is integrated into the process differs across jurisdictions.

Instead of immediately resorting to formal adjudication, some ombudsman schemes use **mediation as an intermediate step**, encouraging complainants and insurers to find a mutually acceptable solution without escalating the dispute. Where

[79] Belgium, The Netherlands, Sect. 11.2.6.5.

[80] Art. 32(1) of the RF Act.

[81] See e.g. France, Sect. 8.3.4.

[82] Ireland, Sect. 10.3.4.4.

[83] Finland, Sect. 7.3.2.2.5.

[84] Belgium, Sect. 5.3.2.1.2, Ireland, Sect. 10.3.4.

this is the case, mediation may be integrated as **a mandatory first step**[85] or as **a discretionary tool**,[86] encouraging dialogue but allowing disputes to proceed to formal adjudication without mediation. Ireland's Financial Services and Pensions Ombudsman (FSPO) represents the former model and begins every dispute with mediation. The Swiss scheme, on the other hand, emphasises mediation but takes a more discretionary approach and attempts to facilitate dialogue only when feasible.

There are also ombudsman schemes where **mediation is less prominent**. For instance, a more legalistic approach is taken in France and Germany, where disputes are resolved primarily through written procedures, emphasising compliance with contractual and legal obligations rather than negotiated settlements. In the Croatian system, in contrast, unresolved cases are referred to external mediation centres, acknowledging the system's limitations in facilitating out-of-court settlements.

It is difficult to determine whether in general ombudsman schemes that emphasise mediation truly resolve disputes faster or lead to higher consumer satisfaction.[87] Yet, beneath this procedural choice lies a fundamental question: should the ombudsperson act as a mediator, fostering dialogue, compromise and mutual agreement, or should they take on the role of a quasi-judicial authority, issuing legally reasoned and/or binding rulings that reinforce contractual obligations and regulatory consistency? The answer is not merely a matter of efficiency; it is a question of what kind of fairness society values more—a system built on negotiation and flexibility, or one anchored in legal certainty and enforcement.

4.4.4 Decision-Making and Outcomes: The Power and Limits of Insurance Ombudsman Decisions

Although the insurance ombudspersons are not judges, their decisions shape the fortunes of individuals and businesses alike. Unlike courts, which are bound by rigid legal principles and determine **what is legally correct**, an insurance ombudsperson should decide **what is fair** in the specific circumstances and, therefore, has a more **equitable mandate**, requiring consideration of not just laws but also fairness and industry standards. Fairness, however, is an elusive concept. To bring order to this ambiguity, various guidelines may help define what "fair" means in practice. Legal principles, jurisprudence, breaches of contract, unfair treatment, maladministration, industry codes, and even advertisements or communication with complainants can all be taken into account. Ultimately, however, the ombudsperson's role is not to mechanically apply the rules but to craft an outcome that feels just.

---

[85] Ireland, Sect. 10.3.4.2.

[86] Belgium, section 0, Switzerland, Sect. 14.3.2.1.2.

[87] However, it is worth noting that in the Netherlands, Kifid reports high consumer satisfaction with mediation, supported by statistical data. See The Netherlands, Sect. 11.2.2.3.1.

This balance between law and fairness is reflected in most of the schemes analysed, with the notable exception of Poland[88] and Germany,[89] where the ombudsperson's decisions are based solely on the applicable law and its procedural rules.

A decision without consequences is little more than advice and that is why the insurance ombudsperson must have real means to ensure that wronged parties receive proper restitution. These means may take different forms. The ombudsperson should be able to demand compensation for direct financial losses and the indirect ripple effects, i.e. expenses that would not have arisen but for the unfair act. Even emotional distress or serious inconvenience should be considered grounds for a financial award. In addition, delays in compensation can further harm the complainant, whether through lost opportunities or the need to borrow money to stay afloat. To counter this, ombudspersons should be able to order interest payments on overdue compensation, ensuring that insurance providers do not benefit from dragging their feet. In this way, fairness is not only about righting past wrongs but also about preventing institutions from turning delay into a strategy. Some of the jurisdictions represented expressly recognise this power. In Finland, France, and Ireland, the ombudspersons are authorised to award compensation. However, limits matter. While there are no caps on the awards under the Finnish and French schemes, one is set under the Irish system: EUR 500,000, or EUR 52,000 per year for annuities.

Lastly, to ensure that fairness is not just financial but also practical, an ombudsperson should have the power to issue "instructions", i.e. orders requiring institutions to take corrective actions.

The degree to which these decisions carry weight, however, depends on their **enforceability**. The power of an ombudsperson's decision hinges on whether it is binding on the insurance provider, the complainant or both. In practice, the schemes implement different models. In most of the schemes analysed, **the ombudsperson's decision is purely advisory**,[90] leaving insurance providers free to ignore unfavourable rulings. This model relies on strong corporate compliance cultures or consumer pressure to ensure firms follow recommendations.

At the other extreme, **binding decisions are imposed on the parties either automatically or upon prior request by both parties**. Among all the analysed schemes, automatically binding decisions are imposed only in Ireland[91] and Croatia. Although this approach may ensure finality, it can also deter complainants from using a new ombudsman scheme they do not yet trust. Therefore, it only works where the ombudsman institution is well-established and the courts are too costly or inaccessible to be a viable alternative. A limited version of this model functions in Germany, where automatically binding effect is reserved for decisions that reject an

[88] Poland, Sect. 12.8.2.4.

[89] Germany, Sect. 9.3.5.

[90] In Belgium, Sect. 5.3.2.1.3, and Switzerland, Sect. 14.3.5, decisions are purely advisory, summarising the legal position without imposing obligations. Similarly in Poland, Sect. 12.8.2.4, and France, Sect. 8.3.5.4, decisions serve as recommendations rather than orders, relying on insurers' willingness to comply. In Finland, Sect. 7.3.5.1, recommendations are the standard.

[91] Decisions made after a formal investigation, Ireland, Sect. 10.3.5.

inadmissible complaint as well as decisions concerning dispute values of up to an amount of EUR 10,000. The Netherlands, in turn, offers a model under which decisions are binding only if both parties agree beforehand.

There is also a middle-ground model where the **enforceability of a decision is conditional.** Complainants are offered a choice: after receiving a written, reasoned decision, they have a set time to accept it. **If they do, the decision will bind both parties, barring further legal action. If they decline or fail to respond, the decision holds no weight, allowing them to pursue the matter in court.** This system encourages consumers to engage with the ombudsman scheme, as they risk nothing by trying.[92]

The binding or purely advisory status of the decision determines **the consequences of disregarding that decision**. In jurisdictions where decisions are non-binding, such as Belgium, Poland and Switzerland, there are no direct penalties imposed on insurance providers who ignore them. In contrast, where the ombudsperson's decisions are binding, a failure to comply entails concrete consequences. For instance, the ombudsperson in Ireland is allowed to seek enforcement through the courts. In Croatia, there is a mild enforcement mechanism, whereby non-compliance with the ombudsperson's rulings can be reported to regulatory authorities. In the Netherlands, persistent non-compliance can also lead to an insurance provider's removal from the scheme. Across the jurisdictions represented, compliance with the respective insurance ombudsperson's decisions is generally high, with insurers following non-binding recommendations in most cases. In Belgium, for instance, non-compliance is rare, with only seven recorded instances of an insurance company or intermediary disregarding the ombudsperson's position. The Croatian rapporteur reports full and unconditional compliance, while the Finnish scheme maintains a 96–100% adherence rate annually. The French scheme boasts an even higher rate, with insurers following the ombudsperson's recommendations in over 99% of cases, with only a handful of exceptions each year. In Germany, binding decisions are followed 100%, though data on recommendations is lacking. Near-total compliance is reported in Ireland, with just one instance of non-compliance since 2018, which was swiftly resolved through court enforcement. This also shows that the approach of insurers towards ombudsman schemes is generally positive.[93] The country reports indicate that, regardless of whether participation in the scheme is mandatory[94] or voluntary,[95] insurers demonstrate a high degree of compliance, with many adjusting their

[92] This model is identified as typical by INFO Network. See *Guide to setting up a Financial Services Ombudsman Scheme*, INFO Network, March 2018, available at: https://www.networkfso.org/resources/Guide-to-setting-up-a%20financial-services-ombudsman-scheme_INFO-Network_March2018.pdf, p. 43. Accessed 16 Apr 2025.

[93] The Dutch scheme monitors financial service providers' satisfaction with the scheme's services. The average satisfaction score in 2023 was 7.4 out of 10. See the Netherlands, Sect. 11.3.

[94] The Netherlands.

[95] Germany.

operating methods based on the ombudsperson's decisions.[96] Across most markets, insurers recognise that mediation offers a faster, more cost-effective alternative to litigation and therefore helps to maintain consumer trust.[97] However, cases in Belgium and France suggest that smaller insurers[98] and/or specialised insurance providers[99] may be less willing to engage with consumer protection standards, potentially undermining the effectiveness of ombudsman schemes in these sectors.

In only a few jurisdictions may the ombudsperson's decisions be **enforced through courts**. As already mentioned, Ireland stands out as a model where the ombudsperson can seek judicial enforcement against non-compliant insurers. Yet, most jurisdictions, including Belgium and France, maintain a clear separation between rulings by the ombudsperson and judicial processes.

4.4.5 The Review Mechanism: Who Watches the Watchdog?

For the system to remain credible, there must be a way to review not just individual decisions but also the process itself. Consumers should have the right to challenge how their case was handled—not necessarily the outcome, but the fairness and quality of the procedure. Without such oversight, the ombudsman scheme risks becoming a self-referential authority, trusted but unchecked.

Yet, across the jurisdictions represented, **the ability to appeal an insurance ombudsperson's decision**—or to seek further legal recourse—varies significantly. In most countries, including Belgium, Croatia, Finland, France and Germany, the legal frameworks governing ombudsman institutions do not provide for formal appeal rights against decisions, effectively making the ombudsperson's decisions final within their process. However, since the decisions are non-binding, dissatisfied complainants can still turn to the courts. A more layered system is used in the Netherlands: non-binding decisions can be disregarded entirely, while binding rulings can only be overturned by a civil court in cases of serious error or procedural defects. The strictest framework can be found in Ireland, where legally binding decisions can only be challenged through a statutory appeal to the High Court within 35 days. The court reviews whether the decision was reached fairly, and if procedural flaws are found, it may amend the ruling or send the case back for reconsideration.

Judicial oversight of ombudsman schemes remains largely absent. The rapporteurs for most of the jurisdictions analysed, including Croatia, Germany and

[96] Finland.

[97] Croatia, Sect. 6.5.1, France, Sect. 8.5.1.3, Switzerland, Sect. 14.5.1.

[98] France, Sect. 8.5.1.3.

[99] Belgium, Sect. 5.1.2, where reference is made to new insurance products, including insurance for electric bikes and multimedia products, such as smartphones and tablets.

Switzerland, confirm that courts have no supervisory authority over the respective ombudsman scheme. In Croatia, oversight is expressly limited to the Ombudsman Council, while the German and Swiss schemes are not subject to judicial review. In respect of other countries, such as Belgium, France, the Netherlands and Poland, it is not clearly stated whether the ombudsman schemes are subject to court supervision, leaving this question open.

The absence of a clear external review procedure may raise concerns—without a strong accountability system, the ombudsman scheme remains a powerful yet largely self-regulated institution. Whether such autonomy fosters efficiency or risks unchecked authority depends on the credibility and trust each ombudsman scheme has earned within its legal and financial ecosystem.

4.5 Market Trends and Practical Observations

The complaints reaching insurance ombudsman offices across Europe reveal trends in consumer dissatisfaction and regulatory gaps. While traditional products like motor and home insurance continue to dominate complaints, new patterns are emerging. For instance, home insurance has overtaken motor insurance as the most complained-about product in Belgium due to the lack of standardised coverage and definitions. Similarly, in France, affinity insurance, i.e. policies bundled with products like smartphones and travel bookings, has seen a sharp rise in disputes, exposing issues concerning limited coverage and inadequate consumer awareness at the point of sale. Across jurisdictions, the most common source of friction remains claims handling, where there are delays, rejections and disputes concerning compensation calculations. Analysis of the data highlights an enduring challenge: consumers often struggle to understand the terms of their policies until they need to make a claim.

Beyond individual products, systemic risks to consumer protection are becoming more evident. The rise of unit-linked life insurance complaints in Switzerland underscores the financial risks consumers face when investment-linked products underperform. In Poland, widespread dissatisfaction stems from the depreciation practices used in motor insurance claims, whereby insurers systematically reduce payouts based on private contracts with repair workshops. The COVID-19 pandemic revealed another structural vulnerability: business interruption insurance disputes surged in Ireland, as policyholders discovered that their coverage was either unclear or inadequate in the face of a global crisis. These trends suggest that consumer grievances are often not just about isolated incidents but about fundamental mismatches between policy expectations and insurer practices.

At the heart of many of these disputes lies a critical issue: consumers' financial awareness and literacy. The rapporteurs' observations suggest a paradox. In theory, information has never been more accessible, with an endless number of reports, digital tools and consumer protection laws aiming to equip individuals with financial knowledge. Yet, across Europe, the reality is far messier. Some ombudspersons, such as in Croatia, report a rise in well-prepared complaints, hinting at progress. While improvements have also been documented in Finland, the complexity of financial products is outpacing financial literacy. Others, for instance in France, lament widespread ignorance, where even basic insurance terms remain elusive. In Switzerland, meanwhile, literacy considerations are embedded into the dispute resolution process, but statistical assessments are avoided due to the lack of necessary data. Ultimately, the illusion seems to persist: access to information does not equate to understanding, and regulation does not guarantee wisdom.

4.6 Beyond the Numbers: What Insurance Ombudsman Complaints Reveal About Market Dynamics

Insurance ombudsman offices serve as the frontline of consumer protection, but they are also a mirror reflecting the deeper realities of an insurance market—its strengths and its failures. The number of complaints, the way they are resolved and who ultimately benefits reveal insights far more complex than simple statistics.

The number of complaints submitted to an insurance ombudsman scheme can reveal far more than just consumer dissatisfaction—it serves as a window into the health of a country's insurance market, the strength of its regulatory framework and the level of trust between insurers and policyholders. A high volume of complaints does not necessarily mean a failing system, just as a low volume does not automatically indicate success. The reality is usually far more nuanced.

Among the jurisdictions analysed, the schemes in France and Germany handle the highest volumes, with 21,500 and 16,000–18,000 complaints per year, respectively. Finland's scheme processes around 9577 cases annually. In countries where complaints are frequent, several explanations may emerge. Beyond the obvious factor of geographical size (the larger the country, the more complaints are likely), high numbers may also indicate that the scheme is accessible and that consumers are well informed about their right to complain. On the other hand, high numbers of complaints can signal **deeper market frictions**—issues like poor claims handling, misleading policy terms or aggressive sales tactics that create widespread dissatisfaction. In some cases, **regulatory gaps** allow insurers to operate with minimal oversight, leading to a surge in complaints as consumers feel compelled to seek external intervention. In exceptional cases where there is no obligation of the policyholder to attempt to resolve the issue with the insurer first, a high complaint rate may also reflect **low confidence in insurers'** willingness to resolve disputes fairly, pushing policyholders to bypass internal processes and go straight to an independent authority.

At the lower end, Croatia's ombudsman scheme received just 22 complaints in 2023. Low complaint numbers could indicate that insurers handle claims efficiently, policy terms are clear and regulations protect consumers effectively. On the other hand, it may also mean that the scheme is inaccessible or consumers are unaware of its existence. In some cultures, consumers may prefer direct negotiation or legal action over mediation, resulting in fewer cases reaching the ombudsman scheme. Fewer complaints may also be reported in countries where legal protection insurance is widespread, as policyholders typically turn to the lawyer provided under their coverage to resolve disputes, rather than to ombudsman schemes. In extreme cases, a general sense of futility may discourage complaints altogether, masking underlying problems rather than proving their absence.

However, volume alone is only part of the equation. Who actually wins these disputes? **The ratio of complaints resolved in favour of insurers versus consumers** provides further insight into both the insurance market and the effectiveness of an ombudsman scheme.

The schemes in the Netherlands and Switzerland stand out, with a significant proportion of cases, 60% and 70% of cases, respectively, resolved in favour of policyholders. In general, a high success rate for complainants may indicate strong consumer protection measures, or a more interventionist ombudsman scheme that actively pushes insurers to settle disputes rather than simply ruling on them. A high proportion of cases decided in favour of consumers might also indicate that insurers routinely engage in unfair practices, such as wrongful claim denials, opaque policy wording or aggressive cost-cutting measures that undermine consumer rights. Furthermore, it might also signal that regulatory enforcement is weak, forcing consumers to rely on the ombudsman scheme to correct insurer misconduct rather than insurers proactively complying with fair business practices.

In contrast, the schemes in Finland, France and Germany show a clear tilt in favour of insurers, with success rates for policyholders hovering around 32–48%.[100] Ireland's scheme stands as an extreme case, with only 10% of legally binding complaints fully upheld in favour of consumers and an additional 7% substantially upheld. The vast majority, 65%, were rejected outright. This may suggest that Ireland's ombudsman scheme follows a highly legalistic approach, requiring strong evidence before ruling against insurers, potentially making it difficult for consumers to succeed unless they have a clear-cut case. In general, however, if a significant majority of cases are decided in favour of insurers, it may suggest that policyholders are frequently filing weak or unjustified claims—perhaps due to misunderstandings about policy coverage, unrealistic expectations, or misleading sales practices that lead consumers to believe they are entitled to benefits not included in their coverage. It may also indicate stricter interpretations of policy contracts, suggesting that insurers operate in a more rule-driven regulatory environment in which the ombudsperson's decisions align closely with contractual obligations rather than broader notions of fairness.

However, the number of complaints or the ratio alone is not enough to diagnose whether a market is fair or broken. Such data must be analysed alongside other factors, such as the types of complaints being filed, the reasoning behind decisions,

[100] France, Sect. 8.4.4, Finland, Sect. 7.4, Germany, Sect. 9.4; However, the numbers for the French scheme change significantly when including spontaneous settlements by insurers, bringing the consumer success rate up to 53%.

whether the ombudsperson's decisions lead to industry-wide improvements, how insurance disputes are handled and whether consumers trust the system. Furthermore, one must consider the size and maturity of the market analysed. A market in which insurers consistently win may be efficient—or it may be biased against consumers. A market in which consumers often prevail may be protective—or it may indicate an industry that routinely tries to deny legitimate claims until it is forced to pay. A scheme with few complaints may be efficient—or it may be silencing its consumers. On the other hand, a scheme flooded with disputes may be failing—or it may be giving policyholders a voice. Ultimately, the real measure of success is whether complaints lead to systemic change, better transparency and a higher standard of fairness in the long run.

4.7 Measuring Effectiveness of Insurance Ombudsman Schemes

Measuring the effectiveness of an insurance ombudsman scheme is no simple task. While this analysis does not claim to offer a definitive assessment, the country reports provide valuable clues about how well their systems function. Complaint volumes, resolution rates and decision outcomes are just a few metrics that may help in measuring the overall effectiveness.

For instance, the **number of complaints submitted** to an insurance ombudsman scheme each year, as discussed above, may shed light on the **accessibility of the ombudsman scheme**. The more accessible the ombudsman scheme is, the more **encouraged consumers** may be to file disputes simply because they are aware of their rights and trust the process. On the other hand, an overly vague and complex process, combined with a lack of awareness of the right to complain, may result in a low number of complaints.

However, the real question is: **how many of these complaints actually lead to a resolution?** At one extreme, the Croatian scheme reports an almost 100% resolution rate—every single complaint received is processed and concluded. However, with only 22 complaints in 2023, the scheme operates on a microscopic scale compared to other jurisdictions analysed. In contrast, the ombudsman schemes in Finland, France, and Germany deal with a high volume of complaints. The French scheme received 21,500 referrals in 2022, but only 33.9% of them were deemed admissible, meaning that a significant proportion never reached the resolution stage. Nevertheless, nearly 8000 cases were settled, indicating a system that, while overwhelmed, still delivers a high number of outcomes. The German scheme receives between 16,000 and 18,000 complaints per year, with over 80% found admissible, which may suggest a structured and effective filtering system. In Finland, the pattern is similar: 9577 cases were handled by the scheme in 2022, with 824 classified as disputes and the rest constituting general enquiries or complaints. Other countries fall somewhere in between. The scheme in Ireland receives around 5331 complaints annually, with an average of 5008 cases closed each year, meaning that it operates at near full capacity. However, formal dispute resolution services only handled 1722 cases in 2022, while others were resolved through mediation or clarification. In the Netherlands, the scheme received between 5000 and 5500 complaints across all financial sectors, with 3000 to 3200 resolved annually. Some ombudsman schemes rely on early-stage resolution mechanisms to prevent complaints from escalating. The Belgian scheme received 7872 requests in 2022, but only 3803 resulted in formal inquiries—the rest were either resolved informally or dismissed. A similar pattern is reported from Switzerland, which received 3000 annual complaints, including telephone calls, letters, and web forms. As this ombudsman scheme only intervenes on the basis of written complaints, 300 out of 1000 complaints within its mandate led to interventions with insurers. What does this tell us? Schemes with high complaint volumes (France, Germany) tend to have a high proportion of dismissed cases, either due to strict admissibility criteria or limited resources to process every complaint. In contrast, where schemes operate close to full capacity (Ireland, the Netherlands), processing nearly as many complaints as they receive, this may suggest an efficient and well-organised scheme that has the capacity to handle its caseload. At the same time, however, these schemes may struggle with longer processing times.

Effectiveness can also be assessed by examining **the ratio of complaints resolved in favour of insurers versus consumers.** If a significant majority of cases are decided in favour of insurers, it could indicate an ombudsman system that leans toward industry interests, either because of regulatory capture, lack of independence or overly rigid interpretations of contracts that favour insurers over fairness.

The **average time taken to resolve disputes** is another crucial metric. A fast resolution process may suggest a responsive, well-resourced and consumer-friendly scheme. Insurance disputes often arise at critical moments—after a car accident, a home disaster or a medical emergency—when policyholders need quick answers. A scheme that delivers decisions swiftly ensures that consumers avoid financial hardship or prolonged uncertainty while waiting for their case to be resolved. schemes that rush cases through at the expense of thoroughness achieve the opposite of effectiveness. If complaints are dismissed too quickly, or if insurers dominate the process, consumers may feel that their cases are not being properly considered. This, in turn, may undermine trust in the ombudsperson's decisions. On the other hand, an overly slow ombudsman process can indicate serious weaknesses—insufficient funding, lack of staff, bureaucratic inefficiencies or an overwhelming case backlog. If consumers must wait months or even years for a decision, the ombudsman scheme risks becoming irrelevant. Long delays may make consumers lose faith in the process and opt for costly litigation instead. Some of the represented jurisdictions pride themselves on rapid dispute resolution. In Croatia, the average case is resolved in three to four weeks. The Swiss scheme follows closely, concluding interventions within four to six weeks.[101] Other schemes operate on moderate time frames, ensuring decisions are made within two to three months. Germany's ombudsman scheme resolves cases in 70 days, while the average resolution time for ADR cases in Finland is 60 days, well within the legally required 90-day limit. Yet, there are also jurisdictions where delays are the norm rather than the exception. In France, where complaints have surged by 63% in a single year, it currently takes seven months to resolve a case, with waiting times expected to rise further. The real outlier however is the Irish scheme, where cases take an average of 10 months, and complex disputes requiring formal procedures can take even longer.

Finally, the rapporteurs provided their own view on the effectiveness of their schemes, with some identifying several **systemic weaknesses limiting their effectiveness**. Among the factors indicated as preventing the system from fully serving its purpose are consumer financial literacy,[102] insufficient budget and human resources,[103] a term of office that is too short to allow for long-term strategic planning[104] and procedural limitations that constrain the ombudsperson's ability to act.[105]

The rapporteurs were also asked about any potential reforms that they would recommend in order to improve the effectiveness of their schemes. In this context, interestingly, the rapporteur for Finland—a country that reports a well-functioning ombudsman scheme with widespread compliance—acknowledges that dispute resolution could be faster, indicating the need for smoother and more timely cooperation from all the parties involved in the proceeding.[106] The French rapporteur points to the ombudsman office's independence. The ombudsman scheme is legally required to be neutral, yet is financially dependent on the very industry it oversees. The professional sector not only funds the ombudsman scheme's work but also plays a role in appointing the ombudsperson. This creates an inherent tension: how can an institution hold insurers accountable when it relies on their goodwill for resources and renewal of the ombudsperson's mandate? In Ireland, meanwhile, reform is approached from an entirely different angle. Instead of focusing on legal and structural barriers, it emphasises innovation, engagement and influence. Its strategic plan does not simply aim to resolve complaints but to shape the entire insurance landscape, raising industry standards and influencing policy so that fewer disputes arise in the first place. This is a vision of an ombudsman scheme that does not merely react to problems; it actively works to prevent them before they escalate.

---

[101] Switzerland, Sect. 14.4; Although complex medical cases take longer due to insurers' limited capacity to provide expert opinions.

[102] Finland, Sect. 7.5.2.

[103] France.

[104] France, Sect. 8.5.2.1.

[105] In Germany, cases that require extensive fact-finding or involve unresolved fundamental legal questions may be rejected, pushing policyholders toward litigation instead. Insurers can also request that unresolved legal questions be left as test cases, though they must cover the complainant's legal costs if the case proceeds to court.

[106] Finland, Sect. 7.5.3.

4.8 Consumer Awareness and Accessibility of Insurance Ombudsman Schemes

How do consumers find out about the existence of insurance ombudsman schemes? Across the schemes analysed, the answer varies. Some jurisdictions mandate omnipresence: insurers in Belgium, Croatia, Finland, France, Germany, Ireland, the Netherlands and Poland are legally obliged to highlight the option of external dispute resolution.[107] The Belgian scheme includes additional measures, such as press appearances and even targeting outreach to compliance officers and law students to raise awareness. In Finland, a hands-on approach is also taken, favouring phone-based accessibility over the prevailing shift toward digital services. However, even the Finnish rapporteur acknowledges that awareness levels remain suboptimal despite these extra initiatives. The digital front is an evolving battlefield. France's ombudsman scheme doubled down on its web presence with a new site, social media (LinkedIn) activity, and an online "claimant space"—a smart move in an era where 60% of its complaints are now submitted online. The Netherlands' Kifid also maximises digital reach,[108] with an intuitive website featuring explainer videos and a complaint quick-checker. By contrast, Germany's ombudsman scheme remains largely offline in terms of social media engagement, a notable outlier. Ireland's FSPO, on the other hand, is fully engaged across Facebook, LinkedIn and outreach events, even appointing an Access Officer to ensure inclusivity. In Croatia and Switzerland, a mixed approach is taken, combining offline and online efforts but without social media presence.[109] As a result, most rapporteurs report that there are no significant barriers to access. Yet, the French rapporteur observes that, despite efforts to increase awareness, access remains skewed toward those who know how to navigate the system.[110]

4.9 Conclusive Remarks: A Reflection on the Evolution and Future of Insurance Ombudsman Schemes

At first glance, the existence of insurance ombudsman schemes across Europe **appears to represent a triumph of consumer protection.** Each represented jurisdiction has developed intricate mechanisms to ensure access to justice and foster industry accountability. Still, beneath the surface, these **schemes reveal some deep structural dilemmas**. For instance: should an ombudsperson be a neutral mediator

[107] Belgium, Sect. 5.6.1, Croatia, Sect. 6.6.1, France, Sect. 8.6.1.3, Finland, Sect. 7.6.1, Germany, Sect. 9.6.1, Ireland, Sect. 10.6.1.1, Netherlands, Sect. 11.5.1, Poland, section.

[108] Kifid is present in social media platforms, such as LinkedIn, Facebook and Instagram.

[109] In Switzerland, there has recently been a change in this regard. Influenced by reports from other countries presented in this book, the Swiss ombudsman scheme has launched its LinkedIn page.

[110] France, Sect. 8.6.1.2.

or an advocate for consumers? Should their funding be industry-driven, or would that risk regulatory capture? Should their decisions carry the force of law, or does strong enforceability compromise flexibility? Such questions go beyond mere technicalities—they reflect broader policy choices that may influence how financial markets operate and evolve.

Furthermore, the analysis of different European experiences offers several lessons. Schemes in some countries, like France and Germany, have developed sophisticated, high-volume complaint-resolution systems that process tens of thousands of cases per year. Others, like in Croatia and Switzerland, operate on a smaller scale, emphasising mediation and informal settlements. Yet, the question must be asked: does the efficiency of an ombudsman scheme truly represent the measure of its success? A jurisdiction with fewer complaints might indicate a well-functioning insurance market—or a lack of awareness among consumers. A system that resolves cases swiftly may prioritise speed over fairness. An ombudsman scheme with broad jurisdiction may enhance consumer protection, but it might also struggle under the weight of its own mandate.

The funding of ombudsman schemes also raises a critical question about independence. The prevailing model, in which insurance businesses finance the dispute resolution mechanism, follows a logical economic rationale: those who generate disputes should pay for resolving them. It makes sense—until the question is asked whether an ombudsman scheme can remain impartial and independent when it is financially dependent on the very industry it oversees.

The insurance ombudsman institution is often seen as a tool for resolving consumer disputes, but this view alone is too narrow. As this analysis suggests, **an ombudsman scheme may, in fact, serve as a mechanism for identifying and correcting market failures**. Perhaps the most profound insight from this comparative study is that consumer complaints are rarely just isolated grievances—they are trends. When a single policyholder fights a claim denial, it is a problem. When thousands of policyholders complain about the same issue, it should be seen as a systemic warning. Affinity insurance complaints in France, unit-linked life insurance disputes in Switzerland or business interruption claim denials during the COVID-19 pandemic in Ireland—each of these is a symptom of a broader problem, and each represents a potential regulatory blind spot. Therefore, the complaints should be understood as a data point or a signal of something bigger, such as systemic issues in policy design, claim-handling inefficiencies, evolution of risk, or regulation. If regulators and insurers paid closer attention to ombudsman complaints, they could see them as diagnostic tools and a blueprint for a better insurance market.

What does the future hold for insurance ombudsman schemes? Should they evolve into stronger regulatory forces, actively shaping market behaviour? Or should they remain dispute-resolution bodies, reactive rather than proactive? The answer likely depends on how societies want to balance market freedom with consumer protection. Furthermore, institutions—no matter how carefully designed—must also continuously adapt to the changing landscapes they seek to govern. In an era of growing financial complexity in which algorithms determine insurance pricing and AI may soon handle claims, the insurance ombudsman institution must also evolve. The question is whether, in the light of this evolution, the ombudsman institution can continue to be just a mediator, or whether it should strengthen its role as a guardian of consumer rights.

Through an exercise in comparison, this analysis reveals how insurance ombudsman schemes reflect deeper societal and market dynamics. They embody each society's interpretation of independence, fairness, accountability and trust in financial institutions—concepts that, in turn, define an intricate balance between market forces and consumer protection. As financial landscapes evolve and new challenges emerge, these insights may hopefully become an inspiration for refining ombudsman models so that they are not just reactive institutions but proactive mechanisms that shape better, fairer insurance markets for the future.

Part III
Country Reports

Chapter 5
Belgium

Insurance Ombudsman Scheme

Laurent de Barsy

5.1 Institutional Framework

5.1.1 Establishment

The Belgian Insurance Ombudsman Scheme was established by the insurance industry in 1987. Initially, the ombudsperson was employed by the Professional Association of Insurers, with an office at its headquarters. The main purpose of establishing an ADR body for insurance was to avoid legal proceedings and to try to understand the negative image of the sector.

At that time, there were very few ombudsman schemes in Belgium, whether public or private. Only the financial institutions had established an ombudsman scheme in 1986.

While the Insurance Ombudsman Scheme and the ombudsman scheme for the financial sector (banking) were created through a "bottom-up" approach, other sectors such as energy, telecommunications and postal services followed in 1991. The approach for these other "economically relevant" sectors was "top down", as in these cases it was an initiative of the Belgian legislature that led to their creation.

Prior to the establishment of the Insurance Ombudsman Service, complaints were addressed to the financial control authority, the Commission Bancaire, Financière et des Assurances (CBFA), which was later renamed Financial Services and Market Authority (hereinafter FSMA).

In 2006, the Ombudsman Service was given a legal framework to operate independently of the insurance industry, and the funding system was restructured

L. de Barsy (✉)
Belgian Insurance Ombudsman, Brussels, Belgium
e-mail: laurent.debarsy@ombudsman-insurance.be

H. Heiss et al. (eds.), *Insurance Ombudsman Schemes*, AIDA Europe Research Series on Insurance Law and Regulation 15,
https://doi.org/10.1007/978-3-032-01500-6_5

accordingly.[1] At the same time, the Ombudsman Service became an independent non-profit association.[2]

In 2014, the legislature established the role and functioning of the Ombudsman Service in art. 302, now art. 322 of the Insurance Act.[3]

The statute of "qualified ADR bodies" was adopted in 2014.[4] The Insurance Ombudsman Service was among the first institutions to be recognised as such.[5] In addition to the conditions set out in the law, such as transparency, free access for the consumers and fixed cycle times, this had two major consequences for the Ombudsman Service: the ombudsperson must publish a comprehensive annual report and is subject to an annual audit by the Ministry of Economic Affairs.

The current framework for the Insurance Ombudsman Scheme in Belgium is set out in art. 322 of the Insurance Act. This legislation defines the funding, role and remit of the Ombudsman Service.

5.1.2 Governance Model

As mentioned above, the Ombudsman Service is now an independent non-profit organisation and is therefore subject to Belgian company law. However, art. 322 of the Insurance Act governs the management of the Insurance Ombudsman Service in a special way.

The Ombudsman Institution consists of four bodies. Firstly, the insurance ombudsperson and their team supervise the general operations. The Governing Board is responsible for appointing the ombudsperson and drawing up the budget. The General Assembly is responsible for approving the budget and the annual accounts. Finally, the Supervisory Committee is responsible for checking the impartiality of the Ombudsman Service and for reporting to the Minister of Economic Affairs on the Ombudsman Scheme's activities.

---

[1] Arrêté royal du 21 juin 2006 modifiant le traitement des plaintes dans le secteur des assurances, défini dans l'arrêté royal du 22 février 1991 portant règlement général relatif au contrôle des entreprises d'assurances et dans l'arrêté royal du 25 mars 1996 portant exécution de la loi du 27 mars 1995 relative à l'intermédiation en assurances et à la distribution d'assurances, M.B. 4 juillet 2006.

[2] Statuts du 5 octobre 2006 ASBL Ombudsman des Assurances, M.B. 9 octobre 2006.

[3] Loi du 4 avril 2014 relative aux assurances, M.B. 30 avril 2014.

[4] Loi du 4 avril 2014 portant insertion du Livre XVI, "Règlement extrajudiciaire des litiges de consommation" dans le Code de droit économique, M.B. 12 mai 2014.

[5] The Insurance Ombudsman Service was recognised on 19 June 2015. For more information, see https://economie.fgov.be/fr/themes/line/belmed-mediation-en-ligne/comment-devenir-une-entite. Accessed 16 Apr 2025.

5.1.2.1 The Ombudsman Service

The ombudsperson is also the Executive Director of the Ombudsman Service's non-profit organisation. Consequently, the ombudsperson is responsible for overseeing all of the operational activities and expenditures. The primary objective of the Service is to provide mediation for disputes between consumers on the one hand and insurance companies, brokers, (sub)agents and ancillary insurance intermediaries on the other.

The Service also publishes an annual report in an entirely independent manner.

5.1.2.2 The Governing Board

The Governing Board is composed of eight members representing the Brokers' Association, the Insurance Association and the Mutuals. The Board is chaired by one of the members, or alternatively by a representative of the brokers or the insurance union, for a period of three years. The Board's primary responsibilities include the appointment of the ombudsperson and the financial control of the Service's operations. The Board in collaboration with the ombudsperson is responsible for preparing the budget, which is then submitted to the General Assembly for approval.

5.1.2.3 The General Assembly

The 2020 revision of Belgian company law has rendered it no longer necessary to separate the members of the governing board of a non-profit organisation from the members of the general assembly. Consequently, the composition of the General Assembly of the Ombudsman Service is identical to that of the Governing Board. The General Assembly is responsible for approving 'the accounts and budget of the Service and the auditor's report. The General Assembly meets at least once a year.

5.1.2.4 The Supervisory Committee

The Supervisory Committee is established by law, and it acts and functions as an independent counterweight to the Governing Board. The Supervisory Committee is responsible for monitoring the functioning of the Ombudsman Service and ensuring its impartiality. The composition of the Supervisory Committee is defined by law as follows:

an independent expert
a representative of brokers
a representative of insurance companies
two representatives of consumers

a representative of the FSMA (supervisory authority)
a representative of the Ministry of Economic Affairs

All members are appointed for a six-year period by the Minister of Economic Affairs.

As is the case with all non-profit organisations, the remit of the Ombudsman Service is based on its statutes. These can be amended by the ombudsperson on the written advice of the Supervisory Committee. However, any such changes must not contradict the ombudsperson's mandate as set out in the Insurance Act.

5.1.3 Coverage

The competences of the Ombudsman Service are defined in Art. 322 of the Insurance Act.[6] Pursuant to this provision, the Ombudsman Service is entitled to examine any complaint arising out of "the present law," which encompasses the entirety of Belgian Insurance Act.

Therefore, any complaint arising out of an insurance contract governed by Belgian law is covered by the Ombudsman Scheme.

The Belgian Insurance Ombudsman Service will not intervene in any insurance policy where a foreign law is applicable, even if the claimant is a Belgian citizen. In the event that the foreign law is covered by the FIN-NET scheme, the Ombudsman Service may transfer the file to another ombudsman scheme in Europe.[7]

5.1.4 Appointment of the Ombudsperson

The ombudsperson is appointed by the Governing Board. The office holder has a permanent contract with the non-profit organisation. The selection process is carried out by an independent headhunter who adheres to the guidelines established by the Board. In practice, the ombudsperson must possess a good reputation, knowledge of the insurance sector and management skills. As the ombudsperson is expected to represent all of the communities in Belgium, they must also have an excellent knowledge of the country's various languages and a good knowledge of English.

[6] Loi du 4 avril 2014 relative aux assurances, M.B. 30 avril 2014.

[7] For more information, see https://finance.ec.europa.eu/consumer-finance-and-payments/retail-financial-services/financial-dispute-resolution-network-fin-net_en. Accessed 16 Apr 2025.

5.1.5 Budget

The budget is drafted by the ombudsperson and subsequently approved by the Governing Board. The Supervisory Committee ensures that the budget is sufficient for the Ombudsman Service to fulfil its mission; it also reports to the Minister.

Art. 322 of the Insurance Act sets out that funding for the Ombudsman Scheme is exclusively derived from contributions from the insurance sector.

The contributions have been divided into three parts:

The first part, representing 10% of the overall budget, is collected by the supervisory authority, FSMA, through the intermediary's yearly licence fee.

The second part, comprising 45% of the total budget, is based on the number of enquiries conducted in the previous year and collected at the beginning of the year. To illustrate, if out of a total of 1000 complaints put to inquiry, an insurer received 100 complaints, it would be required to pay 10% of this part of the budget.

The third part, again comprising 45% of the total budget, is determined by the market share of the insurer in terms of premium collected by them in relation to the total premium collected.

As the Ombudsman Service is a non-profit organisation, any gains made in the previous year are deducted from the overall contribution in advance.

5.1.6 Insurance Ombudsman Functions

The primary role of the Ombudsman Service is to examine and handle complaints made by clients against insurance companies, intermediaries and ancillary insurance intermediaries. In this capacity, the Ombudsman Service will provide the parties with impartial advice and information.

Given that a significant proportion of consumers lack the requisite technical expertise in insurance matters, it is the responsibility of the Ombudsman Service to provide information in clear and understandable language.

In addition to handling complaints, the ombudsperson disseminates information to the public through press releases and other media outlets. Furthermore, the ombudsperson offers guidance to insurance company directors on specific issues affecting their companies. Finally, the ombudsperson can exert influence on legislation through parliamentary questions and recommendations in their annual report.

5.1.7 *Insurance Ombudsman Office*

The Ombudsman Service team currently consists of 13 legal experts, three administrative support staff, and the ombudsperson. All of the members of the Service, including the ombudsperson, are employees with permanent contracts.

The offices are located in central Brussels and there are no regional satellites.

Each year, the Ministry of Economics requests a comprehensive report on the training and courses attended by the Ombudsman Service's employees.

5.2 Insurance Ombudsman Jurisdiction

5.2.1 *Scope*

As previously stated, the Ombudsman Service has a substantive scope that is determined by art. 322 of the Insurance Act. Any complaint filed with regard to the execution of an insurance contract that falls under Belgian law may be examined by the ombudsperson. There is no affiliation process, as a result of which any insurers operating in Belgium are required to collaborate with the Scheme.

In 2024, art. 322 underwent a modification, subjecting all insurers, intermediaries and accessory intermediaries to an obligation to collaborate with the ombudsperson and to provide access to any documents related to the complaint. Furthermore, the latest amendment of art. 322 grants the ombudsperson the authority to consult with experts.

The only exception to the ombudsperson's authority regarding the Insurance Act is set out in § 2.2 of art. 322, in which it is stated that the jurisdiction over mediation held by the Federal Agency for Occupational Risks (FEDRIS)[8] cannot be assumed by the ombudsperson. This implies that while the ombudsperson may intervene in complaints relating to the subscription of work insurance, there is no authorisation to intervene in claims-related issues. In the event of a work-related accident, the victim is required to submit their claim through FEDRIS.

5.2.2 *Personal Scope*

From the outset, it was determined that the Ombudsman Service should be as accessible as possible. The definition of "client-consumer" does not exclude any legal entities (companies, other non-profit organisations) or third parties from filing a

[8] FEDRIS is a public institution that ensures the rights of occupational accidents and diseases. See https://www.fedris.be/en/home.html. Accessed 16 Apr 2025.

complaint with the Ombudsman Service. The Service now accepts complaints from a very wide range of complainants based on the criteria set out in § 2 of art. 322 of the Insurance Act is that "any person having an interest in the execution of the insurance contract" has a right to file a complaint with the Service.

In practice, the majority of complaints are filed by the individual who subscribed to the insurance contract. A small percentage are also introduced by third parties and beneficiaries. In certain fire insurance policies, the remuneration of the expert or surveyor is determined by the terms of the insurance contract. In this case, the surveyor is considered to have an interest in the execution of the insurance contract and can therefore file a complaint on the consumer's behalf.

5.2.3 *Territorial Scope*

There is no territorial scope as such. The complainant is not required to reside in Belgium. The only important aspect is that the insurance contract is regulated by Belgian law.

5.2.4 *Time Limits*

There is no time limit for filing a complaint with the Ombudsman Service. However, the Insurance Act provides general prescription rules for insurance matters. The Ombudsman Service staff must be aware of these rules, as filing a complaint will lead to the suspension of the prescription period. If an insurer invokes the prescription period, the Ombudsman Service will examine this in the same way as any other contention.

5.3 Procedure

5.3.1 *Regulatory Framework*

It should be noted that the Ombudsman Scheme is established by law, whereas the procedure is determined by the Ombudsman Service in its own right. Pursuant to the non-profit organisation's statutes, the ombudsperson may modify the complaints procedure after submitting a revised draft for review to the Supervisory Committee. Until 2020, the Supervisory Committee was required to approve these changes. This has since been amended to allow for more responsive adaptation to societal and product changes. In the event of a disagreement, the Supervisory Committee reserves the right to inform the Ministry of Economics.

As previously stated, the Insurance Ombudsman Service is committed to ensuring that its services are readily accessible to all. In order to submit a complaint, the complainants must provide their name, the name of the insurance professional in question (intermediary or company), and a brief description of the issue.

It has been specified that any complaints must be submitted in writing to the Ombudsman Service.

The Service accepts correspondence in the form of letters and emails, as well as via an online form.

5.3.2 Complaints Handling

5.3.2.1 Process

As is the case with all ombudsman schemes, the first step that the Ombudsman Service will take is to examine whether the complaint falls within the Scheme's remit. Should the complaint be related to a matter that is not related to insurance, the Insurance Ombudsman Service will redirect the complainant to the correct Ombudsman Service. This mainly concerns the fine line between banking and insurance. In the event that a complaint concerns both banking and insurance, a 'gentlemen's agreement' is in place whereby the Ombudsman Service handling the primary aspect of the complaint will assume the lead role and handle any contact with the complainant. The other Ombudsman Service involved will examine the points within their domain and inform the ombudsperson leading the case.

A distinctive feature of the Belgian system is the existence of the Consumer Mediation System, which handles any matters not covered by a specific ombudsman scheme.[9]

Initial Assessment

It is not necessary to have filed a complaint with the insurance company concerned to have access to the Ombudsman Service. Nevertheless, the Ombudsman Service may refer the complainant to the complaints management team within the company in question if they deem that the dispute can be rapidly solved between the parties without their intervention.

In this case, the Ombudsman Service will still provide the consumer with a file number and record the motives and names of the parties in the scheme's database for statistical purposes. Should the complaint not be resolved or if no response is received from the insurance professional, the complainant may inform the Ombudsman Service, who will then initiate a formal inquiry.

[9] See https://consumerombudsman.be/. Accessed 16 Apr 2025.

There are therefore very limited reasons for the Ombudsman Service not to accept a complaint:

The complaint is anonymous.
The complaint is vexatious.
The complaint does not fall within the scope established by law (foreign law, work-related accidents and so on).
The complaint has already been brought before the courts and tribunals.
The complaint could have a significant impact on the Service's operations.

Handling and Mediation

Once the Ombudsman Service has determined that a complaint is admissible and that an inquiry proves essential, they will inform the insurance professional of the complaint and request both a response and the documents related to the complaint.

The insurance professional must grant the Ombudsman Service full access to the file in question and provide a preliminary response within one month of receiving the complaint from the Ombudsman Service. In the event of a lack of collaboration or incomplete responses, the Ombudsman Service will inform the supervisory authority (FSMA). Furthermore, the Ombudsman Service is entitled to visit the insurance professional's premises and inspect the complete file, provided that the Ombudsman Service gives five days' notice and submits a list of the documents that are required. Based on the documents and explanations provided by the insurance professional, the Ombudsman Service will then ascertain whether all the legal and contractual requirements have been met. Should this not be case, the Ombudsman Service will contact the insurance professional again to request further information.

Until last year, the Ombudsman Service did not have a network of experts and field agents. Where discussions were of a technical nature, the Ombudsman Service would advise complainants as to their rights to have an expert and, if necessary, a third arbiter support them in technical discussions. However, following an amendment to art. 322 of the Insurance Act, introduced by art. 75 of the Law of 3 May 2024,[10] the Ombudsman Service now has the authority to call upon experts.

In accordance with the General Data Protection Regulation (GDPR),[11] the transfer of sensitive documents is conducted via a protected extranet, which the ombudsperson shares with insurance professionals. All of the information collected is handled with confidentiality. The transfer of documents from one party to another is only possible upon prior mutual agreement. If information relating to third parties is relevant, their formal agreement will be sought.

---

[10] Loi du 3 mai 2024 portant dispositions diverses en matière d'économie, M.B. 31 mai 2024.

[11] Regulation (EU) 2016/679 of the European Parliament and of the Council of 27 April 2016 on the protection of natural persons with regard to the processing of personal data and on the free movement of such data, and repealing Directive 95/46/EC (General Data Protection Regulation) [2016] OJ L119/1.

Conclusion and Advice

After reviewing the documents received and commenting on and explaining the initial findings to the relevant parties, the ombudsperson will first attempt to mediate in order to find a solution. The ombudsperson's initial findings will be based on the relevant legislation and the insurance contract, as well as on the principle of equity. This point is of particular importance, as it goes beyond a purely legal perspective and introduces a certain degree of creativity and empathy to the discussion. In this phase, the parties can convene to find solutions that extend beyond simply intervening or not.

In certain instances, insurance products other than those under discussion are identified as solutions, and other efforts are made to retroactively cover risks that were overlooked at the time of subscription. One advantage of an ADR scheme is that it encourages the parties to address the underlying issue rather than merely addressing the complaint at hand.

If the mediation is successful, the ombudsperson will include this information in the final statement and close the file.

Given that the final decision of the ombudsperson is not binding, we prefer to refer to it as advice. In the event that the parties are unable to reach a resolution, the advice will recapitulate the positions of the parties and conclude with the legal position taken by the ombudsperson. If the advice is unfavourable to the insurance professional, it is typically communicated to the company's senior management to encourage a change in position. Should the advice be unfavourable to the complainant, a comprehensive explanation is provided with the objective of providing sufficient information to enable an assessment of the likelihood of success in court proceedings.

Once the final advice has been communicated, both parties have the right to initiate judicial proceedings.[12] The decisions are not published; however, the parties may present these as evidence in a court of law.

During the proceedings before the ombudsperson, the prescription period and any recovery proceedings will be suspended. They will start again on the date that the advice is issued.[13]

5.3.2.2 Form

Although the mediation process is primarily conducted in writing, telephone conversations or online meetings may be used to facilitate negotiations. Nevertheless, the insurer is required to provide their initial response in writing within the first 30 days.

[12] Art. 25, Book XVI, Code of Economic Law (*Code droit économique*).

[13] Art. 27, Book XVI, Code of Economic Law (*Code droit économique*).

It is a regulatory requirement that every insurer must have an independent complaints management service that meets the European Insurance and Occupational Pensions Authority's (EIOPA) Guidelines on Complaints-Handling by Insurance Undertakings.[14] This includes the fact that the individual in contact with the ombudsperson was not involved in addressing the initial complaint. Furthermore, these services must be in direct contact with the upper management of their respective companies.

The final advice will always be provided in writing and transmitted to both parties at the conclusion of the mediation process.

5.3.2.3 *Ex officio* Proceedings

The ombudsperson will only act upon a written complaint initiated by a consumer, legal entity, third party or their representatives. However, the full data and lessons that can be taken from the complaints can be used to initiate discussions with companies about structural issues or systemic problems.

5.3.2.4 Collective Proceedings

The ombudsperson does not typically examine joint complaints. The fundamental principle is that each situation is examined on its own merits. This permits reference to be made to the principle of equity during the mediation as the specific circumstances of the complainant may influence the overall interpretation of the contract. This also permits the insurance professional to propose a specific solution without creating a precedent.

However, in very rare cases, the ombudsperson has proposed to an insurance professional that they approach a vast number of complaints structurally and settle a problem globally.

Currently, the ombudsperson has initiated a project with the FSMA with the objective of formalising the possibility of joining cases and accepting joint cases.

5.3.2.5 Complaint Intake

The majority of complaints are currently filed online via the Ombudsman Service website.[15] The Ombudsman Service is referenced in every Belgian insurance policy and on every insurer's website, with direct links provided. Despite this, the

[14] For details, see https://www.eiopa.europa.eu/publications/guidelines-complaints-handling-insurance-undertakings_en. Accessed 16 Apr 2025.

[15] See www.ombudsman-insurance.be. Accessed 16 Apr 2025.

ombudsperson still receives a significant number of complaints via email. Postal complaints account for approximately 5% of all complaints.

Telephone contacts are frequent. The Ombudsman Service staff will redirect consumers to the relevant website or email address. For complaints that can be easily resolved, the administrative staff will redirect consumers to the company's complaints handling team.

5.4 Statistical Data

In 2022, the Ombudsman Scheme received 7872 requests. It is important to note that not every request is a complaint and that not every complaint is admissible.

Of these requests, 2476 were transferred to the complaints management teams of the insurance companies and resolved directly between the insurance company and the complainant. In 779 cases, the ombudsperson was able to advise the consumer of the situation without initiating a formal inquiry.

A total of 814 demands were deemed to fall outside the scope of the Ombudsman Scheme and were therefore transferred to another instance. Finally, the Insurance ombudsperson initiated 3803 formal inquiries with insurance companies and intermediaries. Of these cases, the consumer withdrew from proceedings in only 42 instances.

Out of the 3803 inquiries, a solution was found in 63% of cases. In 1256 cases, the ombudsperson confirmed the position of the insurance professional. In only seven instances did the insurance company or intermediary fail to adhere to the ombudsperson's position.

5.5 Insurance Ombudsman Practice

5.5.1 Market Trends

The majority of all complaints (over 90%) concern insurance companies, with less than 10% being linked to intermediaries. This aligns with the types of complaints received, with approximately 60% of the complaints being claim-related and 15% linked to the termination of the contract, as these points are typically handled by the insurer. With regard to intermediaries, the majority of complaints relate to delays in claims handling (30%) and the provision of inaccurate information upon conclusion or modification of the contract (15%). The ombudsperson actively informs intermediaries of their obligations regarding information and analysis of consumer needs through the specialist press and roadshows. It is noteworthy that intermediaries tend to resolve a higher proportion of complaints than insurance companies. This demonstrates the commercial link between intermediaries and their clients in Belgium, as well as the high percentage of business that continues to be conducted through brokers.

From the outset, the insurance branches that have generated the most complaints have also been the most prevalent on the Belgian market. While motor insurance was previously the branch that generated the most complaints, it has since been surpassed by home insurance. This is due to the continuous improvement in regulations and the extensive agreements between insurers with regard to motor insurance. In contrast, home insurance is less regulated and there is considerable variation in the cover provided by insurers. The lack of uniform definitions and the differences in the cover provided are the primary reasons for the high incidence of complaints pertaining to home insurance in Belgium. In addition to motor and home insurance, medical insurance and life insurance are also the main branches in the market and, for the Ombudsman Service, in complaints.

5.5.2 *Evolution*

Brokers were permitted to join the Ombudsman Scheme in 2001. In the same year, with the creation of Datassur,[16] the sector extended the ombudsperson's competence to include complaints that consumers may have against the Datassur filing system.

In 2006, cover was defined in law to include any litigation a consumer has with insurance companies and insurance intermediaries. For the definition of insurance intermediaries, there is a reference in the Insurance Act to the law on insurance intermediation. This governs brokers as well as agents and subscribers.

In 2019, the Belgian legislature introduced a new category of intermediary into the Insurance Act, specifically in art. 322. This provision expressly refers to accessory insurance intermediaries. This category of insurance intermediary is designed to include any persons engaged in the sale of insurance products in an accessory way. This encompasses the sale of travel insurance by travel agents and the sale of multi-media insurance in stores as a by-product of the sale of smartphones or any other electronic devices.

The Insurance Ombudsman Service in Belgium has recently been confronted with an increase in the number of complaints concerning new insurance products. Such products include insurance for electric bikes and multimedia products, such as smartphones and tablets. As the exclusions are extensive, a significant number of consumers have expressed frustration with these products. Moreover, the manner in which these products are sold in Belgium, as a by-product of a purchase, frequently results in the provision of inadequate information to the consumer at the time of subscription. In certain instances, the ombudsperson has been compelled to determine that a matter was more closely related to illicit sales practices than to insurance law. In previous such instances, the economic inspection services of the Ministry of Economics were informed.

[16] Datassur is a cooperative society set up on the initiative of insurance companies.

5.6 Accessibility and Accountability

5.6.1 Accessibility

As previously stated, the Ombudsman Scheme is promoted through the mandatory inclusion of information regarding its existence in every insurance policy and on every insurance website in Belgium.

Furthermore, the ombudsperson is frequently consulted and interviewed by the press on insurance matters and consumer information. In order to enhance its visibility, the Scheme has initiated a number of initiatives, including the distribution of leaflets to municipalities and the organisation of roadshows for individuals in contact with the public, such as social security workers and debt mediators.

In addition, the ombudsperson also participates in general insurance events with the objective of drawing the attention of the specialised public to the Ombudsman Scheme's existence and to issues concerning the market. In recent years, the ombudsperson has also undertaken to give seminars to compliance officers, aspiring lawyers and law students.

5.6.2 Accountability

It is of significant importance to draw attention to the annual report of the Ombudsman Scheme, which has a direct impact on legislative change and improvement in the insurance sector. The report, which is published once a year, is distributed to all legislators and political decision-makers. Following an analysis of the most frequent reasons behind insurance claims, the ombudsperson submits recommendations for amendments to the Insurance Act, agreements, and codes of conduct that should be implemented by the sector.

The report has been frequently referenced by the Belgian government and parliament, and it is mentioned in several introductory texts of legislation.

Legal Sources

Arrêté royal du 21 juin 2006 modifiant le traitement des plaintes dans le secteur des assurances, défini dans l'arrêté royal du 22 février 1991 portant règlement général relatif au contrôle des entreprises d'assurances et dans l'arrêté royal du 25 mars 1996 portant exécution de la loi du 27 mars 1995 relative à l'intermédiation en assurances et à la distribution d'assurances, M.B. 4 juillet 2006.

Code droit économique, M.B., 29 mars 2013

Loi du 3 mai 2024 portant dispositions diverses en matière d'économie, M.B. 31 mai 2024

Loi du 4 avril 2014 portant insertion du Livre XVI, “Règlement extrajudiciaire des litiges de consommation” dans le Code de droit économique, M.B. 12 mai 2014
Loi du 4 avril 2014 relative aux assurances, M.B. 30 avril 2014
Regulation (EU) 2016/679 of the European Parliament and of the Council of 27 April 2016 on the protection of natural persons with regard to the processing of personal data and on the free movement of such data, and repealing Directive 95/46/EC (General Data Protection Regulation) [2016] OJ L119/1.
Statuts du 5 octobre 2006 ASBL Ombudsman des Assurances, M.B. 9 octobre 2006

Chapter 6
Croatia

The Insurance Ombudsman Scheme

Loris Belanić and Hrvoje Pauković

6.1 Institutional Framework

An important aspect of consumer protection is the option of using alternative (out-of-court) dispute resolution mechanisms to settle disputes arising between consumers and traders, i.e. service providers,[1] aiming at a quick resolution of the so-called consumer disputes at the lowest possible cost, thereby reducing the workload of courts and so on. The importance of alternative dispute resolution in the EU is also evidenced by EU ADR Directive,[2] which imposes on member states the

This chapter has been written with the support of the University of Rijeka Research Project "Legal Aspects of Companies Restructuring and Transition Towards New Corporate Governance Culture" (uniri-drustv-18-43).

[1] Art. 113 of the Consumer Protection Act.

[2] Directive 2013/11/EU of the European Parliament and of the Council of 21 May 2013 on alternative dispute resolution for consumer disputes and amending Regulation (EC) No 2006/2004 and Directive 2009/22/EC (Directive on consumer ADR) [2013] OJ L165/63, Special edition in Croatian: Chapter 15 Volume 028, pp. 214–230.

L. Belanić
Faculty of Law, University of Rijeka, Rijeka, Croatia
e-mail: loris.belanic@pravri.uniri.hr

H. Pauković (✉)
Croatian Insurance Bureau, director, Zagreb, Croatia
e-mail: hrvoje.paukovic@huo.hr

H. Heiss et al. (eds.), *Insurance Ombudsman Schemes*, AIDA Europe Research Series on Insurance Law and Regulation 15,
https://doi.org/10.1007/978-3-032-01500-6_6

establishment of a dispute resolution mechanism, as well as by its complementary EU ODR Regulation.[3]

In Croatian law, the mechanism of the alternative resolution of insurance disputes occurs in two stages. The first stage refers to the procedure of internal dispute resolution before the bodies of the insurer itself (the insurance company). If that stage does not result in a decision with which the consumer is satisfied, the second stage comes into play. This stage refers to the use of the "services" of a third party, i.e., an independent body that helps the consumer and the insurer to resolve the dispute by proposing (or even imposing) a solution in such a way that is meant to convince both parties to reach an amicable resolution to the dispute.[4] An independent body for resolving disputes as referred to above includes the Insurance Ombudsman Service, as well as complementary mediation and conciliation bodies.[5]

6.1.1 Establishment

In Croatia, the institution of the Insurance Ombudsman Scheme, known as *Pravobranitelj na području osiguranja*, operates within the framework of the Croatian Insurance Bureau (*Hrvatski ured za osiguranje,* hereinafter HUO) as the national insurance office. The HUO is a legal entity, established as an association, that represents insurance companies, i.e. insurers in legal transactions with third parties.[6] The Insurance Ombudsman Service is independent of the HUO and is not part of its internal organisation. It is a so-called specialised ombudsman body, operating exclusively in the field (sector) of insurance, where specialist knowledge of insurance is needed to ensure the adequate protection of consumer rights.

The Insurance Ombudsman Scheme started operating on 8 January 2007, pursuant to the Decision on the Establishment and Operation of the Insurance Ombudsman Service[7] adopted by the HUO on 23 May 2005.[8] Today, the position and powers of the Insurance Ombudsman Service are governed by the (new) Decision on the Establishment and Operation of the Insurance Ombudsman Service adopted by the HUO's board of directors on 29 March 2018.[9] This Decision contains two types of

[3] Regulation (EU) No 524/2013 of the European Parliament and of the Council of 21 May 2013 on online dispute resolution for consumer disputes and amending Regulation (EC) No 2006/2004 and Directive 2009/22/EC (Regulation on consumer ODR) [2013] OJ L165/1, Special edition in Croatian: Chapter 15 Volume 028 pp. 202–213; see Grgurić (2014), pp. 23–24.

[4] Pauković (2010), p. 76.

[5] Marin (2018), p. 6.

[6] Art. 352(1) of the Insurance Act (*Zakon o osiguranju*), Official Gazette, n. 30/2015, 112/2018, 63/20 133/20, 151/22.

[7] Odluka o osnivanju i radu Pravobranitelja na području osiguranja.

[8] Pauković (2010), pp. 88–89.

[9] The Decision on the Establishment and Operation of the Insurance Ombudsman Service (hereinafter the Decision) is available at https://huo.hr/hr/zastita-potrosaca/pravobranitelj-na-podrucju-

provisions: 1) organisational provisions on the work of the Insurance Ombudsman Service in the Republic of Croatia, and 2) procedural provisions as well as jurisdictional provisions, to which the ombudsperson adheres in their work. Therefore, the Decision represents the basic organisational and procedural regulation governing the work of the Insurance Ombudsman Service in Croatia.

The HUO's authority to establish an Insurance Ombudsman Scheme derives from the legal provision pursuant to which the HUO's tasks also include dealing with complaints filed by insured persons, i.e. injured persons.[10] The same provision forms the basis for the existence of another out-of-court dispute resolution mechanism that operates within the HUO, namely the Mediation Centre.[11] The establishment of the mechanisms for the out-of-court settlement of disputes by the HUO also fulfils the requirements of the previously mentioned EU ADR Directive.[12]

All members of the HUO accept the Decision on the Establishment and Operation of the Insurance Ombudsman Service as well as the jurisdiction of the ombudsperson. Insurance and reinsurance companies that are not members of the HUO may also accept the Decision and the competence of the ombudsperson by signing the declaration of accession.[13] However, the acceptance of the Decision and the competence of the ombudsperson is in no way a condition that insurance companies must fulfil in order to obtain authorisation to operate.

Members of the HUO are insurance (and reinsurance) companies with their registered office in the Republic of Croatia, insurance companies from EU member states, which have access to the HUO pursuant to the right of establishment and freedom to provide services, insurance companies based in the Swiss Confederation that are authorised to provide insurance services, and branches of insurance companies from third countries that have the approval of the supervisory authority.[14] Membership of the HUO is mandatory for insurance companies providing compulsory motor insurance. Membership of the HUO is voluntary for insurance companies offering other types of insurance.

The Insurance Ombudsman Service operates within the HUO, which provides the scheme with the technical and material conditions for its work.[15] However, the Ombudsman Service is not part of the internal organisation of the HUO, but rather a body independent of the HUO.[16] The ombudsperson makes independent decisions

osiguranja. Accessed 16 Apr 2025.

[10] Art. 353(1) of the Insurance Act.

[11] For more information about the Mediation Centre in Croatian, see https://huo.hr/hr/zastita-potrosaca/centar-za-medijaciju. Accessed 15 Jul 2024, for more information in English, see https://huo.hr/en/consumer-protection/mediation-centre. Accessed 16 Apr 2025.

[12] Grgurić (2014), pp. 28–29.

[13] Third paragraph of art. 3 of the Decision.

[14] Art. 12 of the HUO Statute. The list of current HUO members is available at https://huo.hr/hr/huo/clanovi. Accessed 16 Apr 2025.

[15] Second paragraph of art. 3 of the Decision.

[16] First paragraph of art. 3 and first paragraph of art. 18 of the Decision.

after a procedure in the course of which they impartially consider all the circumstances and factual allegations presented by the parties.

Under Croatian law, the Insurance Ombudsman Service is not an independent legal entity and is not subject to regulations governing financial reporting and audit obligations. The ombudsperson submits an annual report on their activities to the Management Board of the HUO, as detailed below.

6.1.2 Governance Model

The work of the ombudsperson is supervised by the Council of the Insurance Ombudsman Service (*Vijeće Pravobraniteljstva*). The Council of the Insurance Ombudsman Service consists of three members, namely a consumer representative, an independent professional in the field of insurance, finance, or commercial law, and a representative of insurance companies.[17] The consumer representative is proposed by consumer protection associations. The independent professional from the field of insurance, finance, and commercial law is proposed by the regulator (Croatian Financial Services Supervision Agency, HANFA).[18] The insurer representative is proposed by the Management Board of HUO.[19] After receiving their proposals, the Management Board of the HUO appoints the members of the Ombudsman Council for a period of three years with the possibility of re-election.

The Council of the Insurance Ombudsman Service plays a significant role because it monitors and supervises the work of the ombudsperson, and is authorised to propose their dismissal. The council monitors the work of the ombudsperson through joint meetings held at least twice a year, during which the ombudsperson gives an overview of specific cases, which, if necessary, are discussed before the Council. In addition, the Council of the Insurance Ombudsman Service has to study the activity report[20] for the previous year that the ombudsperson must prepare by 30 March at the latest. The Management Board of the HUO decides on whether to accept the activity report,[21] but before it does so, the report is submitted to the Council of the Insurance Ombudsman Service. The Council does not decide on whether to accept the activity report or not, but it may, if it considers it necessary, express its opinion based on the established knowledge about the work of the ombudsperson and propose certain measures.[22] The most severe measure it can

[17] First paragraph of Art. 7 of the Decision.

[18] The website of the regulator/supervisory body (HANFA) is available at https://www.hanfa.hr/en/. Accessed 16 Apr 2025.

[19] Second paragraph of art. 7 of the Decision.

[20] Second paragraph of art. 8 of the Decision.

[21] Second paragraph of art. 18 of the Decision.

[22] Second paragraph of art. 8 of the Decision.

propose is the dismissal of the ombudsperson, which is decided on by the Management Board of the HUO.

6.1.3 Coverage

The jurisdiction of the insurance ombudsperson in Croatia is limited to the insurance sector. The ombudsperson is not competent to resolve consumer disputes in other financial sectors. In insurance disputes, consumers[23] and other natural and legal persons who do not have the status of a consumer can approach the ombudsperson. The ombudsperson handles complaints made by parties to private insurance contracts. Disputes related to social state insurance (pension and health social insurance) do not fall within the ombudsperson's remit.

6.1.4 Insurance Businesses Covered

The ombudsperson can handle complaints against any insurance companies that are members of the HUO. Each respective insurance company is always involved in an out-of-court dispute resolution before the ombudsperson in cases where the ombudsperson has jurisdiction to act, regardless of whether the insurance company agrees to it or not.[24] However, the powers of the ombudsperson can also be extended to encompass insurance companies that are not members of the HUO, if they accept, i.e. accede to the Decision on the Establishment and Operation of the Insurance Ombudsman Service and commit themselves to pay the fee for the work of the Insurance ombudsperson on a regular basis.[25]

6.1.5 Appointment of the Ombudsperson

The conditions which a candidate must fulfil in order to be appointed to the position of insurance ombudsperson are set out in art. 5 of the Decision. These are: a university degree, both theoretical and technical knowledge, extensive experience in the fields of civil and commercial law and the ability to use at least one world language, preferably English. The candidate must not have been legally sentenced to an unconditional prison sentence or be subject to an ongoing investigative procedure.

[23] The definition of a consumer is provided in art. 4(21) of the Consumer Protection Act. Under this provision, a consumer is any natural person who enters into a legal transaction or acts in the market outside their trade, business, craft, or professional activity.

[24] Marin (2018), p. 9.

[25] Third paragraph of art. 3 of the Decision.

The ombudsperson is appointed (and dismissed) by the Management Board of the HUO, for a period of three years with the possibility of re-appointment.[26] However, it is emphasised that such a fact does not affect the impartiality of the ombudsperson,[27] as their work is supervised by the abovementioned Council of the Insurance Ombudsman Service (*Vijeće Pravobraniteljstva*).

The Council of the Insurance Ombudsman Service is authorised to propose the dismissal of the ombudsperson. In addition to the Council of the Insurance Ombudsman Service, the HUO's Management Board itself can dismiss the ombudsperson if the ombudsperson clearly and grossly violates their obligations. The ombudsperson can of course also be dismissed at their own request.[28]

6.1.6 Funding

The insurance ombudsperson's work is financed by the insurance companies themselves, which, in accordance with the HUO's Statutes, pay a fee to finance the HUO's day-to-day activities. Therefore, the ombudsperson's activities are not publicly funded. The funds for the insurance ombudsperson's work are provided for in the HUO's Financial Plan.[29] Parties who initiate proceedings before the ombudsperson, regardless of whether they are natural or legal persons and whether or not the party is a consumer, do not participate in the costs of the ombudsperson's work (the procedure is free of charge).

6.1.7 Insurance Ombudsman Functions

The Ombudsman Service in Croatia, as defined in the Decision on the Establishment and Operation of the Insurance Ombudsman Service, has three functions: 1) a legal protection function, 2) an informative function and 3) an assertive function. These functions are the basis for determining the ombudsperson's competence.

The legal protection function refers to the ombudsperson's authority to resolve disputes in out-of-court procedures between consumers, insured persons and injured parties on the one hand, and insurance companies (insurers) on the other.[30] In such out-of-court procedures, the ombudsperson determines whether, in line with the claims of the complainant (consumer, insured, injured party), the insurance company's actions have violated the Code of Insurance and Reinsurance Business Ethics

[26] First paragraph of art. 6 of the Decision.

[27] Marin (2018), p. 7.

[28] Second paragraph of art. 6 of the Decision.

[29] First and second paragraphs of art. 4 of the Decision.

[30] First paragraph of art. 3 of the Decision.

(hereinafter the Code).[31] The Code is a source of substantive law that the ombudsperson applies in their actions,[32] whereas the Decision on the Establishment and Operation of the Insurance Ombudsman Service is a regulation of an organisational and procedural nature that relates to the activities of the insurance ombudsperson.

The Code was adopted by the Association of Insurance Companies, operating within the Croatian Chamber of Commerce, in 2004. The goals of the Code, as set out in its preamble, deal with the concepts of promoting ethical conduct in accordance with fair business practices and business morals, strengthening a professional approach to parties (for example: consumers, insured persons, injured party) and mutual trust, and raising the overall level of business conduct and collegial cooperation. Every member insurance and reinsurance company of the Association is obliged to comply with the Code.[33] The Code itself is a set of principles and is written in a nomotechnical style, providing an explanation for each principle.[34] In order to fulfil the function of legal protection, the ombudsperson applies the following principles of the Code in particular:

1. the responsibility of companies for other natural or legal persons bound by the contract,
2. the principle of mutual[35] trust and the protection of the rights and interests of the party,[36]
3. informing parties before signing an insurance contract and making them understand the procedures,[37]
4. equality of parties, procedures, damages and payment of the insured amounts,[38]
5. resolving parties' complaints,[39]
6. compliance with legal provisions and rules of the profession.[40]

The informative function of the Ombudsman Service takes two forms: individual and general. In practice, the individual informative function is much more common than the general informative function and consists in providing consumers and any other interested persons with information on the methods of judicial and extrajudicial settlement of insurance disputes.[41] Parties often turn to the ombudsperson to enquire about the protection of their rights even before claims processing has been

---

[31] The Code was adopted by the Association of Insurers of the Croatian Chamber of Commerce on 18 October 2004 and is available at https://huo.hr/hr/zastita-potrosaca/pravobranitelj-na-podrucju-osiguranja. Accessed 16 Apr 2025.

[32] Marin (2018), p. 11.

[33] Art. 2.1 of the Code.

[34] Marin (2018), p. 11.

[35] Art. 2.2 of the Code.

[36] Art. 2.4 of the Code.

[37] Art. 3.1 of the Code.

[38] Art. 3.2 of the Code.

[39] Art. 3.3 of the Code.

[40] Art. 3.4 of the Code.

[41] First paragraph of art. 3 of the Decision.

completed and before their complaints and objections are resolved. The ombudsperson then informs the interested parties about the possibilities of internal dispute resolution before the insurance companies' bodies responsible for the out-of-court resolution of consumer disputes. The ombudsperson informs the parties that they can claim the right to out-of-court dispute resolution by submitting complaints to insurance companies in accordance with arts. 377 and 378 of the Insurance Act.

Furthermore, in cases where the ombudsperson is not competent to resolve disputes between parties and insurance companies (e.g. property legal disputes), the ombudsperson will inform the parties about other possibilities for out-of-court dispute resolution, e.g. by referring them to the Mediation Centre at the HUO, which is competent to resolve property legal disputes (although they may also be referred to other mediation centres). Finally, once all of the possibilities for an out-of-court dispute resolution have been exhausted, the ombudsperson will inform the parties about dispute resolution within the court system, refraining from providing legal assessments of the insurance disputes and of possible outcomes. The ombudsperson can also inform interested parties about the possibility of lodging a complaint with the supervisory body (HANFA).

When the need arises or when a public interest is concerned, the Ombudsman Service carries out its general informative function.[42] The ombudsperson informs the public about their work and competence and provides the public with the established facts. This function is also fulfilled by publishing professional or scientific papers on legal issues that have arisen in the course of the ombudsperson's performance of their duties.

The assertive function of the Ombudsman Service comes into play in cases of frequent identical violations of certain provisions of the Code. If the ombudsperson deems it appropriate, they may send general non-binding recommendations and opinions to the insurance companies, to which the insurance companies may respond.[43]

It is important to emphasise that the ombudsperson is not authorised to provide legal advice to parties in order to resolve disputes arising from insurance contracts. In addition, the ombudsperson is not tasked with educating consumers and parties to insurance contracts. However, the ombudsperson assists in the early detection and prevention of disputes. This is achieved through the aforementioned informational function, which involves providing information about out-of-court dispute resolution to consumers and other parties. The role in dispute prevention is further supported by the presentation of the ombudsperson's annual report to representatives of insurance companies that are members of HUO. In the report, insurance companies are informed about observed violations of the Code and are urged to prevent similar violations in the future.

[42] Fourth paragraph of art. 18 of the Decision.

[43] Fifth paragraph of art. 18 of the Decision.

6.1.8 *Insurance Ombudsman Office*

The Ombudsman Office consists of the ombudsperson and the office manager. The ombudsperson communicates with the parties, responds to enquiries, and issues decisions on cases. The office manager handles the post, keeps records of cases, collates statistics, drafts the annual report on the ombudsperson's activities, and prepares meetings with the Council of the Insurance Ombudsman Service. The HUO provides technical, material, and financial support to the Ombudsman Service. Both the ombudsperson and the office manager participate in professional training sessions on insurance law.

6.2 Insurance Ombudsman Jurisdiction

6.2.1 *Substantive Scope*

The ombudsperson's primary task involves determining whether there has been a violation of the Code of Insurance and Reinsurance Business Ethics by the insurance company (insurer), as previously discussed (Sect. 6.1.7 above). The ombudsperson must examine the claims of the complainant (consumer, insured, or claimant) and determine whether there has been a breach of the Code. In practice, the Code violations that fall within the ombudsperson's jurisdiction include:

- lack of communication between the complainant and the insurer,
- inadequate explanations in decisions on compensation claims,
- delays in processing compensation claims,
- failure to provide pre-contractual information and insurance terms.

The ombudsperson's jurisdiction extends to insurance contracts as well as the relations between liability insurers and third-party claimants who are not parties to the insurance contract. The ombudsperson deals with complaints relating to all stages of insurance (contract conclusion, contract duration, claim processing).

At first glance, the ombudsperson seems to have considerable power in deciding on the violations of the Code in extrajudicial procedures. However, the Decision on the Establishment and Operation of the Insurance Ombudsman Service imposed significant limitations on the ombudsperson's activities.

The most important limitation on the ombudsperson's remit is the inability to decide on property legal disputes arising between the insured and insurance companies. It is expressly stated in the third paragraph of art. 9 of the Decision that the ombudsperson is not authorised to issue any decisions in a property legal dispute between the complainant and the insurance company, and in particular prohibits them from assessing the merits of the compensation claim and/or its amount. The complainants (consumers, insured persons, injured parties) are the least familiar with the exact limitations on the ombudsperson's competence in resolving property legal disputes. Complainants often request for the ombudsperson to issue a determination to the effect that an insurance contract is invalid or that they are entitled to the insurance money, i.e. for the ombudsperson to order insurance companies to pay damages. They may also ask the ombudsperson to amend or overrule a decision made by an insurance company, suspend executions, amend their insurance policies, conclude a new contract with a party, terminate an insurance contract and so on. The ombudsperson often even receives such requests from the parties' legal representatives, who do not take into account the abovementioned limitation on the ombudsperson's competence and believe that property legal disputes constitute a violation of the Code. It should be highlighted that the ombudsperson is only competent for the violations of the Code that are referred to in art. 9(3) of the Decision. Therefore, requests to decide on a property legal dispute or on a compensation claim are beyond the ombudsperson's remit. The ombudsperson cannot determine whether a violation of the Code represents an alleged infringement of rights arising from a property legal relationship, because this necessarily requires a determination to be made on the property legal relationship between a party and an insurance company, a matter which, as stated above, exceeds the ombudsperson's remit. Property legal disputes are excluded because another body is authorised to decide on them, namely the Mediation Centre at the HUO. However, mediation is only possible if both parties, i.e. the complainant and the insurance company, agree to it. If the insurance company rejects a mediation proposal, it will not be possible to settle a property legal dispute out of court.[44] For this reason, arguments have been propounded in legal literature in favour of expanding the ombudsperson's competence to property legal disputes in cases where there are undeniable facts and the value of the dispute does not exceed the amount of HRK 10,000.00 (EUR 1 = HRK 7.53).[45]

Although there is no provision in the Decision on the Establishment and Operation of the Insurance Ombudsman Service expressly stating that the ombudsperson does not provide legal assistance, does not give legal advice or legal opinions, and does not represent parties in procedures against insurance companies or claims processing procedures before insurance companies. These limitations need to be emphasised as parties often expect the ombudsperson to act exactly in this way. As stated above, the ombudsperson is prevented from giving legal advice and opinions on property legal disputes primarily by virtue of the provision on the exclusions from the ombudsperson's competence in the third paragraph of art. 9 of the Decision. However, the restriction on providing legal assistance, advice, and representation, in fact, stems from the provisions governing legal services, pursuant to which only lawyers are authorised to provide legal assistance.[46] The ombudsperson is only authorised to inform the parties and interested persons about the methods of judicial and extrajudicial dispute resolution in insurance matters (art. 3(1) of

[44] Marin (2018), p. 9.

[45] Marin (2018), p. 10.

[46] Art. 5 of the Law on Advocacy.

the Decision), which represents the so-called informative function discussed earlier in the chapter.

There are further limitations regarding the ombudsperson's activities, referred to as procedural obstacles, due to which it is impossible to initiate a procedure before the ombudsperson. There are three types of such procedural obstacles. The first obstacle is the absence of a decision issued by the insurance company on a party's complaint in an out-of-court procedure. The decision regarding a complaint is a prerequisite for initiating a procedure before the ombudsperson.[47] The insurance company should have the opportunity to review its decision and the way it handled the complaint in general[48] before the party is allowed to address the ombudsperson. The second procedural obstacle refers to *lis pendens*, i.e. the existence of simultaneous civil proceedings concerning a complaint lodged with the ombudsperson, in which case the ombudsperson is not authorised to act.[49] Finally, the third obstacle is the limitation period. Pursuant to art. 10 of the Decision, the ombudsperson does not review complaints if more than one year has elapsed between the event, which, according to the complainant, constitutes a violation of the Code, and the date of submission of the complaint.

6.2.2 *Personal Scope*

The Insurance Ombudsman Service provides legal protection to a wide range of interested persons, namely consumers and other persons with certain rights and/or obligations arising under an insurance contract. This includes not only parties to an insurance contract but also injured parties to a non-contractual compensation claim filed with an insurance company.[50] In addition to natural persons as consumers, legal persons who do not have consumer status can also be parties to a claim. However, legal persons as insureds or policyholders belong to a group of persons with specific rights or obligations arising under an insurance contract and are recognised as parties in a procedure before the ombudsperson. Legal persons can be companies, various institutions and associations, cities, municipalities, ministries, and the like. Since the procedure is initiated by filing a complaint, the group of interested persons described is often referred to as the complainant.

On the other hand, there is the insurance company that appears as a party to a procedure before the ombudsperson. The insurance company is a legal person licensed by a competent supervisory body (in this case HANFA) to conduct insurance business.[51] In practice, complaints are often filed against insurance brokers and

[47] First and second paragraphs of art. 11 of the Decision.

[48] Ćurković (2016), p. 53.

[49] Second paragraph of art. 9 of the Decision.

[50] First indent of art. 2 of the Decision.

[51] Second indent of art. 2 of the Decision.

representatives. In this case, it is the insurance company associated with the insurance broker or representative that is party to the procedure. Pursuant to art. 2.2. of the Code, if a natural or legal person violates the provisions of the Code while conducting insurance business, the Code shall be deemed to have been violated by the company in whose name and on whose account the natural or legal person acted, i.e. the company that allowed such behaviour.

6.2.3 *Territorial Scope*

The ombudsperson's territorial jurisdiction covers insurance companies that are members of the HUO. These are insurance companies with their head offices in Croatia. Only complaints against such insurance companies may be submitted to the ombudsperson. The place of residence or registered office of the complainant is not an obstacle to approaching the ombudsperson. Anyone who lives or has a residence or any legal entity with a registered office in the Republic of Croatia or abroad can contact the ombudsperson. It is essential that the complaint concerns an insurance company that is a member of the HUO and has its registered office in the Republic of Croatia.

6.2.4 *Time Limits*

There is a prescribed time limit within which a complaint must be filed with the ombudsperson, which is one year from the date of the violation of the Code. The starting point of this period is considered to be the time when the violation occurred according to the complainant's claim. The ombudsperson will not consider complaints if more than one year has elapsed between the date on which the alleged violation was committed by the insurance company and the date on which the complaint was submitted.[52]

6.3 The Procedure

6.3.1 *Regulatory Framework*

The rules of procedure before the ombudsperson are governed by the Decision on the Establishment and Operation of the Insurance Ombudsman Service, specifically in arts. 9 to 17. The following procedural rules are included:

---

[52] Art. 10 of the Decision.

- the jurisdiction of the ombudsperson to decide (art. 9),
- statute of limitations (art. 10),
- filing a complaint with the ombudsperson (art. 11),
- response to the complaint (art. 12),
- review procedure (art. 13),
- hearing before the ombudsperson (art. 14),
- dispute resolution through direct communication between the complainant and the insurance company (art. 15),
- the ombudsperson's decision (art. 16),
- and procedural costs (art. 17).

The aforementioned Decision was adopted by the Management Board of the HUO and may be amended by it. In other words, the ombudsperson is not authorised to make or amend procedural rules. It is important to emphasise that the content of the Decision is published on the HUO website.[53] This is crucial to safeguard the transparency of the procedural rules before the ombudsperson.

6.3.2 *Complaints and Enquiry Handling Process*

6.3.2.1 Complaints Handling Process

A procedure before the ombudsperson is initiated by filing a complaint. After receiving a complaint, the ombudsperson will consider whether it can be acted upon. It is important to emphasise that not all enquiries sent to the ombudsperson constitute a complaint. This particularly applies to complaints where complainants express their dissatisfaction with the decision on its merits and/or with the amount of the compensation claim without indicating any potential violations of the Code or providing facts, circumstances or other evidence based on which the ombudsperson can conclude that the party is complaining about a Code violation. Therefore, if a party is merely dissatisfied with the decision on its merits and/or with the amount of the compensation claim, the ombudsperson will inform the complainant that they have not jurisdiction to act on the complaint and will refer it to the Mediation Centre.

If the ombudsperson determines that the complaint may be acted upon, they will submit it to the insurance company, requesting a response to the complaint.[54] The insurance company is required to provide a written response to the complaint within 15 days of receipt, with a possibility of receiving an additional 15-day extension.[55] The insurance company is required to respond to all of the allegations of Code vio-

[53] Information about the insurance ombudsperson is available at https://huo.hr/hr/zastita-potrosaca/pravobranitelj-na-podrucju-osiguranja. Accessed 16 Apr 2025; the Decision is available at https://huo.hr/upload_data/site_files/odluka-o-osnivanju-i-radu-pravobraniteljstva-na-podrucju-osiguranja-1-.pdf. Accessed 16 Apr 2025.

[54] First paragraph of art. 12 of the Decision.

[55] Second paragraph of art. 12 of the Decision.

lations outlined in the complaint and to provide relevant evidence for the purposes of confirming the accuracy of the allegations in the response.[56] The ombudsperson may request additional statements or documentation from the complainant or the insurance company at any time if they deem such additional information necessary to decide on a dispute.[57]

The complaint must include complete information about the complainant and be duly signed. The ombudsperson does not consider anonymous complaints.[58] The complaint must be submitted in writing, including via email. It must include the request and the facts on which it is based, as well as the evidence supporting these facts.[59] To assist complainants in preparing their complaints and accompanying documents, a complaints form is provided on the HUO website.[60] Appellants are advised to begin their complaint by briefly stating why they are filing it and then proceed by presenting the relevant facts and circumstances in a chronological order, before finally addressing their request. The complaints form emphasises that it is in the complainant's best interest to present all of the evidence supporting the factual allegations, namely the insurance policy (if it exists and is available), proof of addressing the insurer to resolve the dispute in an internal procedure, any relevant decisions made by the insurer, any documents from other competent authorities (police report, investigation report, etc.), photographs, and so on. The ombudsperson accepts plain copies of documents, so there is no need to submit the original documents or their certified copies.

Should the complaint filed with the ombudsperson be unclear or incomprehensible, the Ombudsman Service will assist the complainant in completing the complaint in a precise manner. If the complainant is unable to do so, an appropriate deadline will be set, so that they can do it by themselves with a warning that the complaint will not be taken into consideration if they do not proceed as the ombudsperson has requested.[61]

The out-of-court dispute resolution procedure before the ombudsperson is based on the principles of efficiency, expediency and economy.[62] For this reason, the ombudsperson is obliged to consider complaints in a prompt manner and to investigate and establish facts and evidence relevant to determining a dispute at each stage of the procedure.[63] The procedure before the ombudsperson typically does not require an oral hearing for the presentation of evidence. An oral hearing is an

---

[56] Third paragraph of art. 12 of the Decision.

[57] Fourth paragraph of art. 12 of the Decision.

[58] Fourth paragraph of art. 11 of the Decision.

[59] Fifth paragraph of art. 11 of the Decision.

[60] The complaints form is available at https://huo.hr/hr/zastita-potrosaca/pravobranitelj-na-podrucju-osiguranja. Accessed 16 Apr 2025.

[61] Seventh paragraph of art. 11 of the Decision.

[62] Second paragraph of art. 13 of the Decision.

[63] First paragraph of art. 13 of the Decision.

exception, convened only when necessary and expedient for making a decision.[64] In other words, the procedure before the ombudsperson is carried out in writing, and any specific secondary procedural issues can be resolved through the proper application of the Civil Procedure Act.[65] However, it is necessary to bear in mind the flexibility of the procedure before the ombudsperson, which ensures that complainants are not in any way limited in obtaining legal protection before the ombudsperson.[66]

The procedure before the ombudsperson is free of charge, with the complainant and the insurance company each bearing their own costs, including the fees of their legal representatives, i.e. lawyers.[67]

6.3.2.2 Form

The ombudsperson does not conduct mediation; instead, the process is exclusively concerned with whether there has been a violation of the Code by the insurance company. The ombudsman procedure is informal, with the main goal of highlighting any Code violations to the insurance company in order to improve the provision of insurance services. However, there are certain formal elements in the process. The insurance company must designate a contact person for the ombudsperson. The ombudsperson will send complaints and decisions in cases to this contact person. Furthermore, as previously mentioned, the insurance company must respond to the complaint within 15 days (the deadline can be extended by an additional 15 days if necessary). The response must be comprehensive and address all of the issues raised in the complaint. It is expected that the response will include evidence supporting the insurer's claims. If the ombudsperson issues a recommendation to the insurance company, the time limit for implementing the recommendation is 15 days. Failure to comply with the recommendation is considered a violation of the Code, and the ombudsperson will inform the supervisory authority (HANFA) about it.[68]

6.3.2.3 Ex officio Proceedings

The procedure is initiated exclusively by the dissatisfied party (consumer, insured) who files a complaint. The ombudsperson cannot initiate proceedings *ex officio*. This is due to the informal nature of the procedure before the ombudsperson.

---

[64] First and second paragraphs of art. 14 of the Decision.

[65] Third paragraph of art. 13 of the Decision. Civil Procedure Act (*Zakon o parničnom postupku*), Official Gazette, n. 53/91., 91/92., 112/99., 129/00., 88/01., 117/03., 88/05., 2/07., 96/08., 84/08., 123/08., 57/11., 148/11., 25/13., 89/14., 70/19., 80/22., 114/22., 155/23.

[66] Marin (2018), p. 13.

[67] Art. 17 of the Decision.

[68] Third paragraph of art. 16 of the Decision.

6.3.2.4 Collective Proceedings

Collective consumer protection is not specifically provided for in the procedure before the ombudsperson and is not practised.

6.3.2.5 Complaint Intake

Complaints are submitted via email.[69] However, the complainant may also send the complaint by regular post. In this case, the complaint documentation will be scanned and digitalised for the purpose of the proceedings held by the ombudsperson. Complaints cannot be submitted by telephone or orally.

6.3.2.6 Limitation Periods

Submitting a complaint to the ombudsperson does not affect the running of limitation periods. The ombudsperson cannot determine issues relating to the statute of limitations, preclusion, or expiry of time limits for exercising rights arising under the insurance contract or the right to compensation.

6.3.2.7 Enquiry Handling Process

In the ombudsman procedure, enquiries relate to requests made by parties for decisions on the validity and amount of compensation claims against and property disputes with the insurer. In such cases, the ombudsperson will inform the parties of the lack of jurisdiction to determine compensation claims and property disputes. The ombudsperson also directs them to other options for out-of-court dispute resolution with the insurer before competent bodies (e.g. mediation). Enquiries from parties also concern legal advice. In such cases, the ombudsperson will inform the parties of the lack of authorisation to provide legal advice and direct them to seek legal advice from a lawyer.

6.3.3 Admissible Complaints

The procedure before the ombudsperson is initiated by filing a complaint. The Decision on the Establishment and Operation of the Insurance Ombudsman Service does not define what constitutes a complaint before the ombudsperson. The content of the complaint is not specifically prescribed, but a complaint form is available on

[69] To the generic email address: pravobranitelj@huo.hr.

the website, the use of which is not mandatory but is recommended to the complainant. There are no personal restrictions on who can lodge a complaint. A complaint can be filed by a consumer who is party to the insurance contract, an injured third party and beneficiaries of rights arising under the insurance contract. It can also be filed by other persons who do not have consumer status, for example, institutions, companies, commercial enterprises and local administrative units (municipalities, cities, counties) that have the status of the insured or injured party.

It has already been emphasised that a complaint can only be lodged against an insurance company's decision (in relation to a complaint made to the insurance company) in an out-of-court (internal) dispute resolution procedure,[70] as well as in cases in which a complainant has previously initiated an out-of-court dispute resolution procedure with the insurance company, but the insurance company has not provided them with an answer within the prescribed period.[71] Consumers, i.e. the insured and injured parties, must receive a response to their complaints within 15 days of receipt, as prescribed by law.[72]

There is no minimum amount or value of the dispute required as a precondition for filing a complaint with the ombudsperson. The ombudsperson may dismiss a complaint without consideration if there is no evidence that the internal dispute resolution procedure with the insurer has been carried out beforehand (e.g. a decision issued based on a submitted complaint or objection).

6.3.4 *Obtaining Information and Collecting Evidence*

The complainant is required to provide any evidence and information required for consideration of the complaint. The ombudsperson may request additional information and evidence from the complainant if this is necessary to form an opinion on the complaint. The burden of proof to prove the facts stated in the complaint rests with the complainant.

When the insurer responds to the ombudsperson's request for a statement on the complaint, in its response, it must provide any evidence and information relevant to the facts stated by the complainant. If the information provided is not sufficient to establish the facts, the ombudsperson is entitled to request additional evidence and necessary documentation from the insurance company. To date, insurers have always provided the requested documentation.

It is important to note that the ombudsperson does not have investigative powers and cannot request information and evidence from third parties. The ombudsperson can use information publicly available on the Internet or in publicly accessible databases.

---

[70] First paragraph of art. 11 of the Decision.

[71] Third paragraph of art. 11 of the Decision.

[72] Art. 378(2) of the Insurance Act.

Only the data for which the complainant has given consent can be used in the procedure. Insurance companies must comply with data protection regulations and cannot provide the ombudsperson with third-party data without consent.

6.3.5 *Outcome of the Process*

The procedure before the ombudsperson is concluded with the issuance of a decision. If the ombudsperson determines that there has been a violation of the Code, the decision will contain recommendations on how to rectify the violation (see more under Sect. 6.3.6 below).

In addition to the ombudsperson's decision, the procedure can also be concluded by an agreement made between the parties to resolve the dispute. The Decision on the Establishment and Operation of the Insurance Ombudsman Service provides for the possibility of resolving disputes by means of direct communication between the complainant and the insurance company. Such "direct communication" refers to a situation in which the ombudsperson submits a request for clarification to the insurance company, which then directly contacts the party (the complainant) in order to resolve the dispute. The party's requests may then be fully granted, or the party and the insurance company may reach an agreement, i.e. a compromise. In direct communication, the parties reach an agreement (similar to a settlement) to end the dispute and inform the ombudsperson. Throughout the procedure, the ombudsperson can encourage the parties to resolve the dispute through direct communication.[73] Once the parties inform the ombudsperson that they have resolved the dispute by means of direct communication (the complainant usually states that they are withdrawing the complaint), this will be noted in the file, and the ombudsperson will immediately inform the complainant and the insurance company that the case is considered closed.[74] This also ends the procedure before the ombudsperson.

6.3.6 *The Ombudsperson's Decisions*

The procedure before the ombudsperson ends with a written, reasoned decision, which is issued when the facts and legal circumstances have been sufficiently clarified for a dispute to be decided.[75]

The ombudsperson can issue three types of decision. These are:

[73] First paragraph of art. 15 of the Decision.

[74] First paragraph of art. 15 of the Decision.

[75] First paragraph of art. 16 of the Decision.

1. a decision rejecting a complaint if there is no jurisdiction to resolve the dispute or some other procedural obstacle (*lis pendens*, limitation period),[76]
2. a decision rejecting a complaint as unfounded, establishing at the same time that the insurance company did not violate the Code,[77]
3. a decision accepting a complaint as well-founded, establishing at the same time that the insurance company did violate the Code.[78]

In practice, it is often the case that the complainant makes multiple requests, so that it is possible to make a decision that partly rejects the complaint and partly accepts it. This happens when the matters detailed in the complainant's requests fall within the ombudsperson's jurisdiction while other matters in the requests do not.[79]

If a decision issued by the ombudsperson establishes that the Code was violated, it will also contain recommendations on the measures to take in order to correct the violation. Recommendations can be either specific or general.[80] The aim behind a specific recommendation is to correct the violations of the Code in a specific case brought by the complainant (e.g. asking the insurance company to answer previously unanswered questions raised by the complainant). If it is not possible to correct the violation, it is recommended to the insurer to write an apology to the complainant. The aim behind a general recommendation is to take measures to prevent a repetition of the same or similar violations of the Code in the future (e.g. the recommendation that decisions on compensation claims should contain instructions for out-of-court dispute resolution). Therefore, the aim of general recommendations is to improve the position and the rights of parties in general.[81] When the ombudsperson issues recommendations, they also set an appropriate deadline by which the insurance company is obliged to inform them about the recommendations it has implemented, i.e. the measures it has taken. In practice, the insurance company usually has 15 days to comply. If the insurance company does not act in accordance with the recommendations issued, this is considered a violation of the Decision and the Code and the ombudsperson will inform the supervisory authority (HANFA) about it.[82] The possibility of reporting an insurance company to the supervisory authority (HANFA) is provided for as a consequence of non-compliance with the ombudsperson's decision. This means that the ombudsperson's decisions are binding for insurers. However, in practice, all insurance companies comply with the ombudsperson's decisions, and there is no need to report them to the supervisory authority.

---

[76] Fourth paragraph of art. 16 of the Decision.

[77] Fifth paragraph of art. 16 of the Decision.

[78] First paragraph of art. 16 of the Decision.

[79] Marin (2018), p. 14.

[80] First and second paragraphs of art. 16 of the Decision.

[81] Marin (2018), p. 14.

[82] Third paragraph of art. 16 of the Decision.

The ombudsperson's decision, along with the insurance company's response, is delivered to the complainant.[83] This can be beneficial to the complainant, even if the decision is unfavourable. In particular, by receiving the response (together with the ombudsperson's decision), the complainant receives a document containing the insurance company's position on the matter of dispute, which is essential for any future legal proceedings.

The procedure before the ombudsperson is informal in nature. However, in order to maintain standards in decision-making, the most important legislative provisions in the fields of insurance, consumer protection and insurance contracts (Insurance Act, Consumer Protection Act, Civil Obligations Act), and court practices are taken into account when necessary. Yet, these provisions are not strictly applied; rather, in making decisions, the ombudsperson strives to act in accordance with the principle of equity. By referring to various legislative provisions and court practices in its decisions, the ombudsperson contributes to providing transparency and information to consumers, as well as to other insured parties and injured third parties, about their rights. The ombudsperson only applies Croatian law in the proceedings and cannot consider complaints that are subject to the application of foreign law.

As emphasised above, the ombudsperson determines whether the insurance company has violated the Code of Insurance and Reinsurance Business Ethics. The ombudsperson is not authorised to decide on the validity of claims and the amount of compensation to be awarded, nor on any other property law claims arising from the insurance contract (e.g. premium payment, contract termination, enforcement of the insurer's claims). In this respect, the ombudsperson cannot order the payment of certain amounts in favour of the complainant. Consequently, the ombudsperson's decisions cannot become enforceable documents. The ombudsperson's decisions are not published and made public; they are delivered exclusively to the parties involved in the procedure (the insurance company and the complainant).

6.3.7 Oversight by Courts

There are no legal remedies against the ombudsperson's decisions; however, a decision does not constitute a procedural or any other obstacle to the initiation of another judicial or extrajudicial dispute resolution procedure. In this sense, it can be said that the ombudsperson's decision is final. There is no judicial control over the work of the ombudsperson, which is exclusively supervised by the Ombudsman Council, as discussed earlier in this chapter.

[83] Fifth paragraph of art. 12 of the Decision.

6.4 Statistical Data

Statistical data are included in the annual reports on the activities of the ombudsperson, which, as already mentioned, are submitted to the Council of the Insurance Ombudsman Service and the Management Board of the HUO. The activity report includes data on the number and type of decisions issued, an expert assessment of the situation regarding the protection of the consumer rights, the degree of protection parties receive in the field of insurance and expert proposals for its improvement.[84]

The total number of complaints or cases dealt with in each year and the number of complaints in which it was determined that insurance companies had acted contrary to the provisions of the Code are detailed in Table 6.1.

In addition to complaints, the Ombudsman Service receives written and telephone enquiries from parties. These are detailed in Table 6.2.

Written and telephone enquiries are handled by the Ombudsman Service immediately upon receipt. Decisions on complaints are issued within an average of three to four weeks, depending on how long it takes to receive the insurance company's response. All of the complaints received by the Ombudsman Service in a year are resolved within the specified time, i.e. the ombudsperson does not have a backlog of cases. All of the recommendations the ombudsperson proposes to insurance companies in decisions where they are found to be in violation of the Code are implemented within one to a maximum of two weeks.

Insurance companies fully and unconditionally comply with the ombudsperson's decisions and act in accordance with the recommendations issued. The insurance company regularly reports to the ombudsperson on the implemented recommendations, providing explanations of the measures taken to address the identified violations of the Code.

Table 6.1 Number of complaints and violations of the Code 2019–2023

Year	Total number of complaints	Number of complaints in which a violation of the Code was found
2019	29	7
2020	21	6
2021	25	7
2022	20	5
2023	22	4

[84] Third paragraph of art. 18 of the Decision.

Table 6.2 Number of written and telephone enquiries 2019–2023

Year	Number of written enquiries	Number of telephone enquiries
2019	171	50
2020	219	97
2021	176	60
2022	141	61
2023	132	85

Table 6.3 Amount of premiums paid and % of total gross premium per insurance type

Type of insurance	Amount of premiums paid (EUR)	% of the total gross premium
Motor third-party liability insurance	428.6 million	25.5%
Life insurance	282 million	16.8%
Comprehensive vehicle insurance	210.4 million	12.5%
Other property insurance	141.4 million	8.4%
Property insurance against fire and natural disasters	116.8 million	6.9%

6.5 Insurance Ombudsman Practice

6.5.1 *Market Trends*

With regard to the types of insurance involved, most complaints addressed to the ombudsperson mostly concerned automobile third-party liability insurance (approximately 40% of the cases per year) and property insurance (approximately 30% of the cases per year), and to a lesser extent life insurance, travel insurance, accident insurance and supplementary health insurance.

The Ombudsman Service in Croatia does not keep statistical records on which areas of insurance are high-risk for consumers. It should be noted that in 2022, the total gross insurance premiums in Croatia amounted to EUR 1.682 billion, of which EUR 1.3 billion were attributed to non-life insurance and only EUR 0.377 billion to life insurance. The amount of premiums paid by type of insurance were as follows in Table 6.3:[85]

From the data presented, it can be seen that the highest annual insurance premium in Croatia is achieved by motor vehicle liability insurance.

Regarding the relationship between the insurers and the ombudsperson, insurers are aware that cooperation with the ombudsperson contributes to adherence to the Code and to consumer rights, thereby enhancing the reputation and trust in insurance companies. Moreover, insurers recognise that resolving disputes with the help

[85] Statistical data on the insurance market in Croatia over several years are available at https://huo.hr/en/publications (English) and https://huo.hr/hr/publikacije/statisticke-publikacije/ (Croatian). Accessed 16 Apr 2025.

of the ombudsperson avoids lengthy court proceedings wherever possible. Therefore, insurance companies always act in accordance with the ombudsperson's decisions and recommendations.

6.5.2 Limitations

The effectiveness of the Ombudsman Service depends to a large extent on cooperation with insurance companies. The insurance companies and the Ombudsman Service have successfully cooperated for many years, since the establishment of the Ombudsman Service in 2007. This cooperation is reflected in the provision of various statements and necessary documentation that insurance companies submit to the ombudsperson upon request. Furthermore, insurance companies regularly accept the recommendations made by the ombudsperson when a breach of the Code is identified. On the other hand, communication with complainants is constant and two-way. If essential documentation is missing, the ombudsperson provides instructions to the parties on how to gather the documentation needed to submit a clearer and more complete complaint. In view of the above, we conclude that there are no limitations that would hinder the functioning of the system.

The ombudsperson does not monitor issues concerning the level of financial literacy and financial awareness of consumers. Recently, there has been an increase in the submission of well-prepared complaints, which suggests that the level of consumer financial literacy is improving.

6.5.3 Examples from the Practice of the Ombudsperson

Among the reasons for complaints, the following stand out in particular:

- inadequate communication with the complainants;
- failure to comply with the prescribed time limits for processing claims and making decisions on compensation claims and complaints submitted by the insured/injured parties;
- insufficient explanations provided in the response to a compensation claim, i.e. the response to complaints;
- incomplete responses to complaints made by the complainants;
- failure to comply with the obligations arising from the insurance contract;
- failure to provide pre-contractual information, lack of legal instruction on the out-of-court dispute resolution mechanism that should be provided in the insurance company's final decision.

6.5.3.1 Poor Communication of the Insurance Companies with Consumers

Inadequate communication or a complete absence of any communication is a common reason for filing a complaint with the ombudsperson. This can happen when the insurance company does not respond to enquiries at all, or when communication takes place but is unprofessional and inappropriate. In cases of verbal or telephone communication, it is more difficult to prove unprofessional or inappropriate behaviour. Therefore, it is crucial to have written communication through the exchanging of letters or e-mails. The complete absence of communication between a complaining party and the insurance company, as well as an insurance company's silence on the issues raised by a party, constitute a violation of the Code, namely of the provisions in art. 2.4. (the principle of mutual trust and the protection of the rights and livelihood of the party) and often those in art. 3.2. (equality of parties, processing and compensation of damages, and payment of the insured amount). If parties are in active communication, with several exchanged e-mails or telephone conversations, a single unanswered e-mail or enquiry does not constitute a violation of the Code. In such a case, it is clear that the insurance company is willing to maintain communication with the party, so there can be no talk of a violation of the Code.

In practice, there are cases where parties complain that they have not received the insurance company's response to their complaint within the prescribed period. Such negligence would indeed constitute a violation of the Code (art. 3.3), and of the legal provision pursuant to which the insurance company is obliged to respond in writing to the party's complaint within 15 days of receipt.[86] The same applies to insurance intermediaries.[87] However, insurance companies cannot be held responsible for the activities of the postal service if the response was sent by post, which can be proven by providing proof it was sent by registered post (available to ombudsperson upon request and availability), although it should also be noted that insurance companies are not legally obliged to send their responses to complaints in that manner. It should also be noted that insurance companies are not legally obliged to send their responses to complaints by registered post.

The Code contains specific provisions on the form a response to a complaint must take, requiring parity of form.[88] If a party has sent a written complaint, they must receive a response in writing, whereas if complaints have been sent by e-mail, then an e-mail response is considered to be in accordance with the Code. However, the final response from the insurance company must be in writing (e.g. the response of a second instance commission regarding a claim for compensation).

---

[86] Art. 378(2) of the Insurance Act.

[87] Art. 427(2) of the Insurance Act.

[88] Subparagraph (b) of the second paragraph of Art. 3.3 of the Code.

6.5.3.2 Lack of Explanation in the Insurance Company's Decisions

If the insurance company's decision dismisses a compensation claim, in whole or in part, it must contain an adequate explanation that makes the reasons for the dismissal clear to the party. The complainant will then be able to examine the reasons for such a decision. In addition, by providing a sufficient explanation, the insurance company avoids arbitrariness in decision-making, which is not compatible with the insurance profession. An explanation is deemed adequate if the reasons for the dismissal are based on the law (Civil Obligations Act, Compulsory Traffic Insurance Act, insurance terms and conditions, applicable case law) and if evidence is cited to support the decision that the compensation claim is wholly or partially unfounded. If there is no explanation at all, or if the explanation provided is very brief or inadequate, then this constitutes a violation of the Code and is a frequent reason for complainants to turn to the ombudsperson. This constitutes a violation of art. 2.4 of the Code (the principle of mutual trust and protection of the rights and livelihood of the party) and of art. 3.2(2) of the Code, pursuant to which insurance companies should act professionally, efficiently, fairly and without delay when processing compensation claims and payments.

One case involved a supplementary health insurance contract. The contract was concluded for an indefinite period (until termination). The complainant was dissatisfied with what she considered to be a unilateral increase in the monthly premium amounts by the insurance company. She was also unhappy with the manner of communication—the complainant did not receive any notification of the increase, but instead received payment slips for the higher premium amount. The insurance company, on the other hand, argued that the possibility of a unilateral premium increase was provided for in the insurance terms and conditions provided to the complainant at the time of the conclusion of the contract. In addition, the insurance company argued that the increased payments required did not ensue from an increase in the premium, but rather from the expiry of a promotional discount that was in place at the time the contract was signed. The insurance company also asserted that all notifications were sent to the complainant's registered address using an external delivery service. In the ombudsman procedure, it was not possible to verify the correctness of the delivery method, but the written communications between the parties, which were made available to the ombudsperson, clearly showed a lack of trust between the parties and visibly strained relations. The ombudsperson therefore recommended that the insurance company send the complainant a special letter with detailed information on the options for terminating the supplementary health insurance contract. Given that it was a contract of indefinite duration, it was recommended that the letter should include, among other things, information on how and where to terminate the contract, whether there was a period of notice and its length, and the complainant's rights and obligations during the period of notice.

6.5.3.3 Delay in Processing the Compensation Claim

Delays in the payment of insurance money call into question the very purpose and meaning of insurance. To prevent such occurrences, there are laws prescribing time limits for the processing of compensation claims. The time limit for processing a compensation claim and paying the insurance money is no sooner than 14 days and no later than 30 days from receipt of a compensation claim or a notification of the occurrence of the insured event.[89] In the case of compulsory motor insurance, the time limit is 60 days from receipt of the compensation claim,[90] or three months if the traffic accident occurred in an EU Member State.[91] Failure to meet these time limits is a common reason for turning to the ombudsperson. Under the Code, any delay on the part of an insurance company in processing a compensation claim and paying out the insurance money is considered to be contrary to the social function of insurance, which is particularly important in the case of automobile liability insurance.[92] However, the claimant (the injured/insured) can facilitate the insurance company's task of handling the claim by submitting all of the relevant documentation necessary to determine the insurer's obligations (e.g. a European Accident Report, a police report if available, any photographs of the damage from the scene of the accident, information about witnesses if there are any, medical documentation or repair/work invoices). This does not mean that the claimants are under an obligation to submit a so-called documented compensation claim, but if an insurance company fails to collect sufficient evidence to establish its obligation within the prescribed time limit, it is entitled to issue a decision rejecting the compensation claim. If an insurance company issues such a decision within the prescribed time limit, it will not be in violation of the Code's provisions on the duty to avoid delay in resolving a compensation claim (art. 3.2(2)). The description provided above is cause for confusion among claimants who often believe that an insurance company's decision is in breach of the Code simply because it is negative, i.e. because it dismisses the claim on the grounds that this prolongs the claims processing procedure. There is no violation of the Code in a decision of a negative nature if it is adequately explained and delivered to the parties within the prescribed time limit.

In one case, the complainant objected to the delay in resolving the compensation claim. The ombudsperson concluded that the insurance company involved had acted in accordance with the provisions in art. 12 of the Road Traffic Insurance Act. Under this provision, an insurance company is required to provide a reasoned offer to the claimant within 60 days of receiving the compensation claim (if liability for the damage and the amount is undisputed), or a substantiated response (if liability for the damage and the amount is disputed). Alternatively, if it is not possible to

[89] Art. 943(1) and (2) of the Civil Obligations Act (*Zakon o obveznim odnosima*) Official Gazette, n. 35/05, 41/08, 125/11, 78/15, 29/18, 126/21, 114/22, 156/22, 155/23.

[90] Art. 12(2) of the Compulsory Automobile Insurance Act.

[91] Art. 50(1) of the Compulsory Automobile Insurance Act.

[92] Second paragraph of Art. 3.2 of the Code.

determine the final amount of the damage within this period, the insurance company must pay the undisputed amount as an advance. As the compensation claim in this specific case was submitted on 2 April 2019, and the offer was provided on 27 May 2019, the ombudsperson concluded that the insurance company acted in accordance with the prescribed time limits. Even if it were argued that the offer was not reasoned, it can still be considered that the amount offered represents the undisputed part and thus complies with the statutory time limits.

6.5.3.4 Lack of Pre-contractual Information and Lack of Explanation/Advice

Complainants frequently cite the failure to provide insurance terms and conditions and other pre-contractual information as reasons for complaints. In addition, they emphasise that the insurance company's representative did not explain to them in detail the meaning of certain terms and legal institutes used in the insurance conditions, i.e. the representative did not provide them with adequate advice.

The failure to provide or distribute pre-contractual information and insurance terms and conditions, as well as information during the term of the insurance contract, constitutes a breach of the legal provisions.[93] Insurance companies (insurers) and distributors are legally obliged to provide pre-contractual information and insurance terms and conditions. Such failure renders them liable for a misdemeanour.[94] It also represents a violation of art. 3. 1. of the Code, which sets out the duty to provide customers with information before they sign an insurance contract and to ensure the clarity of procedure. However, a problem arises when trying to prove such negligence, because by signing an insurance policy, customers confirm the receipt of the disputed pre-contractual information and insurance terms and conditions, so it is virtually impossible to establish any violation of the Code.

On the other hand, the Civil Obligations Act and the Insurance Act contain no provision under which the insurance company is obliged to individually advise interested parties on insurance cover and the meaning of certain provisions in the insurance conditions. The provisions of the Code do not provide grounds for acting in such a way. Under the Insurance Act, insurance brokers may provide consulting services.[95] However, before signing an insurance contract, brokers must inform parties of whether they also provide consulting services.[96]

In one case involving property insurance, damage was caused by a water leak caused from a burst water pipe. The insurance company rejected the compensation claim, an outcome with which the policyholder was dissatisfied. The complainant (policyholder) argued that the insurance company referred to pre-contractual

[93] Arts. 380 and 381 of the Insurance Act.

[94] Art. 438(1)(35)-(39) and art. 439(6)(2)-(5) of the Insurance Act.

[95] Art. 401(3)(1) of the Insurance Act.

[96] Art. 431(1) of the Insurance Act.

information using different numerical references than those used for the pre-contractual information listed on the insurance policy. Furthermore, the complainant claimed that the latter information, as listed on the policy, was never provided to them.

In the procedure before the ombudsperson, a discrepancy was observed between the numerical references of the pre-contractual information cited by the insurance company and the numerical references of the pre-contractual information listed on the policy provided by the complainant. This discrepancy was also confirmed by the insurer. The ombudsperson recommended that the insurance company apologise to the complainant (policyholder) and provide the pre-contractual information with the same number as listed on the insurance policy. It was also recommended to provide the complainant with an appropriate explanation as to why the insurance company referred to pre-contractual information with numerical references different from those listed on the insurance policy, which is a part of the insurance contract.

6.6 Accessibility and Accountability of the Ombudsman Scheme

6.6.1 Accessibility

Insurers are obliged to inform consumers and insured persons in general of the option of out-of-court dispute resolution. Furthermore, consumers and insured persons should be made aware that they may contact the insurance ombudsperson if they are not satisfied with the insurer's actions. Information about the Ombudsman Scheme is most often provided in insurance companies' decisions on compensation claims or in decisions concerning any other rights derived from the insurance contract.

In addition, consumers and other interested persons may obtain information about the role and activities of the insurance ombudsperson in a section related to consumer protection on the official website of the HUO.[97] The website provides information on the ombudsperson's competences, on filing a complaint and on the procedures for considering and deciding on a complaint. The complaints form with instructions is also made available, as are the documents containing the legal bases on which the ombudsperson issues decisions, namely the Decision on the Establishment and Operation of the Insurance Ombudsman Service and the Code of Business Insurance and Reinsurance Ethics.

---

[97] Information on the insurance ombudsman in Croatia is available in Croatian at https://huo.hr/hr/zastita-potrosaca/pravobranitelj-na-podrucju-osiguranja. Accessed 16 Apr 2025. The English version is available at https://huo.hr/en/consumer-protection/insurance-ombudsman. Accessed 16 Apr 2025.

6.6.2 *Accountability*

The ombudsperson submits an annual report on their activities by the end of March for the previous year (see Sect. 6.1.2 above). The report is submitted to the Council of the Insurance Ombudsman Service and the Management Board of the HUO. Any insurance companies that are members of the HUO, as well as the supervisory authority (Croatian Financial Services Supervisory Agency, HANFA), will have access to the report. In addition, the ombudsperson submits a semi-annual brief report on their activities twice a year (usually in January and July) to the Council of the Insurance Ombudsman Service. This report is acknowledged but not subject to a separate decision.

The annual report provides data on the number of complaints, written enquiries, and telephone enquiries received. It also shows the trend in the number of complaints and enquiries over a specific multi-year period. Furthermore, the report provides details of the structure of complaints received based on the type of insurance. It summarises the violations identified and referenced by the complainants and discusses the general cooperation with insurance companies. The semi-annual brief reports highlight specific cases that the ombudsperson has received and decided upon. All of the data is presented in a way that maintains the confidentiality of the parties involved.

The Ombudsman Service's budget is not published in the annual report. The funds for the Ombudsman Service's operations are provided in the budget of the HUO, as previously mentioned (see Sect. 6.1.6 above).

6.7 Conclusion

The Insurance Ombudsman Service undoubtedly represents an important mechanism for resolving out-of-court disputes between consumers and insurers. From the presented analysis of Croatian law, it can be concluded that the procedure conducted before the ombudsperson is speedy, ending well before the 90 day time limit laid down in the EU ADR Directive. This is because the ombudsman procedure is based on the principles of written form and efficiency. There is no need to collect evidence in addition to that already provided in documentation. There is no discussion, no hearings of parties and witnesses, and no expert testimonies. Under Croatian law, the ombudsperson's decisions are final, and there is no possibility of appealing against them. Communication with parties is informal, often by e-mail and telephone, and devoid of formal delivery rules. Therefore, the procedure before the ombudsperson bypasses a whole range of procedural actions that are characteristic of court cases, and it is in this way more suitable for the resolution of individual consumer insurance disputes, which are frequent and require swift settlement.

The analysis of Croatian law reveals the existence of certain procedural preconditions that must be met in order to initiate a procedure before the insurance ombudsperson. These procedural preconditions pertain to the following issues:

1. *lis pendens* (prohibition of initiating a procedure before the ombudsperson if court proceedings are already underway),
2. previously carried out internal procedure of resolving a complaint before the insurance company's bodies,
3. limitation period (impossibility of initiating a procedure before the ombudsperson if more than a year has elapsed since the insurance company's final decision),
4. absence of restrictions regarding the types of entities that can initiate a procedure before the ombudsperson (consumers, but also other legal persons).

Under Croatian law, the ombudsperson's competence is strictly limited to "examining" whether an insurance company's actions have been taken in accordance with the Code of Business Insurance and Reinsurance Ethics. The ombudsperson is not competent to decide on property legal relations between parties, such as issues of damage compensation and payments from the insurance contract.

Legal Sources

Civil Obligations Act (*Zakon o obveznim odnosima*), Official Gazette, n. 35/05, 41/08, 125/11, 78/15, 29/18, 126/21, 114/22, 156/22, 155/23

Code of Insurance and Reinsurance Business Ethics (2004) (*Kodeks poslovne osiguravateljne i reosiguravateljne etike*), https://huo.hr/upload_data/site_files/kodeks-poslovne-osiguravateljne-i-reosiguravateljne-etike-1-.pdf. Accessed 15 July 2024

Compulsory Automobile Insurance Act (*Zakon o obveznim osiguranjima u prometu*), Official Gazette, n. 151/05, 36/09, 75/09, 76/13, 152/14

Consumer Protection Act (*Zakon o zaštiti potrošača*), Official Gazette, n. 19/22, 56/23

Decision on the Establishment and Operation of the Insurance Ombudsman Service (2018) (*Odluka o osnivanju i radu Pravobraniteljstva na području osiguranja*) https://huo.hr/upload_data/site_files/odluka-o-osnivanju-i-radu-pravobraniteljstva-na-podrucju-osiguranja-1-.pdf. Accessed 15 July 2024

Directive 2013/11/EU of the European Parliament and of the Council of 21 May 2013 on alternative dispute resolution for consumer disputes and amending Regulation (EC) No 2006/2004 and Directive 2009/22/EC (Directive on consumer ADR) [2013] OJ L165/63, Special edition in Croatian: Chapter 15 Volume 028 pp. 214–230

Insurance Act (*Zakon o osiguranju*), Official Gazette, n. 30/15, 112/18, 63/20, 133/20, 151/22

Law on Advocacy (*Zakon o odvjetništvu*), Official Gazette, n. 9/94, 117/08, 50/09, 75/09, 18/11, 126/21

Regulation (EU) No 524/2013 of the European Parliament and of the Council of 21 May 2013 on online dispute resolution for consumer disputes and amending Regulation (EC) No 2006/2004 and Directive 2009/22/EC (Regulation on consumer ODR) [2013] OJ L165/1, Special edition in Croatian: Chapter 15 Volume 028 pp. 202–213

References

Ćurković M (2016) Vozač – odgovornost za štetu, naknada štete i osiguranje (Driver - Liability for Damage, Compensation for Damage and Insurance). Hrvatski autoklub, Zagreb

Grgurić N (2014) Direktiva i Uredba Europskog parlamenta i Vijeća Europske unije o alternativnom i online načinu rješavanja potrošačkih sporova (Directive and Regulation of the European Parliament and the Council of the European Union on alternative and online resolution of consumer disputes), Zbornik radova s međunarodne znanstveno-stručne konferencije Dani hrvatskog osiguranja, Hrvatski ured za osiguranje, Hrvatska gospodarska komora, pp 23–31

Marin J (2018) Izvansudsko rješavanje sporova iz osiguranja (Out-of-court settlement of insurance disputes). https://eu.pravo.hr/_download/repository/JASENKO_MARIN_-_IZVANSUDSKO_RJESAVANJE_SPOROVA_IZ_OSIGURANJA.pdf, pp 1–21

Pauković H (2010) Instituti zaštite pravnog položaja ugovaratelja osiguranja i osiguranika u hrvatskom i europskom pravu (The Protection of the Legal Status of Insurance Policyholders and Insureds in Croatian and European law). Pravni fakultet Sveučilišta u Rijeci, Rijeka

Chapter 7
Finland

FINE: Finnish Financial Ombudsman Bureau

Anu Koskenvuo

7.1 Introduction

7.1.1 Establishment

The origins of the Finnish Financial Ombudsman Bureau FINE (*FINE Vakuutus- ja rahoitusneuvonta*, hereinafter FINE), and the Insurance Ombudsman Scheme, in particular, originally date back to 1971, when the Consumers Insurance Agency (*Kuluttajien vakuutustoimisto*) and the Insurance Complaints Board (*Vakuutuslautakunta*) were established. At that time, there was no consumer protection legislation, nor any consumer agencies or consumer complaint boards. However, there had been a growing public interest in consumer issues. The need to arrange consumer protection in the insurance business was obvious.[1]

The Consumers Insurance Agency and the Insurance Complaints Board functioned back then much like FINE does today. The Insurance Complaints Board was assigned to handle disputes arising from the application and interpretation of terms of insurance contracts. The dispute had to be raised by a policyholder, a party who had suffered a loss or the insurance company involved. As an outcome, the Board issued statements with appropriate and written arguments. The scope of the Board was limited to voluntary life and non-life insurance. The scope of the Consumers Insurance Agency was even wider. The core function of the entity was and still is to

[1] For more on the early phases of the founding of the Consumers Insurance Agency, see Sisula-Tulokas et al. (2001), p. 257. See also Luukkonen et al. (2018), p. 345.

A. Koskenvuo (✉)
FINE – the Finnish Financial Ombudsman Bureau, Helsinki, Finland
e-mail: info@fine.fi

H. Heiss et al. (eds.), *Insurance Ombudsman Schemes*, AIDA Europe Research Series on Insurance Law and Regulation 15,
https://doi.org/10.1007/978-3-032-01500-6_7

answer enquiries and help consumers.[2] During the next few decades, the Consumers Insurance Agency and the Insurance Complaints Board handled an increasing number of cases and gained recognition among consumers and other customers as well as within the insurance industry. The Agency and the Insurance Complaints Board have had a significant impact on the development of consumer protection, providing guidelines and comparisons. It has also created and implemented soft law practices in its scheme in Finland.[3]

Meanwhile, a collaborative arrangement to form a Banking Customer Advice Office within banking industry was founded in 1997.[4] The respective arrangement to form a Securities Board was made in 2001.[5] Both of these organisations functioned closely together. In 2009, it was decided that the advisory offices and complaint boards in the financial sector were to form a new collaborative arrangement, FINE. At the time, there were also other organisations or federations within the financial industry that were reorganised to form a single federation. In this respect, the founding of FINE can be seen as a natural consequence of this development.

Since then, FINE has existed as a voluntarily established advisory and dispute resolution organisation operating in the financial sector under the agreement between the Finnish Competition and Consumer Authority, the Financial Supervisory Authority and the Federation of Finnish Financial Services. The signatories have adopted the FINE Regulations.[6] The present Code of Conduct also applies to FINE's dispute resolution activities in addition to the Regulations.

FINE respects the obligations set out in the Act on Alternative Dispute Resolution (1696/2015),[7] which is based on the respective EU Directive. FINE is currently the only institution in Finland subject to the Act.[8] FINE's actual functions and procedures are not regulated by law. The Insurance Board is merely referred to in the Insurance Contract Act (543/1994),[9] where it is mentioned in connection with time limits.

FINE is not supervised by a financial regulator. It is instead overseen and guided by its Executive Board. However, FINE is supervised by a financial regulator, the Financial Supervisor Authority, as part of its governance model. In addition, the alternative dispute resolution (ADR) obligations are overseen by the Ministry of Justice.

---

[2] See Sisula-Tulokas et al. (2001), p. 259.

[3] For more on soft law practices and FINE in Hyvä vakuutustapa ja Vakuutuslautakunta (2017).

[4] See more Sisula-Tulokas et al. (2011), pp. 242–248.

[5] See more Sisula-Tulokas et al. (2011), pp. 249–253. The Securities Board was later turned into the Investment Board.

[6] See FINE, Regulations and Code of Conduct. Available at https://www.fine.fi/en/about-us/regulations-and-code-of-conduct.html. Accessed 16 Apr 2025.

[7] Laki muussa kuin viranomaisessa tapahtuvasta kuluttajariitojen ratkaisemisesta (1696/2015).

[8] See Government Proposal on Alternative Dispute Resolution Act, HE 74/2015, chapter 4.3.

[9] Vakuutussopimuslaki (543/1994).

7.1.2 Governance Model

FINE is a financial sector organisation comprising the Finnish Financial Ombudsman Bureau and the three Complaints Boards for Insurance, Banking and Investment issues, as well as the Executive Committee and the Supervisory Board.

FINE represents a collaborative arrangement between the authorities, customer organisations and the financial sector. The Consumer Agency, the Financial Supervisory Authority and the Federation of Finnish Financial Services (nowadays Finance Finland, FFI) founded FINE on 1 January 2009, thereby merging the operations of the formerly separate Consumers Insurance Agency, Insurance Complaints Board, Banking Customer Advice Office and the Securities Board. The establishment of FINE was achieved through the implementation of a contractual agreement.

The governance body to oversee the operations of FINE consists of the Supervisory Board and the Executive Committee, see Fig. 7.1.

The Supervisory Board comprises a chairperson, three members representing the signatory parties as well as members invited by the signatory parties. The Chairperson is not a representative of the parties but is unanimously appointed by them. The Chairperson is authorised to sign for FINE. The signatory parties, that is the Financial Supervisory Authority, the Finnish Competition and Consumer Authority and Finance Finland (FFI) each appoint one Supervisory Board member and a deputy member. In addition, these signatories may collectively invite Board Members representing the ministries that fall within the sphere of operation of FINE. Currently, there are two invited members in the Supervisory Board, one from the Ministry of Finance and one from the Ministry of Social Affairs and Health.[10]

The tasks of the FINE Supervisory Board include the following:

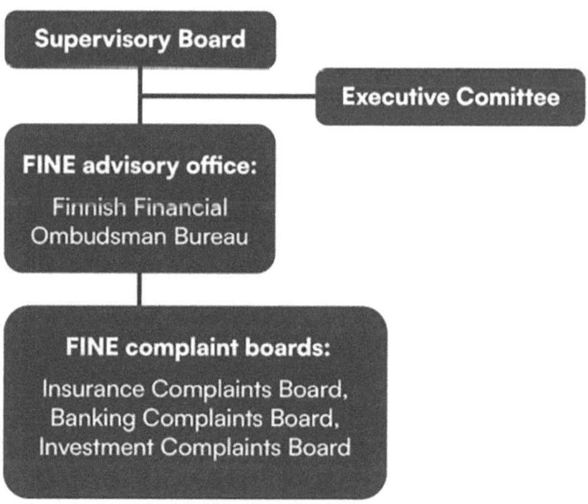

Fig. 7.1 FINE Governance Body

[10] See FINE, Regulations and Code of Conduct, Regulations, art. 2. See also Rantala and Kivisaari (2020), p. 145.

1. adopting the FINE budget and financial statements, including the annual report;
2. appointing the members to the Executive Committee and determining the remunerations payable to them;
3. electing the auditor;
4. adopting the FINE strategy and deciding on the general terms of employment of the personnel;
5. appointing the managing director and the director of FINE;
6. deciding on other persons authorised to sign for FINE; and
7. acting as the superior decisive body, directing and controlling FINE operations.

The Executive Committee has eight members and eight deputy members. Half of the members of the Executive Committee represent the authorities and organisations, while the other members are appointed by FFI. The Executive Committee elects the Chairperson and the Vice-Chairperson from among its members.[11]

FINE's Executive Committee shall:

1. provide the Supervisory Board with an annual proposition for a budget and action plan;
2. present the Supervisory Board with an annual report and account for the funds allocated to the organisation's operations;
3. appoint the chairpersons and members of FINE's Complaints Boards and determine the remunerations payable to the Complaints Boards;
4. carry out other tasks entrusted to it by the Supervisory Board.

The Supervisory Board and the Executive Committee convene at the invitation of their respective chairpersons. The Supervisory Board may also decide to meet at regular intervals. A Supervisory Board Member can request that the Board be convened to discuss a specific issue. The Supervisory Board and the Executive Committee constitute a quorum when the Chairperson or Vice-Chairperson and at least half of the members or deputy members are present.

7.1.3 Coverage and Insurance Business

FINE's scheme is not exclusively for the insurance sector. FINE's core operations include its advisory, information and dispute resolution services in the insurance, banking and investment sectors.

Insurance companies participate automatically in the Insurance Ombudsman Scheme if they are members of FFI. As a result, even though insurance companies in Finland are not under an obligation to participate in the Insurance Ombudsman Scheme, they become participants by virtue of their membership of FFI. In practice, almost all Finnish insurance companies are members of FFI. Insurance companies

[11] See FINE, Regulations and Code of Conduct, Regulations, art. 3.

that are not FFI members,[12] insurance agents and insurance brokers can participate in the Insurance Ombudsman Scheme if they have made a separate agreement with FINE.

7.1.4 Appointment of the Ombudsperson

FINE respects the obligations under the Act on Alternative Dispute Resolution (1696/2015) when examining the consumer disputes referred to in the Act.

Each person responsible for dispute resolution, that is a person who is responsible for dispute resolution in the issues handled by the Office, has the professional and legal expertise required for the purpose and has an employment contract with the FINE.

There is no single ombudsperson in the Ombudsman Scheme. The entity of FINE and its Complaint Boards form the entity of the Ombudsman Scheme. This differs from many other countries. The FINE Supervisory Board appoints the Managing Director, who is responsible for dispute resolution. The Managing Director appoints other persons responsible for dispute resolution at the Office. These persons are Chief Senior Lawyers and department managers.[13] The names of these persons are disclosed to the Ministry of Justice.

As mentioned above, the Complaints Boards are also included in the Ombudsman Scheme. Each Complaints Board has a Chairperson and Members who are independent in the performance of their dispute resolution duties. Each Complaints Board elects its respective Vice Chairperson from among its members. The handling of disputes in boards is a centuries old tradition in the Nordic countries.

FINE asks the signatory parties to the organisation to nominate the candidates for Complaints Board Members and their personal Deputies. The candidates must possess the professional and legal competency required by the task.

The Complaints Boards will make their decisions on the basis of the preparatory proposals made by the Secretary who acts as the referring official and who is an ombudsperson in the Office.

The Ombudsman Office, that is the FINE bodies, the Complaints Boards and the Office personnel in charge of dispute resolution, serves terms of office of three calendar years at a time.[14] As the persons responsible for dispute resolution are employed by the Office, their terms of office are, in practice, valid for as long as they work for the Office with the same job description. If a Chairperson, Vice Chairperson, Member or Deputy Member or a member of personnel in charge of dispute resolution resigns in the middle of a term, a new person will be appointed

[12] Mostly foreign insurance companies who have a minor presence in Finland.

[13] Currently, there are nine persons responsible of dispute resolution in FINE.

[14] See FINE, Regulations and Code of Conduct, Regulations, art. 16.

for the remainder of the term. The removal of a person responsible for the dispute resolution before the appointed time requires a compelling reason.

7.1.5 *Funding*

FFI covers the costs of FINE. Service providers who are not members of FFI must, however, contribute to FINE's costs when they use FINE's services.[15] The funding is determined in an annual budgeting process.

FINE's services are available to customers at no charge.[16]

7.1.6 *Insurance Ombudsman Functions*

The purpose of FINE is to promote the interests of customers and enhance their trust in the financial operations, to improve financial literacy among consumers and, otherwise, to develop the everyday practices in the financial sector in line with sound development principles.[17]

FINE's core operations include its advisory, information and dispute resolution services. However, FINE does not provide investment advice, nor does it carry out any comparison of individual products or services.

7.1.6.1 The Office

FINE shall fulfil the following tasks independently:[18]

1. provide advice and assistance to consumers, small businesses and other comparable customers on insurance, banking and investment issues;
2. conciliate customer disputes relating to insurance, banking and investment issues and make recommendations for the resolution of such disputes in the areas of competence of FINE's Complaints Boards;
3. promote general financial literacy through the production of information materials targeted at customers;
4. provide information on issues arising from the daily operations of FINE;
5. prepare comparisons of financial products and contribute to the preparation of the legislation related to the financial sector;

---

[15] See FINE, Regulations and Code of Conduct, Regulations, art. 18.

[16] See FINE, Regulations and Code of Conduct, Regulations, art. 17.

[17] See FINE, Regulations and Code of Conduct, Regulations, art. 1.

[18] See FINE, Regulations and Code of Conduct, Regulations, art. 5.

6. make proposals and issue opinions on questions related to legislation, contractual terms, customer information as well as services provided by financial sector companies, based on observations made during daily operations;
7. act as the secretariat for the Supervisory Board, the Executive Committee and FINE's Complaints Boards;
8. carry out any other tasks entrusted to it by the Supervisory Board or the Executive Committee.

To perform its advisory functions, the Office provides guidance and information to customers. Customers are offered information on the applicable contractual terms and legal provisions as well as on the practices of the dispute resolution bodies. In addition, the Office will inform customers about the means of appeal and dispute resolution available to them.

Even though FINE informs customers about the means of appeal and dispute resolution, FINE does not pursue the actual case for a customer. In comparison to insurance companies, customers are given a bit more advice in practice, for example, regarding which documents to provide.

FINE meets with insurance companies regularly on a yearly basis. During these meetings, FINE presents, in an anonymised form, the figures and the most relevant issues and topics of the previous year. FINE also provides each company with its own data and feedback received from customers, as well as observations made in the Office.

7.1.6.2 Insurance Complaints Board

The role of the Complaints Boards is to promote good practice in the operation of the financial sector, i.e. insurance, banking, securities markets and crowdfunding sectors by issuing recommendations on the resolution of questions related to liability for damages or other disputes.[19]

The activities of the Insurance Complaints Board are divided into Sections. Currently, there are five Sections.[20]

- Section I examines life and personal accident insurance issues, with the exception of investment-type insurance policies, as well as issues relating to personal injuries under travel and general liability insurance policies.
- Section II examines travel insurance issues as well as general liability and legal expenses insurance issues in cases where the policyholder, the insured or the injured party is deemed to be a consumer.
- Section III examines issues relating to household, voluntary motor vehicle, agricultural, property, animal, motor liability and boat insurance policies. It also

[19] See FINE, Regulations and Code of Conduct, Regulations, art. 6.

[20] See FINE, Regulations and Code of Conduct, Regulations, art. 7.

covers other consumer-related lines of insurance not falling within the remit of Sections I, II or V.

- Section IV examines issues relating to policies covering corporate and self-employed persons' property and operations, as well as liability insurance issues in cases where the injured party is also a business or a self-employed person.
- Section V examines issues relating to pharmaceutical injuries insurance policies.

For particular reasons, the Chairperson can order a specific Section to examine a case.

The Insurance Complaints Board is composed of the Chairperson and Section Chairs. The Chairperson of the Insurance Complaints Board also chairs one of the Sections, as well as the Extended Section. Each Section Chairperson chairs one or more Sections and acts as Deputy to the Complaints Board Chairperson.

Each of the Sections I, II, III and V is composed of a Section chairperson and four members, with deputies. Section IV is composed of a chairperson, six members and their deputies, plus additional members and their deputies. They are responsible for the examination of forward liability and consultation liability issues. Complaints Board members and deputies can also serve in Sections other than the one to which they have been appointed.

The FINE Executive Committee will appoint the chairpersons of the Complaints Board and the Sections as well as the members and their deputies. The Executive Committee will appoint the members of Sections I, II and III from the pool of candidates proposed by the Finnish Competition and Consumer Authority and FFI. The Executive Committee will appoint the members of Section IV from the pool of candidates proposed by FFI, the Federation of Finnish Enterprises, the Confederation of Finnish Industries EK and the Federation of Finnish Commerce, while deputy member candidates are proposed by FFI, the Association of Finnish Lawyers, the District Court of Helsinki and the Central Chamber of Commerce. The additional members and their deputies will be appointed from the pool of candidates nominated by the Finnish Freight Forwarders' Association and the Finnish Association of Consulting Firms SKOL. The Executive Committee will appoint the members of Section V from the pool of candidates nominated by the Ministry of Social Affairs and Health, Pharma Industry Finland PIF and FFI.

The Board does not issue any publication on its own; all such publications are issued by the FINE Office.

7.1.7 The Insurance Ombudsman Office

The staff consists of about 30 people in total. About two-thirds of the staff have a legal education background.

The Insurance Ombudsman Office's staff structure consists of different kind of investigators: advisors, senior advisors, chiefs of departments and chief legal counsels. In addition, there is a support team of four people to provide support in customer service, IT, communication and HR-issues and there are also occasional trainees. Chiefs of departments and chief legal counsels hold a Law's degree. About half of the advisors are lawyers, while the remainder typically hold other university-level degrees.

In order to participate in the ADR process, an employee must hold a Law degree.

The Ombudsman Office's employees are required to take ongoing training to develop their skills and knowledge. This can include participating in different courses and educational programmes or in-house training and education.

7.2 Insurance Ombudsman Jurisdiction

7.2.1 Substantive Scope

The substantive scope of FINE's Insurance Ombudsman Scheme is wide. It basically covers all types of non-statutory life and non-life insurance with few exceptions. Insurance enquiries or disputes typically concern home insurance, car insurance, third party liability, accident and health insurance or legal expenses insurance. FINE's operations do not apply to statutory pensions nor to statutory health or unemployment insurance policies. However, the Office can handle simple enquiries even on some types of statutory insurance when it seems appropriate.[21]

The role of FINE in relation to disputes is limited to those based on existing contracts. It does not extend to commercial decisions. Furthermore, FINE may not initiate a proceeding *ex officio*.

The Insurance Complaints Board issues recommendations to resolve disputes concerning the interpretation of the legislation and insurance terms that are related to the insurance relationship and brought to the Complaints Board by the policyholder, insured or injured party, beneficiary or the insurance company in question. The Insurance Complaints Board does not examine issues related to the statutory accident insurance and patient insurance policies. Issues related to statutory motor liability insurance are examined by the Insurance Complaints Board only if the dispute is of a private-law nature and outside the jurisdiction of the Traffic Accident and Patient Injury Board or similar bodies.[22]

FINE is entitled to dismiss a dispute being processed in the Office or the Complaints Boards without examination if the dispute does not involve a monetary or other financial interest.

[21] For example, there may be a question concerning third party motor liability where FINE can give general information or advise the customer on whom to contact about any given issue. With regard to the substantive scope, see Luukkonen et al. (2018), pp. 347 and 349.

[22] See FINE, Regulations and Code of Conduct, Regulations, art. 6.

7.2.2 Personal Scope, Territorial Scope and Time Limits

FINE provides advice and assistance to consumers, small businesses and other comparable customers in insurance matters. Cases will be taken up on the condition that the financial service provider, party to the dispute, is domiciled in Finland or has a Finland-based subsidiary or branch office. Furthermore, the service provider must be a member of FFI. In other instances, the condition applies that the service provider must have made a specific agreement with FINE on the use of its services. In the absence of a specific agreement with FINE, cross-border disputes based on the freedom to provide financial services will be examined in accordance with the principles followed by the FIN-NET scheme, which has been promoted by the European Commission.

FINE is entitled to dismiss a dispute being processed in the Office or the Complaints Boards without examination if, in an insurance case, the three-year period for filing a suit under the Insurance Contracts Act has expired before FINE receives the complaint.[23]

7.3 Procedure

7.3.1 Regulatory Framework

In examining disputes, FINE adheres to the principles of a fair trial, such as the independence and neutrality[24] of the persons appointed to settle the dispute and the right of both litigant parties to be heard. As mentioned earlier, FINE respects the obligations laid down in the Act on Alternative Dispute Resolution (1696/2015) when examining the consumer disputes referred to in the Act.

FINE's dispute resolution framework is governed by law. In their dispute resolution operations, the FINE Office and Complaints Boards also observe the principles of good insurance practice, good banking practice and good securities market practice, the guidelines and norms issued by the Financial Supervisory Authority as well as the self-regulation norms of the financial sector, such as the Insurance Companies' Claims Handling Guidelines and General Principles of Selection of Risks in Insurance Operations, adopted by the Federation of Finnish Financial Services.[25]

The cross-border disputes based on the freedom to provide financial services will be examined in accordance with the principles followed by the FIN-NET scheme, which has been promoted by the European Commission. In general, the ombudsperson applies Finnish law.

---

[23] See FINE, Regulations and Code of Conduct, Regulations, art. 10.

[24] See more on the independence and impartiality of FINE in FINE 50 vuotta pp. 276–294.

[25] See FINE, Regulations and Code of Conduct, Code of Conduct, art. 2.1.

7.3.2 *Enquiries and Complaints Handling Process*

The handling process used at FINE is partly informal and partly formal. For example, parties may present documentation quite freely and informally and the time limits for presenting documents are not binding. In the context of complaints handling, the hearing of both parties and the written procedure in dispute resolutions are examples of a formal process.

An appeal to FINE interrupts the limitation period for bringing a claim to court.

7.3.2.1 Enquiry Handling Process

Enquiries account for about 90% of FINE's interactions with the public. Enquiries are typically questions regarding the terms of insurance cover or a question on a claims decision. An enquiry can be an actual complaint. However, the ombudspersons will determine whether it is to be handled in an enquiry process or in a dispute process. Usually, complaints that necessitate the gathering of additional documentation or the conducting of further investigation start as an enquiry handling process. If it is obvious that the case cannot be resolved without a dispute resolution process, it is then transferred directly into that process. Typically, complaints that are clear in terms of both the actual interest and the legal question, and where efforts have been made to settle the case with the insurance company, are sent straight to a dispute process.

The enquiry handling process is an informal process. A customer may initiate the process by telephone, via an electronic form, email or letter. The telephone is the most commonly used and, in most cases, the best way to start the process. Many enquiries can be answered over the telephone.

In some cases, a deeper investigation or intervention may be necessary. Hence, these cases are complaints. The complaint handling process starts in the same manner as an enquiry handling process. There may be interactions with the insurance company, as well as the necessity to ask the customer additional questions. The ombudsperson always acts impartially, and the process is transparent; the other party is always informed of the interaction and the content of the interaction. In fact, the process may be fairly similar to a dispute resolution process. A complaint can also turn into a real dispute case that initiates a dispute handling process.

7.3.2.2 Dispute Handling Process

Procedure in the Office

About 10% of FINE's interactions concern dispute cases. A dispute is initiated at FINE when a complaint is received in writing or in electronic form. The customer must specify the service provider constituting the adversary party and the monetary claim, request for a declaratory statement or other claim, stating the reasons.

Dispute handling can take place both in the Office and in the Insurance Board. Cases that can be handled in the Office and for which recommendations can be given are generally simpler in nature.[26] FINE will seek to resolve disputes between the parties and provide recommendations for resolutions in cases with an established resolution practice or cases which are unambiguous in terms of the application of the law or contractual terms.[27] The aim is to provide an effective resolution to the dispute and to shorten the time required for handling a case.

More complex cases are handled by the Insurance Complaints Board.

Simplified Procedure at the Complaints Boards

The Complaints Boards can apply a simplified procedure to issues that have an established resolution practice or are unambiguous in terms of the application of the law or contractual terms.

In the simplified procedure, the Board is represented by the Chairperson alone. The decision to apply the simplified procedure to a case is made by the Secretary, who acts as the presenting official for the Section in question. If necessary, the Chairperson can decide to refer the case to the relevant Complaints Board or Section.

Extended Section of the Insurance Complaints Board

In the event that it is deemed necessary and at the initiative of the Section Chairperson, the Extended Section will discuss matters pertaining to the interpretation and application of the law or contractual terms and conditions, which may potentially be raised in various Sections or which are of fundamental importance. The Extended Section means that the Chairperson of the Section in question is joined by the Chairpersons of the other Sections.

---

[26] Rantala and Kivisaari (2020), p. 144.

[27] See FINE, Regulations and Code of Conduct, Regulations, art 7.

Decision to Dismiss the Case Without Examining Its Merits

The Complaints Board, the referring official appointed as the Head of Section of the Board, the FINE Managing Director or the Director may decide to dismiss a dispute without examining its merits pursuant to art. 10 of FINE's Regulations and Code of Conduct or on the grounds that the issue does not fall within FINE's remit.[28]

Procedure in the Insurance Complaints Board

Written proceedings are used by the Complaints Board unless it, in its composition examining the dispute, decides, for a particular reason, to hear the litigants or other parties orally. The decisions made in the Complaints Board meetings will be recorded in the form of transcripts.[29]

The Complaints Board may, at its discretion, hear experts or request an expert opinion. The expert must not be a person with an employment or similar relationship to the service provider whose product is under examination, nor may they be a person who cannot be heard as an expert under the Code of Judicial Procedure.[30] For example, medical experts are consulted in cases concerning health insurance and technical experts in some cases relating to car and home insurance.

A dispute case may be initiated at FINE only after the parties have attempted to resolve the case through direct contact.[31] A written decision or a reply to a complaint from the insurance company, bank or other service provider is required. A customer is normally asked to provide a written decision before the process can start.

A case can be initiated through a free-form letter, fax or by using the online form available at the FINE website. Complaints may be made in Finnish, Swedish or English. However, oral resolution recommendations cannot be requested.[32]

In order to process a customer's personal data, FINE is required to obtain the customer's consent in accordance with the Personal Data Act. This consent must be documented by means of a signed complaint, or a resolution recommendation should be requested by using FINE's online form.[33]

FINE respects the rules of insurance and banking secrecy. Releasing a customer's information to a third party, such as a lawyer, requires the customer's consent. Consequently, a power of attorney given by the customer or another document demonstrating the customer's consent is required when a customer wishes to engage the services of a lawyer, public legal aid counsel or other representative.[34] FINE's

[28] See FINE, Regulations and Code of Conduct, Regulations, art. 7.

[29] See FINE, Regulations and Code of Conduct, Regulations, art. 9.

[30] See FINE, Regulations and Code of Conduct, Code of Conduct, art. 2.3.1.

[31] See FINE, Regulations and Code of Conduct, Code of Conduct, art. 1.1.

[32] See FINE, Regulations and Code of Conduct, Code of Conduct, art. 1.2.

[33] See FINE, Regulations and Code of Conduct, Code of Conduct, art. 1.2.

[34] See FINE, Regulations and Code of Conduct, Code of Conduct, art. 1.3.

requests do not override any duty of confidentiality that insurance businesses owe to third parties unless written consent is provided.

If the injured party has requested a resolution recommendation in a general liability insurance case, FINE will reserve the opportunity for the policyholder to be heard, as provided for in s. 68 of the Insurance Contracts Act. Other parties who may be heard include, for example, competing beneficiaries.

The policyholder or other party heard will be furnished with the documents sent to FINE by the party requesting the resolution recommendation and the response from the insurance company, with the exception of potential detailed data concerning the state of health of the customer requesting the resolution recommendation.[35] This is a very core element of the procedure and is necessary to keep the process as open as possible to all parties involved.

Nature of the Procedure

FINE's dispute resolution process adheres to common principles. In their dispute resolution operations, the FINE Office and Complaints Boards also observe the principles of good insurance practice, good banking practice and good securities market practice, as well as the guidelines and norms issued by the Financial Supervisory Authority. Furthermore, they comply with the self-regulation norms of the financial sector, such as the Insurance Companies' Claims Handling Guidelines and General Principles of Selection of Risks in Insurance Operations, which have been adopted by the Federation of Finnish Financial Services.[36]

Preliminary Ruling

It is not permitted for consumers to submit their complaints collectively to FINE. However, a preliminary ruling procedure exists.[37]

If a Complaints Board receives or the Board Secretariat expects to receive multiple complaints pertaining to a similar interpretative issue or another matter involving a specific service provider, the Complaints Board may, in order to facilitate the expeditious examination of these cases, consider taking up one or two of these comparable cases for a preliminary ruling. Since such decisions by the Complaints Board constitute preliminary rulings, they are deliberately issued with the intention of providing guidance.

Once the preliminary ruling procedure has started, any further complaints on the same issue shall be stayed pending the preliminary ruling. The parties to the cases

[35] See FINE, Regulations and Code of Conduct, Code of Conduct, art. 1.4.

[36] See FINE, Regulations and Code of Conduct, Code of Conduct, art. 2.1.

[37] See FINE, Regulations and Code of Conduct, Regulations, art. 13.

being heard as well as other customers, who are similarly affected by the issue, will be informed of this.

7.3.3 Admissible Complaints

The Complaints Board, the referring official appointed as the Head of Section of the Board, the FINE Managing Director or the Director may decide to dismiss a dispute without examining its merits pursuant to art. 10 of FINE's Regulations or on the grounds that the issue does not fall within FINE's jurisdiction.

The case will be annulled if the customer does not specify the complaint, despite being invited to do so, or withdraws it. Furthermore, the case will also be annulled if the customer's agent does not present an appropriate authorisation from the customer.

Disputes processed in the Office or the Complaints Boards must adhere to the following criteria:

1. The customer must first seek resolution of the issue through direct contact with the service provider;
2. In an insurance case, the three-year period for filing a suit under the Insurance Contracts Act should not have elapsed prior to FINE receiving the complaint;
3. The same dispute cannot be examined or cannot be tried at the same time by a court of law or the Consumer Complaints Board, the Traffic Accident and Patient Injury Board or a similar alternative dispute resolution body;
4. The dispute must involve a monetary or other financial interest;[38]
5. The dispute is not unfounded or motivated by a wish to cause intentional harm;
6. The reliable resolution of the dispute does not require oral evidence, the conduct of a party to the dispute does not constitute a threat, or the nature of the dispute would not, otherwise, significantly impede the efficient operation of FINE.[39]

If a dispute processed in the Office or the Complaints Boards does not comply with these criteria, FINE may dismiss the dispute without examination.

A dispute case can be initiated at FINE only after the parties have tried to resolve the case through direct contact. A written decision or a response to a complaint from the insurance company, bank or other service provider is required.[40] There is a 30 day period within which the Insurance Company should handle all claims and that also applies to complaints. After a period of 30 days, insurance companies are obliged to pay penalty interest on any compensation that may be delayed.[41]

[38] However, there are no specific minimum or maximum amounts.

[39] See FINE, Regulations and Code of Conduct, Regulations, art. 10.

[40] See FINE, Regulations and Code of Conduct, Code of Conduct, art. 1.1.

[41] Insurance Contract Act, art. 70.

FINE's right to acquire and process the customer's personal data is based on the Personal Data Act.[42]

As mentioned above, FINE respects the rules of insurance and banking secrecy. The customer's consent is required to release a customer's information to a third party, such as a lawyer.

All members of FINE's Supervisory Body, Executive Committee and Complaints Boards as well as FINE officials are bound by the same duty of confidentiality as those set out in the Act on Credit Institutions, the Insurance Companies Act, the Act on Common Funds and the Act on Investment Services.

7.3.4 *Obtaining Information and Collecting Evidence*

7.3.4.1 Active Role and Burden of Proof

The insurance ombudsperson has the power to require information and documents relevant to deciding a case by law. Due to open and fair practices, however, FINE always informs customers in advance about the sources and the scope of information contained in the documents that FINE will acquire from the insurance company.

Under the EU ADR Directive,[43] the parties must be able to act in an alternative dispute resolution procedure without relying on legal counsel.

Consumers or corresponding customers cannot, in practice, be expected to have legal expertise, and, therefore, the alternative dispute resolution bodies must play an active role in these cases. The FINE Office and the Complaints Board can also rest their decision in favour of the consumer or corresponding customer on facts that the customer has not noted or has not been able to provide. In this case, the parties concerned, or other potential interested parties, are reserved an opportunity to give the necessary opinions before the decision on the case is made.

The financial sector service providers are expert organisations in their field of operations. In their responses and other writs, the service providers must present all the arguments they deem necessary for the resolution of the case. In their handling of the case, the FINE Office or Complaints Boards do not pay attention to other facts supporting the service provider's case, unless the customer's claim is deemed to be unjustified.[44]

---

[42] Personal Data Act, s. 6, sub-ss. 1 C and F.

[43] Directive 2013/11/EU of the European Parliament and of the Council of 21 May 2013 on alternative dispute resolution for consumer disputes and amending Regulation (EC) No 2006/2004 and Directive 2009/22/EC (Directive on consumer ADR) [2013] OJ L165/63.

[44] See FINE, Regulations and Code of Conduct, Code of Conduct, art. 2.2.

7.3.4.2 Evidence

The examination of a dispute is based on the written documentation submitted to FINE, or other information such as telephone, video or other recordings. The FINE Office or Complaints Boards will only hear the parties concerned or other parties present oral arguments for specific reasons.[45]

7.3.4.3 Expert Opinions

At its own discretion and expense, FINE can ask for an expert opinion, for example, on medical or construction engineering issues, should it be deemed necessary to assess the evidence presented by the parties or, otherwise, clarify the case.

The medical experts used by FINE do not conduct physical examinations of customers; rather, they issue their opinions on the basis of the documentation submitted in each case.

The expert opinions acquired by FINE will be sent to both parties for their information prior to a decision on the case being made.[46]

7.3.5 Outcome of the Process: Insurance Ombudsman Decision and Oversight by Courts

7.3.5.1 Resolution Recommendation

The resolutions made by the FINE Office and Complaints Board are recommendations. They are not binding on the parties and are not enforceable in courts.[47] Consequently, the decision of the Ombudsman Scheme cannot be appealed against in court. In this sense, the Ombudsman Scheme's decision is final[48] and not subject

---

[45] See FINE, Regulations and Code of Conduct, Code of Conduct, art. 2.3.

[46] See FINE, Regulations and Code of Conduct, Code of Conduct, art. 2.3.1.

[47] See FINE, Regulations and Code of Conduct, Regulations, art. 3.1.

[48] According to art. 12 of the Regulations, the Ombudsman can rectify errors. FINE will re-examine a case that has already been resolved if there is good cause to do so. Good cause may relate to decisions that have been based on clearly erroneous or incomplete information or a manifestly incorrect application of law or situations where a procedural error has occurred in the decision-making process. The parties will be informed of the review. The presenting official appointed as the Head of Section of the Complaints Board may correct any obvious typographical or calculation errors or similar clear errors in the Board's decision. The Head of Section may also decide whether or not the Complaints Board will re-examine a case that has already been resolved. The member of the Office personnel in charge of dispute resolution may correct any obvious typographical or calculation errors or similar clear errors in a decision issued through the procedure in the Office, or they may decide upon a re-examination of a case that has already been resolved.

to judicial review by the courts. Nevertheless, either party may choose to pursue the case further in court.

There is no maximum amount that the Ombudsman Scheme can award. The amounts in disputes vary considerably, from cases where a mere principle is the only issue in question and the actual interest is very low, to cases where the possible interest could amount to millions of euros. On average, the interest owed ranges from several hundred euros to several thousands of euros.

The redress powers are seldom required, as the recommendations are generally adhered to within the insurance sector. In the event that a party fails to comply with the recommendation, the ombudsperson may attempt to contact and negotiate with that party. Furthermore, there is a public and media interest that can be seen and used as a redress power.

7.3.5.2 Issuing the Resolution Recommendation and Returning of Evidence

The resolution recommendation is issued in the language used in the complaint, either in Finnish, Swedish or English.

In accordance with the FINE Regulations, the FINE Office resolution recommendations are signed by the person appointed for dispute resolution and the presenting official. The resolution recommendations issued by a Complaints Board are signed by the Chairperson of the Board or its Section, and the Secretary acting as the presenting official. Furthermore, the recommendation includes the names of the Complaints Board members who have participated in the decision-making process.

Signed recommendations will be sent to the parties concerned. The recommendations sent to service providers will be addressed to the person issuing the response on behalf of the service provider, unless otherwise agreed upon.

Original receipts, photographs, medical certificates and other documents will be returned to the parties and sent together with the recommendation, unless they have already been returned. Resolution recommendations containing identifying data about the parties, opinions or other documents may not be sent in a non-encrypted email for data security reasons.[49]

7.3.5.3 Publication of Resolution Recommendations

The resolution recommendations published in the online database containing the Complaints Boards' recommendations are anonymous. They will be edited in such a way that the parties cannot be identified on the basis of details regarding the event, location, or other specific elements.[50]

[49] See FINE, Regulations and Code of Conduct, Code of Conduct, art. 3.2.

[50] See FINE, Regulations and Code of Conduct, Code of Conduct, art. 3.3.

7.4 Statistical Data

FINE receives and resolves approximately 10,000 enquiries, complaints and actual disputes per year. A total of 9577 cases were recorded in 2022.[51] Enquiries and non-complex complaints that are not actual disputes account for approximately 90% of the cases. Insurance enquiries form a majority, with 6399 cases in 2022. The remaining cases are actual disputes that require formal handling by the Office or Complaints Board. Out of 9577 cases in 2022, 824 were classified as disputes, while the remainder were enquiries and complaints. Of the total number of disputes, 723 cases were insurance related. Only a small number of enquiries or complaints were declined.

The ratio of complaints resolved in favour of the complainant per year is usually one third (2022: 33%). Accordingly, the ratio of complaints resolved in favour of the insurance business per year is usually two thirds (2022: 63%).

The average time taken to resolve disputes falls within the timeframe stipulated by ADR legislation. This means that the disputes must be resolved within 90 days upon receipt of all documentation and comments pertaining to the case. The time taken to resolve an insurance dispute in ADR cases averaged approximately 60 days in 2022.

7.5 Insurance Ombudsman Practice

7.5.1 Market Trends

Home insurance, personal accident insurance and liability insurance are the insurance products for which the most complaints are received. In addition to queries regarding whether a product has been sold properly with the provision of sufficient information, most cases concern claims. Usually, complaints about home insurance are more like enquiries in nature. The majority of actual disputes concern personal accident or liability insurance, given that causality and, in cases involving personal injuries, insurance-specific medical evaluations are often difficult for consumers to understand.[52] In general, Finnish consumer protection legislation and soft law practices are taken into account in the insurance industry.

The signatory parties find it important that financial sector service providers comply with FINE's resolution recommendations.[53] The insurance sector is highly committed to recognising FINE, customers are well informed of the opportunity to seek recommendations from FINE, and there is a high degree of compliance by

[51] FINE, FINE Vuosikertomus 2022. Available at https://www.fine.fi/tietoa-finesta/vuosikertomukset/fine-vuosikertomus-2022.html. Accessed 16 Apr 2025.

[52] See more on FINE, FINE Vuosikertomus 2022.

[53] See FINE, Regulations and Code of Conduct, Regulations, art. 14.

insurance businesses with the recommendations issued. The compliance rate for the recommendations is usually 96–100% on an annual basis (2022: 96%).

7.5.2 Limitations

The legal and institutional framework of the Insurance Ombudsman Scheme does not impose any constraints on the effective functioning of the Scheme.

The main limitation is the financial illiteracy that impedes consumers from knowing their rights. Consequently, in addition to handling complaints, FINE assesses consumers' financial awareness and literacy in a number of ways, namely by:

1. promoting general financial literacy by producing information material targeted at the customers;
2. providing information on the issues raised during the daily operations of FINE;
3. preparing comparisons of financial products and contributing to the preparation of legislation related to the financial sector;
4. making proposals and offering opinions on matters pertaining to legislation, contractual terms, customer information, and services provided by financial sector companies, based on observations made during daily operations.

In general, there has been an increase in consumer financial awareness over time. However, products and related problems have also become more complicated over the years.

7.5.3 De lege ferenda Postulates

In our experience, the Ombudsman Scheme functions quite well in Finland. As mentioned earlier, insurance businesses broadly comply with the recommendations in a co-operative manner. Working in Complaints Boards in dispute cases is also a very essential part of FINE's culture. The experts involved are highly committed and the Boards add an extra layer of impartiality to the process as a case will be seen by multiple people. In the current situation, there are few changes that can be suggested. The average time taken to resolve disputes could of course be shorter so that consumers do not to have to wait for so long. In order to reduce the time taken to resolve disputes, it is essential that all of the parties involved demonstrate a high level of cooperation and commitment to providing all the answers and documentation needed in a timely manner.

7.6 Other

7.6.1 Accessibility

There are no barriers to accessing the Insurance Ombudsman Service or the barriers to doing so are minimal. For instance, as a part of each claims decision, insurance businesses are obliged to inform consumers of the various avenues available for seeking a recommendation or an appeal. In this context, FINE is mentioned first, along with the general Consumer Disputes Board and common courts.

Access to FINE has been made as easy as possible by offering services via different channels, with a particular focus on telephone support, in contrast to the increasing prevalence of digital and online services. FINE has its own website[54] that is frequently visited, with over 300,000 visits per year. FINE also holds seminars and gives interviews. Nevertheless, the knowledge of FINE and its services could still be promoted more. Each year, a number of initiatives are undertaken with the objective of increasing awareness of FINE and the importance of promoting financial literacy.

7.6.2 Accountability

FINE presents a detailed account of its activities to the Supervisory Board and the Executive Committee. Additionally, FINE publishes an annual report on its website.

The FINE scheme budget is subject to an approval procedure. In practice, the Managing Director and the Chairperson of the Supervisory Board conduct the preliminary discussions regarding the budgetary requirements for the forthcoming year. The Managing Director presents the draft budget to the Executive Committee, which may suggest alterations to it. Subsequently, the Executive Committee makes a decision, which is then presented to the Supervisory Board. Ultimately, the Supervisory Board is responsible for approving the budget.

The actual collection of funds follows a proceeding accepted by the negotiating parties. The funding of the FFI members is divided between the insurance, banking and investment sector. The funding of the non-FFI members happens according to the agreements made with FINE.

The funding for the year is allocated in advance in accordance with the estimated need. The estimated funding is balanced towards the end of the year. FINE is a non-profit organisation.

[54] See www.fine.fi. Accessed 16 Apr 2025.

Legal Sources

Directive 2013/11/EU of the European Parliament and of the Council of 21 May 2013 on alternative dispute resolution for consumer disputes and amending Regulation (EC) No 2006/2004 and Directive 2009/22/EC (Directive on consumer ADR) [2013] OJ L165/63

FINE, Regulations and Code of Conduct. https://www.fine.fi/en/about-us/regulations-and-code-of-conduct.html

Laki muussa kuin viranomaisessa tapahtuvasta kuluttajariitojen ratkaisemisesta (1696/2015)

Vakuutussopimuslaki (543/1994)

Documents

FINE 50 vuotta. Grano 2021

FINE, FINE Vuosikertomus 2022. https://www.fine.fi/oppaat/julkaisu/fine-vuosikertomus-2022.html

Government Proposal on Alternative Dispute Resolution Act – Hallituksen esitys eduskunnalle kuluttajariitojen vaihtoehtoista ratkaisemista koskevaksi lainsäädännöksi (HE 74/2015). https://finlex.fi/fi/esitykset/he/2015/20150074

Hyvä vakuutustapa ja Vakuutuslautakunta - FINE - Vakuutus- ja rahoitusneuvonta (2017). https://www.fine.fi/

References

Luukkonen I, Mäntyniemi L, Pekonen-Ranta M, Raulos V, Santavirta P (eds) (2018) Vakuutuslainsäädäntö. Hansaprint Oy, Turenki

Rantala J, Kivisaari E (2020) Vakuutusoppi. Finva/Hansaprint Oy, Turenki

Sisula-Tulokas L, Luukkonen I, Saario M (eds) (2001) Kuluttajien vakuutustoimisto & vakuutuslautakunta 30 vuotta. Gummerus Kirjapaino Oy, Jyväskylä

Sisula-Tulokas L, Luukkonen I, Sirén E, Raulos V (eds) (2011) Vakuutus- ja rahoitusneuvonta 40 vuotta. Kariston Kirjapaino Oy, Hämeenlinna

Chapter 8
France

Insurance Ombudsman Scheme

Arnaud Chneiweiss

8.1 Institutional Framework

8.1.1 Establishment

8.1.1.1 Background of the Scheme

La Médiation de l'Assurance (LMA) [the French Ombudsman Service] was created by the industry on 1 September 2015, at the same time as insurers joined forces to form a unified Federation. LMA resulted from the merger of the previous mediation schemes offered by the *Fédération Française des Sociétés d'Assurances* (FFSA)—which primarily comprised insurers incorporated as limited companies, whether listed on the stock exchange or not, and the *Groupement des Entreprises Mutuelles d'Assurance* (GEMA), which brought together mutual insurers. It is an association comprising all insurers governed by the French Insurance Code. Association members include public limited companies (such as AXA, Allianz and Generali), mutual insurers (such as Covea, Groupama and Macif) and insurance subsidiaries of banking groups (such as Cardif, a subsidiary of BNP Paribas, Assurances du Crédit Mutuel and Crédit Agricole Assurances). Brokerage associations are also members.

The purpose of LMA is:

– to provide the public with a free system for the out-of-court settlement of consumer disputes in accordance with the requirements of independence, impartial-

A. Chneiweiss (✉)
La Médiation de l'Assurance, Paris, France
e-mail: arnaud.chneiweiss@mediation-assurance.org

H. Heiss et al. (eds.), *Insurance Ombudsman Schemes*, AIDA Europe Research Series on Insurance Law and Regulation 15,
https://doi.org/10.1007/978-3-032-01500-6_8

ity, effectiveness and transparency set forth in EU ADR Directive;[1] the system provides a free and impartial means of settling disputes that may arise between individuals and insurance companies or insurance intermediaries; the system is designed to facilitate the search for amicable solutions to disputes in which a consumer is pitted against an insurance company or insurance broker operating in France;
- to appoint the ombudsperson and guarantee their independence by ensuring that they have the material and human resources necessary to carry out their mission.

Our mediation service is first and foremost a mediation for private individuals, who account for 95% of cases. In December 2020, an agreement between the government and the insurance industry expanded the LMA's remit to encompass disputes involving small and medium-sized enterprises (SMEs). This announcement was made in a press release from the Ministry of Finance.[2]

Finally, in September 2023, it was decided that LMA's remit would be expanded to encompass disputes between local authorities and their insurers. Once more, this new option of applying to LMA was announced by the Minister of Finance.

8.1.1.2 Basis of the Insurance Ombudsman Scheme

It is a legal requirement for all insurance companies and brokers to have a mediation system. This is in accordance with the EU ADR Directive, which was transposed into French law in 2015.[3] French insurers have opted for a sector-specific ombudsman scheme, but there is still no complete unification. LMA is by far the leading mediation body in the sector, with approximately 30,000 members and more than 36,500 cases submitted in 2024. However, there is also a mediator for mutual health insurance companies and one for provident institutions.

In my estimation, it would be advantageous for the industry as a whole to move towards a unified mediation system. Such a system would undoubtedly prove to be simpler, clearer and potentially more efficient.

We work within the framework of the EU ADR Directive. Its transposition into French law led to the creation of the *Commission d'évaluation et de contrôle de la médiation de la consommation* (CECMC), a public body, with the mandate to approve or revoke referenced mediators.

---

[1] Directive 2013/11/EU of the European Parliament and of the Council of 21 May 2013 on alternative dispute resolution for consumer disputes and amending Regulation (EC) No 2006/2004 and Directive 2009/22/EC (Directive on consumer ADR) [2013] OJ L165/63.

[2] See https://www.economie.gouv.fr/renforcement-engagements-assureurs-entreprises-affectees-covid-19. Accessed 16 Apr 2025.

[3] *Ordonnance n°2015-1033 du 20 août 2015 relative au Règlement Extra-judiciaire des litiges de la consommation.* https://www.legifrance.gouv.fr/loda/id/JORFTEXT000031070940. Accessed 16 Apr 2025.

The CECMC is presided over by a member of the *Conseil d'Etat*. Its Vice-Chairman is from the *Cour de Cassation*, the country's highest judicial court. Four representatives of consumer associations, together with a Professor of Consumer Law and two representatives of employers, constitute the Board. Its secretariat is provided by a department of the Ministry of Finance.

8.1.1.3 Establishment of the Insurance Ombudsman Scheme

The French Insurance Federation (*Fédération France Assureurs*) was the driving force behind the establishment of LMA as an association. It was subsequently joined by associations of brokers, asset managers and others.

A Board of Directors has been constituted, comprising representatives from all the aforementioned organisations. The Board is currently chaired by an individual who previously chaired the Financial Sector Consultative Committee, which brings together consumer associations, professionals and public authorities.

In my opinion, it would have been preferable to include consumer representatives on the Board; however, this was not permitted due to the fact that they are members of the CECMC, which oversees all ADR schemes. They therefore felt that it would be a conflict of interest to be present at the various stages of governance.

The ombudsperson reports to the CECMC, which was established by the 2015 law to oversee all ombudspersons, rather than to the *Autorité de contrôle prudentiel et de resolution* (ACPR), which oversees insurers. However, informal discussions may be held with the latter, as well as with the Treasury Directorate of the Ministry of Finance and other Departments within the Ministry.

Furthermore, the ombudsperson is occasionally interviewed by Members of Parliament or Senators who seek to gain a comprehensive understanding of a particular subject matter (for example, local authorities' insurance).

8.1.2 Governance Model

LMA is subject to the authority overseeing the Insurance Ombudsman Service (*Médiateur de l'Assurance*), as referenced by the CECMC.

The governance structure is as follows:

- Supervisory Authority: CECMC. Consumer associations are represented in this Commission.
- LMA Board: The Board of Directors is comprised of one representative from each of the LMA's institutional members, the Chairman of the Financial Sector Consultative (*Comité Consultatif du Secteur Financier*, hereinafter CCSF), two members from the insurance industry, and up to three qualified individuals recognised for their expertise, particularly in insurance or consumer law.

8.1.3 *Coverage*

The remit of LMA is limited to the resolution of insurance-related matters. We can, of course, also conduct informal exchanges with our counterparts in the banking and financial sectors.

8.1.4 *Insurance Business Covered*

The insurance providers are obliged to provide all consumers access to a consumer mediation scheme with a view to resolving any disputes amicably. This obligation stems from the EU ADR Directive and the 2015 French law which transposed the Directive. It is set out in art. L. 612-1 of the French Consumer Code.

The insurers operating within the framework of the Insurance Code[4] (i.e. AXA, Allianz, Generali, Credit Agricole, Credit Mutuel, BNP Paribas, Covea, Groupama, Aema and so on) have voluntarily decided to join LMA, an ombudsman service established by the insurance industry in accordance with legal requirements.

All the members of the French Insurance Federation (*France Assureurs*) have consented to becoming members of LMA and to engage in mediation proceedings when a policyholder requests such an action.

The ACPR, which supervises the activities of insurers and brokers, ensures that the entity under audit is in compliance with its obligations by informing policyholders of the competent ombudsman service in the event of a dispute.

8.1.5 *Appointment of the Ombudsperson*

The insurance ombudsperson is appointed unanimously by an Appointments Committee, comprising the Chairperson of the Financial Sector Consultative Committee, a representative appointed by the institutional members and two qualified persons. The Committee is responsible for selecting candidates for the role, which is subject to a renewable three-year term. In order to be eligible, the person concerned must be below the age of 65 on the day of their appointment or renewal.

The ombudsperson is an independent and impartial individual, distinguished for their qualities and skills within the domain of mediation and their knowledge of insurance issues. The ombudsperson fulfils their duties with diligence and competence; they receive no instructions from any party. The individual in question is furnished with all the requisite assistance, resources, and powers required to carry out their mission.

---

[4] *Code des assurances*. https://www.legifrance.gouv.fr/codes/texte_lc/LEGITEXT000006073984/. Accessed 16 Apr 2025.

The ombudsperson is registered on the list of mediators notified to the European Commission, in accordance with art. L.615-1 of the French Consumer Code.[5]

The ombudsperson may be dismissed during their term of office by the CECMC:

- in the event of force majeure;
- in the event of withdrawal from the list of mediators by the CECMC, in accordance with art. L615.2 of the French Consumer Code.

If the ombudsperson considers that certain circumstances may potentially compromise their independence or impartiality, they are obliged to consult with the CECMC.

The ombudsperson is bound by an obligation of confidentiality. This obligation may not be invoked against the CECMC in the context of its inspections.

8.1.6 Funding

Recourse to mediation is free of charge for the consumer. Consequently, LMA's operating budget is wholly financed by the insurance professionals who are members of LMA. 2% of LMA's budget is made up of the annual flat-rate fee paid by all members. The remaining 98% is financed by a variable contribution calculated on an annual basis for each member, based on the number of admissible cases involving that member.

The funding of LMA's budget is therefore divided among its members. For example, if 10% of LMA's admissible cases concern an insurance group, the latter will be required to contribute the same percentage to the budget, in addition to the flat-rate contribution.

The Board of Directors is responsible for approving LMA's financing arrangements on an annual basis.

The budget for 2024 is approximately EUR 11 million. LMA currently employs 80 people and plans to expand its workforce to 90 to respond to the significant increase in complaints. Personnel costs represent two-thirds of the budget.

As at mid-2024, we have received more than 35,000 complaints, representing a 63% increase in the volume of files to be processed year-on-year.

8.1.7 Insurance Ombudsman Functions

The ombudsperson is responsible for the day-to-day running of the LMA and may delegate their powers to any person to represent them in matters pertaining to accounting. The LMA employees are placed under the functional authority of the ombudsperson.

---

[5] *Code de la consummation*. https://www.legifrance.gouv.fr/codes/texte_lc/LEGITEXT000006069565/. Accessed 16 Apr 2025.

The role of the ombudsperson, who is independent of insurers and insurance intermediaries, is to examine and attempt to settle disputes between policyholders and their insurers.

Cases are referred to the ombudsperson by policyholders, and the insurer is then requested to provide explanations and documents. At the end of the mediation process, the ombudsperson issues an opinion that is not binding for the parties, but which, if adhered to, can bring the dispute to an amicable end, avoiding the inconvenience and expense of legal proceedings. The ombudsperson's intervention is provided free of charge to the policyholder. Our decisions are almost always adhered to by insurers and brokers. This high level of acceptance is a crucial factor in establishing LMA's credibility.

The cases examined by the insurance mediation service reveal the tensions that exist in society: distrust of experts and institutions, in this case embodied by insurers, and sometimes violent expression. Furthermore, there is a lack of financial education, difficulties in purchasing power, and an increased desire to assert one's rights.

Mediation thus appears to be a useful safety valve for our legal system. This is fully consistent with the development of an "amicable settlement policy" that is desired by the Minister of Justice. Moreover, for disputes concerning sums of less than EUR 5000, it is now compulsory to attempt mediation or conciliation before going to court.

In a French society that is more defiant than ever, and where insurance issues are essential to social cohesion, the "LMA has an important role to play. This is to propose a settlement on a case-by-case basis, with a primary focus on legal principles but occasionally also on equity. It is also to explain, pacify and play the role of a trusted third party. And sometimes, it is to denounce the conduct of insurers or the clauses used in the contracts that do not respect the legal framework.

The findings and recommendations of LMA over the previous few years were the starting point for the CCSF's work and have resulted in significant advancements for consumers. They have resulted in the harmonisation of the conditions that must be met to terminate insurance contracts, by extending the scope of contracts that can now be cancelled "at any time." Furthermore, in affinity insurance (for instance mobile phone insurance) the withdrawal period has been extended, the manner of obtaining consent has been modified and the content of annual information to be provided has been reinforced. These represent concrete advancements that have been made by the ombudsperson.

In addition, the ombudsperson has called upon the insurance industry to ensure that vague exclusion clauses, which have been condemned by the French Supreme Court (*Cour de Cassation*), are deleted from all contracts, and to improve the clarity of contracts.

The definitions of what constitutes an "accident" or a "break-in" are sometimes very restrictive, which can lead to disputes, misunderstanding and frustration among policyholders, which is not good for anyone. The ombudsperson has called for definitions to be clearer and more in line with everyday language.

8.1.8 Insurance Ombudsman Office

The ombudsperson is supported by a team of more than 80 people as at mid-2024, whose roles include the administrative processing of complaints and the drafting of proposed solutions. More than 50 individuals on the team are legal experts in insurance law. That number is due to increase to 90 people in the next few months, in response to the sharp increase in the number of files to be processed.

LMA is structured into the following departments: property and casualty insurance; life insurance and pensions; health and provident insurance. A legal studies unit provides support. The legal experts have different backgrounds, with the majority having considerable experience in law and the world of insurance in particular (master's degrees in insurance law, legal studies, etc.).

To propose solutions, the ombudsperson relies on the analysis of cases carried out by legal experts. They are also supported by file managers, who are responsible for the administrative processing of complaints.

As soon as it was set up, LMA joined the GIE GPSA (*Gestion professionnelle des services de l'assurance*). This resource pool is managed by *Fédération France Assurance*. It is responsible for the management of all resources required by its member professional bodies (human resources, IT, accounting-finance, general and logistical resources, premises).

The LMA team is entirely dedicated to the ombudsperson's mission: resolving disputes.

8.2 Insurance Ombudsman Jurisdiction

8.2.1 Substantive Scope

8.2.1.1 Definition of Scope

The LMA's remit is defined in the Insurance Ombudsman Charter, which can be consulted on our website.[6] Any consumer, policyholder or beneficiary may refer to the LMA any dispute relating to the conclusion, interpretation or application of an insurance contract. Under the provisions of art. L.612-2 of the French Consumer Code, the matter cannot be referred to the LMA if:

- the consumers are unable to prove that they have previously tried to resolve their disputes directly with the professional by means of a written complaint, where applicable, in accordance with the procedures set out in the contract;
- the claim is manifestly unfounded or vexatious;

[6] https://www.mediation-assurance.org/. Accessed 16 Apr 2025.

- the dispute has already been examined or is in the process of being examined by another ombudsman scheme or by a court;
- the consumer submitted their request to the LMA more than one year after their written complaint to the trader;
- the dispute does not fall within the ombudsperson's remit (for instance it is a banking issue, not an insurance question).

8.2.1.2 Activities Covered

LMA covers all insurance activities, both life and non-life. As mentioned previously, we can now be contacted by private individuals (95% of cases) and by SMEs (5%) and local authorities.

8.2.1.3 Relation to Commercial Decisions

Our role is to examine the insurance contract concluded between the insured and the insurer, and to determine whether it has been correctly applied by the insurer. No opinion is provided on the cost of the contract or the insurer's commercial policy. We invite the policyholders to take advantage of the competition—which is real on the French market on most products—if their contract no longer suits them.

8.2.1.4 Enquiries and Disputes Handled

A priori, we do not conduct "investigations". It should be noted that in 2021, the Minister of Finance requested a report on the issue of operating losses for retailers and SMEs in the context of the COVID-19 crisis. The report which included findings and proposals, was published in July 2021, and is available online.[7] In July 2024, we also received a request by the Minister of Finance to submit proposals for assisting local authorities in finding an insurer.

8.2.1.5 Claim Amount

Unfortunately, there is no minimum amount for claims that can be referred to LMA. We are sometimes called upon for symbolic amounts. The investigation of the matter may require a significant investment of time, similar to that required for more challenging and difficult situations.

[7] See https://www.economie.gouv.fr/files/files/2021/Rapport_Mediateur_assurances_professionnelles.pdf. Accessed 16 Apr 2025.

8.2.2 Personal Scope

SMEs, shopkeepers, craftsmen and other tradesmen have been able to call on us since December 2020, when an agreement was reached between the Ministry of Finance and the insurance sector at the height of the COVID-19 crisis. However, we only look at situations where a contract exists between the insurer and the insured.

Our members are insurers that are subject to the French Insurance Code and brokers who have decided to use our services. It is possible that some brokers may have chosen an alternative mediator. All our members are supervised by the French supervisory authority, the ACPR.

The ombudsperson, a competent and independent individual, has full discretion in the examination of the cases referred to them. In the course of fulfilling their duties, the ombudsperson is entitled to communicate directly with any and all insurance companies and insurance intermediaries that are members of the LMA's member organisations. The ombudsperson is responsible for issuing fully independent and reasoned opinions.

8.2.3 Territorial Scope

We examine disputes that are subject to French law. The vast majority of contracts are drafted in French, but if they are drafted in English (e.g. expatriate healthcare costs) or even another language, we also examine them.

Regardless of where the claim occurred, we look at whether or not the contract should cover it.

8.2.4 Time Limits

The work carried out by CCSF in 2021 led to changes in the regulations aimed at the financial sector.

The revised ACPR Recommendation 2022-R-01 of 9 May 2022 on the handling of complaints,[8] which amends the previous recommendation dating from November 2016, came into force on 31 December 2022.

It simplifies access to mediation by allowing consumers to complain to the ombudsperson after a period of two months after having first expressed dissatisfaction in writing without receiving a response, irrespective of the entity to which the

[8] https://acpr.banque-france.fr/sites/default/files/media/2022/05/17/20220517_recommandation_2022-r-01_traitement_reclamations.pdf. Accessed 16 Apr 2025.

dissatisfaction is addressed to (the insurer itself, a broker, a management delegate, etc.) and regardless of the claims mechanism provided for in their contract.

This represents a major change in philosophy, as we are moving away from compliance with a multi-level escalation procedure to a time limit of two months. This is a significant reduction compared with past practices for handling complaints.

Today, at LMA, we respond on average within seven months. This time frame is likely to increase due to a surge in claims. By mid-2024, we received 63% more admissible requests in the preceding 12 months than for the same period last year. It is clear to us that the reform of the complaints procedure mentioned above is key to understanding this surge: the reform enables policyholders to refer cases to the ombudsperson more quickly. We will likely reach 37,000 referrals in 2024, compared with 21,500 in 2022 (before the reform), and 15,000 in 2019.

8.3 Procedure

8.3.1 Regulatory Framework

We work within the framework of the EU ADR Directive, transposed into French law in 2015.[9] The key rules are set out in law, and we act under the supervision of the CECMC.

It is our responsibility to define the practical way of working with insurers and policyholders. We share information with other mediators to get the best ideas and use new technologies to be as efficient as possible.

8.3.2 Complaints and Enquiry Handling Process

Policyholders must express their dissatisfaction to their usual contact (insurer or broker) before contacting the ombudsperson. Complainants should also check that their insurer or broker is a member of LMA.[10]

To avoid wasting time, it is also useful to check that the case is "admissible". This means that it can be examined by the ombudsperson (see the Mediation officer's charter, available online on our website).[11]

[9] Ordonnance n°2015-1033 du 20 août 2015 relative au Règlement Extra-judiciaire des litiges de la consommation.

[10] https://formulaire.mediation-assurance.org/Societes. Accessed 16 Apr 2025.

[11] https://www.mediation-assurance.org/la-charte-du-mediateur/. Accessed 16 Apr 2025.

Once these preliminary steps have been taken, the file should be sent to the ombudsperson with a copy of the contract, a copy of the complaint dating back less than one year and longer than two months, and any response from the professional. Upon receipt of the file, LMA will conduct a more detailed "admissibility" analysis.

If this check is conclusive, the parties will be informed of the complaint's admissibility via electronic means or regular mail (art. R.612-2 of the French Consumer Code). If necessary, the LMA will ask for additional documents that may be useful to the ombudsperson in the examination of the case.

All subsequent exchanges with LMA are carried out by post or electronically.

Policyholders are provided with a claimant's section on our website to simplify the transmission of these documents.

At the request of one of the parties, all or some of the documents in the case file may be communicated by the ombudsperson (art. R.612-3 of the French Consumer Code).

In examining a case, the ombudsperson considers the documents provided by the parties involved.

Once this has been done, a "proposed solution" is sent to the policyholder and the professional (insurance company or broker) within three months of the date on which the complaint was accepted. This period may be extended in the case of complex disputes (art. R.612-5 of the French Consumer Code).

8.3.3 Admissible Complaints

8.3.3.1 Complaints

A complaint is a dissatisfaction expressed in writing by the insured to the insurer. If policyholders are not satisfied with the insurer's response, they can contact us. The subject of the dissatisfaction must, of course, relate to the insurance contract.

8.3.3.2 Lodging a Complaint

Complainants must first try to resolve their dispute with the insurer by expressing their dissatisfaction in writing. The insurer or its representative has a maximum period of two months to respond. If there is no response within this two-month period, or if the response is not satisfactory to the policyholder, they may refer the matter to us.

8.3.3.3 Claim Amount

There is no minimum amount of money that is required for a claim to be referred to the insurance ombudsperson. For disputes concerning an amount of less than EUR 5000, policyholders must go through the process with us (or a conciliation procedure) before going to court.

8.3.3.4 Complaint Dismissal

The insurance ombudsperson cannot dismiss a complaint without considering its merits. We look at all the 35,000 referrals we receive each year. Complaints are dismissed if:

- the dispute is not with the insurer (it is in fact a banking matter, for example);
- the policyholder has not tried to resolve the dispute with the insurer first;
- the policyholder's claim appears to be vexatious or fanciful (e.g. they want to be reimbursed for a penny).

8.3.4 Obtaining Information and Collecting Evidence

8.3.4.1 Written Form and Power to Obtain Information

The mediation procedure is conducted in written form. It is not our practice to convene physical meetings with consumers and insurers. Furthermore, at this stage, we do not contact the parties by telephone or by video conference.

The insurance ombudsperson has no special power to obtain documents if one of the parties sends us very little or nothing at all. In very rare cases, this leads us to determine that, in the absence of documents from both sides, we cannot examine the case.

8.3.4.2 Insurers Obligation to Provide Information

By joining our mediation service, insurers undertake to participate in mediation and to support the process by providing their arguments. Failure to do so systematically could result in exclusion. In practice, difficulties sometimes arise. We subsequently review the situation with the insurer concerned to remind it of its commitments and obligations, and to date things have always worked out.

8.3.4.3 Duty of Confidentiality

The mediation procedure is confidential. We sometimes remind insurers of this when they are reluctant to send us certain information, for example regarding fraud.

8.3.5 Insurance Ombudsman Decision

8.3.5.1 Proposal for a Solution

At the end of the mediation procedure, the ombudsperson makes a "proposal for a solution", as it is referred to in legislation—in practice, this can be called an opinion or recommendation. This proposal is accepted by insurers and brokers in 99.7% of cases.

The "proposal for a solution" is based on law or equity. The complaint may be upheld (in favour of the policyholder), partially upheld or dismissed (in favour of the professional).

In 32% of cases, our proposed solution is favourable to the insured. Hence, the position of the insurer is confirmed in 68% of cases. But note that the insurer often makes a proposal for an amicable settlement in the weeks following the referral by the insured. So much so that in more than one in two cases (53% in 2023), the insured obtains satisfaction, in whole or in part, by calling upon us.

The ombudsperson examines the case on the basis of the documents provided by the parties. Once this has been done, a "proposal for a solution" is sent to the policyholder and the professional (insurance company or broker) within three months of the date on which the case was accepted. This period may be extended in the case of complex disputes (art. R.612-5 of the French Consumer Code).

Non-binding Nature

The "proposal for a solution", established in law or in equity, may differ from a dccision that may bc madc by a judgc. It is not binding on thc partics. This proposal is final: the ombudsperson cannot respond to new requests from the parties concerning the same dispute. If the disagreement persists after our proposal, recourse to the courts remains possible.

Law and Equity

LMA is a flexible, pragmatic system that provides speedier results than court proceedings, and is free of charge for policyholders, since we are entirely financed by insurers and brokers as a result of the EU ADR Directive, which allows us to take equitable positions.

In this way, we can take the policyholder's side to "re-establish fairness" in a way that is not available to judges, who adhere to the rule of law. When we believe that the strict application of the contract leads to an absurd situation, given the circumstances of the claim, we take a position in equity. In 2023, this was the case in 4% of cases.

8.3.5.2 Cross-border Complaints

The LMA has been a member of FIN-NET network since its creation in 2001. FIN-NET is a network of national organisations responsible for the out-of-court settlement of consumers' complaints concerning financial services. The network covers the countries of the European Economic Area (EU, Iceland, Liechtenstein, Norway.[12]

When a claimant, residing in France, brings to the attention of the LMA a dispute with an insurance company governed by the law of another member state (for instance Luxemburg or Malta), LMA will forward the complaint to the competent body in the foreign country.

Conversely, LMA can deal with complaints from nationals of member countries in dispute with an insurance company governed by French law. The complaint may be submitted directly by the consumer or via the ombudsman scheme of the country concerned. Within this framework, LMA can be contacted in either French or English. The solution proposed by the insurance ombudsperson (*Médiateur de l'Assurance*) is written in French.

In practice, we have very few disputes involving cross-border issues.

8.3.5.3 Powers of Redress

The ombudsperson is not a judge. The decisions rendered by the ombudsperson are not binding on the parties, despite the fact that they are almost always respected by insurers and brokers. This includes instances where a position in equity is taken to "re-establish what is right".

To achieve this result, we have to convince the professionals of the quality of our services, by demonstrating our competence and independence. We must also demonstrate that it is in the interests of the insurance profession to use the LMA, a flexible system that is far less costly than legal action, as a means of redress.

There is no maximum limit to the amount the insurance ombudsperson can award. Generally speaking, compensation amounts range from a few hundred to a few thousand euros. Sometimes, the amount can reach several hundred thousand

[12] Cf. European Commission. About FIN-NET. https://finance.ec.europa.eu/consumer-finance-and-payments/retail-financial-services/financial-dispute-resolution-network-fin-net/about-fin-net_en. Accessed 16 Apr 2025.

euros or in exceptional cases more than one million—and such awards have always been accepted by the insurer to date.

8.3.5.4 Nature of the Decision

In our "proposal for a solution", we remind the parties that they are free to accept or refuse the proposal within one month. If the insurance company or broker refuses, its general management must inform the ombudsperson (the requirement that the company's general management inform the ombudsperson of its refusal to accept our solution is intended to ensure that this decision is not taken lightly), and provide the reasons for its refusal; if no response is received within the period specified, the proposed solution is deemed to have been accepted.

The parties are also reminded that recourse to mediation does not prevent them from taking recourse to a court of law and that the LMA solution may differ from the decision that would be taken by a judge.

The insurance ombudsperson's decision-making procedures and those of the courts are distinct. The solution proposed by the ombudsperson is confidential and, if one of the two parties refuses it, the decision cannot be presented to a judge. This limitation is regrettable.

While the decisions of the insurance ombudsperson are not published because the procedure is confidential, a ranking is published in the annual report of the insurers who have been involved in the most disputes. This must of course be put into perspective by taking into account market shares.

8.4 Statistical Data

8.4.1 Complaints Received per Year

In 2022, the proportion of admissible complaints received was 33.9%. This figure was too low, and other mediations in the banking and insurance sectors had comparable figures. This is why consumer associations called for a reform to make access to the LMA easier for consumers. This reform has been described above. Consequently, should a consumer remain unsatisfied with the response to their complaint two months after expressing their dissatisfaction to the insurer, they can refer the matter to LMA.

The reform came into force at the beginning of 2023. Following the implementation of the reform, the acceptance rate has risen to 44%. This figure may still seem low. This is due to the fact that we still receive a lot of premature complaints (policyholders refer to us without having first tried to resolve their dispute with their insurer) or irrelevant referrals (for instance, if the dispute concerns a banking issue).

8.4.2 Average Time for Dispute Resolution

By mid-2024, insureds will have received a response, on average, within seven months. This time frame is unfortunately likely to increase due to a strong surge in complaints (63% more admissible requests than for the same period in 2023), following the reform of the complaint procedure, which enables policyholders to refer cases to the ombudsperson more quickly. We will probably exceed 35,000 referrals this year.

8.4.3 Complaints Resolved per Year

In 2023, LMA made close to 5000 "proposals for a solution". In addition to such proposals, it is necessary to include amicable settlements that are "spontaneously" proposed by insurers when they learn that their policyholder has approached us. In 2023, a total of nearly 8000 cases were settled. In 2024, to maintain our response times, we would have had to produce 10,000 proposals for a solution, which is an impossible task even if we were to strongly increase our staff; hence, we regrettably expect our response times to worsen.

8.4.4 Proportion of Complaints Resolved

In 2023, 32% of the proposals for a solution formulated by LMA were, in whole or in part, favourable to the policyholder, including 4% on the grounds of fairness (decisions made in equity). If we add the "spontaneous" amicable settlements made by insurers when they learn that their policyholder has contacted us, policyholders have obtained favourable solutions, in whole or in part, in 53% of cases.

In 68% of the solutions delivered, LMA confirmed the insurer's position and helped the policyholder to understand it better by explaining why the position taken by the insurer was correct. The insurance ombudsperson then plays the role of a trusted third party, confirming to the policyholder that the contract has been correctly applied by the insurer.

8.4.5 Adherence to Proposals

In 2023, the insurance ombudsperson's proposals were adhered to by professionals (insurers or brokers) in more than 99% of cases. In the very rare cases (a dozen per annum) where an insurer does not wish to follow the proposal made by LMA, the policyholders can take their dispute to court by presenting the insurance ombudsperson's arguments to the judge (but not the proposal itself, which remains confidential).

8.5 Insurance Ombudsman Practice

8.5.1 Market Trends

8.5.1.1 Most Common Complaints

Two thirds of complaints concern property and casualty insurance. Unsurprisingly, around 30% of policyholder complaints relate to motor insurance (liability in a car accident, cover for bodily injury and property damage, etc.) and 30% concern home insurance (water damage, natural disasters, etc.). However, we are always surprised to see the importance of so-called "affinity insurance" (mobile phone insurance, travel cancellation, credit card insurance), which accounts for more than 20% of cases.

The remaining third concerns life and health insurance. Of this, 25% is for "health and provident" subjects (loan insurance, death, incapacity, disability, long-term care insurance, funeral insurance, etc.); and 8% for life insurance and retirement savings.

8.5.1.2 Highest Risk Areas of Insurance Business

In my recent experience, the biggest irritants in terms of consumer protection have been mobile phone insurance and travel cancellation insurance. Cover is very limited, and policyholders are disappointed when they discover how limited their guarantees are.

Another very important issue is to make progress on the clarity of contracts. This must include definitions of terms such as "accident", a situation of "dependence", a "break-in", which are often surprising and far removed from the language of everyday life. Clarity is also required in respect of the conditions of the guarantee or the exclusion clauses. If there is any doubt, the contract must be interpreted to the benefit of the consumer under French law.

8.5.1.3 Approach Adopted Towards Insurance Businesses

Insurance businesses generally adopt a cooperative stance when engaging with the Insurance Ombudsman Service, with the exception of a few small players. Insurers play the game: they are aware of the advantages of mediation, which is quicker, less costly and more pragmatic than going to court. When we reach the end of the dispute and draft up a "proposed solution", we confirm the insurers' position in 68% of cases (in 2023).

8.5.2 *Limitations*

8.5.2.1 Legal and Institutional Limitations

In terms of the framework, there are two constraints: financial constraints and independence. The former is an issue given the sharp increase in complaints (more than 35,000 over the last 12 months), it is necessary to obtain approval from the Board of Directors for the human and financial resources required. This is a normal process, common to all organisations, which requires us to document and prove the need for additional resources.

In 2023, the CECMC issued a press release in the summer, calling on each profession to provide the ombudsperson with sufficient resources to carry out their work.

As previously stated, our services are provided free of charge to consumers, and we do not receive any subsidies from the government. Therefore, we depend entirely on the resources provided by the insurance industry. Our budget for 2024 is close to EUR 11 million.

The second constraint concerns independence. The ombudsperson's term of office is three years, which seems a little short to plan for the future, both in terms of the organisation of LMA and the substance of the issues, even if the mandate is renewable without limit.

8.5.2.2 Consumer Financial Awareness and Literacy

With regard to consumers' financial awareness and literacy, the level unfortunately does not appear to be improving over time. Thanks to the Internet, however, information is much more readily available so that policyholders understand how a contract works and know how to assert their rights. Information is provided by public authorities, consumer associations, by LMA, and of course by the professionals themselves.

Nevertheless, there is still a great deal of ignorance about how an insurance contract works, about the general principles of law, and there are many problems in understanding the vocabulary ("deductible", "waiting period", the definition of disability, what is an "accident" and so on).

It is difficult to determine where there has been an improvement over time. People often believe that all insurance contracts are the same and that it is a waste of time to scrutinise them, but it is of course necessary to invest time to understand the contract and check if it suits the customer's needs.

8.5.3 *De lege ferenda Postulates*

To improve the effectiveness of the existing Ombudsman Scheme, one key suggestion would be to strengthen the ombudsperson's independence. Firstly, we are totally financially dependent on the professional sector in which we operate. Access to our services is free for policyholders, and we receive no public subsidies.

Secondly, in the process of nominating an ombudsperson, it is the professional sector that proposes a name, which the CECMC then approves or rejects.

This creates a delicate situation for the ombudsperson, who is required by law to be neutral, impartial, independent. At the same time, they are dependent on the professional sector to obtain the human and financial resources necessary to carry out their mission; and for their possible renewal.

8.6 Other

8.6.1 Accessibility

8.6.1.1 Informing Consumers

Our website, which was updated in 2021, has improved our visibility and accessibility.[13] It presents our missions and activities. As at mid-2024, more than 60% of all complaints to us are now made online, compared with only a third four years ago. In March 2021, we also created a LinkedIn page, which now has more than 10,000 followers.[14] On his personal LinkedIn page, the Ombudsman only posts about his professional practice as *médiateur* and has more than 18,000 followers.

In early 2022, we created a "claimant space" on our website. Policyholders can use it to submit the documents we need to investigate their case. We offer a range of educational materials on how mediation works, the mechanisms of insurance contracts and the legal rules that govern them. Each year, we publish around thirty case studies, as well as two "*Cahiers de la Médiation*", which present technical subjects in greater detail, and short educational videos.

Finally, we publish an annual report that reviews developments over the preceding year and includes all of our case studies—this is combined with holding a press conference to provide visibility and to deliver our messages. Journalists often ask when the annual report will be published in order to allow them to prepare for its publication.

8.6.1.2 Barriers to Access

There do not appear to be significant barriers to accessing LMA. Our services are free of charge for the consumer and can be accessed via the Internet (more than 60% of cases today).

Nevertheless, we are well aware that the consumers who turn to us are often those who have the energy to do so, and often have the financial or legal knowledge to doubt the insurer's position.

[13] See https://www.mediation-assurance.org/. Accessed 16 Apr 2025.

[14] See https://fr.linkedin.com/company/la-mediation-de-l-assurance. Accessed 16 Apr 2025.

8.6.1.3 Insurers' Obligation to Provide Information

It should also be noted that the ACPR recommendation on complaints handling (Recommendation 2022-R-01 of 9 May 2022), which came into force on 1 January 2023, applies to various financial professionals including insurance companies and credit institutions. This recommendation emphasises the importance of customer protection and proposes best practices for efficient, transparent, and harmonised complaint management. It obliges insurers, when responding to a complaint, to indicate that in the event of persistent disagreement, the policyholder may refer the matter to LMA. Our website and address are provided in this reply letter.

The recommendation stipulates that response times should not exceed two months and emphasises the need for clear and accessible information on complaint and mediation procedures. It also requires professionals to train employees in identifying and processing complaints, record and monitor complaints, analyse the quality of the handling system, and submit annual reports to governance bodies. Importantly, the recommendation defines complaints as expressions of dissatisfaction towards a professional, which can be made by anyone, even without a contractual relationship, while noting that requests for service or information are not considered complaints.

8.6.2 Accountability

8.6.2.1 Reporting

The ombudsperson is accountable to the CECMC. As a rule, a hearing is held once a year to review the LMA's activities. In addition, LMA's Board of Directors convenes on a quarterly basis (or more frequently if so required due to current events and activities) to monitor developments and take any necessary decisions, for instance about the need to augment resources. It is only the ombudsperson who receives renumeration during the course of their term of office; Board members perform their role pro bono.

8.6.2.2 Publications

The insurance ombudsperson releases various publications throughout the year:

- a case study is published every 15 days on the website and LinkedIn page,
- a *Cahier de la Médiation* on a particular theme, is published two or three times a year,
- Motions, a new format (short videos combining animation and voice-over) and an educational tool for policyholders, are released
- an annual report is published at the end of August.

In the annual report, which is available free of charge on our website, the ombudsperson shares their findings and recommendations for improvement. For example, in last year's report, the lack of confidence in the experts sent by insurers, the problems of vocabulary misunderstood by policyholders and the need to respect the decisions of the High Court were highlighted.

The rankings of our main financiers, who are also the insurers with the highest number of disputes arising, are published, with a distinction made between property and casualty insurance and life and health insurance.

Each year, the ombudsperson prepares a report, the contents of which are made available to the public. The ombudsperson is frequently invited to present their activities at external events.

8.6.2.3 Budget Approval

With regard to the budget, it is first approved by the LMA Board of Directors, then validated by the General Assembly of the Association's members.

The General Meeting is convened once a year by the Chairman of the Board of Directors by simple letter or by email sent to each member at least 20 days in advance, to approve the annual accounts, the criteria for determining the contributions due by the members, and the arrangements for their collection.

The General Assembly is composed of all the institutional members and all the members of LMA. Each member has one vote, and the decisions are made by a two-thirds majority of the members present or represented.

Legal Sources

Code de la consommation. https://www.legifrance.gouv.fr/codes/texte_lc/LEGITEXT000006069565/

Code des assurances. https://www.legifrance.gouv.fr/codes/texte_lc/LEGITEXT000006073984/

Directive 2013/11/EU of the European Parliament and of the Council of 21 May 2013 on alternative dispute resolution for consumer disputes and amending Regulation (EC) No 2006/2004 and Directive 2009/22/EC (Directive on consumer ADR) [2013] OJ L165/63

Ordonnance n°2015-1033 du 20 août 2015 relative au Règlement Extra-judiciaire des litiges de la consommation. https://www.legifrance.gouv.fr/loda/id/JORFTEXT000031070940

Chapter 9
Germany

The Insurance Ombudsman Scheme

Wilhelm Schluckebier and Constantin Graf von Rex

9.1 Institutional Framework

9.1.1 Establishment

The activity of the *Versicherungsombudsmann e. V.* (Insurance Ombudsman Association) began in 2001,[1] the year in which the Association was founded. As a registered association, it is a legal entity and therefore has legal capacity. This means that the Association is its own organisation and is institutionally independent.

With the establishment of the *Versicherungsombudsmann e. V.*, the insurance industry took up and implemented two ideas that are increasingly gaining attention in today's society. The first is consumer protection. In the event of a dispute about an insurance contract, insured consumers should be able to clarify the legal situation without the risk of incurring costs. The second is to enable insurers to clarify differing opinions with their customers objectively and without further straining the customer relationship.

The existence of the *Versicherungsombudsmann e. V.* gives complainants the opportunity to have the decisions of their contractual partners reviewed by an independent and neutral body with legal expertise. The same standard applies here as

[1] Versicherungsombudsmann e. V. (2001) Presseinformation vom 25.09.2001: Ombudsmann nimmt ab 1. Oktober 2001 Kundenbeschwerden entgegen. https://www.versicherungsombudsmann.de/pressemitteilung/ombudsmann-nimmt-ab-1-oktober-2001-kundenbeschwerden-entgegen. Accessed 16 Apr 2025; see also Schluckebier (2020), p. 2.

W. Schluckebier · C. Graf von Rex (✉)
Versicherungsombudsmann e. V., Berlin, Germany
e-mail: info@versicherungsombudsmann.de; v.Rex@versicherungsombudsmann.de

H. Heiss et al. (eds.), *Insurance Ombudsman Schemes*, AIDA Europe Research Series on Insurance Law and Regulation 15,
https://doi.org/10.1007/978-3-032-01500-6_9

before a state court, namely the rule of law. Experience has shown that, given the large number of processes involved in processing contracts and services, incorrect decisions by insurers are difficult to avoid. They can be corrected quickly, reliably and in accordance with the legal system. However, should the insurer's decision be upheld, the result will be justified in plain language and explained to the complainant. If the positions of both parties are justified, the ombudsperson's neutrality may encourage an appropriate compromise. With its pacifying elements, the ombudsman procedure can help to ensure that the complainant stays with the company as a customer.

When designing the rules of procedure, the insurance industry has taken great care to ensure that the ombudsman procedure is aligned with the interests and possible claims of customers. For complainants, the procedure is free of charge and can be undertaken without legal assistance. The ombudsperson can also help to enforce justified claims, because decisions against insurers are binding for complaints with a value of up to EUR 10,000.

With the Ombudsman Scheme, the members of the Insurance Ombudsman Association voluntarily created a neutral authority with far-reaching powers on the basis of private law. By joining the Association, insurance companies agree to participate in the arbitration procedure, acknowledge the ombudsperson's rules of procedure as binding and submit to the ombudsperson's determination claims with a value of up to EUR 10,000. This allows the ombudsperson to oblige the insurer to pay.

In 2007, the *Versicherungsombudsmann e. V.* was assigned its tasks on a legal basis. The Federal Ministry of Justice has recognised the Association as an arbitration board for the out-of-court settlement of disputes between insurance brokers and policyholders in connection with the brokerage of insurance contracts. In August 2016, the state granted the *Versicherungsombudsmann e. V.* the status of a consumer arbitration board in accordance with the recently created Consumer Dispute Settlement Act (hereinafter VSBG).[2]

Versicherungsombudsmann e. V. is the Arbitration Board. In accordance with the *Versicherungsombudsmann e. V.*'s Articles of Association, the German Insurance Association (hereinafter GDV) and its member companies may join the *Versicherungsombudsmann e. V.*

The Arbitration Board also carries out other tasks assigned to it by the legislature. Since 2007, the *Versicherungsombudsmann e. V.* has been legally obliged to handle complaints regarding insurance contracts concluded by means of distance selling between a consumer and a member company. This task is governed by § 214(1)(1) of the Insurance Contract Act (hereinafter VVG).[3]

The Arbitration Board is empowered to conduct and confirm a conciliation attempt, as provided for under § 15a of the Introductory Act to the Code of Civil

[2] *Verbraucherstreitbeilegungsgesetz (VSBG) vom 19. Februar 2016*, BGBl. I S. 254, 1039, as amended. https://www.gesetze-im-internet.de/vsbg. Accessed 16 Apr 2025.

[3] *Versicherungsvertragsgesetz (VVG) vom 23. November 2007*, BGBl. I S. 2631, as amended. https://www.gesetze-im-internet.de/vvg_2008. Accessed 16 Apr 2025.

Procedure (EGZPO).[4] In certain cases, the admissibility of a lawsuit is contingent upon the completion of such conciliation proceedings. In this capacity, the Arbitration Board is equivalent to a state conciliation board.

A further task that has been assigned by the legislature concerns the procedure for bringing complaints against insurance intermediaries in accordance with § 214(1)(2) VVG. The *Versicherungsombudsmann e. V.* is recognised as an arbitration board for the out-of-court settlement of disputes arising between insurance intermediaries or insurance advisors and policyholders in connection with the procurement of insurance contracts. In this regard, the General Assembly of the *Versicherungsombudsmann e. V.* adopted Rules of Procedure for Complaints against Insurance Intermediaries (VermVO)[5] subsequent to a prior decision by the Advisory Board. A separate set of procedural rules was deemed necessary due to the significant divergence in design between the procedure in question and the complaints procedure offered by the member companies to their customers.

The member companies meet at least once a year and determine the basic affairs of the Insurance Ombudsman Association at the General Meeting. The responsibilities of the General Meeting include the determination of the budget, the approval of the annual accounts, and the election of the members of the Board as well as the members' representatives to the Advisory Board. The General Assembly, in conjunction with the Advisory Board, is responsible for the appointment of the ombudsperson and for amending the rules of procedure. It is the head of the Association and constitutes one of its bodies, along with the Board of Directors.

The Board of Directors is responsible for all matters pertaining to the *Versicherungsombudsmann e. V.*, unless such matters are assigned in the Articles of Association to another body, namely the advisory council or the executive director. The Executive Board is responsible for a number of key tasks, including the external representation of the Association, the nomination of candidates for the position of the ombudsperson and the preparation of the General Meeting and the economic plan.

The Executive Board consists of a minimum of five and a maximum of eleven individuals. These individuals hold their positions on an honorary basis and, at the time of their election, must belong to the executive body of a member company, for example, its executive board or supervisory board. The members of the Executive Board are elected at the General Meeting for a period of four years. The Executive Board appoints the Chairperson from among its members.

The remit of the insurance ombudsperson covers all of the private insurance industry sectors in which insurance contracts may be concluded by consumers, with the exception of health and long-term care insurance. It does not extend to other financial sectors.

---

[4] *Gesetz betreffend die Einführung der Zivilprozeßordnung (EGZPO)*, Gesetz vom 30.01.1877, RGBl. S. 244, as amended. https://dejure.org/gesetze/EGZPO. Accessed 16 Apr 2025.

[5] Verfahrensordnung für Beschwerden im Zusammenhang mit der Vermittlung von Versicherungsverträgen (VermVO) im Sinne von § 214 Abs. 1 Nr. 2 VVG. https://www.versicherungsombudsmann.de/wp-content/uploads/vermvo.pdf. Accessed 16 Apr 2025.

It is not mandatory for insurance companies to become affiliated with the *Versicherungsombudsmann e. V.*, which serves as the Arbitration Board.

9.1.2 Governance Model

The *Versicherungsombudsmann e. V.* is an independent, recognised consumer arbitration board that provides free services to consumers and has the legal form of a registered association. Despite its founding by large parts of the insurance industry and the GDV, the Insurance Ombudsman Association maintains its independence. The Association's committees appoint an ombudsperson for a term of five years. This process is supported by the Association's office and its employees.

9.1.3 Coverage

Over 300 insurance companies and the GDV are members of the *Versicherungsombudsmann e. V.* In other words, more than 90 percent of insurance companies offering insurance contracts in the Federal Republic of Germany are subject to the arbitration service provided by the Insurance Ombudsman Association.

9.1.4 Insurance Businesses Covered

With the exception of health and long-term care insurance, any branches of the private insurance industry in which consumers can conclude insurance contracts fall within the jurisdiction of the Insurance Ombudsman Association. This means that the *Versicherungsombudsmann e. V.* can deal with disputes concerning legal protection, life insurance, occupational disability insurance, motor vehicle third party liability insurance, motor vehicle comprehensive insurance, liability insurance, accident insurance, buildings insurance, travel insurance, household contents insurance, mortgage insurance and other types of insurance. A distinct ombudsman service is responsible for matters pertaining to private nursing and health insurance. In the event that the *Versicherungsombudsmann e. V.* receives a dispute that falls under the remit of the Ombudsman Service responsible for private nursing and health insurance, the complainant will be informed of the relevant consumer dispute resolution body.

9.1.5 Appointment of the Ombudsperson

In order to be elected to the office of ombudsperson, a person must meet a number of special requirements. It is essential that the ombudsperson be independent both personally and institutionally, and that they display neutrality in order to fulfil the task for which they have been elected. Only if both parties to the procedure acknowledge the professional competence and personal integrity of the ombudsperson will they entrust them with solving their insurance problems, accept their arbitration proposals and, last but not least, accept the decisions and recommendations.

It is of the utmost importance that the individual in question should be able to demonstrate the requisite qualifications for judicial office and possess a particular degree of experience in matters pertaining to insurance. It is imperative that the person in question has not been employed on a full-time basis by an insurance company for a period of three years prior to assuming the aforementioned position. In light of the extension of duties pertaining to complaints regarding intermediaries, this criterion also encompasses previous work as an insurance intermediary or as a consultant.

The neutrality of the ombudsperson is guaranteed by virtue of their independent position. The ombudsperson is not an employee of the Insurance Ombudsman Association; rather, they have full discretion with regard to their decisions, procedures and official conduct within the framework of the rules of procedure. They are not subject to any instructions. In their capacity as ombudsperson, they operate with the same level of independence as a judge. There is also a similarity with regard to the decision-making framework used by the ombudsperson, which is based on the law. From a professional standpoint, they hold the authority to give instructions to the employees of the Arbitration Board.

The ombudsperson is appointed at the recommendation of the Association's Board of Directors and by resolution of the General Assembly and the Advisory Board.

The ombudsperson's term of office is a maximum of five years. Re-election is possible only once.

In the event of manifest and serious misconduct, the ombudsperson can only be dismissed prematurely by a two-thirds majority of the Advisory Board.

9.1.6 Funding

The *Versicherungsombudsmann e. V.* is funded by its members. An annual contribution is levied on a pay-as-you-go basis. The amount of the contribution is determined by the financial requirements as they result from the economic plan approved at the General Meeting. This levy is distributed among all members of the Insurance Ombudsman Association, with the amount of each member's contribution depending on the ratio of the gross annual contribution income of all member companies. In addition, the member insurance companies pay a case fee for admissible complaints. The *Versicherungsombudsmann e. V.* is not funded by the state or by any financial supervisory authority.

Filing complaints is free of charge for complainants. Insurance companies pay a case fee for admissible complaints in accordance with the Rules of Procedure for Insurance Companies (VomVO).[6] The members of the Insurance Ombudsman Association finance the work of the Arbitration Board. This funding comes from membership fees and case fees for processed complaints. Case lump sums are charged for complaints filed against the companies. For complaints that are admissible under the Rules of Procedure (VomVO), a flat-rate case fee is charged at the end of the procedure. It does not matter whether the complaint was legally justified or not. This is provided for in the Articles of Association. Case fees are also subject to a cost regulation. There are no free cases per year offered to the members of the Association.

Complaints to insurance intermediaries are free of charge for the intermediaries.

9.1.7 Insurance Ombudsman Functions

The Arbitration Board allows complainants to have the decisions taken by their contractual partner reviewed by an independent and neutral body. As with a state court, the review is based on principles of law and justice. In this way, incorrect decisions, which experience shows, are almost inevitable given the large number of procedures involved in the processing of contracts and benefits, can be avoided. They can be corrected quickly, reliably and in accordance with the legal system. However, if the insurer's decision is upheld, the outcome will be justified and explained to the complainant in plain language. If the positions of both parties are well-founded, the ombudsperson's neutrality may encourage an appropriate compromise. Consequently, the pacifying elements of the ombudsman procedure can assist in retaining the complainant as a customer of the company.

In the event that clarification is required, the role of the Insurance Ombudsman Service is to explain to consumers the content of the contract and the ensuing rights and obligations. This can prove challenging in the context of insurance contracts. This has the effect of providing the customer with information relevant to the particular circumstances of their cases.

The Insurance Ombudsman Association's website publishes a selection of anonymised decisions, which are accessible to the general public.[7] This enables the parties involved in the proceedings to modify their expectations regarding the potential outcome in accordance with the legal reality at an early stage. Furthermore,

---

[6] *Verfahrensordnung des Versicherungsombudsmann e. V. (VomVO).* https://www.versicherungsombudsmann.de/wp-content/uploads/2017/05/verfahrensordnung.pdf. Accessed 16 Apr 2025.

[7] https://www.versicherungsombudsmann.de/entscheidungssuche/. Accessed 16 Apr 2025.

it permits potential complainants to study the assessment of a comparable case and determine whether they want to file a complaint at all.

For obvious reasons, there is no repetition of similar cases, hence the published decisions are not representative of the most common issues dealt with by the ombudsperson.

A close exchange is maintained with the member companies. When necessary, representatives of the *Versicherungsombudsmann e. V.* and representatives of a member company convene (for the most part, virtually) to hold a meeting.

The ombudsperson and the Managing Director of the *Versicherungsombudsmann e. V.* also take every opportunity to give presentations about the Association and the insurance ombudsman procedures. This is done with the aim of informing either the interested public or representatives of the insurance industry and to be available for questions.

9.1.8 Insurance Ombudsman Office

Complaints are processed in two distinct units of the Insurance Ombudsman Association: in the service centre and in the legal department. In the service centre of the Insurance Ombudsman Office, insurance clerks are responsible for the receipt and processing of complaints. The employees receive the conciliation applications and enter the information into the Association's IT system. They assist consumers in formulating the objective of the complaint and in compiling the documents necessary for the procedure. Furthermore, they ascertain the admissibility of the complaint in accordance with the procedural regulations and inform the complainants if the matter falls outside the remit of the ombudsperson's duties.

In the legal department, fully qualified legal experts, namely legal advisors, support the ombudsperson in the assessment of complaints. They examine whether the complainants' concerns fall within the ombudsperson's jurisdiction, conduct the legal correspondence, explore settlement options and in consultation with and on behalf of the ombudsperson, determine whether the individual complaint is justified. The legal experts are assigned to different insurance sectors.

The *Versicherungsombudsmann e. V.* employs additional staff in the office, specifically in the fields of administration, business organisation and information technology.

A total of 14 insurance clerks are employed within the service centre. More than 20 fully qualified legal experts work in the Association's legal department.

Employees in each of the Association's departments participate in different training programmes every year, with the objective of maintaining the highest possible standards of qualification among its members. For example, all members of the legal department engage in an annual exchange with university professors and/or judges from the field of insurance law.

9.2 Insurance Ombudsman Jurisdiction

9.2.1 Substantive Scope

Any branches of the private insurance industry in which consumers can conclude insurance contracts fall within the jurisdiction of the insurance ombudsperson, with the exception of health and long-term care insurance. Insofar as a complaint is related to the consumer status of an insurance customer, said customer is entitled to use the conciliation body. The services provided by the Ombudsman Office makes it possible for consumers to settle disagreements without the risk of incurring costs.

An ombudsman procedure is not initiated in the event that:[8]

the complaint's value exceeds EUR 100,000;
the complaint is related to a health or long-term care insurance contract;
a consumer arbitration board has already carried out a procedure to settle the dispute or the dispute is pending with another consumer arbitration board;
a court has already made a substantive decision on the dispute, or the dispute is pending before a court;
the complaint clearly has no prospect of success or appears vexatious, in particular in the event that the claim is already statute-barred at the time the application is made, and the respondent invokes the statute of limitations;
the dispute has already been settled or an application for legal aid has already been rejected because the intended legal action does not offer sufficient prospects of success or appears vexatious.

Matters pertaining to commercial decisions fall outside the remit of the *Versicherungsombudsmann e. V.* The initiation of proceedings requires that the complaint concerns a separate claim arising from an insurance contract, a contract that has a close economic connection with an insurance contract, a real estate credit contract, the mediation or the initiation of such a contract, or that the subject matter of the complaint is the existence of such a contract.

The ombudsperson can be called upon by consumers. Under the German Civil Code, a consumer is any natural person who enters into a legal transaction for purposes that are predominantly neither commercial nor self-employed.

If small entrepreneurs or freelancers are in a "consumer-like situation", they may also receive assistance from the ombudsperson. The specific economic activity (type and scope) concerned, the insurance contract and the claim made are of crucial importance in this regard.

For disputed claims to fall within the insurance ombudsperson remit, they must arise from an insurance contract that has been concluded with a company that is a member of the *Versicherungsombudsmann e. V.* Furthermore, the complaint must be

[8] *Satzung des Vereins Versicherungsombudsmann e. V.* https://www.versicherungsombudsmann.de/wp-content/uploads/SATZUNG.pdf. Accessed 16 Apr 2025.

admissible at each stage of the procedure in accordance with the Rules of Procedure. There is no minimum amount for claims that can be referred to the ombudsperson.

In order for the procedure to be conducted, it is necessary for the complainant to have first filed their claim with their insurer and for the insurer to have rejected their claim.

Claims are subject to the statute of limitations set out in the German Civil Code. In the event that the statute of limitations has elapsed and is invoked by the respondent, the insurance ombudsperson will refrain from taking action.

9.2.2 Personal Scope

The Insurance Ombudsman can be called upon by consumers. Pursuant to the German Civil Code (§ 13 BGB), a consumer is defined as any natural person who enters into a legal transaction for purposes that are predominantly outside their trade, business or profession. The insurance ombudsperson can deal with complaints from other persons who are in a situation similar to that of a consumer. The economic activity (type and scope) in question, along with the insurance contract and the asserted claim, are determining factors. In the absence of a claim from the complainant directed towards the respondent, the insurance ombudsperson will be unable to continue with the proceedings. Once a claim has been asserted, the respondent can apply for the proceedings to be suspended if no more than six weeks have elapsed since the initial assertion and the respondent has neither recognised nor rejected the claim during that period.[9]

9.2.3 Territorial Scope

The territorial scope of the insurance ombudsperson's jurisdiction covers complaints about activities of insurance companies that are members of the *Versicherungsombudsmann e. V.* Furthermore, the insurance contracts concluded with consumers must be governed by German law. There are no jurisdictional restrictions with regard to the residence of a complainant. The language of the proceedings is German.

---

[9] See *Verfahrensordnung des Versicherungsombudsmann e. V. (VomVO)*. https://www.versicherungsombudsmann.de/das-schlichtungsverfahren/verfahrensordnungen/vomvo/. Accessed 16 Apr 2025.

9.2.4 *Time Limits*

In cases where an appeal lacks the prospect of success or appears to be vexatious, and especially in instances where the claim in question was already time-barred at the time of filing it, no proceedings will be held before the insurance ombudsperson.

In the event that the value of the complaint exceeds the amount of EUR 100,000, the principles set forth in the Code of Civil Procedure (ZPO)[10] regarding the amount in dispute shall be used to determine the value. In the instance of a disclosed partial complaint, the recognisable total value shall be taken into account. Furthermore, proceedings before the ombudsperson shall not be initiated.

The insurance ombudsperson is not responsible for complaints pertaining to claims arising from a health or long-term care insurance contract. Furthermore, the ombudsperson is not empowered to intervene if a consumer arbitration board has already conducted proceedings to settle the dispute or the dispute is pending before another consumer arbitration board. The same applies where a court has already made a decision on the merits of the dispute or the dispute is pending before a court, unless the court orders the suspension of the proceedings in accordance with § 278a(2) ZPO with regard to the proceedings before the consumer arbitration board. Finally, the ombudsperson does not have jurisdiction in instances where the dispute has already been settled or an application for legal aid for the dispute has already been rejected on the grounds that the intended legal action lacks sufficient prospect of success or appears to be unreasonable.[11]

9.3 Procedure

9.3.1 *Regulatory Framework*

Depending on whether the procedure is directed against an insurance company or against a broker of insurance contracts, either the Rules of Procedure for Complaints in Connection with the Brokerage of Insurance Contracts (VermVO) or the Rules of Procedure of the Insurance Ombudsman (VomVO) apply. In addition, the rules of the Consumer Dispute Settlement Act (VSBG) apply.

As stated in the Articles of Association,[12] the aim of the complaints procedure is to settle disputes out of court, and further details shall be governed by Rules of Procedure. The Executive Board, Advisory Council and General Assembly were

---

[10] *Zivilprozessordnung (ZPO).* https://www.gesetze-im-internet.de/zpo/. Accessed 16 Apr 2025.

[11] *Verfahrensordnung des Versicherungsombudsmann e. V. (VomVO).* https://www.versicherungsombudsmann.de/das-schlichtungsverfahren/verfahrensordnungen/vomvo. Accessed 16 Apr 2025.

[12] *Satzung des Vereins Versicherungsombudsmann e. V.* https://www.versicherungsombudsmann.de/wp-content/uploads/SATZUNG.pdf. Accessed 16 Apr 2025.

involved in the drafting of the two procedural rules and continue to be so in the event of any amendments.

9.3.2 Complaint and Enquiry

The procedure begins with an appeal to the *Versicherungsombudsmann e. V.*, which may be made verbally, in writing, or in any other appropriate format. The employees in the service centre acknowledge receipt of the complaint to the complainant. If necessary, they assist the complainant in specifying the objective of the complaint. Furthermore, the complainant is informed which documents still have to be submitted. At each stage of the procedure, the personnel of the service centre verify the admissibility of the complaint.

The complaint is forwarded from the service centre to the respondent (the insurance company and/or insurance intermediary) for the provision of a statement.

As soon as the respondent's statement is available, it will be forwarded to the complainant for information and, if necessary, comment. Once the file is complete and the facts are verifiable, the file is handed over to the legal department. There, the matters of the complaint are examined, and the decision is taken. In the case of complaints that are either fully or partially justified, we ask the member company for (partial) redress. In instances where this is granted, no decision is made. In instances where complex, difficult-to-clarify factual questions or fundamentally important legal questions that have not yet been decided by the courts arise, we do not resolve the complaint but can make a settlement proposal (arbitration proposal).

According to certain submission criteria, the decision must be submitted to the ombudsperson by the respective colleague from the legal department.

Given that the processing of complaints is governed by two sets of procedures, it can be classified as a formal procedure.

No proceedings are initiated *ex officio* by the ombudsperson. The insurance ombudsperson will only act upon request.

The procedural rules for complaints procedures against insurance companies do not allow for collective appeals by multiple policyholders.

In the event of complaints against insurance intermediaries, the procedural rules provide for the right of consumer protection organisations to lodge complaints.

The submission of a complaint to the insurance ombudsperson interrupts the limitation period for bringing a claim to court.

Enquiries about the status of the complaint will be answered by the department in which the complaint is currently being processed (service centre or legal department). Further enquiries can be made verbally or by any other means of communication (via fax, email, letter or the Insurance Ombudsman Association's website).

9.3.3 Admissible Complaints

The Rules of Procedure set out which complaints are admissible. Firstly, the complaints must be submitted by a consumer or at least by an entrepreneur in a consumer-like position.

The Rules of Procedure for complaints against insurance intermediaries do not impose this restriction.

The fundamental requirement for conducting the proceedings is the unsuccessful filing of a claim by the complainant with the respondent (insurance company or intermediary).

Insurance companies and insurance intermediaries are required to promptly attend to the claims notifications of their policyholders. Nevertheless, the general workload must be taken into account. In principle, any claims submitted are subject to the standard limitation period set forth in German law.

There is not a minimum amount for which claims can be referred to the insurance ombudsperson; a claim may, however, not exceed EUR 100,000.

For amounts up to EUR 10,000, the ombudsperson can issue a decision that is binding on insurance companies. In cases where the amount in question falls between EUR 10,000.01 and EUR 100,000, the Insurance Ombudsman can issue a recommendation. In cases where the sum exceeds EUR 100,000, the ombudsperson is no longer competent.

There is no limit set on the value of complaints against insurance intermediaries, however the ombudsperson is only in a position to make recommendations where intermediaries are concerned.

The proceedings shall be terminated if the complainant does not pursue the matter further. This may occur if a complainant does not take up the matter despite being given a deadline. Should the complainant come forward at a later date, the proceedings may be reopened.

9.3.4 Obtaining Information and Collecting Evidence

The parties to the proceedings shall be given the right to be heard and to present facts and assessments. The ombudsperson can investigate the facts of the case *ex officio*, provided that this is necessary for the decision-making process. The ombudsperson is independent in their assessment of the evidence. They do not gather any evidence other than documentary evidence. The proceedings before the insurance ombudsperson are purely documentary proceedings. The facts of the case and all documents relevant to the case and thus to the damage must be available or presented in paper or written form. Witness or expert evidence is reserved for court proceedings.

The procedural rules established by the *Versicherungsombudsmann e. V.* provide that the complainant should make a clear and unambiguous request and communicate any facts appropriate and necessary for the assessment of the case. In addition, the complainant is obliged to enclose or attach the necessary documents. The complainant is assisted in this process by the colleagues from the service centre. Should further clarification be required, the ombudsperson may contact the respondent to obtain the necessary information.

If the insurance companies fail to provide any documents and/or otherwise respond, the ombudsperson can make a decision based solely on the information provided in the submission, provided that the complainant's submission is conclusive.

The proceedings do not automatically suspend any confidentiality obligations of the parties to the proceedings vis-à-vis third parties.

If, for example, highly personal health data have to be part of the procedure, the individual whose personal data is concerned must explicitly and in writing release the respective doctor from the obligation of medical confidentiality.

9.3.5 Outcome of the Process

The ombudsperson will reject inadmissible complaints and state the reasons for the decision.

If applicants withdraw their application or object to the further course of the procedure, the proceedings end when the ombudsperson receives their statement.

In the event that the complaint is not suitable for conciliation, conciliation is unsuccessful or the dispute cannot be settled otherwise, the ombudsperson shall decide on the complaint. If the complaint is worth up to EUR 10,000, the ombudsperson will issue a decision. In instances where the monetary value of the complaint exceeds EUR 10,000 but does not surpass EUR 100,000, the ombudsperson will issue a recommendation.

The refusal to proceed, the decision and the recommendation shall be communicated in writing, accompanied by an explanation of the reasons. If the dispute is resolved (remedy, settlement) or if the proceedings end by dismissal, due to a refusal to proceed or with the issuance of a decision on the complaint, the ombudsperson will inform the parties to the proceedings accordingly. Termination takes effect when the complainant takes note of the final statement, at the latest three days after it has been sent.

Mediation proposals are sent to the parties involved in the proceedings in written form. It also furnishes the parties with information regarding the legal consequences of accepting such a proposal. It is also communicated that the decision may differ from that of a court. Furthermore, it is indicated that, should the proposal not be accepted, an appeal can be made to ordinary courts.

A procedure that has been concluded may be resumed where it is justified in individual cases at the discretion of the ombudsperson if there is a new factual information or the legal situation changes.

There are three different types of decisions made by the insurance ombudsperson: a refusal to conduct proceedings, a decision and a recommendation.

A decision to reject a complaint on the grounds of inadmissibility has binding effect on the complainant. A decision rendered by the ombudsperson for sums up to an amount of EUR 10,000 is binding on both parties involved in the proceedings, provided that the insurance company's obligation was expressly stated in the decision.

A consumer still has the option to take their complaint to state courts in Germany.

The insurance companies have voluntarily joined the *Versicherungsombudsmann e. V.* This entails the acceptance of the Rules of Procedure, which consequently entails the automatic acceptance of the ombudsperson's decisions and their implementation.

The ombudsperson is bound by the law in their decisions. They base their decisions on the two Rules of Procedure (VomVO and VermVO) and the Consumer Dispute Settlement Act (VSBG).

The proceedings are subject to German law and are conducted in German. In case of a claim arising from an insurance contract based on a legal system other than German, the German insurance ombudsperson will have no jurisdiction. In such cases, the complainant is advised to contact the insurance ombudsperson of the country whose legal system applies to the insurance contract.

Individual powers of appeal do not exist in the process.

The decisions made by the *Versicherungsombudsmann e. V.* are not subject to the judicial review by courts.

9.4 Statistical Data

The Insurance Ombudsman Association receives an average of between 16,000 and 18,000 complaints over the course of a year. On average over 80 % of these complaints are found to be admissible.

The average time required by the *Versicherungsombudsmann e. V.* to conclude a complaint is 2.3 months (equivalent to 70 days). The success rate in life insurance is 34%, while in all other lines of insurance, it is 48%. In the case of life insurance, the ratio of complaints decided in favour of the insurance company is 66%. In all other lines of insurance, this figure is 52%. Decisions that are binding on insurance companies are adhered to 100% of the time. With regard to the recommendations, there is a lack of reliable data.

9.5 Insurance Ombudsman Practice

9.5.1 Market Trends

The sector with the highest number of complaints is currently that of life insurance. Prior to this, it was legal expenses insurance for a long time. This is followed by automobile insurance, which has a lower number of complaints but a consistently high volume over the years. There is no particular insurance product that is the subject of most complaints.

In principle, all member companies of the *Versicherungsombudsmann e. V.* are interested in a long and mutually successful insurance contract relationship with consumers. If they are unable to resolve disputes, they are happy to refer their policyholders to the Insurance Ombudsman Association as a means of settling disputes out of court. Insurance companies are voluntary members of the *Versicherungsombudsmann e. V.* Consequently, they actively follow all of the proceedings that take place and are open and positive towards the idea of mediation.

At the time of writing, no limitations can be identified that result from the legal and/or institutional framework of the Insurance Ombudsman Scheme that hinder the effective functioning of the Association. If this were the case, the procedural rules would be adapted in order to ensure the smooth running of the procedure. The only limitations to our procedure are matters that have not yet been decided by the highest court.

We have a relatively constant number of incoming complaints. Therefore, it can be stated that consumers are in part well informed and aware of their rights. Nevertheless, this does not allow us to conclude that consumers are better financially informed. No discernible changes are evident at this time. It would appear that there is still scope for improvement in terms of consumer awareness of the institution of Insurance Ombudsman.

In any printed matter concerning an insurance product and an insurance contract, members of the *Versicherungsombudsmann e. V.* must indicate the existence of the Insurance Ombudsman Scheme as an independent consumer dispute resolution body for the settlement of consumer complaints. In addition, the *Versicherungsombudsmann e. V.* is also referenced on the websites of all of the members.

The ombudsperson represents the Arbitration Board externally. The insurance ombudsperson's active public relations work includes the publication of an annual report, which is submitted each year. All annual reports are available to the general public on the Insurance Ombudsman Association's website.[13] The Association's website also offers a range of other information. The Arbitration Board provides

[13] https://www.versicherungsombudsmann.de/downloads/. Accessed 16 Apr 2025.

transparent information on all essential matters. For example, the annual report contains very comprehensive descriptions of complaint activity across all insurance sectors, along with comprehensive information on complaint statistics and the Association's profit and loss account.

The ombudsperson primarily provides information to the press and comments on current events, explains the special features of complaints handling process and the development of case law, to the extent that this is relevant for the Arbitration Board. In addition, the Managing Director of the Insurance Ombudsman Association is available to provide information regarding statistical data and organisational matters.

Otherwise, the initiative for reporting regularly comes from the media representatives. Every year, the ombudsperson's interviews and statements are reproduced in magazines and online articles. Furthermore, the ombudsperson participates in live broadcasts on television and radio.

In order for the insurance ombudsperson to take up a complaint, certain admissibility requirements must be met. Moreover, the dispute must be resolvable exclusively on the basis of documentary evidence. Other than that, there are no obstacles to referring a complaint to the ombudsperson.

Under the Articles of Association and the VSBG, Association members are obliged to provide their customers with certain information in accordance with the legal requirements when concluding a contract or sending contract documents, as well as when a dispute cannot be settled.

The *Versicherungsombudsmann e. V.* does not maintain a social media presence; however, it does maintain a well-functioning website.

The most significant publication is the annual report, which is submitted each year. The ombudsperson presents and explains the report to interested media.

In addition to the annual report, the insurance ombudsperson provides information about the activities of the previous year within the first few months of the year in an activity report as defined by the VSBG. The activity report is also published annually.

Decisions are only published in anonymised form on the Insurance Ombudsman Association's website. Different statistics regarding the volume of complaints are either published on the Association's website or are included in the annual and activity reports, which are also available on the website. Furthermore, the ombudsperson and the Managing Director of the Association incorporate statistical data and factual information into their lectures for the benefit of the interested public.

The annual budget is drafted by the Managing Director of the Insurance Ombudsman Association supporting the insurance ombudsperson, approved by the Association's Board of Directors and adopted by the General Assembly.

In addition, the annual financial statement is approved, and the Board and Executive Director are discharged by the members of the Association at the Annual General Meeting.

9.5.2 Limitations

In the event that the handling of a dispute has the potential to seriously impact the effective operation of the Arbitration Board, the insurance ombudsperson may refuse to carry out or continue the procedure. This may occur in instances where the facts or legal questions cannot be reasonably clarified without undue effort or a complex fact-finding procedure involving the taking of evidence, or when a fundamental legal question that is relevant to the assessment of the dispute has not been clarified,

Where, in light of the overall circumstances, it appears appropriate to propose an amicable settlement to the parties involved in the procedure, the insurance ombudsperson can bring the procedure to a conclusion, stating the reasons for doing so. The respondent may, at any stage of the procedure, request that the ombudsperson leave a complaint undecided as a test case, provided that the respondent can demonstrate that it plausibly concerns a question of fundamental legal importance. Nevertheless, the respondent must reimburse the complainant for the first instance court costs and legal fees, even if the respondent were to prevail in court. The ombudsperson may also refuse to carry out the procedure in cases where the contract concerned provides for a suitable alternative procedure for resolving disputes concerning the subject of the complaint and this procedure has not yet been used.

9.6 Accessibility and Accountability

9.6.1 Accessibility

The process commences with a communication to the insurance ombudsperson, which may be oral, written or in any other appropriate form. It is imperative that there are no impediments to contacting the ombudsperson. At the same time, it is of paramount importance for policyholders to be aware that they have the option of contacting the ombudsperson. On the one hand, the member companies highlight this information on their respective websites, in their contract documents and in their communication with policyholders. On the other hand, the ombudsperson and the Insurance Ombudsman Association's employees draw the attention of consumers to the procedure. Articles are published and lectures are given as are radio and/or television interviews. Finally, the *Versicherungsombudsmann e. V.* maintains a user-friendly website, accessible in German and English.

9.6.2 Accountability

The *Versicherungsombudsmann e. V.* meets its accountability obligations in different ways. Information about the composition of the committees, their meetings and any key resolutions can be found in the annual reports. Information on the Insurance Ombudsman Association's finances and on further developments of the Association or the insurance ombudsperson is also published there. In addition, an activity report containing the key figures for the preceding year in relation to the complaint procedures is published at the beginning of each year.

Legal Sources

Gesetz betreffend die Einführung der Zivilprozeßordnung, Gesetz vom 30.01.1877, RGBl. S. 244, as amended. https://dejure.org/gesetze/EGZPO

Satzung des Vereins Versicherungsombudsmann e. V. https://www.versicherungsombudsmann.de/wp-content/uploads/SATZUNG.pdf

Verbraucherstreitbeilegungsgesetz (VSBG) vom 19. Februar 2016, BGBl. I S. 254, 1039, as amended. https://www.gesetze-im-internet.de/vsbg

Verfahrensordnung des Versicherungsombudsmann e. V. (VomVO). https://www.versicherungsombudsmann.de/wp-content/uploads/2017/05/verfahrensordnung.pdf

Verfahrensordnung für Beschwerden im Zusammenhang mit der Vermittlung von Versicherungsverträgen (VermVO) im Sinne von § 214 Abs. 1 Nr. 2 VVG. https://www.versicherungsombudsmann.de/wp-content/uploads/vermvo.pdf

Versicherungsvertragsgesetz (VVG) vom 23. November 2007, BGBl. I S. 2631, as amended. https://www.gesetze-im-internet.de/vvg_2008

Zivilprozessordnung (ZPO). https://www.gesetze-im-internet.de/zpo/

Documents

Versicherungsombudsmann e. V. (2001) Presseinformation vom 25.09.2001: Ombudsmann nimmt ab 1. Oktober 2001 Kundenbeschwerden entgegen. https://www.versicherungsombudsmann.de/pressemitteilung/ombudsmann-nimmt-ab-1-oktober-2001-kundenbeschwerden-entgegen

Reference

Schluckebier W (2020) Aktuelles zur Tätigkeit des Ombudsmanns. In: Düsseldorfer Vorträge zum Versicherungsrecht 2020. VVW, Karlsruhe, p 1

Chapter 10
Ireland

Financial Services and Pensions Ombudsman

Sadhbh Kurzawska

10.1 Institutional Framework

10.1.1 Establishment

The Office of the Financial Services and Pensions Ombudsman (hereinafter the FSPO) was established in January 2018 by the Financial Services and Pensions Ombudsman Act 2017[1] (hereinafter the FSPO Act). The organisation was formed from the merger of the Financial Services Ombudsman Bureau[2] and the Office of the Pensions Ombudsman.[3] This occurred as part of the Public Service Reform Programme 2014,[4] where the Financial Services Ombudsman Bureau and the Office of the Pensions Ombudsman were included on a critical review list of bodies that might be amalgamated.

[1] Financial Services and Pensions Ombudsman Act 2017. https://www.irishstatutebook.ie/eli/2017/act/22/enacted/en/pdf. Accessed 16 Apr 2025.

[2] Central Bank and Financial Services Authority of Ireland Act 2004. https://www.irishstatutebook.ie/eli/2004/act/21. Accessed 16 Apr 2025.

[3] The Pensions (Amendment) Act 2002. www.irishstatutebook.ie/eli/2002/act/18. Accessed 16 Apr 2025.

[4] Public Service Reform Programme 2014. https://reformplan.per.gov.ie/2014/resources/Action-Plan.pdf. Accessed 8 Aug 2024.

S. Kurzawska (✉)
Financial Services and Pensions Ombudsman, Dublin, Ireland
e-mail: Sadhbh.Kurzawska@fspo.ie

H. Heiss et al. (eds.), *Insurance Ombudsman Schemes*, AIDA Europe Research Series on Insurance Law and Regulation 15,
https://doi.org/10.1007/978-3-032-01500-6_10

The role of the FSPO is to resolve complaints from consumers, including small businesses and other organisations, against regulated financial service providers[5] and pension providers.

Financial service providers and pension providers must be licensed with the supervisory authority, the Central Bank of Ireland (CBI), to carry out business in Ireland. The CBI serves the public interest by maintaining monetary and financial stability while ensuring that the financial system operates in the best interests of consumers and the wider economy.[6] The CBI does not investigate individual complaints from consumers; however, the ombudsperson can refer legally binding decisions to the CBI (s. 18 of the FSPO Act). Referrals take place for a variety of reasons including in circumstances where a complaint raises the possibility of a potentially systemic issue, which may warrant consideration by the regulatory authorities.

The FSPO cannot investigate complaints against non-regulated financial service providers or pension providers.

The FSPO provides an independent, fair, impartial, confidential and free service to resolve complaints through either informal mediation, leading to a potential settlement agreed between the parties, or formal investigation and adjudication, leading to a legally binding decision.

When any consumer, whether an individual, a small business or an organisation, is unable to resolve a complaint or dispute about the conduct of a financial service provider or a pension provider, they can refer their complaint to the FSPO.

We deal with complaints informally at first, by listening to both parties and engaging with them to facilitate a resolution that is acceptable to both parties. Much of this informal engagement takes place by telephone. Where these early interventions do not resolve the dispute, the FSPO formally investigates the complaint and issues a decision that is legally binding on both parties, subject only to a statutory appeal to the High Court.

The ombudsperson has wide-ranging powers to deal with complaints against financial service providers. The ombudsperson can direct a provider to rectify the conduct that is the subject of the complaint and there is no limit to the value of the rectification that can be directed. The ombudsperson can also direct a provider to pay compensation to a complainant of up to EUR 500,000.

In addition, the ombudsperson can publish anonymised decisions and can also publish the names of any financial service provider that has had at least three complaints against it upheld, substantially upheld, or partially upheld in a year.

In terms of dealing with complaints against pension providers, the ombudsperson's powers are more limited. While the ombudsperson can direct rectification, the legislation governing the FSPO sets out that such rectification shall not exceed any actual loss of benefit under the pension scheme concerned. Furthermore, the ombudsperson cannot direct a pension provider to pay compensation.

---

[5] A financial service provider is a business that provides financial services, such as banking, savings, insurance, loans or stockbroking.

[6] See https://www.centralbank.ie/about. Accessed 16 Apr 2025.

The ombudsperson can only publish case studies in relation to pension decisions (not the full decision), and they cannot publish the names of any pension provider irrespective of the number of complaints they may have had upheld, substantially upheld, or partially upheld against it in a year.

Formal investigation of a complaint by the FSPO is a detailed, fair and impartial process carried out in accordance with fair procedures. For this reason, documentary and audio evidence and other material, together with submissions from the parties, is gathered by the FSPO from those involved in the dispute and exchanged between the parties.

Unless a decision is appealed to the High Court, the financial service provider or pension provider must implement any direction made by the ombudsperson in a legally binding decision. Decisions appealed to the High Court are not published while they are the subject of an appeal.

10.1.2 Governance Model

Part 4 of the FSPO Act sets out the role of the Financial Services and Pensions Ombudsman Council (FSPOC), which has two main areas of responsibility: firstly, it is responsible under the legislation for setting the levy to be paid by financial service providers; secondly, it has certain oversight responsibilities in relation to the work of the FSPO, including its responsibilities in relation to:

- Approval of the FSPO's annual budget
- Approval of the ombudsperson's strategic plan
- Keeping under review the efficiency and effectiveness of the ombudsperson

The FSPOC consists of a chairperson and six members, all of whom are appointed by the Minister for Finance following a recruitment process undertaken by the Public Appointments Service.

10.1.3 Coverage

The role of the FSPO is to resolve complaints from consumers, including small businesses and other organisations, against regulated financial service providers and pension providers. This includes service sectors of banking, insurance and investment. Here are some examples of the types of providers we can receive complaints about:

- banks
- credit unions
- credit intermediaries
- insurance companies (life and non-life)

- health insurance companies
- e-money providers
- payment service providers
- stockbrokers/investment intermediaries
- money lenders/high-cost credit providers
- consumer credit/hire-purchase providers
- Buy Now Pay Later providers
- household goods credit providers/retail credit firms
- mortgage brokers, insurance brokers and other intermediaries
- pawnbrokers
- loan owners/credit servicing firms
- debt management firms
- home reversion firms

10.1.4 Insurance Business Covered

The powers of the ombudsperson are set out in s. 47 of the FSPO Act. Under this provision, the ombudsperson may require any person, who in the opinion of the ombudsperson, is in possession of information, or has a document or thing in their power or control, that is relevant to the investigation, to provide evidence to the investigation. Such a person may be obliged to provide that information either orally or in writing.

A person to whom a requirement is addressed under the powers above, shall be entitled to the same immunities and privileges as if they were a witness before the High Court.

Information provided by a person in response to a request by the ombudsperson is not admissible as evidence against that person in criminal proceedings other than in respect of perjury or an offence committed by obstructing the work of the ombudsperson.

A person does not have to produce information or produce a document, or a copy of a document, if the communication of it is subject to legal professional privilege.

The ombudsperson has wide-ranging powers to deal with complaints against financial service providers. The ombudsperson can direct a provider to rectify the conduct that is the subject of the complaint and there is no limit to the value of the rectification that can be directed. The ombudsperson can also direct a provider to pay compensation to a complainant of up to EUR 500,000.

In terms of dealing with complaints against pension providers, the ombudsperson's powers are more limited. While the ombudsperson can direct rectification, the legislation governing the FSPO sets out that such rectification shall not exceed any actual loss of benefit under the pension scheme concerned. Furthermore, the ombudsperson cannot direct a pension provider to pay compensation.

Unless a decision is appealed to the High Court, the financial service provider or pension provider must implement any direction made by the ombudsperson in a legally binding decision. Decisions appealed to the High Court are not published while they are the subject of an appeal.

10.1.5 Appointment of the Ombudsperson

In s. 8 of the FSPO Act it is provided that the Minister for Finance, having consulted the Minister for Public Expenditure and Reform, will appoint an ombudsperson for a period of five years following an open competition run by the Public Appointments Service. The criteria for recruitment of an ombudsperson are determined by the Public Appointments Service.

The Public Appointment Service may refer up to three candidates to the Minister for Finance for the role of ombudsperson.

The Minister for Finance may reappoint the ombudsperson following the expiration of the 5-year appointment period.

The ombudsperson shall hold office subject to such terms and conditions (including terms and conditions relating to remuneration, allowances for expenses and superannuation) as may be determined by the Minister, with the consent of the Minister for Public Expenditure and Reform.

In s. 11 of the FSPO Act, it is stated that the Minister for Finance may remove the ombudsperson from office where, in the Minister's opinion, the ombudsperson has become incapable through ill-health of performing their functions, or has committed stated misbehaviour, or their removal appears to the Minister to be necessary for the effective performance of the functions of the office.

10.1.6 Funding

The FSPO is funded by levies on financial services providers and by a government grant. The levy amounts are set by the FSPOC, with the consent of the Minister for Finance. The amount of the government grant is approved by the Minister for Finance. It is free for any person to submit a complaint to the FSPO.

The FSPOC is responsible under s. 40 of the FSPO Act for setting the levy to be paid by financial service providers.

The FSPOC approves the FSPO's annual budget which is linked to the organisation's Strategic Plan.[7] This annual budget is then funded through two distinct sources; the financial services complaints are funded by a levy on the financial services industry and the pensions complaints are funded by the Exchequer, through the Department of Finance. The levy is enacted through a statutory instrument.[8]

---

[7] Financial Services and Pensions Ombudsman (2021) Strategic Plan 2021–2024 Connecting and Innovating. https://www.fspo.ie/documents/Strategic-Plan-2021-2024-Connecting-and-Engaging.pdf. Accessed 16 Apr 2025.

[8] Financial Services and Pensions Ombudsman (2023) S.I. No. 6 of 2023, Financial Services and Pensions Ombudsman Act 2017 (Financial Services and Pensions Ombudsman Council) Financial Services Industry Levy Regulations 2023. https://www.fspo.ie/documents/SI-6-of-2023-FSPO-Industry-Levy.pdf. Accessed 16 Apr 2025.

Table 10.1 Budget 2023 with funding breakdown[a]

Budget 2023	€	€
Approved Funding Requirement		11,981,674
Less:		
Funding from Department of Finance	-479,267	
Total to be collected by way of Financial Services Industry Levy		**11,502,407**

[a]Financial Services and Pensions Ombudsman (2023) Understanding the Financial Services Industry Levy 2023, p. 3. https://www.fspo.ie/documents/Understanding-the-Financial-Services-Industry-Levy-Report-2023.pdf. Accessed 16 Apr 2025

Our publication, "Understanding the Financial Services Industry Levy"[9] provides information on how the levy on the financial services industry is determined, calculated and collected.

10.1.6.1 Determining the Overall Levy Requirement

The proportion of funding provided by the Exchequer is based on the ratio of pensions-related complaints to financial services complaints. This ratio is 5% for 2023, meaning that once the FSPOC approved the FSPO's budget for the year, and the overall budget was reduced by the surplus carried forward from the previous year, 5% of the total budget was drawn down from the Exchequer directly, with the remaining funding collected through the financial services industry levy (see Table 10.1).

10.1.6.2 Apportioning the Levy by Category

The categories of financial service provider subject to a levy by the FSPO are based on authorisations held by each entity with the Central Bank of Ireland and as prescribed in s. 43 of the FSPO Act. The FSPO does not have a role in relation to the authorisation held by financial service providers with the Central Bank of Ireland.

To ensure standardisation and ease of comparison, the labelling of categories of financial service providers used by the FSPO match the Central Bank register.

In order to ensure an equitable distribution of the levy among financial service providers, a rebalancing exercise was carried out ahead of the issuing of the levy in 2023. This exercise, which occurs on an annual basis, ensures that the proportion of

[9]Financial Services and Pensions Ombudsman (2023) Understanding the Financial Services Industry Levy 2023. https://www.fspo.ie/documents/Understanding-the-Financial-Services-Industry-Levy-Report-2023.pdf. Accessed 16 Apr 2025.

Table 10.2 Aggregated Total of Complaints Received (2019, 2020, 2021)[a]

Sector 1	Banking 61%
Sector 2	Insurance 33%
Sector 3	Investment 6%

[a]Financial Services and Pensions Ombudsman (2023) Understanding the Financial Services Industry Levy 2023, p. 4. https://www.fspo.ie/documents/Understanding-the-Financial-Services-Industry-Levy-Report-2023.pdf. Accessed 16 Apr 2025

Table 10.3 Financial Services Industries by Sector[a]

Financial Services Industry by Sector	
Sector 1: Banking	€ 6,432,271
Sector 2: Insurance	€3,487,056
Sector 3: Investment	€ 678,439
All other categories of financial service provider	€904,641
	€ 10,597,766

[a]Financial Services and Pensions Ombudsman (2023) Understanding the Financial Services Industry Levy 2023, p. 4. https://www.fspo.ie/documents/Understanding-the-Financial-Services-Industry-Levy-Report-2023.pdf. Accessed 16 Apr 2025

the levy applicable to each category reflects the volume of complaints received by the FSPO in the previous three-year period.

The complaints handling experience for the three-year period from January 2019 to December 2021[10] across the three major sectors of banking, insurance and investments is depicted in Table 10.2.

For those categories of financial service providers which cannot be readily categorised under Sectors 1, 2 or 3, or which may fall across sectors, arrangements in relation to the appropriate allocation base are set out per category in the schedule to the relevant Statutory Instrument. The share-out of the total levy among the categories of regulated entities being charged is set out in Table 10.3.

Within each sector, the funding required is apportioned across the categories of financial service provider included in each sector as regulated by the Central Bank of Ireland.

10.1.7 Insurance Ombudsperson's Functions

The functions of the ombudsperson are set out under s. 12 of the FSPO Act.

The ombudsperson is independent in the performance of their functions.

[10]Complaints made in 2022 were not included in the 2023 levy exercise as the calculation of the levy was completed before year end. As such, complete data for 2022 was not available.

The principal function of the ombudsperson is to investigate complaints in an appropriate manner proportionate to the nature of the complaint by informal means, mediation, formal investigation (including oral hearings if required), or a combination of informal and formal methods.

The ombudsperson shall endeavour to be accessible to the public and ensure that complaints about the conduct of financial service providers or pension providers are dealt with in an informal manner, efficiently, effectively and fairly.

The ombudsperson should also improve public understanding of the role and functions of the ombudsperson and improve public understanding of issues related to complaints considered by the ombudsperson by publishing decisions and guidance notes on procedures and processes.

The ombudsperson is also required to engage with financial service providers and pension providers to promote active engagement and consumer education in respect of their internal dispute resolution practices. The ombudsperson does not have a role in the financial education of customers.

The ombudsperson's role is to establish and maintain efficient and effective systems and procedures for the investigation and adjudication of complaints in a timely and effective manner.

The ombudsperson should also publish accessible information in relation to how to make a complaint to the FSPO and the services offered by the FSPO, including guidelines to using each aspect of its service.

The ombudsperson may, when requested by the Minister, provide advice in relation to any proposals for legislative change, or any other policy matters, concerning financial services or pensions and relating to the functions of the Ombudsman.

The ombudsperson, when dealing with a particular complaint, shall act in an informal manner and according to equity, good conscience and the substantial merits of the complaint without undue regard to technicality or legal form.

10.1.7.1 Publication of Ombudsperson's Decisions

The ombudsperson has the power to publish legally binding decisions in relation to complaints concerning financial service providers under s. 62 of the FSPO Act.

The legislation requires that decisions should be published in a manner that ensures that a complainant is not identified by name, address or otherwise, and a provider is not identified by name or address.

Publication must also comply with data protection legislation and regulations.[11] Decisions appealed to the High Court are not published while they are the subject of legal proceedings.

When the ombudsperson issues a legally binding decision, that decision may be challenged by way of statutory appeal to the High Court within 35 calendar days from that date. For this reason, the ombudsperson does not publish decisions before

[11] For more information, see https://dataprotection.ie/. Accessed 16 Apr 2025.

the elapse of the 35-day period available to the parties to issue a statutory appeal to the High Court. In addition, decisions which have been appealed to the High Court are not published, pending the outcome of any such court proceedings.

Before any legally binding decision is published by the ombudsperson, it undertakes a rigorous and stringent review to ensure that the non-identification requirements of the FSPO Act are adhered to in order to protect the confidentiality of the parties.

The FSPO Act also provides the FSPO with the power to publish case studies of decisions relating to pension providers, but not the full decision.

To provide full access to the ombudsperson's decisions, the FSPO has created an online database of anonymised legally binding decisions.[12] This database holds the full text of over 2,400 of the ombudsperson's published decisions issued since January 2018 in relation to complaints against financial service providers. Recent decisions are added on an ongoing basis, typically once a month.

The ombudsperson also publishes Digests of Decisions,[13] which contain summaries of decisions made in relation to complaints against financial service providers and case studies of decisions made in relation to complaints against pension providers.

The ombudsperson has published 8 Digests of Ombudsman's Decisions to date, four of which are themed digests. Of particular interest may be volume 6,[14] which contains insurance complaints from businesses, volume 7[15] concerns complaints relating to travel insurance and volume 8[16] concerns complaints made relating to private health insurance. The four remaining digests contain a selection of decision summaries across all sectors, showing the wide breadth of complaints which are received by the FSPO.

Some details within the summaries referenced in the Digests, such as names and locations, have been altered in order to protect the identity of the complainants. It is important to keep in mind that these are only short summaries of the decisions concerned.

By publishing these decisions and Digests of Decisions, the ombudsperson aims to enhance transparency and understanding of their powers and the services of the FSPO. Providing access to the ombudsperson's decisions contributes to an enhanced

---

[12] For more information, see https://www.fspo.ie/complaint-outcomes/investigation-services/legally-binding-decisions/. Accessed 16 Apr 2025.

[13] Financial Services and Pensions Ombudsman (2022) Ombudsman's Digests of Legally Binding Decisions, Volumes 1–8. https://www.fspo.ie/publications/. Accessed 16 Apr 2025.

[14] Financial Services and Pensions Ombudsman (2021) Ombudsman's Digest of Legally Binding Decisions, Volume 6. https://www.fspo.ie/documents/Ombudsmans_Digest_of_Decisions_2021_Vol6.pdf. Accessed 16 Apr 2025.

[15] Financial Services and Pensions Ombudsman (2022) Ombudsman's Digest of Legally Binding Decisions Travel Insurance, Volume 7. https://www.fspo.ie/documents/Digest-of-Decisions-Volume-7-Final.pdf. Accessed 16 Apr 2025.

[16] Financial Services and Pensions Ombudsman (2021) Ombudsman's Digest of Legally Binding Decisions Health Insurance, Volume 8. https://www.fspo.ie/documents/Digest-of-Decisions-Volume-8-Final.pdf. Accessed 16 Apr 2025.

consumer protection framework and is a valuable tool for providers and consumers alike in understanding the ombudsperson's decisions.

The Digests of Decisions published in 2022 highlight the broad range of issues leading to complaints made to the FSPO and the redress directed by the ombudsperson.

10.1.7.2 The Overview of Complaints

The ombudsperson publishes an Overview of Complaints[17] for the previous year by the end of Q1 each year, as set out in s. 25(2) of the FSPO Act, which includes a summary of all complaints made to the FSPO; a review of trends and patterns in the complaints made to the FSPO; a breakdown of the method by which all complaints made to the FSPO were dealt with; and a summary of the outcome of all complaints concluded or terminated.

In accordance with s. 25 of the FSPO Act, the ombudsperson can also report every regulated financial service provider, which, in the preceding year, had at least three complaints against it upheld, substantially upheld, or partially upheld. This report on named financial service providers excludes any decision upholding a complaint if that decision is the subject of a statutory appeal at the time of publication.

During 2022, the ombudsperson referred 10 legally binding decisions to the Central Bank of Ireland (CBI),[18] because of the ombudsperson's concerns regarding potentially systemic issues. This is an important part of our role, and these referrals, in addition to the ongoing sharing of information with the CBI on areas of mutual interest, help to ensure that issues and conducts evident in complaints made to this Office can be considered from a regulatory perspective. Consumers place their trust in financial providers when using their services. It is a serious matter where that trust is breached.

The ombudsperson also shared a copy of every legally binding decision issued concerning a complaint about a tracker mortgage rate of interest with the Central Bank of Ireland (CBI). Copies of 134 tracker mortgage decisions were sent by the FSPO to the CBI during 2022.

The same approach was adopted for 19 legally binding decisions issued in complaints concerning declined insurance claims for business interruption losses, to share the perspective of the ombudsperson with the CBI as regulator of financial service providers, with a view to promoting the best interests of consumers and strengthening the consumer protection framework. The ombudsperson is aware of the CBI's expectation of financial service providers to consider the terms of any

---

[17] Financial Services and Pensions Ombudsman (2023) Financial Services and Pensions Ombudsman Overview of Complaints 2022. https://www.fspo.ie/documents/Overview-of-Complaints-2022.pdf. Accessed 16 Apr 2025.

[18] Financial Services and Pensions Ombudsman (2023) The Financial Services and Pensions Ombudsman Overview of Complaints 2022, p.10. https://www.fspo.ie/documents/Overview-of-Complaints-2022.pdf. Accessed 16 Apr 2025.

Table 10.4 Complaint handlers, as at year end, 31 December 2019–2023

	2019	2020	2021	2022	2023
Total	60.6	72.6	69.6	68.6	74

Table 10.5 Number of staff by grade as of 31 December 2023[a]

Ombudsperson	1
Deputy Ombudsperson	1
Principal Officer	3
Assistant Principal Officer	19
Higher Executive Officer	22
Executive Officer	42
Clerical Officer	10
Total	86

[a]Financial Services and Pensions Ombudsman (2024) Financial Services and Pensions Ombudsman Annual Report 2023. www.fspo.ie/publications. Accessed 16 Apr 2025

decision issued by the ombudsperson and apply that outcome to similarly impacted customers.

The Act provides that the ombudsperson may make recommendations to the Central Bank of Ireland (CBI) in relation to measures that the CBI might take in order to effectively deal with persistent patterns of complaints. The FSPO and the CBI have agreed a Memorandum of Understanding (MoU)[19] which sets out the terms under which both parties give effect to these provisions.

10.1.8 Insurance Ombudsman Office

10.1.8.1 Staff

The majority of staff employed with the FSPO are deemed to handle complaints, primarily as assigned case owners (Tables 10.4, 10.5 and 10.6). The exceptions to this are staff working in support areas, such as Corporate Services, HR and ICT.

Following the approval of the FSPO's Workforce Plan in December 2023, the sanctioned staff complement in the FSPO was increased from 90.2 to 128. As at 1 February 2024, the number of staff (FTE) is 93. Arising from the approval of the FSPO's Workforce Plan by the Minister for Finance, there are 35 further roles to be recruited, of which 30 relate to complaint handling roles (this excludes support staff). This recruitment process has commenced.

[19] Memorandum of Understanding between the Central Bank of Ireland and the Financial Services and Pensions Ombudsman (2023), https://service.betterregulation.com/sites/default/files/2024-05/MoU-from-CBI.pdf. Accessed 16 Apr 2025.

Table 10.6 Organisation Structure 2023

Council	Executive
Council Chairperson	Financial Services and Pensions Ombudsman
Council Member	Deputy Financial Services and Pensions Ombudsman
	Director of Dispute Resolution Services
Council Member	Director of Customer Operations and Information Management
Council Member	Director of Customer Operations and Information Management
Council Member	Director of Investigation Services
Council Member	Director of Corporate and Communication Services

10.1.8.2 Training and Development

Our core strategic pillar, 'Developing our people, building our capability', is supported by a diverse range of training programmes which are made available to staff. The FSPO is a learning organisation, facilitating and focusing on ongoing training and upskilling of staff through in-house training, externally delivered training courses, membership of professional bodies and professional development. Over 30 training opportunities were provided to groups of staff during 2022, with a focus on core skills and knowledge including management training, mediation training, financial services knowledge, cyber security and communications.

In line with our People Strategy,[20] the FSPO also delivers mandatory ethics training to all new staff.

10.1.8.3 People Strategy

The FSPO launched its People Strategy 2022–2025[21] in early 2022. The Vision of the FSPO's People Strategy is 'to support and empower our people to deliver an excellent customer experience'. Our People Strategy allows us to support the delivery of our Strategic Plan 2021–2024, 'Connecting and Innovating'.

A programme for implementation will pinpoint the parallels and connect the priorities across our Strategic Plan, our People Strategy and our Customer Action Plan.[22]

---

[20] Financial Services and Pensions Ombudsman (2022) FSPO People Strategy 2022–2025. www.fspo.ie/governance/funding.asp. Accessed 16 Apr 2025.

[21] Financial Services and Pensions Ombudsman (2022) FSPO People Strategy 2022–2025. www.fspo.ie/governance/funding.asp. Accessed 16 Apr 2025.

[22] Financial Services and Pensions Ombudsman Customer Action Plan, https://www.fspo.ie/about-us/customer-service/customer-action-plan.asp. Accessed 16 Apr 2025.

During the term of the People Strategy 2022–2025, we will be focused on three strategic pillars to realise our People Vision and support the ongoing development of our organisation. They are 'Culture and Strategy', 'Employee Experience', 'Leadership and Learning'. We recognise that considerable emphasis is required on a fourth, underpinning foundational pillar - Human Resources (HR) Infrastructure.

As an organisation, we are committed to continued investment in our HR operating model to build our capacity, grow our expertise and assess the quality of our delivery. Doing this will allow us to enhance our functional impact on the changing needs of employee and customer expectations.

We are fully committed to implementing each of the pillars of the strategy and working collectively as a team to support our people to deliver the right outcomes for our customers, key stakeholders and for our growth—both personally and organisationally.

10.2 Jurisdiction

10.2.1 Substantive Scope

The scope of the FSPO is set out in the FSPO Act. The FSPO helps resolve complaints from consumers, including small businesses and other organisations, concerning the conduct of financial service providers and pension providers.

As an impartial complaints body, the FSPO cannot offer advice. However, there are several other bodies which can be contacted to provide information to consumers. In relation to insurance complaints these are:

- Competition and Consumer Protection Commission (CCPC)
- The CCPC's role and function includes:
  - Personal finance information and education—The CCPC has a specific role under legislation to provide personal finance information and education to consumers. This includes providing information through their consumer helpline and website, running public awareness campaigns and financial education programmes for schools and workplaces.
  - Informing consumers about their rights—The CCPC empowers consumers by providing information to them on their rights through their helpline and website. The CCPC also runs public awareness campaigns and uses various media channels to communicate their message.
- Insurance Ireland
- Motor Insurer's Bureau of Ireland
- Health Insurance Authority
- Citizens Information Services

There is no minimum amount for claims that can be referred to the FSPO. The ombudsperson can direct a provider to rectify the conduct that is the subject of the complaint. There is no limit to the value of the rectification that can be directed. The ombudsperson can also direct a financial service provider to pay compensation to a complainant of up to EUR 500,000.

In terms of dealing with complaints against pension providers, the ombudsperson's powers are more limited. While the ombudsperson can direct rectification, the legislation governing the ombudsperson sets out that such rectification shall not exceed any actual loss of benefit under the pension scheme concerned. Furthermore, the ombudsperson cannot direct a pension provider to pay compensation.

Consumers must make a complaint to their provider first. If they have complained to their provider and the issues have not been resolved, they can then make a complaint to the ombudsperson. If a complaint concerns a joint account or joint policy, all owners must make the complaint.

The ombudsperson does not deal with complaints which have arisen because of a commercial decision by a provider. Commercial decisions could include a refusal to provide credit or insurance.

The ombudsperson cannot deal with complaints that are currently the subject of legal proceedings or have been in the past.

Some complaints can only be dealt with by other bodies. For example, complaints under the Equal Status Acts 2000–2015 that prohibit discrimination in the provision of goods and services, are dealt with by the Workplace Relations Commission.

Complaints about issues of data protection or data access are a matter for the Data Protection Commission.

The ombudsperson cannot investigate complaints that are not made within the time limits.

10.2.1.1 What Is a Financial Service Provider?

A complaint can be made against a financial service provider that is authorised by the Central Bank of Ireland. The regulation status of a provider can be checked via the Central Bank register.[23]

10.2.1.2 Credit Intermediaries

A complaint can be made against a credit intermediary and other providers authorised by the Competition and Consumer Protection Commission (CCPC). To check whether the provider is authorised, reference can be made to the CCPC register.[24]

---

[23] Central Bank of Ireland (2023) Central Bank of Ireland's Registers. https://registers.centralbank.ie/. Accessed 16 Apr 2025.

[24] Competition and Consumer Protection Commission (2024) Authorised Credit Intermediaries, https://www.ccpc.ie/business/credit-intermediaries/authorised-credit-intermediaries/. Accessed 16 Apr 2025.

10.2.1.3 Certain Providers Subject to The Consumer Credit Act (1995)

Complaints can be made against certain providers subject to the Consumer Credit Act (1995).[25] If a credit agreement was made under the Consumer Credit Act, a complaint can be brought to the ombudsperson. The Consumer Credit Act covers hire-purchase agreements, consumer hire agreements and moneylending agreements. This Act does not cover the giving of credit, or otherwise, to businesses.

A list of the providers can be found in Sect. 10.1.3 above.

10.2.2 Personal Scope

The personal scope of the ombudsperson covers complainants. The definition of 'complainant' is set out in s. 2 of the FSPO Act and includes:

- a consumer
- an actual or potential beneficiary (including surviving dependant) of a consumer
- a legal personal representative of a consumer who has died
- a widow, widower or surviving spouse or civil partner of a consumer who has died or a person acting on behalf of an actual or potential beneficiary
- any person who is contractually entitled to benefit from a long-term financial service
- a consumer who has a credit agreement, such as a mortgage or loan, with a financial service provider, that is serviced by a credit servicing firm
- an employee, or a former employee, entitled to benefit from an income continuance plan
- A consumer is a private individual—for example a personal policy holder or account holder

or

- a limited company, a sole trader, a trust, a club, a charity or a partnership subject to a turnover limit of EUR 3 million in the preceding financial year.
- In addition, a consumer must be one of the following: a customer of a financial service provider;
- a person or body to whom a financial service provider has offered to provide a financial service; or
- a person or body who has sought the provision of a financial service.

If a complaint is made about a pension scheme, the consumer must be

- a member, an external member, or a former member of a pension scheme, which is not an overseas pension scheme

[25] Consumer Credit Act 1995, https://www.irishstatutebook.ie/eli/1995/act/24. Accessed 16 Apr 2025.

- a surviving dependant of a member who has died
- any person claiming to be a member or a surviving dependant of a member who has died
- a contributor to a PRSA
- a legal personal representative of a deceased member or deceased contributor
- a widow, widower or surviving spouse or civil partner of a member or contributor who has died
- any person with an entitlement under a scheme, for example, the holder of a Payment Adjustment Order

10.2.3 Territorial Scope

The functions of the ombudsperson are governed by the provisions of the FSPO Act. The ombudsperson can investigate any consumer complaint made about the conduct of a "financial service provider" which has a specific definition under the Act, and which makes reference to the separate provisions of the Central Bank Act 1942,[26] as amended.

This definition includes financial service providers that are regulated in this country by the Central Bank of Ireland. It also includes other financial service providers which are regulated by a competent regulatory authority in another member state of the European Economic Area (EEA), but which provide services across EU borders, to make their services available to Irish consumers on what is known as a "freedom of service" basis. This is also referred to as "passporting".

When investigating complaints, the ombudsperson must consider the regulatory status of the financial service provider whose conduct is the subject of the consumer complaint to ensure that it is a regulated entity meeting the definition under the Act.

In addition, however, the ombudsperson must also consider the particular law specified by the contract to be the governing law of that contractual arrangement in place between the consumer and the financial service provider.

10.2.3.1 Consumer-Held Financial Services Contracts That Are Not Governed by Irish Law

When the consumer contract is not governed by Irish law, the ombudsperson does not ordinarily investigate and adjudicate on that complaint, as this would call for the ombudsperson to interpret and apply the laws of a foreign jurisdiction in the course of an investigation under the Act, leading to a legally binding outcome.

[26] The Central Bank Act 1942. https://www.irishstatutebook.ie/eli/1942/act/22/enacted/en/html. Accessed 16 Apr 2025.

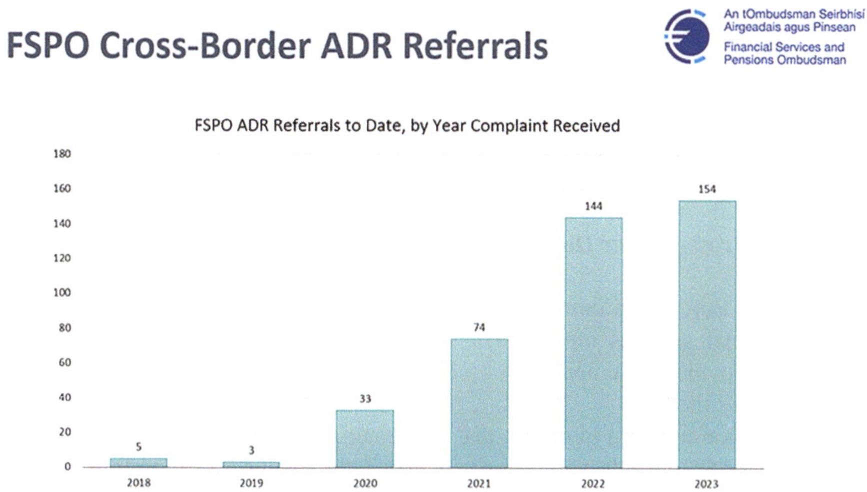

Fig. 10.1 FSPO Cross-Border ADR Referrals (Financial Services and Pensions Ombudsman (2024) Cross Border Referrals. https://www.fspo.ie/our-services/cross-border-referrals.asp. Accessed 16 Apr 2025.)

When that happens, the ombudsperson will refer the complaint to the appropriate Alternative Dispute Resolution (ADR) body in the relevant country as the competent authority to adjudicate the complaint in relation to the contractual issue arising.

This includes referrals to ADR bodies within the EEA area, in accordance with the FIN-NET Memorandum of Understanding on a Cross-Border Out-of-Court Complaints Network for Financial Services.[27]

The increased number of such complaint referrals by the ombudsperson to other ADR bodies from 2018 to end of December 2023 are depicted in Fig. 10.1 below.

10.2.3.2 An Alternative to Referring the Complaint to an ADR Body in Another European Country

The ombudsperson is conscious that when the governing law of the contract is not Irish law, a consumer may have a preference to use the services of the FSPO, rather than pursuing a complaint through a complaint resolution body in another country. Therefore, before referring the complaint to the appropriate ADR body of outside Ireland, and with a view to providing an option to the parties, it is the practice of the FSPO to seek the consent of both parties to the investigation and adjudication of the complaint by the FSPO, pursuant to the laws of Ireland.

[27] FIN-NET Memorandum of Understanding on a Cross-Border Out-of-Court Complaints Network for Financial Services (2016). https://finance.ec.europa.eu/document/download/7b30f574-0413-4620-a970-f7bf67813b9c_en?filename=memorandum-of-understanding_en.pdf. Accessed 16 Apr 2025.

This consent is sought from both parties on the basis that such an agreement to enable the FSPO to make its complaint resolution services available to the parties will not in any manner alter the underlying governing law of the contract.

In some instances, both parties make the required written consent available and the FSPO investigation can then proceed in accordance with the laws of Ireland.

10.2.3.3 Cross-Border Disputes

As part of a European Commission initiative, FIN-NET, the FSPO cooperate with other financial services ombudsman schemes in the European Economic Area (EEA) to provide consumers with access to a cross-border complaints resolution service across the EEA.

Cooperation will aim to ensure that consumer complaints with regard to cross-border disputes are dealt with effectively and in the interest of supporting a cross-border market in financial services through recourse to high-quality out of court settlement.

Each participating scheme cooperates in areas which it normally covers according to its terms of reference and/or its legal obligations. They also cooperate and act in accordance with the ADR Directive and other relevant legislation or recommendations.

The FSPO will not progress a complaint where the contract is governed by the law of another jurisdiction. Where possible the FSPO will direct the consumer to an appropriate ADR body in that other jurisdiction.

In accordance with s. 10 of the European Union (Alternative Dispute Resolution for Consumer Disputes) Regulations 2015,[28] the FSPO is obliged to publish an annual activity report on its website within 6 months of the end of each calendar year. It must also submit a two-year activity report to the Competition and Consumer Protection Commission (CCPC) every two years. The CCPC is designated as the competent authority in the State for the purposes of these Regulations and the Directive.

10.2.4 Time Limits

Under s. 51 of the FSPO Act, complaints must be made to the ombudsperson within 6 years of the date of the conduct complained of.

There is an alternative time limit for complaints about a long-term financial service[29] or about a pension provider. Those complaints must be made within 3 years

[28] European Union (Alternative Dispute Resolution for Consumer Disputes) Regulations 2015, SI 343/2015. https://www.irishstatutebook.ie/eli/2015/si/343/made/en/print. Accessed 16 Apr 2025.

[29] Financial Services and Pensions Ombudsman Act 2017, s. 2. https://www.irishstatutebook.ie/eli/2017/act/22/enacted/en/print#sec2. Accessed 16 Apr 2025.

from the date of awareness, or the date the consumer should reasonably have become aware, of the conduct complained of.

There are some additional requirements that the ombudsperson must consider when applying the time limits to complaints about a long-term financial service or about a pension provider:

- The conduct complained of must have occurred on or after 1 January 2002 for a complaint about a long-term financial service, and the long-term financial service must not have expired more than six years before the date of the complaint to the ombudsperson.
- The conduct complained of must have occurred on or after 13 April 1996 for a complaint about a pension provider.

In certain circumstances, the ombudsperson has discretion to consider a complaint that falls outside these time frames.

Where a question arises as to whether a complaint has been made to the ombudsperson within the time limits, the FSPO may carry out a jurisdictional assessment.

10.3 Procedure

10.3.1 Regulatory Framework

In s. 44 of the FSPO Act, it is stated that complaints should be received in writing or in any other format the ombudsperson considers appropriate. The legislation also directs the ombudsperson to provide the financial service provider or the pension provider, with details of the complaint as soon as possible after receiving a complaint in relation to its conduct.

The procedures for carrying out its services are otherwise set by the ombudsperson.

10.3.2 Complaint and Enquiry Handling Process

10.3.2.1 Receiving a Complaint

The ombudsperson may only commence an investigation upon receipt of a complaint. Complaints may be received in writing on our paper-based complaint form or our online complaint form. In 2022, 80% of all complaints received were via our online complaint form. This is due to improvements in our website, our online complaint form and a general switch towards digital delivery channels by many of our customers over the course of the pandemic.

A complainant who has difficulty with either of these options may contact us and they will be assisted in making their complaint by our Access Officer.

When we receive a complaint, it is reviewed and assessed by our Registry and Assessment team.

The team checks that the consumer has provided all the information we need to progress the complaint and whether the provider has been given the opportunity to resolve the complaint first.

If we need more information to progress the complaint, a member of the team will contact the consumer.

Some complaints require a more detailed assessment. For example,

- to understand whether the conduct being complained of falls within the statutory time-limits,
- to check that consent has been provided by all of the relevant parties, or
- we may need to check if the provider is a regulated provider.

In some circumstances, the team may need to refer a complaint to our Legal Services team for a detailed legal review.

Once the team has completed its process, the complaint is either referred to Dispute Resolution Services for mediation, or, where the complaint cannot progress any further, it will be closed.

Here are the steps a consumer should follow before making a complaint to the ombudsperson:

1. They should speak or write to the person they usually deal with or ask for the complaints manager to make a complaint. They should make it clear that they are making a complaint. They should explain their complaint and suggest how their provider can resolve the issue.

   They should provide detailed information, including:

   - relevant dates, places and times
   - details of any phone conversations and meetings, for example, who was involved, when they took place and what was said
   - copies of relevant documents, such as contracts, statements, emails, letters, invoices and receipts.

2. The provider should deal with the complaint through its complaint handling process. In accordance with the Central Bank of Ireland's Consumer Protection Code 2012,[30] the provider may take up to **40 working days** to deal with the complaint.

The provider should fully investigate the complaint in accordance with its Internal Dispute Resolution process (IDR process). At the end of IDR, the provider will detail its position regarding the complaint by issuing a final response letter for financial service complaints or a notice of determination for pension complaints.

[30] Central Bank of Ireland (2015) Consumer Protection Code 2012 (as amended). https://www.centralbank.ie/docs/default-source/regulation/consumer-protection/other-codes-of-conduct/4-gns-4-2-7-cp-code-2012.pdf. Accessed 16 Apr 2025.

10.3.2.2 Final Response Letter/Notice of Determination

A final response letter or notice of determination should set out what the provider has done to investigate the complaint through its complaint handling process. The letter should advise the consumer to contact the FSPO as their next step, if they remain unsatisfied.

If a consumer has difficulty getting a final response letter from the provider and 40 working days have passed since they made their complaint, or if their provider is not engaging with them, the consumer can advise the FSPO and we will follow up on the complaint for them.

The ombudsperson may, in some limited circumstances, investigate a complaint against a financial service provider or pension provider before the IDR process is complete. This may happen if the provider has failed to complete the IDR process, so as to allow a complaint to be made within the time limits, as set out in the FSPO Act, or where the ombudsperson determines that a complaint is of such importance that it warrants waiving the IDR procedure.

10.3.2.3 How to Make a Complaint to the FSPO

Once the consumer has completed the two steps outlined in Sect. 10.3.2.1, to refer a complaint to us, a completed complaint form should be furnished along with a copy of the final response letter, so that we can assess the complaint to see whether we can deal with it. If a consumer cannot get a final response letter from the provider within 40 working days, the consumer should contact us.

10.3.2.4 Dispute Resolution Services

Dispute Resolution is a confidential mediation service provided by the FSPO. We facilitate the process between the consumer and the financial service provider. Our aim is to help the consumer and the provider to design and agree a solution they are both satisfied with.

Mediation is voluntary and completely confidential. We ask that all parties who enter the mediation process have a genuine intention to try to resolve the complaint. However, the process can be ended by any party at any time.

Mediation begins on the telephone and if needed, the FSPO mediator will invite both the consumer and their provider to attend a meeting. We will discuss the complaint with them and explore how they both consider it could be resolved and aim to help them to reach an agreement.

The outcome of mediation will usually be one of three things:

- A settlement is agreed between the parties.
- The consumer receives clarification from the provider around the issues they raised, which solves their complaint.

- If they do not reach a settlement, the complaint may be transferred within the FSPO for formal investigation.

During the dispute resolution process, we may identify issues which might stop the complaint proceeding to the formal investigation process.

The Dispute Resolution Service strives for best practice in dispute resolution using mediation techniques. The Financial Services and Pensions Ombudsman Code of Ethics for Mediation[31] provides a professional framework for our Dispute Resolution Officers and explains the FSPO mediation process for those who choose to take part. Each of our Dispute Resolution Officers is a qualified mediator. In 2022, the FSPO resolved 1722 complaints through Dispute Resolution Services.

Where the complaint is not resolved in mediation, the complaint is referred to Investigation Services. The investigation process is a detailed gathering of all evidence and leads to a legally binding decision.

If the complaint is upheld, the ombudsperson may direct the payment of compensation to the complainant or may direct the provider to rectify the issue complained of. There is no limit to the value of the rectification that can be directed. The ombudsperson can also direct a financial service provider to pay compensation to a complainant of up to EUR 500,000.

In terms of dealing with complaints against pension providers, the ombudsperson's powers are more limited. While the ombudsperson can direct rectification, the legislation governing the FSPO sets out that such rectification shall not exceed any actual loss of benefit under the pension scheme concerned. Furthermore, the ombudsperson cannot direct a pension provider to pay compensation.

10.3.2.5 Investigation Services

The FSPO resolves a majority of complaints at an early stage through mediation within the Dispute Resolution Service. When a complaint is not resolved through mediation, it may be transferred for formal investigation.

When this happens, no details of the engagement which took place between the parties during the confidential mediation are available for the formal investigation process. This is to ensure that the engagements between the parties during mediation can cause no prejudice to either party if a formal investigation is required.

Subject to any issues of suitability, the investigation process begins with the FSPO issuing a formal Summary of Complaint to the provider. This document identifies the conduct of the provider which has given rise to the complaint, and it asks targeted questions of the provider, which are designed to gather information regarding the issues. The FSPO also seeks certain specified items of evidence from the

[31] Financial Services and Pensions Ombudsman (2022) Financial Services and Pensions Ombudsman Code of Ethics for Mediation. https://www.fspo.ie/documents/FSPO-Code-of-Ethics-for-Mediation-October-2022.pdf. Accessed 16 Apr 2025.

provider. Sometimes the complainant will also be asked, separately, to clarify an aspect of their complaint or may be required to supply further documents.

The processes of the FSPO for formal investigation ensure that all information and evidence gathered from the complainant and the provider during the investigation, is shared between the parties. This ensures that both have possession of all the evidence, and each party can take the opportunity to offer any comments or observations regarding the evidence and records made available to the FSPO.

When the parties have concluded their submission of evidence and observations, all these details are considered in the adjudication of the complaint, which may ultimately lead to a legally binding decision.

The ombudsperson may uphold, substantially uphold, partially uphold, or reject a complaint. The ombudsperson has wide-ranging powers when adjudicating complaints.

If a complaint against a financial service provider is upheld, a financial service provider can be directed to rectify the conduct complained of, whatever the value of that rectification. In addition, the financial service provider can be directed to make a compensatory payment to a complainant, up to a maximum of EUR 500,000. During 2022, the ombudsperson issued 439 legally binding decisions.

10.3.3 Admissible Complaints

When a complaint is received, the Registry and Assessment team reviews and assesses it. This initial assessment provides an opportunity for the FSPO to determine if the complainant has provided all the necessary information to progress the complaint and to ensure the provider has been given the opportunity to resolve the complaint first. In many cases, this preliminary work allows the complaint to close, if the complainant is subsequently satisfied with the provider's resolution of the complaint.

The complaint is assessed to confirm that it is admissible for the statutory jurisdiction of the FSPO. Not all complaints are admissible for investigation by the FSPO and so the assessment of the complaint's admissibility takes place at the earliest possible stage. This may include determining whether the conduct complained of falls within the statutory time limits, checking that consent has been provided by all of the account or policy owners, or we may need to check if a financial service provider is regulated.

This early assessment service has enabled the FSPO to use its resources in the most efficient manner. More importantly, this service has enabled the FSPO to provide a greatly improved customer experience, ensuring the complainant is informed early on in the process if their complaint falls outside the FSPO's remit.

In some circumstances, the Customer Operations and Information Management (COIM) team may need to refer a complaint to our Legal Services team for a detailed legal review. Once the COIM team has completed its assessment, the complaint is either referred to Dispute Resolution Services for mediation or, where the complaint cannot progress any further, it will be closed.

Consumer Protection Code 2012

The Central Bank of Ireland's Consumer Protection Code (2012), ss. 10.7–10.12[32] sets out the obligations of the regulated provider in terms of complaint resolution and referral to the FSPO, as below.

10.7 A regulated entity must seek to resolve any complaints with consumers.

10.8 When a regulated entity receives an oral complaint, it must offer the consumer the opportunity to have this handled in accordance with the regulated entity's complaints process.

10.9 A regulated entity must have in place a written procedure for the proper handling of complaints. This procedure need not apply where the complaint has been resolved to the complainant's satisfaction within five business days, provided however that a record of this fact is maintained. At a minimum this procedure must provide that:

(a) the regulated entity must acknowledge each complaint on paper or on another durable medium within five business days of the complaint being received;
(b) the regulated entity must provide the complainant with the name of one or more individuals appointed by the regulated entity to be the complainant's point of contact in relation to the complaint until the complaint is resolved or cannot be progressed any further;
(c) the regulated entity must provide the complainant with a regular update, on paper or on another durable medium, on the progress of the investigation of the complaint at intervals of not greater than 20 business days, starting from the date on which the complaint was made;
(d) the regulated entity must attempt to investigate and resolve a complaint within 40 business days of having received the complaint; where the 40 business days have elapsed and the complaint is not resolved, the regulated entity must inform the complainant of the anticipated timeframe within which the regulated entity hopes to resolve the complaint and must inform the consumer that they can refer the matter to the relevant Ombudsman, and must provide the consumer with the contact details of such Ombudsman;
(e) within five business days of the completion of the investigation, the regulated entity must advise the consumer on paper or on another durable medium of:

(i) the outcome of the investigation;
(ii) where applicable, the terms of any offer or settlement being made;
(iii) that the consumer can refer the matter to the relevant Ombudsman, and
(iv) the contact details of such Ombudsman.

[32] Central Bank of Ireland (2015) Consumer Protection Code 2012 (as amended), ss. 10.7-10.12. https://www.centralbank.ie/docs/default-source/regulation/consumer-protection/other-codes-of-conduct/4-gns-4-2-7-cp-code-2012.pdf. Accessed 16 Apr 2025.

10.10 A regulated entity must maintain an up-to-date log of all complaints from consumers subject to the complaints procedure. This log must contain:

(a) details of each complaint;
(b) the date the complaint was received;
(c) a summary of the regulated entity's response(s) including dates;
(d) details of any other relevant correspondence or records;
(e) the action taken to resolve each complaint;
(f) the date the complaint was resolved; and
(g) where relevant, the current status of the complaint which has been referred to the relevant Ombudsman.

10.11 A regulated entity must maintain up to date and comprehensive records for each complaint received from a consumer.

10.12 A regulated entity must undertake an appropriate analysis of the patterns of complaints from consumers on a regular basis including investigating whether complaints indicate an isolated issue or a more widespread issue for consumers. This analysis of consumer complaints must be escalated to the regulated entity's compliance/risk function and senior management.

10.3.4 Obtaining Information and Collecting Evidence

The powers of the ombudsperson are set out in s. 47 of the FSPO Act. Under s. 47 of the FSPO Act, the ombudsperson may require any person to provide evidence to the investigation if the ombudsperson is of the opinion that that person holds information or a document relevant to an investigation. Such a person may be obliged to provide that information either orally or in writing.

- The ombudsperson can require any person to attend an oral hearing either voluntarily, or by way of summons, and may examine them under oath.
- The ombudsperson has the power to set the procedures and method of investigation as they see fit.
- The ombudsperson has the power to enter and inspect any business premises occupied by the financial service provider and inspect any document or thing in or on the premises.
- The ombudsperson shall, for the purposes of the investigation of a complaint, have all the powers, rights and privileges vested in the High Court or a judge of that court on the hearing of civil proceedings in respect of the examination of witnesses, including the administration of oaths and affirmations and the examination of witnesses outside the State.

A person to whom a requirement is addressed under the powers above, shall be entitled to the same immunities and privileges as if they were a witness before the High Court.

Information provided by a person in response to a request by the ombudsperson is not admissible as evidence against that person in criminal proceedings other than in respect of perjury or an offence committed by obstructing the work of the ombudsperson.

A person does not have to produce information or produce a document, or a copy of a document, if the communication of it is subject to legal professional privilege.

10.3.4.1 FSPO Complaint Processes

All providers of financial services and pension products are encouraged to adopt an approach of seeking, where possible, to resolve complaints quickly with their customers. In many instances, complaints are resolved promptly when the provider receives an initial contact from the FSPO, requesting a final response letter or simply advising of the receipt of the complaint.

There are several such case studies in the FSPO's Overview of Complaints 2022[33] publication, published in March 2023, which describe how the complaint was resolved once the complaint was made to the FSPO.

Providers seeking to resolve complaints at the earliest stage would not only contribute in a positive way to the vision of this Office of a progressive financial services and pension environment built on trust, fairness and transparency, where complaints are the exception; it would also make a significant difference to the customers of those providers, by removing the necessity for complainants to use the services of the FSPO.

The functions and powers of the ombudsperson are prescribed by the FSPO Act.

When a complaint is received, it is initially assessed to confirm that it falls within the statutory jurisdiction of this Office. Not all complaints are admissible for investigation by the ombudsperson and so the assessment of a complaint's admissibility takes place at the earliest possible stage.

When a complaint is received, the Registry and Assessment team of Customer Operations and Information Management (COIM) reviews and assesses it. This may include determining whether the conduct complained of falls within the statutory time limits, checking that consent has been provided by all of the relevant parties, or we may need to check if a financial service provider is regulated.

Where an issue requiring a more detailed legal assessment arises, the matter is referred to the Legal Services team for a formal jurisdictional assessment to determine whether the complaint, or elements of the complaint, can proceed to investigation.

The FSPO makes every effort to assist the parties in understanding the extent and limits of the ombudsperson's statutory jurisdiction, being mindful that the legislation contains some provisions which are complex.

[33] Financial Services and Pensions Ombudsman (2023) The Financial Services and Pensions Ombudsman Overview of Complaints 2022. https://www.fspo.ie/documents/Overview-of-Complaints-2022.pdf. Accessed 16 Apr 2025.

The parties to the complaint are invited to offer their comments and to submit all relevant details during this assessment process, before the ombudsperson's final determination on jurisdiction is ultimately set out for the parties.

Various issues of jurisdiction can arise when a consumer seeks to make a complaint to the FSPO. The Overview of Complaints 2022 provides case studies on pages 62–67 which provide examples of the types of jurisdictional issues which can arise.[34]

In some instances, it was determined that the complaints could not proceed to investigation as they did not come within the ombudsperson's remit. In other instances, some or all elements of the complaint were determined to be admissible for progression by way of a formal investigation of the merits of the complaint.

10.3.4.2 Dispute Resolution Services

Dispute Resolution is a confidential mediation service. Mediation is a process where we aim to help the complainant and the provider to design and agree a solution that they are both satisfied with. Mediation is voluntary and completely confidential and the complainant, the provider, or we, may end the process at any time.

Mediation begins on the telephone and if needed, the FSPO mediator will invite both the complainant and the provider to attend a meeting. All documents created for the purpose of the mediation process are considered confidential and are not shared outside the mediation process, even within the FSPO.

10.3.4.3 Investigation Services

If the complaint is not resolved through mediation in our Dispute Resolution Service, we may formally investigate it. Any details of what happened during the mediation process will not be disclosed or be part of the formal investigation, as those details are confidential.

The investigation process is a detailed gathering and examination of all relevant evidence. All communications between the complainant and the investigating team must be in writing so that documents can be exchanged with the provider.

We will review the complainant's complaint file to make sure that it is suitable for formal investigation. If a question arises as to whether we can investigate their complaint, we may refer the complaint file to our Legal Services team for assessment.

If the complaint is suitable for formal investigation, we start an investigation by issuing a formal document, called a Summary of Complaint, to the provider. We ask questions about the issues that have led to the complaint. We ask for certain

[34] Financial Services and Pensions Ombudsman (2023) The Financial Services and Pensions Ombudsman Overview of Complaints 2022. https://www.fspo.ie/documents/Overview-of-Complaints-2022.pdf. Accessed 16 Apr 2025.

evidence, which may include documents and audio evidence. We send a copy of the Summary of Complaint to the complainant for their information.

When we receive the provider's formal response to the Summary of Complaint, we will share it with the complainant, and they can give us their comments on the provider's response. The complainant can also submit any other evidence or comments that they want us to consider. We will make sure that both the complainant and the provider receive a copy of all evidence submitted by both parties, so that everyone holds the same information. The complaint will proceed to adjudication only when both parties have finished this sharing of comments and evidence.

10.3.4.4 Oral Hearings

When we are conducting our adjudication, we may need to ask the complainant and their provider to give us their evidence verbally. This is called an oral hearing. We may do this if there is a dispute about a fact between the complainant and the provider that we find difficult to resolve without hearing that evidence orally. We do not need an oral hearing for every complaint. The ombudsperson will decide if oral evidence is needed. If we have a hearing and if the complainant gives us oral evidence, they will then be cross-examined about what they have said. In the same way, witnesses from the provider will also be cross-examined.

10.3.4.5 Potential Costs

Bringing a complaint to us is a straightforward and free process. A consumer does not need to hire a solicitor or any other professional assistance to handle their complaint, but if they choose to, then any costs incurred for these services are their responsibility.

10.3.4.6 Financial Obligations

A complaint may be about a financial product for which a consumer makes regular payments or repayments, such as an investment, an insurance policy or a mortgage. Making a complaint to us does not change a consumer's financial obligations and they should continue to make payments as normal.

10.3.5 Outcome of the Process

There are three potential outcomes of Dispute Resolution:

1. A settlement agreed between the complainant and their provider.
2. Clarification from the provider around the issue(s) which the complainant complained about, which solves their complaint.

3. No settlement agreed and the complaint transfers to investigation

There are four potential outcomes of a formal investigation. The complaint is:

- upheld
- substantially upheld
- partially upheld
- not upheld

When a financial service complaint is upheld, substantially upheld or partially upheld, the legally binding decision may direct the provider to pay compensation to the complainant, or to fix or correct the issue.

The ombudsperson can direct a financial service provider to pay compensation of up to EUR 500,000, or EUR 52,000 per annum in the case of annuities.

The ombudsperson's statutory powers are more limited when dealing with complaints against pension providers. The ombudsperson can direct a pension provider to fix or correct an issue, but any direction cannot exceed any actual loss of benefit under the pension scheme concerned. Therefore, no additional compensation can be directed for pension complaints.

The provider must implement any direction set out in the ombudsperson's legally binding decision, unless the decision is appealed to the High Court, by the complainant or the provider, within a period of 35 days.

If the complaint is not upheld, the ombudsperson cannot direct the provider to take any action or to pay compensation.

10.3.6 Insurance Ombudsperson's Decision

As mentioned above, decisions by the ombudsperson are legally binding. Once a legally binding decision is issued, the provider must implement any direction set out in the ombudsperson's legally binding decision unless the complainant or the provider challenges the decision in the High Court, within a period of 35 days. Pursuing an appeal to the High Court can lead to the complainant becoming liable for legal costs.

In the event of an appeal to the High Court, all of the evidence put forward to the ombudsperson for the purpose of the adjudication, is examined to assess whether the ombudsperson came to the decision correctly, and whether the procedures offered to the parties in the course of that decision-making process were fair. Should the Court take the view that the decision of the ombudsperson is not sound, any such decision can be amended as is considered appropriate by the Court, or the complaint may be sent back to the ombudsperson for fresh consideration of the issues.

Where a provider does not comply with the ombudsperson's decision, the ombudsperson can apply to the Circuit Court for an order requiring the financial service provider or the pension provider concerned to comply with the direction within a period, or by a date.[35]

10.3.6.1 Publishing Legally Binding Decisions

The ombudsperson publishes legally binding decisions in relation to complaints concerning financial service providers under s. 62 of the FSPO Act.

The legislation requires that decisions should be published in a manner that ensures that a complainant is not identified by name, address or otherwise, and a provider is not identified by name or address.

Publication must also comply with data protection legislation and regulations. The legislation also provides the ombudsperson with the power to publish case studies of decisions relating to pension providers, but not the full decision.

Decisions appealed to the High Court are not published while they are the subject of legal proceedings.

When the ombudsperson issues a legally binding decision, that decision may be challenged by way of statutory appeal to the High Court within 35 calendar days from that date. For this reason, the ombudsperson does not publish decisions before the elapse of the 35-day period available to the parties to issue a statutory appeal to the High Court. In addition, decisions which have been appealed to the High Court are not published, pending the outcome of any such court proceedings.

To ensure transparency and ease of access to these decisions, the FSPO has an online database of the ombudsperson's legally binding decisions. This database holds the full text of the vast majority of ombudsperson's decisions in relation to complaints against financial service providers, issued by the ombudsperson since January 2018. At the end of 2023, our database held over 2300 legally binding decisions.

The regular publication of decisions means that decisions are published shortly after the time limit for a statutory appeal to the High Court has passed and a review of each decision has been conducted to ensure compliance with the provisions of the Financial Services and Pensions Ombudsman Act.

10.3.6.2 Report on Named Financial Service Providers

In accordance with s. 25 of the FSPO Act, the ombudsperson may identify every regulated financial service provider, which, in each year, had at least three complaints against it upheld, substantially upheld, or partially upheld. The report excludes any decision upholding a complaint if that decision is the subject of a statutory appeal at the time of publication.

---

[35] Financial Services and Pensions Ombudsman Act 2017, s. 65. https://www.irishstatutebook.ie/eli/2017/act/22/enacted/en/print#sec65. Accessed 16 Apr 2025.

In the report,[36] the financial service providers are listed in order of the combined total number of complaints upheld, substantially upheld or partially upheld. The name of the business group is provided where the financial service provider is a member of a business group.

10.3.7 Oversight by the Courts

Decisions by the ombudsperson are legally binding. Once a legally binding decision is issued, the provider must implement any direction set out in the ombudsperson's legally binding decision unless the complainant or the provider challenges the decision in the High Court within a period of 35 days. Pursuing an appeal to the High Court can lead to the complainant becoming liable for legal costs.

In the event of an appeal to the High Court, all of the evidence put forward to the ombudsperson for the purpose of the adjudication, is examined to assess whether the ombudsperson came to the decision correctly, and whether the procedures offered to the parties in the course of that decision-making process were fair. Should the Court take the view that the decision of the ombudsperson is not sound, any such decision can be amended as is considered appropriate by the Court, or the complaint may be sent back to the ombudsperson for fresh consideration of the issues.

10.4 Statistical Data

10.4.1 Complaints Received and Closed 2018–2022

The FSPO receives on average 5,331 complaints per year and closes on average 5,008 complaints per year (see Table 10.7).

An average of 1,486 insurance complaints are received per year (see Table 10.8).

208 inadmissible complaints are received on average per year. Complaints are considered to be inadmissible where they are intended for a different ombudsperson or relate to non-financial products and services, or service providers that do not fall within the remit of this Office. Where possible, the complainant is redirected to the appropriate body.

[36] Financial Services and Pensions Ombudsman (2024) Overview of Complaints 2022. https://www.fspo.ie/documents/Overview-of-Complaints-2022.pdf. Accessed 16 Apr 2025.

Table 10.7 Complaints received and closed 2018–2022[a]

Year	2018	2019	2020	2021	2022
Complaints received	5692	5275	5395	4658	4781
Complaints Closed	4443	4569	6193	5010	4647

[a]Financial Services and Pensions Ombudsman (2023) The Financial Services and Pensions Ombudsman Overview of Complaints 2018–2022. https://www.fspo.ie/publications/overview-of-complaints.asp. Accessed 16 Apr 2025

Table 10.8 Complaints received by sector 2018–2022

Complaints received by Sector	2018	2019	2020	2021	2022
Banking	3104	2862	2782	2660	2640
Insurance	**1843**	**1660**	**1579**	**1257**	**1129**
Investment	278	233	278	352	366
Pension	363	214	179	186	233

Table 10.9 Percentage of complaints closed in DRS in 2022[a]

Time open	Percentage of complaints closed in DRS in 2022
2 months or less	6.4%
2–4 months	38.6%
4–6 months	27.4%
Over 6 months	27.5%

[a]Financial Services and Pensions Ombudsman (2023) The Financial Services and Pensions Ombudsman ADR Annual Activity Report 2022, p. 15. https://www.fspo.ie/documents/FSPO-ADR-Regulations-Annual-Report-2022.pdf. Accessed 16 Apr 2025

10.4.2 *Average Time to resolve Disputes*

The average time from receipt of complaint to closure was 10 months for complaints that closed in 2022 (see Table 10.9). 47% of complaints were closed at an early stage in Customer Operations and Information Management, while a further 35% were closed in Dispute Resolution Services. In total, more than 80% of complaints that closed in 2022 were closed within 12 months of the complaint being made. Complaints that require a formal process can take considerably longer.

During 2022, 36 complaints were settled during the formal investigation process as an outside settlement (Table 10.10). The value to complainants of these settlements is unquantifiable, but nevertheless provides an agreed outcome for the complainant and the provider.

Table 10.10 Percentage of complaints closed in Investigation Services in 2022[a]

Time open	Percentage of complaints closed in DRS in 2022
2 months or less	6.4%
2–4 months	38.6%
4–6 months	27.4%
Over 6 months	27.5%

[a]Financial Services and Pensions Ombudsman (2023) The Financial Services and Pensions Ombudsman ADR Annual Activity Report 2022, p.16. https://www.fspo.ie/documents/FSPO-ADR-Regulations-Annual-Report-2022.pdf. Accessed 16 Apr 2025

10.4.3 Complaints Resolved

As mentioned in Sect. 10.4.1 above, the FSPO closes on average 5,008 complaints per year. Closures can happen for a variety of reasons and at different points in our processes.

In 2022, the FSPO resolved 1,722 complaints through Dispute Resolution Services. 1,137 complaints reached a confidential mediation settlement, and a further 505 complaints were settled where a clarification was accepted by the complainant.

The total value to complainants of mediated settlements was EUR 3,425,443 in 2022. The ability to reach such settlements in a short time frame makes the informal mediation process an attractive option for complainants and providers.

A total of 20 complaints were closed when the parties reached a settlement themselves and 35 were withdrawn by the complainant.

In some 7 complaints, contact was made with the complainant only, the complaint was intended for another ombudsperson or the complainant resolved their issue without the provider.

16 were closed within Dispute Resolution Services at an early stage as the complainant did not provide enough information to proceed, or the complaint could be immediately resolved.

The FSPO resolves a majority of complaints at an early stage through mediation within the Dispute Resolution Service. When a complaint is not resolved through mediation, it may be transferred for a formal investigation.

During 2022, the ombudsperson issued 439 legally binding decisions, which included the following outcomes:

> The combined value of compensation directed in 90 of the 96 legally binding decisions where the complaint was upheld, substantially upheld or partially upheld, was EUR 616,686.
>
> An additional amount of EUR 965,527 was paid to complainants by providers across 116 complaints which were resolved before the conclusion of the FSPO's formal investigation process.

> A further amount of EUR 174,495 in redress from providers, noted by the ombudsperson as available for acceptance by complainants, was paid across 74 complaints. This resulted in the complaints in those legally binding decisions not being upheld, because the offer in question was reasonable and adequate to redress the conduct giving rise to the complaint, and no formal direction by the ombudsperson was required.
>
> 269 legally binding decisions were issued where on the merits of the complaint, the ombudsperson considered on the evidence that the complaint should not be upheld, and no redress was directed.
>
> 16 legally binding decisions where the ombudsperson made a direction for rectification of the conduct complained of. This may have been in addition to compensation or instead of compensation. The financial value of a direction for rectification, whilst potentially very significant, is difficult to quantify and, on occasion, remains unknown. Examples include:
>
> - A direction to the provider concerned to immediately notify the CCR that the complainant's loan balance was written off, with effect from the date of the complainant's discharge from bankruptcy, and to request the CCR to amend its records accordingly. (Decision 2022-0151[37])
> - A direction to the provider concerned to immediately admit and assess the complainant company's December 2020 insurance claim for business interruption losses, and to make an advance payment of policy benefit of EUR 8,000 to the complainant company, pending the assessment of any further benefit payable. (Decision 2022-0368[38])
> - A direction to the provider concerned to arrange the write-off of a mortgage loan and any interest accrued since the date of the complainant's wife's death, and to correct any adverse credit record associated with this remedy, including making appropriate arrangements with the new loan owner who purchased the outstanding loan balance. (Decision 2022-0036[39])
> - A direction to the provider concerned to recalculate the mortgage balance by reference to a particular interest rate differential, over a certain period. (Decision 2022-0150)
> - A direction to the provider concerned to reinstate annuity payments from May 2020 until May 2024, or until the complainant's death if earlier. (Decision 2022-0234[40])

From 2018–2022, 2,183 legally binding decisions were issued. 226 decisions were upheld, 148 were substantially upheld, 396 were partially upheld, and 1,413 decisions were rejected.

[37] For the full decision, see https://www.fspo.ie/complaint-outcomes/decisions/documents/2022-0151.pdf. Accessed 16 Apr 2025.

[38] For the full decision, see https://www.fspo.ie/complaint-outcomes/decisions/documents/2022-0368.pdf. Accessed 16 Apr 2025.

[39] For the full decision, see https://www.fspo.ie/complaint-outcomes/decisions/documents/2022-0036.pdf. Accessed 16 Apr 2025.

[40] For the full decision, see https://www.fspo.ie/complaint-outcomes/decisions/documents/2022-0150.pdf. Accessed 16 Apr 2025.

10.4.4 Non-compliance with Decisions

Since 2018, there has only been one instance where a financial service provider has not complied with a legally binding decision issued against it. An enforcement application was made to the Circuit Court and the compensation was paid thereafter.

10.5 Insurance Ombudsman Practice

10.5.1 Market Trends

10.5.1.1 Risks to Consumer Protection

Under s. 25 of the FSPO Act, and by the end of Q1 each year, the ombudsperson publishes an Overview of Complaints for the previous year. This includes a summary of all complaints made to the FSPO; a review of trends and patterns in the making of complaints to the FSPO; a breakdown of the method by which all complaints made to the FSPO were dealt with; and a summary of the outcome of all complaints concluded or terminated.

Table 10.11 Insurance complaints received 2018–2022

Total complaints received	7,468
Motor	1,913
Health, accident, to include income protection insurance	1,436
Home and or property	658
Travel	968
Life	849
Consumer Credit, Mortgage Protection	808
Commercial	435
Miscellaneous[a]	347
Multiple Product/Service	54

[a]Miscellaneous includes categories not readily falling into the other categories and could include, for example, marine, farm, gadget, computer, mobile phone and pet insurance

10.5.1.2 Insurance Complaints

The FSPO received 7,468 insurance related complaints from 2018–2022 (see Table 10.11). The insurance product most complained about was motor insurance (1913 complaints), followed by the category ‘health, accident, to include income protection insurance’ (1,436 complaints).

The conduct most complained of from 2018–2022 was ‘claim handling’, followed by ‘rejection of claim’ and then ‘customer service’.

10.5.1.3 COVID-19

The beginning of the COVID-19 pandemic in 2020 led to an increase in the number of complaints submitted to the FSPO as consumers struggled with the financial impact of the pandemic. The complaints received since that time have highlighted that the circumstances surrounding COVID-19, particularly in relation to business interruption insurance claims, were exceptionally difficult for many of those businesses that brought their complaints to us.

600 complaints identified as related to COVID-19 were received in 2020, 275 were received in 2021, but this then fell to 69 new complaints in 2022. 37 of these complaints concerned insurance and 32 concerned banking.

During the pandemic, we prioritised complaints concerning business interruption insurance in recognition of the importance to policyholders of achieving a swift understanding as to whether they were entitled to benefits payments. In 2022, concluding COVID-19 related complaints remained a priority, and at the end of 2022, this Office had reduced the number of COVID-19 related complaints on hand to 132.

10.5.1.4 Approach of Insurance Businesses

The FSPO received a record number of complaints in 2023 (6,182 complaints), representing a 29% increase on the number received in 2022. It is clear that the FSPO needs to further grow its capacity to meet the growing challenges.

In this regard, 2023 was an important year for the organisation, as the Minister for Finance provided sanction to increase its workforce by 42% from 90 to 128. This increase in resources, combined with the work of the FSPO to continuously increase efficiency will significantly impact on the capacity of the Office to deliver for its customers.

It is also important for providers to consider what measures they can take to reduce the number of complaints arising. An increase of almost 30% in the number of complaints being made to the FSPO in just one year should be a cause for reflection amongst providers.

Where appropriate, the FSPO will do what it can to assist providers in their work to reduce complaints. It meets with providers and their representatives to discuss trends in complaints received. The ombudsperson has published over 2,400 legally binding decisions in relation to complaints against financial service providers on its website.

The ombudsperson's annual Overview of Complaints and their Digests of Decisions, which provide analyses and examples of complaints and decisions are also useful resources for both providers and consumers.

In addition to encouraging providers of financial services and pension products to work to reduce the number of complaints arising, the ombudsperson also encourages them to adopt an approach of seeking, where possible, to resolve complaints quickly with their customers.

It is clear that many of the consumers making complaints to the FSPO could have had their complaints addressed by their provider at an earlier point in time. Even after a complaint has been made to the FSPO, there continue to be opportunities for providers and consumers to resolve their complaints informally.

Mediation has been central to the efforts of the FSPO to resolve complaints at the earliest stage and since the introduction of mediation as the default complaint resolution process used by the FSPO, it has achieved very considerable success in facilitating the resolution of complaints by agreement, directly between providers and their customers. Typically, more than 70% of complaints referred to mediation are successfully resolved through the mediation process.

10.5.2 Limitations

When investigating complaints, the FSPO must consider the regulatory status of the financial service provider whose conduct is the subject of the consumer complaint, to ensure that it is a regulated entity falling with its territorial scope as described in Sect. 10.2.3 above.

In addition, however, the FSPO must also consider the particular law specified by the contract to be the governing law of that contractual arrangement in place between the consumer and the financial service provider.

When the consumer contract is not governed by Irish law, the FSPO cannot investigate and adjudicate on that complaint, as this would call for the FSPO to interpret and apply the laws of a foreign jurisdiction in the course of an investigation under the Act, leading to a legally binding outcome.

When that happens, the FSPO will refer the complaint to the appropriate Alternative Dispute Resolution (ADR) body in the relevant country as the competent authority to adjudicate the complaint in relation to the contractual issue arising.

This includes referrals to ADR bodies within the EEA area, in accordance with the FIN-NET Memorandum of Understanding on a Cross-Border Out-of-Court Complaints Network for Financial Services.

The FSPO has no remit to assess consumers' financial awareness and literacy.

10.5.3 De lege ferenda Postulates

The FSPO's Mission is 'providing an impartial, accessible, and responsive complaint resolution service that delivers fair, transparent and timely outcomes, and enhances the financial services and pensions environment'.[41]

Its Vision is of 'a progressive financial services and pension environment built on trust, fairness and transparency, where complaints are the exception'.[42]

The FSPO is a values-driven organisation. Our values are embedded in our processes and procedures. At the heart of our values is a deep desire to consistently deliver the best possible service for our customers and stakeholders.

Its values are:

Fairness

- We will adopt an impartial, independent, objective approach, dealing with each complaint based on its own merits.
- We will listen to all parties in dispute, asking questions to redress the balance between them.Integrity

- We will uphold the highest ethical standards.
- We will earn trust by delivering our services in an unbiased, transparent and professional manner.
- We will respect the confidentiality of those seeking our services.Independence

- We will be independent in how we handle complaints, yet accountable to the people and the Oireachtas (Irish national parliament).Accessibility

- We will be responsive to the needs of our customers.
- We will communicate clearly and in a professional manner.
- We will provide guidance and support to access our services.Effectiveness

- We will continuously seek ways of improving how we communicate and deliver our services.
- We will seek to deal with every complaint in the most effective, efficient and timely manner.

Strategic Plan

We launched our second Strategic Plan, 'Connecting and Innovating',[43] in 2021. The Strategic Plan provides a high-level framework of strategic priorities, gives

---

[41] The Financial Services and Pensions Ombudsman (2021) Strategic Plan 2021–2024 Connecting and Innovating, p.8. https://www.fspo.ie/documents/Strategic-Plan-2021-2024-Connecting-and-Engaging.pdf. Accessed 16 Apr 2025.

[42] The Financial Services and Pensions Ombudsman (2021) Strategic Plan 2021–2024 Connecting and Innovating, p.8. https://www.fspo.ie/documents/Strategic-Plan-2021-2024-Connecting-and-Engaging.pdf. Accessed 16 Apr 2025.

[43] Financial Services and Pensions Ombudsman (2021) Strategic Plan 2021–2024 Connecting and Innovating. https://www.fspo.ie/documents/Strategic-Plan-2021-2024-Connecting-and-Engaging.pdf. Accessed 16 Apr 2025.

clear direction to the work of the FSPO and sets out how we will measure our success in achieving these priorities.

Covering the period 2021–2024, the Strategy sets out the following strategic priorities:

Evolving and Innovating

We will adapt and evolve our service, using innovation to respond to the changing needs and expectations of all our customers, maintaining a relentless focus on delivering fair, impartial, timely outcomes.

Connecting and Engaging

We will connect with consumers, providers, regulatory bodies and others to help build a better understanding of what we do, and how people can best access and make use of our service should they need us.

Sharing and Influencing

We will play our full part in helping to raise standards in complaints handling and resolution, and to inform legislative, regulatory and policy developments so that customer complaints are prevented from arising where possible, and fair outcomes are achieved.

Developing our People, Building our Capability

We will build on our values-led culture to truly embrace diverse perspectives at all levels of our organisation. We are committed to fostering a truly inclusive culture, where every one of our team members believes that they belong and that they have equal opportunity to thrive as part of a diverse workforce that is reflective of the customers we proudly serve.

Our strategic priorities reflect our ambition to evolve and innovate our services and the organisation, with a strong focus on our customers, external stakeholders and audiences.

Critical to the delivery of our third strategic priority is effective engagement, communication and collaboration with our stakeholders. During 2023, the FSPO had 38 stakeholder engagements with regulatory bodies, government departments, Oireachtas Committees, industry groups, peer groups and consumer groups. Key areas for discussion were FSPO insights and pipeline data, financial literacy and engagement on the Consumer Protection Code review.

A presentation of the FSPO to the Consumer Advisory Group of the Central Bank of Ireland (CBI) facilitated greater insight into the role and functions of the FSPO. The role of the Consumer Advisory Group is to advise the CBI on the performance of its functions and the exercise of its powers in relation to consumers of financial services.

10.6 Other

10.6.1 Accessibility

10.6.1.1 Consumer Awareness

Our second strategic priority "Connecting and Engaging" commits the FSPO to effectively communicate with all its stakeholders, to create awareness of its role and to build a better understanding of what it does. To assist in achieving this aim, it gathers data through surveys, meeting the public through outreach events and having a clear focus on improving both its physical and digital accessibility.

The FSPO is committed to providing equality of access to its services for all people. The FSPO has an Access Officer, whose role is to coordinate assistance and guidance for persons with disabilities to ensure they can access our services and the information we provide. The role of Access Officer is an important part of creating a society where everyone is treated with dignity, has access to human rights and does not suffer from discrimination.

Regulated providers are obliged, under the Consumer Protection Code 2012,[44] to tell customers they may contact the FSPO if they are not satisfied with its resolution of their complaint and to provide the FSPO's contact details.

10.6.1.2 Website

The FSPO website, www.fspo.ie, plays a critical role in meeting our commitments under the Strategic Plan to provide clear and accessible information to consumers, financial service providers, pension providers, industry bodies and public bodies.

In addition to the above, the FSPO is continually working to improve the accessibility of the documents available, and the website content in general, so that information may be accessed by users of all abilities.

10.6.1.3 Digital Marketing

Our first digital marketing campaign commenced in 2022. Since then, digital marketing has played an important role in the delivery of the FSPO's communications strategy. It has provided the opportunity to target identified audiences and demographics, with in-depth, ongoing measurement of campaign performance.

[44] Central Bank of Ireland (2015) Consumer Protection Code 2012 (as amended), s. 10. https://www.centralbank.ie/docs/default-source/regulation/consumer-protection/other-codes-of-conduct/4-gns-4-2-7-cp-code-2012.pdf. Accessed 16 Apr 2025.

Digital channels also offer better value for money in comparison to traditional forms of media. Organic digital campaigns increased significantly during 2023 as a result of increased resources within the communications team.

Our campaigns focused on awareness, careers and public events. We also continued with our paid digital marketing campaign across a range of platforms during 2023, with regular measurement and review to ensure optimum performance.

To complement our existing social media presence on Facebook,[45] we launched a LinkedIn[46] page in mid-2023. This has been well received and provides access to an alternate demographic for raising awareness about our services. The LinkedIn page allows us to communicate our services, publications, events and in particular, it provides an excellent platform for announcing recruitment campaigns.

10.6.1.4 Youth Awareness

The FSPO is a proud sponsor of the Graduate.ie programme, a government, local government and EU-funded Citizenship & Democracy programme for second level students and members of Youth Reach Centres or Youth Clubs in Ireland. The free, online competition encourages second level students to learn about important local and national topics, such as entrepreneurship, the environment, sustainability, health and fitness, and financial literacy. Sponsorship of this programme raises awareness of the FSPO and its service and empowers young people to learn about their rights. Students who complete the competition can be entered to win one of many educational trips to Brussels, Luxembourg and the European Parliament in Strasbourg each year. During 2023, almost 28,000 students registered for the programme, with just over 8,760 taking part in the weekly quiz.

10.6.1.5 Events

We are committed to growing awareness of our role and increasing our visibility amongst the public, particularly amongst sectors of the population which would have low awareness of our functions. Our communications strategy supports our Strategic Plan in this regard, through the identification of events at which our team can engage with attendees to explain our role and function.

[45] https://www.facebook.com/FSPOIreland. Accessed 16 Apr 2025.

[46] https://www.linkedin.com/company/fspo. Accessed 16 Apr 2025.

10.6.1.6 Media Relations

The FSPO publishes articles in external publications each year. In early January 2023, one such article was published and served to enhance public awareness of the kinds of complaints we receive in relation to private health insurance, the common issues consumers experience, and what they should be aware of when buying private health insurance.

This article followed on from the earlier release of the Ombudsman's Digest of Legally Binding Decisions, volume 8, which was released in late 2022.[47] This Digest provided summaries of decisions issued between 2018 and 2022 and highlighted the difficult circumstances experienced by consumers which led to a complaint to the FSPO.

Another article focused on raising awareness with consumers through our attendance at the 50 Plus Show, on how to resolve financial service complaints with a provider, and how a complaint can be made to the FSPO, where the consumer remains unsatisfied following a complaint to the business itself.

The ombudsperson and deputy ombudsperson also participated in radio and television interviews in relation to the release of the Overview of Complaints 2022, released in March 2023, and to promote our attendance at the 50 Plus Show in Limerick.

The Overview of Complaints details the activities of the FSPO each year and provides easy access to case studies and summaries of decisions to grow awareness of the kinds of complaints which the FSPO received and the outcomes of its decisions.

10.6.2 Accountability

The FSPO operates a Customer Charter and Customer Action Plan, which outline the standard of service and behaviour underpinning all interactions with customers and describe the FSPO's policy of encouraging feedback from its customers, evaluating that feedback and, where possible, continuously improving the quality of service offered.

While the Minister has no role in the investigation of complaints brought to the FSPO under the FSPO Act, it is advised that there is a Service Level, Oversight and Performance Delivery Agreement in place between the Department of Finance and the Office of the Financial Services and Pensions Ombudsman, in accordance with the Code of Practice for the Governance of State Bodies (2016),[48] which sets out the

[47] Financial Services and Pensions Ombudsman (2022) Ombudsman's Digest of Legally Binding Decisions on Health Insurance. https://www.fspo.ie/documents/Digest-of-Decisions-Volume-8-Final.pdf. Accessed 16 Apr 2025.

[48] The Department of Public Expenditure and Reform (2016) The Code of Practice for the Governance of State Bodies. https://hea.ie/assets/uploads/2017/05/Code-of-Practice-for-Governance-of-State-Bodies-2016.pdf. Accessed 16 Apr 2025.

arrangements for oversight, monitoring and reporting and also sets out the FSPO's commitments regarding the operational roles, responsibilities, outputs and outcomes.

Under s. 40 of the FSPO Act, the FSPOC has the function to keep under review the efficiency and effectiveness of the ombudsperson.

Each year, the FSPO prepares an annual report[49] on the performance of its functions during the previous year. Once its accounts have been certified by the Comptroller and Auditor General, the annual report is submitted to the Minister for Finance and the Minister for Social Protection pursuant to s. 24(2) of the FSPO Act.

Once the annual report is laid before the Houses of the Oireachtas, the report must be published, in both English and Irish, as soon as possible.

Under s. 25 of the FSPO Act, and by the end of Q1 each year, the ombudsperson publishes an Overview of Complaints for the previous year. This includes a summary of all complaints made to the FSPO, a review of trends and patterns in the making of complaints to the FSPO; a breakdown of the method by which all complaints made to the FSPO were dealt with; and a summary of the outcome of all complaints concluded or terminated.

Other reports may be published throughout the year, such as the Ombudsman's Digests of Legally Binding Decisions.[50] These reports include short summaries of a selection of decisions in relation to complaints against financial service providers, and case studies of decisions in relation to complaints against pension providers.

The ombudsperson is accountable to the Public Accounts Committee and to other Oireachtas Committees under ss. 22 and 23 of the FSPO Act.

Budget Approval

The FSPOC approves the FSPO's annual budget which is linked to the organisation's Strategic Plan. This annual budget is then funded through two distinct sources; the financial services complaints are funded by a levy on the financial services industry and the pensions complaints are funded by the Exchequer, through the Department of Finance.[51] The levy is enacted through a statutory instrument.

---

[49] For more details, see the Financial Services and Pensions Ombudsman's Annual Reports 2018–2022. https://www.fspo.ie/publications/annual-report.asp. Accessed 16 Apr 2025.

[50] For more details, see Ombudsman's Digests of Legally Binding Decisions Vols 1–8, https://www.fspo.ie/publications/. 16 Apr 2025.

[51] For more details, see Understanding the Financial Services Industry Levy 2018–2022. www.fspo.ie/governance/funding.asp. 16 Apr 2025.

Legal Sources

The Department of Public Expenditure and Reform (2016) The Code of Practice for the Governance of State Bodies. https://www.gov.ie/pdf/?file=https://assets.gov.ie/138835/1d213280-29b8-41ec-92c4-ca8974db5224.pdf#page=null.pdf. Accessed 20 December 2024.

Financial Services and Pensions Ombudsman (2022) Financial Services and Pensions Ombudsman Code of Ethics for Mediation. https://www.fspo.ie/documents/FSPO-Code-of-Ethics-for-Mediation-October-2022.pdf. Accessed 14 August 2023

Financial Services and Pensions Ombudsman (2023) S.I. No. 6 of 2023, Financial Services and Pensions Ombudsman Act 2017 (Financial Services and Pensions Ombudsman Council) Financial Services Industry Levy Regulations 2023, https://www.fspo.ie/documents/SI-6-of-2023-FSPO-Industry-Levy.pdf. Accessed 24 July 2023

FIN-NET (2016) FIN-NET Memorandum of Understanding on a Cross-Border Out-of-Court Complaints Network for Financial Services. https://finance.ec.europa.eu/system/files/2023-02/memorandum-of-understanding_en.pdf. Accessed 15 August 2023

Memorandum of Understanding between the Central Bank of Ireland and the Financial Services and Pensions Ombudsman (2023), https://www.fspo.ie/documents/MoU-from-CBI.pdf. Accessed 8 August 2024

Documents

Financial Services and Pensions Ombudsman (2019) The Financial Services and Pensions Ombudsman Annual Report 2018. https://www.fspo.ie/documents/FSPO_AnnualReport_2018.pdf. Accessed 28 August 2023

Financial Services and Pensions Ombudsman (2019) The Financial Services and Pensions Ombudsman Overview of Complaints 2018. https://www.fspo.ie/documents/FSPO-Overview-of-Complaints-2018.pdf. Accessed 14 August 2023

Financial Services and Pensions Ombudsman (2020) The Financial Services and Pensions Ombudsman Annual Report 2019. https://www.fspo.ie/documents/FSPO_AnnualReport_2019.pdf. Accessed 28 August 2023

Financial Services and Pensions Ombudsman (2020) The Financial Services and Pensions Ombudsman Overview of Complaints 2019. https://www.fspo.ie/documents/Complaints_Overview_2019-v2.pdf. Accessed 14 August 2023

Financial Services and Pensions Ombudsman (2021) Ombudsman's Digest of Legally Binding Decisions, Volume 6, https://www.fspo.ie/documents/Ombudsmans_Digest_of_Decisions_2021_Vol6.pdf. Accessed 14 August 2023

Financial Services and Pensions Ombudsman (2021) Ombudsman's Digest of Legally Binding Decisions Health Insurance, Volume 8. https://www.fspo.ie/documents/Digest-of-Decisions-Volume-8-Final.pdf. Accessed 14 August 2023

Financial Services and Pensions Ombudsman (2021) Strategic Plan 2021–2024 Connecting and Innovating. https://www.fspo.ie/documents/Strategic-Plan-2021-2024-Connecting-and-Engaging.pdf. Accessed 14 August 2023

Financial Services and Pensions Ombudsman (2021) The Financial Services and Pensions Ombudsman Annual Report 2020. https://www.fspo.ie/documents/FSPO-Annual-Report-2020.pdf. Accessed 28 August 2023

Financial Services and Pensions Ombudsman (2021) The Financial Services and Pensions Ombudsman Overview of Complaints 2020. https://www.fspo.ie/documents/Overview_of_Complaints_2020_Final.pdf. Accessed 14 August 2023

Financial Services and Pensions Ombudsman (2022) FSPO People Strategy 2022–2025. https://www.fspo.ie/governance/funding.asp. Accessed 24 July 2023

Financial Services and Pensions Ombudsman (2022) Ombudsman's Digest of Legally Binding Decisions Travel Insurance, Volume 7. https://www.fspo.ie/documents/Digest-of-Decisions-Volume-7-Final.pdf. Accessed 14 August 2023

Financial Services and Pensions Ombudsman (2022) The Financial Services and Pensions Ombudsman Annual Report 2021. https://www.fspo.ie/documents/FSPO-Annual-Report-2021.pdf. Accessed 28 August 2023

Financial Services and Pensions Ombudsman (2022) The Financial Services and Pensions Ombudsman Overview of Complaints 2021. https://www.fspo.ie/documents/Overview-of-Complaints-2021.pdf. Accessed 14 August 2023

Financial Services and Pensions Ombudsman (2023) Cross Border Referrals. https://www.fspo.ie/our-services/cross-border-referrals.asp. Accessed 15 August 2023

Financial Services and Pensions Ombudsman (2023) Financial Services and Pensions Ombudsman Overview of Complaints 2022. https://www.fspo.ie/documents/Overview-of-Complaints-2022.pdf. Accessed 14 August 2023

Financial Services and Pensions Ombudsman (2023) The Financial Services and Pensions Ombudsman Annual Report 2022. https://www.fspo.ie/documents/Annual-Report-2022.pdf. Accessed 28 August 2023

Financial Services and Pensions Ombudsman (2023) The Financial Services and Pensions Ombudsman ADR Annual Activity Report 2022. https://www.fspo.ie/documents/FSPO-ADR-Regulations-Annual-Report-2022.pdf. Accessed 14 August 2023

Financial Services and Pensions Ombudsman (2023) Understanding the Financial Services Industry Levy 2023. https://www.fspo.ie/documents/Understanding-the-Financial-Services-Industry-Levy-Report-2023.pdf. Accessed 24 July 2023

Public Service Reform Programme 2014, https://reformplan.per.gov.ie/2014/resources/Action-Plan.pdf. Accessed 8 August 2024

Chapter 11
Netherlands

Kifid: Dutch Institute for Financial Disputes

Eveline Ruinaard and Colinda Guijt

11.1 Institutional Framework[1]

11.1.1 Establishment

Kifid,[2] the Dutch Institute for Financial Disputes, was established in 2007 and is based in The Hague. It combines the activities of four predecessors, namely the four organisations that for years were responsible for alternative (i.e. out-of-court) resolution of disputes in the fields of (1) banking, (2) mortgages, (3) insurance, and (4) securities. All these organisations, which operated on the basis of self-regulation, merged in 2007 to form Kifid and so to improve accessibility for consumers.

Kifid also operates on the basis of self-regulation. It was set up by the financial sector itself in liaison with the Dutch Consumer Association. Although there was no statutory obligation at that time to establish an alternative dispute resolution body for the financial sector, the benefits of bringing this fragmented landscape together under a single roof were evident. Since then, consumers have been able to contact a single institution, Kifid, if they have a complaint about any financial product or

[1] This chapter reflects Kifid's legal and institutional framework as at the end of 2023. Readers should note that changes were implemented in 2024 that are not presented here. For the most current information, consult Kifid's website: https://www.kifid.nl. Accessed 16 Apr 2025.

[2] In full: Stichting *Klachteninstituut Financiële Dienstverlening*.

E. Ruinaard (✉)
Arbitration Commission and Kifid, Den Haag, The Netherlands
e-mail: consumenten@kifid.nl

C. Guijt
Kifid, Den Haag, The Netherlands
e-mail: consumenten@kifid.nl

H. Heiss et al. (eds.), *Insurance Ombudsman Schemes*, AIDA Europe Research Series on Insurance Law and Regulation 15,
https://doi.org/10.1007/978-3-032-01500-6_11

service. Establishing a single alternative dispute resolution body is a way of combining expertise and so improving the quality of services offered to consumers and financial service providers alike.

The Financial Supervision Act (hereinafter Wft)[3] is the legislative framework for the Dutch financial sector and determines how financial service providers operate in the consumer market. This legislation requires financial service providers to have an internal complaints procedure and also to be affiliated to a body designated by the Minister of Finance for the resolution of disputes relating to their payment and other financial products and services (art. 4:17 Wft).

By the decree of 22 December 2006, the Minister of Finance designated Kifid as the dispute resolution body in accordance with the Financial Supervision Act (Wft). This created the legal basis for Kifid.[4]

Kifid's purpose is set out in art. 3 of its Articles of Association, as published on its website.[5] Its purpose is to operate a mediation body approved by the minister, together with a body able to issue binding rulings on complaints relating to the provision of financial services, as defined in the Financial Supervision Act (Wft). Its purpose is also to provide information on internal complaints procedures, to establish uniform review frameworks for such arrangements, and to do everything related or conducive to this in the broadest sense. Pursuant to art. 3, Kifid has sought to achieve this purpose by, among other things, establishing an Arbitration Commission and an Appeals Board, along with the accompanying regulations, and ensuring an adequate management support organisation. Lastly, under art. 3, the foundation and its bodies (i.e. the Managing Board, the Arbitration Commission and the Appeals Board) must perform their activities independently and impartially.

11.1.2 Governance Model

Kifid was established as a private foundation. Rather than being formed as a government organisation, Kifid is an independent organisation with its own Managing Board. The composition of the Managing Board and its responsibilities are set out in Kifid's Articles of Association. The Managing Board reports to the Minister of Finance.

[3] *Wet op het financieel toezicht*. For details, see https://wetten.overheid.nl. Accessed 16 Apr 2025.

[4] See https://zoek.officielebekendmakingen.nl/stcrt-2007-5-p22-SC78744.html. Accessed 16 Apr 2025.

[5] 2020 Articles of Association. For details, see Kifid. 2020. Statuten per 14 augustus 2020 van de stichting: Kifid, Stichting Klachteninstituut Financiële Dienstverlening, met zetel in de gemeente 's-Gravenhage. https://www.kifid.nl/wp-content/uploads/2020/08/Statuten-Kifid-Stichting-Klachtenintituut-Financiele-Dienstverlening-vanaf-14-augustus-2020.pdf. Accessed 16 Apr 2025.

The statutory framework within which it operates is set out in the 2015 Alternative Dispute Resolution for Consumer Disputes Implementation Act[6] which is the legislation implementing the EU ADR Directive.[7] This legislation, referred to in the rest of this report as the 'Implementation Act', comprises provisions for ensuring access to alternative (i.e. out-of-court) dispute resolution methods and imposes requirements on the bodies and procedures used to resolve disputes in such manner. For the financial sector, these provisions have been elaborated in the Decree on the Supervision of the Conduct of Financial Enterprises *(Besluit Gedragstoezicht financiële ondernemingen* hereinafter BGfo).[8] Pursuant to this decree, based on the Financial Supervision Act (Wft), the Minister of Finance is responsible for supervising Kifid.

Kifid's Managing Board is a non-executive Board ('Supervisory Board model') and comprises three to five natural persons; under art. 5 of the Articles of Association, these persons are not permitted to work in the financial sector. Managing Board members are appointed for a period of four years and may be reappointed for a further period of four years; being a Managing Board member is an ancillary activity. The Managing Board is responsible for ensuring its own composition, including the recruitment of new members.

The manner in which Managing Board members are appointed and reappointed and the requirements they have to meet are set out in art. 5 of Kifid's Articles of Association. An (re)appointment takes place by decision of the Board. This decision requires a qualified majority of two-thirds of the votes cast.

The Articles of Association also state that the procedures for appointing and reappointing Managing Board members must be approved in writing by the Minister of Finance. This requirement derives from the Decree on the Supervision of the Conduct of Financial Enterprises (arts. 46 and 48a BGfo). The appointments, and any reappointments, must be approved by the Minister of Finance.

The Managing Board determines the remuneration of its members and records this in its remuneration policy, which has to be approved by the Minister of Finance (art. 8.1). The Managing Board members' tasks and responsibilities are detailed in art. 9 of the Articles of Association. The Managing Board is responsible for managing the foundation. The Managing Board explicitly does not become involved in the procedural handling or substantive assessment of and decisions on complaints submitted to Kifid.

The Chair of the Arbitration Commission, who is also a managing director, is responsible for day-to-day management of Kifid, as set out in art. 19 of the Articles of Association. Under authorisation by the Managing Board, the Chair of the

---

[6] *Implementatiewet buitengerechtelijke geschillenbeslechting consumenten*. For details, see https://wetten.overheid.nl. Accessed 16 Apr 2025.

[7] Directive 2013/11/EU of the European Parliament and of the Council of 21 May 2013 on alternative dispute resolution for consumer disputes and amending Regulation (EC) No 2006/2004 and Directive 2009/22/EC (Directive on consumer ADR) [2013] OJ L165/63.

[8] *Besluit Gedragstoezicht financiële ondernemingen*. For details, see https://wetten.overheid.nl. Accessed 16 Apr 2025.

Arbitration Commission represents the foundation. The Chair of the Arbitration Commission reports to the Managing Board and prepares the annual budget, annual financial statements and annual report, as well as attending meetings of the Managing Board.

The Minister of Finance supervises Kifid in the sense that the Decree on the Supervision of the Conduct of Financial Enterprises (BGfo) vests various responsibilities in this minister as the authorised minister. This will be set out in the following sections of this chapter.

11.1.3 Coverage

Kifid has been set up to resolve consumer complaints about financial products and services.

Under the EU ADR Directive, Kifid has been appointed as the body responsible for resolving disputes between consumers and financial service providers in the Netherlands. It is recognised by the Minister of Finance as a mediator and can also issue binding rulings. Kifid provides a broad range of alternative dispute resolution services because we handle complaints about financial products and services provided by banks, life and general insurers, intermediaries, mortgage advisers, asset managers and investment advisers.

Alongside Kifid, there is an ADR body that handles health insurance disputes only. There is also an ADR body that handles complaints about pension funds.

In other words, consumers can contact Kifid regarding any other financial disputes they may have. The complaints that Kifid handles are very varied, ranging from complaints about online fraud and excessive charges on insurance policies to complaints about the handling of fire-related damage and complaints about execution-only investments and interest charged on revolving credits and other lending.

The term 'consumer' is defined in Question 5 of the Arbitration Commission regulations[9] as a natural person who uses a financial service for private purposes, i.e. not for trading, business, professional or other comparable activities. If a natural person also uses a financial service for commercial purposes, the latter must not be the dominant activity. Question 5 includes various examples of situations in which Kifid is also authorised to handle a complaint, even when it does not meet the definition above.

Kifid does not only serve consumers. We have also been able to handle small businesses' complaints about bank loans since 1 July 2018, complaints about

[9] *Reglement Geschillencommissie Kifid.* For details, see Kifid. 2024. Reglement voor de behandeling van klachten door de Geschillencommissie Financiële Dienstverlening van de Stichting Klachteninstituut financiële dienstverlening (Kifid). https://www.kifid.nl/wp-content/uploads/2024/05/Kifid_Reglement-Geschillencommissie-vanaf-1-april-2024-1.pdf. Accessed 16 Apr 2025.

alternative forms of finance since 1 July 2019 and complaints about financial advice since 1 May 2021, and complaints about short-term business loans since 1 October 2023. The authority of Kifid to handle these kinds of complaints made by small businesses is based on self-regulation. First the banking sector introduced Kifid as an easily accessible expert and impartial dispute resolution body for this target group. This initiative was later followed by establishing an organisation for SME financing. The main reason was to provide the same services for small businesses as for consumers.

Kifid primarily handles complaints submitted by consumers. In 2023, for example, we handled a total of 3201 complaints, seven of which were submitted by small businesses. Lastly, we have been able to handle complaints about registrations at the Credit Registration Office (BKR)[10] for both consumers and small businesses since 1 October 2021.

Kifid is only authorised to handle complaints about financial services governed by Dutch law and involving financial service providers established in the Netherlands, active in the Dutch consumer market, and affiliated to Kifid.

11.1.4 Insurance Business Covered

Under the Financial Supervision Act (Wft), financial service providers operating in the Dutch consumer market have to be affiliated to Kifid. In other words, they have a statutory duty to be affiliated with Kifid as the designated alternative dispute resolution body (art. 4:17 Wft).

The Dutch Authority for the Financial Markets (*Autoriteit Financiële Markten* (hereinafter AFM)),[11] imposes this obligation when granting a licence to operate in the Dutch consumer market. The AFM is responsible for monitoring compliance with licensing conditions. This applies to general and life insurers, pension insurers, insurance intermediaries and advisers, as well as pension advisers and premium pension institutions. Should problems arise with a financial service provider while a complaint is being handled, whether by Kifid's Arbitration Commission or its Appeals Board, the Chair of the relevant body can report this to the AFM.

This means that Kifid can handle complaints relating to a very wide range of insurance products:

General insurance: home insurance, theft insurance, fire insurance, liability insurance, travel insurance, cancellation insurance, motor vehicle insurance, vessel insurance, telephone insurance, pet insurance, horse insurance, legal expenses insurance, accident insurance and disability insurance.

Life insurance: pension insurance, term life insurance, unit-linked insurance and funeral insurance.

---

[10] For details, see https://www.bkr.nl. Accessed 16 Apr 2025.

[11] For details, see https://www.afm.nl/en/over-de-afm. Accessed 16 Apr 2025.

11.1.5 Appointment of Kifid Dispute Resolvers

Kifid's organisation comprises an Arbitration Commission and an Appeals Board, together with various management support services. Kifid does not have an ombudsperson.

The work of all the members of the Arbitration Commission or Appeals Board for Kifid is an ancillary activity.[12] Members of the Arbitration Commission and Appeals Board are not allowed to work in the financial sector while working for Kifid or during the twelve months immediately beforehand. Many of them work in the legal sector, either as lawyers or academics. They are selected for their expertise in financial, legal, actuarial, economic or medical matters. Relevant information (in Dutch) about the background of Commission and Board members is published on www.kifid.nl.[13] The principle requiring the Arbitration Commission and Appeals Board to operate impartially is laid down in our Articles of Association and regulations.

The provisions guaranteeing the expertise, independence and impartiality of our dispute resolvers are laid down in art. 5 of the Implementation Act, where it is stated that the dispute resolution body must ensure that dispute resolvers:

- have the required knowledge and expertise in resolving consumer disputes in and out of court, and have a general understanding of the law;
- are appointed for a term of office that is sufficiently long to ensure they act independently and that they cannot be relieved of their duties without a valid reason;
- are not required to accept instructions from one of the two parties to a dispute or their representatives;
- receive remuneration that is not dependent on the outcome of the procedure.

Pursuant to art. 5 of the Implementation Act, dispute resolvers must immediately notify the dispute resolution body of any circumstances that could or could be seen to influence their independence or impartiality or that could cause a conflict of interests with one of the parties to the dispute submitted for resolution.

In arts. 21 and 22 of Kifid's Articles of Association, there is an explicit reference to the requirements for independence and impartiality, which are identical for members of the Arbitration Commission and members of the Appeals Board. The relevant sections in these Articles are worded as below.

- Members of the Arbitration Commission perform their duties independently and as they see fit, and do not accept instructions from anyone regarding performance of these duties.
- From the moment at which they accept appointment to the position, members of the Arbitration Commission must not be employed by or hold any position at a

[12] The only exception is the Chair of the Arbitration Commission, who is responsible for leading the organisation and is also a managing director, employed by Kifid.

[13] For details, see https://www.kifid.nl/organisatie. Accessed 16 Apr 2025.

professional organisation for financial enterprises or at a financial enterprise in respect of which complaints can be submitted to the foundation for resolution. During a period of one (1) year before accepting appointment to the position, they must also not have been employed by or worked in any comparable role or held any position at a professional organisation for financial enterprises or at a financial enterprise in respect of which complaints can be submitted to the foundation for resolution.
- Members of the Arbitration Commission undertake, for a period of one (1) year after their appointment ends, not to work for an affiliated or previously affiliated organisation or for a professional or business organisation of which an affiliated or previously affiliated organisation was or is a member.

In order to ensure compliance with the need for independence and impartiality, art. 5 of the Implementation Act requires the alternative dispute resolution body to have arrangements in place for a dispute resolver to withdraw in the event of a conflict of interest or for parties to be able to raise concerns about a dispute resolver's potential bias.

Kifid meets this requirement by including two options in the regulations of the Arbitration Commission[14] and Appeals Board:[15]

1. The option for Commission members themselves to excuse themselves;[16]
2. The option for complainants to challenge or object to Commission members, as set out in the objections protocol included as an appendix in both sets of regulations. This protocol explains how objections can be submitted and are handled.[17]

Dispute resolvers are expected to keep their expertise up to date. Kifid offers a programme for continuing professional development in which dispute resolvers can also participate. In this way, Kifid complies with the requirement, referred to above, in art. 5 of the Implementation Act.

The Managing Board appoints members to the Arbitration Commission and Appeals Board upon nomination by the responsible Chair (arts. 21 and 22 of the Articles of Association). The Managing Board verifies whether nominations meet the requirements of expertise, independence and impartiality. The Managing Board also appoints the Chairs to these bodies. The latter appointments, and any reappointments, must be approved by the Minister of Finance.

Commission members are always appointed for a period of five years, with the opportunity to be reappointed for further periods of five years at a time, until they

[14] *Reglement Geschillencommissie Kifid.*

[15] *Reglement Commissie van Beroep Kifid.* For details, see Kifid. 2024. Reglement voor de behandeling van beroepen door de Commissie van Beroep Financiële Dienstverlening van de Stichting Klachteninstituut financiële dienstverlening (Kifid). https://www.kifid.nl/wp-content/uploads/2024/05/Kifid_reglement-Commissie-van-Beroep-vanaf-1-april-2024.pdf. Accessed 16 Apr 2025.

[16] See Question 24.5 of the Arbitration Commission Regulations and Rule 11.5 of the Appeals Board Regulations.

[17] Appendix to the Arbitration Commission Regulations and Appeals Board Regulations.

reach the age of 70. From the age of 70, reappointments of commission members are for one year at a time and end on the date on which the member reaches the age of 74.

The Managing Board determines the remuneration of members of the Arbitration Commission and Appeals Board and records this in a remuneration policy that has to be approved by the Minister of Finance (art. 8.3 of the Articles of Association).

New dispute resolvers are recruited by advertising a vacancy on our website. In this way, Kifid makes clear the requirements to be met by commission members. If a vacancy requires specific expertise, Kifid will also use a recruitment agency. The relevant Chair decides whether a candidate for appointment to the Managing Board should be nominated.

Dispute resolvers' activities are structured as follows: complaints handled by the Arbitration Commission are heard by a single assessor or by a panel of three people, while cases relating to matters of principle are heard by a five-member panel. Cases submitted to the Appeals Board are generally heard by a panel of five.

11.1.6 Funding

Kifid is a private foundation funded by the affiliated financial service providers. It does not receive any financial support from the government. Every year, it prepares a budget, which is then used as the basis for setting the annual contributions payable by affiliated financial service providers. The budget is prepared by the Chair of the Arbitration Commission for the Managing Board, which then submits it to five sector organisations for financial service providers. These sector organisations represent the interests of the affiliated financial service providers and can ask questions about and comment on the budget, to which Kifid then responds. The budget, together with the questions, comments and responses, is then sent to the Minister of Finance. Once it has been approved, the budget is adopted by the Managing Board.

This procedure is set out in art. 27 of the Articles of Association and elaborates the provisions of the Decree on the Supervision of the Conduct of Financial Enterprises (art. 48f(4) BGfo).

After the budget has been adopted, Kifid calculates the annual contributions payable by the individual financial service providers. Kifid collects these contributions itself by sending an invoice to each affiliated financial service provider. Kifid calculates the annual contributions due, as set out in its *Kostenreglement* or Expenses Regulations, published annually on www.kifid.nl.[18]

Kifid is a private, non-profit foundation. If there is a budget surplus for any one year, the surplus is offset (as a refund) against the annual contributions due for the year two years after the surplus is recorded (art. 9, Expenses Regulations). If, by

[18] For details, see Kifid. 2024. Kostenreglement Kifid 2024. https://www.kifid.nl/wp-content/uploads/2023/12/Kostenreglement-2024.pdf. Accessed 16 Apr 2025.

contrast, there is a budget shortfall for any one year, this results in an increase in the annual contributions due for the year two years after the shortfall is recorded (i.e. a supplementary charge) (art. 8, Expenses Regulations).

Kifid's budget for 2023 was EUR 10,830,000. Its funding is based on the annual contributions paid by affiliated financial service providers, and it has little other income. It should be noted that the Arbitration Commission handles complaints free of charge, and no fees are payable by consumers. Consumers wishing to submit an appeal to the Appeals Board have to pay a fee of EUR 500, while financial service providers pay a maximum of EUR 5000. As only around 50 appeals are handled each year, this does not generate substantial amounts of income.

The system of annual contributions is based on solidarity. Annual contributions do not depend on whether there were complaints submitted against an individual financial service provider in the previous year nor whether any are expected during the next year. The financial sector has accepted this system because of the common interest in having a sufficiently well-equipped body with the necessary expertise to resolve disputes in the sector. A financial service provider against whom a complaint or appeal is filed does not have to pay a fee. A fee is therefore payable only if the financial service provider itself submits an appeal to the Appeals Board.

Each year, Kifid prepares its financial statements and submits these, together with an auditor's report and the Managing Board's report, to the Minister of Finance for approval. Together, these documents comprise Kifid's annual report. This procedure is set out in art. 26 of the Articles of Association and represents an elaboration of the provisions of the Decree on the Supervision of the Conduct of Financial Enterprises (art. 48f(5) and (6) BGfo).

11.1.7 Kifid's Functions

11.1.7.1 Dispute Resolution

Kifid's main activity is to resolve disputes. Disputes can be resolved through mediation and, if it is unsuccessful, they can be resolved through rulings, which are usually binding. Our work and approach are described below.

When signing up to Kifid, a financial service provider has to decide whether to accept Arbitration Commission rulings as binding or non-binding. Similarly, consumers submitting a complaint have to decide whether they want rulings issued by the Arbitration Commission to be binding or non-binding. A ruling is only binding when both parties accept the ruling as binding. Rulings by the Appeals Board are always binding. Details of the difference between binding and non-binding rulings can be found below in Sect. 11.2.6 concerning Kifid's decisions.

Kifid is not authorised to conduct independent research of its own and can only investigate facts relevant to a complaint submitted. It can engage external experts, where necessary (Question 21 of the Arbitration Commission regulations).

11.1.7.2 Provision of Information

Kifid's responsibilities include providing broad-ranging information on issues arising during its complaints-handling activities. It does this by answering questions by telephone or e-mail on a daily basis. A list of frequently asked questions can be found on our website.[19] The website also provides information in the form of easy-to-understand knowledge documents (under 'Kifid kennis'[20]) to explain how we deal with issues that are often the subject of complaints. These documents are widely consulted, not only by consumers, but also by financial service providers, lawyers, academics, students, and other interested parties.

Twice a year, the Chair of Kifid's Managing Board and the Chair of the Arbitration Commission meet representatives of various consumer and financial sector organisations. Twice a year, Kifid also arranges a meeting with the supervisory authorities (i.e. representatives of the Dutch Central Bank, the AFM and the Ministry of Finance). During these meetings, Kifid gives a presentation on recent developments in its complaints-handling activities, as well as discussing trends that the various parties themselves have seen in the financial sector.

Kifid also provides information by publishing news items on important rulings, as well as through lectures, articles in specialised publications, contributions to academic guidelines and meetings, and sometimes media appearances by the Chair of the Arbitration Commission. Kifid collaborates with two universities and arranges part of their Master's programmes in Financial Law. At the request of consumers, sector and professional associations and financial training institutes, Kifid also provides lectures on aspects of its complaints-handling activities of relevance to these organisations. Kifid itself is not, however, a training institute for the financial sector.

11.1.7.3 Feedback

Lastly, Kifid also has a feedback role. If certain trends become evident during its handling of complaints, it reports on these trends to the outside world, as outlined above. If certain trends become evident during its handling of a complaint against a specific financial service provider, Kifid reports this to the provider.

11.1.8 Kifid's Office

Kifid is a private foundation with a non-executive Managing Board ('Supervisory Board model'), an Arbitration Commission and an Appeals Board. These bodies are supported by the office organisation, see Fig. 11.1.

[19] For details, see https://www.kifid.nl/veelgestelde-vragen. Accessed 16 Apr 2025.

[20] For details, see https://www.kifid.nl/kennis. Accessed 16 Apr 2025.

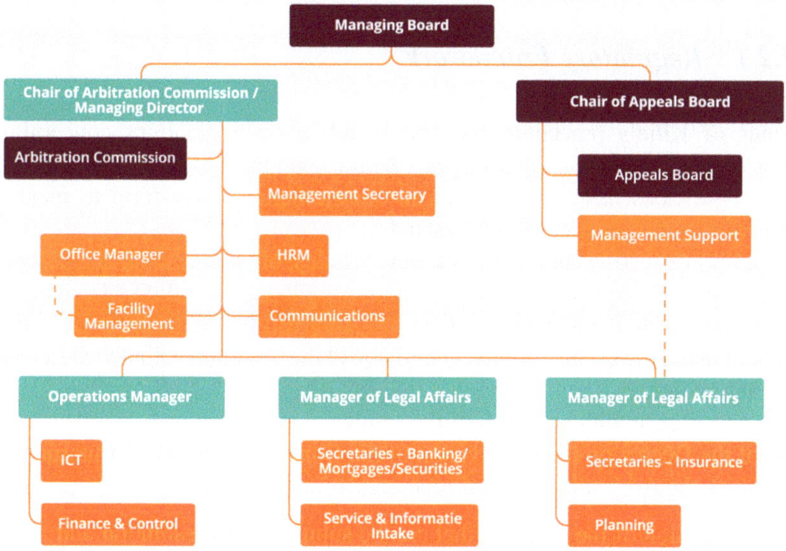

Fig. 11.1 Kifid's office organisation structure

It should be noted that the work performed by members of the Managing Board, members of the Arbitration Commission, and the Chair and members of the Appeals Board for Kifid constitutes an ancillary activity. These individuals are not employed by the Kifid foundation. In 2023, the Arbitration Commission had 47 members (including the Chair), and the Appeals Board had 16 (including the Chair).

The Chair of the Arbitration Commission is employed by the Kifid foundation and responsible for managing the organisation. This Chair is also a managing director and, together with three managers, comprises the management team. The management team is supported by an executive secretary, an office manager, the HRM department and the Communications department. All of the case officers have a law degree and are divided into two thematic teams: banking/mortgages/securities and insurance. The case officers work together in the complaints process, with the Service & Information, Intake and Planning departments supporting the case officers. The whole complaints process is assisted by the ICT and Finance & Control departments.

In 2023, the organisation had 77 employees, 40 of whom were case officers. Case officers have to ensure they keep their expertise up to date, in terms of both professional knowledge and skills (including their discussion and mediation skills). They do so by taking external courses and training, while Kifid itself also provides a programme for continuing professional development.

11.2 Procedure

11.2.1 Regulatory Framework

Details of Kifid's procedures can be found in the regulations concerning the Arbitration Commission[21] and Appeals Board[22] on the website. Since 1 April 2022, these regulations have been written in question-and-answer form to make them easier for users to access and understand.

Under arts. 21(2) and 22(2) of our Articles of Association, the Arbitration Commission and Appeals Board regulations are adopted by Kifid's Managing Board after approval by the Minister of Finance. Approval by the Minister of Finance is required under the Decree on the Supervision of the Conduct of Financial Enterprises (art. 48a BGfo).

In accordance with arts. 6–8 of the Implementation Act and the relevant provision of the Decree on the Supervision of the Conduct of Financial Enterprises (art. 48 BGfo), the Arbitration Commission regulations contain:

- a description of the disputes that can be submitted for resolution and by whom (ss. 1 and 2);
- various provisions to be aware of before submitting a complaint to Kifid, such as how we assess complaints, how we deal with evidence, and what choices are available to consumers in terms of whether a ruling is binding and what the consequences of these choices are (s. 3);
- rules on how to submit a complaint and on interacting with Kifid (s. 4);
- rules on whether complaints can be handled and the opportunities for an appeal (s. 5);
- rules on how Kifid handles complaints and who is involved (s. 6);
- various provisions covering other relevant aspects, including the option to withdraw complaints, what happens if a party does not cooperate, and details of the opportunities for objecting (s. 7); and
- provisions for adopting the regulations (closing provisions).

The Appeals Board regulations consist of:

---

[21] *Reglement Geschillencommissie Kifid.* For details, see Kifid. 2024. Reglement voor de behandeling van klachten door de Geschillencommissie Financiële Dienstverlening van de Stichting Klachteninstituut financiële dienstverlening (Kifid). https://www.kifid.nl/wp-content/uploads/2024/05/Kifid_Reglement-Geschillencommissie-vanaf-1-april-2024-1.pdf. Accessed 16 Apr 2025.

[22] *Reglement Commissie van Beroep Kifid.* For details, see Kifid. 2024. Reglement voor de behandeling van beroepen door de Commissie van Beroep Financiële Dienstverlening van de Stichting Klachteninstituut financiële dienstverlening (Kifid). https://www.kifid.nl/wp-content/uploads/2024/05/Kifid_reglement-Commissie-van-Beroep-vanaf-1-april-2024.pdf. Accessed 16 Apr 2025.

- provisions detailing the tasks of the Appeals Board and who is involved in the procedure (s. 1);
- rules on cases in relation to which an appeal is possible (s. 2);
- various provisions to be aware of before submitting an appeal to the Appeals Board, such as the rules on the fees payable and how expertise and independence are assured (s. 3);
- rules on how appeals are handled (s. 4);
- rules on how rulings are issued (s. 5);
- various provisions covering other aspects relating to appeals, including the option to object (s. 6); and
- provisions for adopting the regulations (s. 7).

For brevity's sake, only the Arbitration Commission regulations are discussed below in more detail, given that the Arbitration Commission handles over 3000 cases a year, whereas the Appeals Board handles only around 50.

11.2.2 Complaints and Enquiry Handling Process

11.2.2.1 Steps in the Complaints Handling Process

Kifid's complaints-handling is a formal process, details of which are recorded in the Arbitration Commission regulations. The steps are depicted in Fig. 11.2. The process starts when we receive a complaint from a consumer or small business. Parties wanting to submit a complaint can do so by filling in a complaint form on the website through 'Mijn Kifid'[23] or by printing the form available on the website and completing it in writing, as stated in Question 28 of the Arbitration Commission regulations. As stated in Question 3.4 of the Arbitration Commission regulations, it is not possible to submit group complaints to Kifid. Kifid is also not allowed to initiate proceedings *ex officio*. Submitting a complaint to Kifid interrupts the limitation period for bringing a claim to court.

Although complaints by consumers and small businesses are handled identically, the conditions applying to Kifid's powers vary, depending on the type of complaint submitted by a small business. These conditions can be found in our regulations. Different rules also apply to the form in which we issue rulings; these can be binding or non-binding. We will not discuss these different rules in more detail here[24] but will instead limit ourselves to discussing complaints submitted by consumers.

After receiving a complaint, Kifid assesses whether it complies with the requirements set out in Question 2 of the Arbitration Commission regulations and is therefore admissible to be handled by the Arbitration Commission. A complaint to be handled will be assigned to a case officer, who will then contact the consumer to

[23] For details, see Kifid. Mijn Kifid. https://mijn.kifid.nl. Accessed 16 Apr 2025.

[24] For details, see Sect. 11.2.6.

Fig. 11.2 Complaints handling process

discuss the contents of the complaint and explain what the consumer can expect from the Kifid procedure. The case officer will aim to establish as clearly as possible what the problem is and how the consumer would like it to be resolved.

The case officer oversees the written procedure on the Arbitration Commission's behalf and investigates whether mediation is possible (Question 34 of the Arbitration Commission regulations). If a solution is reached, Kifid will close the file. If the complaint is not resolved, the Arbitration Commission will continue the procedure. In the latter case, too, however, the case officer or Arbitration Commission can examine at any point whether the complaint could be resolved in consultation.

11.2.2.2 Basic Principles for Handling Complaints

Kifid knows how important it is for both parties—consumers and financial service providers alike—to feel that our officers are taking them and their complaints seriously. Our aim, therefore, is to:

- deal with a consumer's *actual* complaint(s);
- handle complaints effectively and investigate them properly;
- allow both parties to speak and be heard;
- communicate with the parties actively and clearly;
- make the procedure transparent and as clear as possible for the parties;

- seek to reach an amicable settlement (through mediation) rather than issue a ruling.

The main difference between Kifid and a court is that, as an ADR body, Kifid can interpret its tasks more widely. This makes Kifid more accessible to consumers. Yet although our work starts with a focus on mediation, there are also some other differences.

Identifying the Complaint Behind a Complaint

If consumers claim that a financial service provider, such as an insurer, is at fault, it is important to find out exactly what they mean. This is why Kifid sets out to identify the 'complaint behind a complaint'. We are more proactive than courts are in this respect. Our case officer phones the consumer to find out whether the complaint set out in the registration form is really the issue at stake. This may result in the complaint being supplemented or reworded before the form is sent to the financial service provider. The benefit of this is that the discussions between the parties will then be about what really matters to the consumer. This, in turn, will ensure that our officers work efficiently and provide a solution to the actual problem.

Active Management

Complaints submitted to Kifid are often of a specialised nature. However, many consumers have less knowledge of the subject than financial service providers. Kifid therefore takes this into consideration, without losing sight of the need to remain impartial. Our officers make sure, for example, that consumers do not unwittingly say too little in their own defence or, in legal terms, do too little to substantiate their claims. We outline the procedure and continue to question to ensure that the parties feel that there is a level playing field. If necessary, we explain to consumers what the documents submitted by financial service providers mean. On the other hand, and if necessary, we explain to financial service providers what we expect of them. They will obviously also be kept informed of interactions with the consumer, and vice versa.

11.2.2.3 Mediation, Written Procedure, Oral Hearing and Ruling

Mediation (Question 34 Arbitration Commission Regulations)

The Arbitration Commission actively focuses on mediation, where one-to-one contact with the consumer or the financial service provider is arranged or, alternatively, where the consumer and the financial service provider are both invited to a mediation meeting to discuss a possible solution. During an oral hearing, parties may also be given the opportunity to discuss matters with each other. In 2023, a successful result was achieved in 52% of cases, and consumers gave our mediation services a score of 8 or higher out of 10.

Written Procedure (Question 35 Arbitration Commission Regulations)

Under the Arbitration Commission's written procedure (see Fig. 11.3), a financial service provider has four weeks in which to respond to a complaint. If necessary for handling the complaint, the consumer is given the opportunity to respond to the financial service provider's statement. In turn, the financial service provider may respond, in a counter-response, to any statement made by the consumer. In each case, parties have two weeks in which to respond to statements made by other party.

What Happens After the Written Procedure? (Question 39 Arbitration Commission Regulations)

The next step is for Kifid to appoint a commission to handle the complaint. The members of this commission will depend on the nature and contents of the complaint. If the commission considers it necessary, the complaint will be discussed orally. Otherwise, the commission will issue its ruling based on the documents submitted.

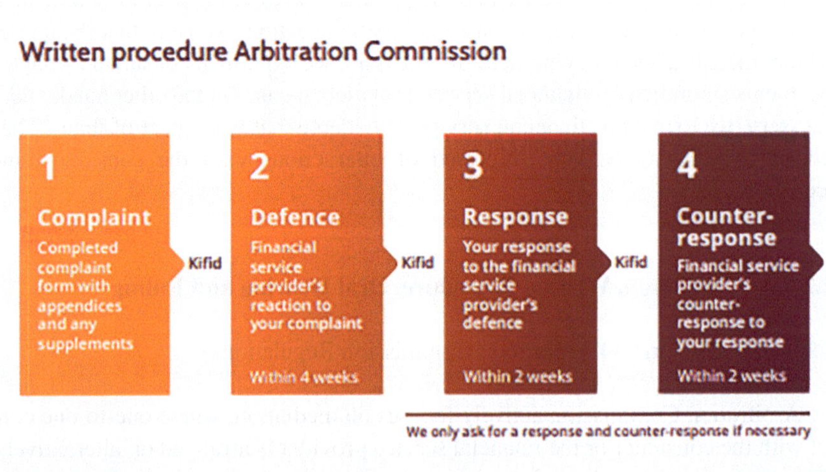

Fig. 11.3 The Arbitration Commission's written procedure

Oral Hearing (Question 40 Arbitration Commission Regulations)

Oral hearings are held at Kifid's offices or by video call or telephone. During an oral hearing, the commission can put questions to the party submitting the complaint and to the financial service provider, as well as investigating whether the dispute can still be resolved through mediation.

What Happens After the Oral Hearing? (Question 45 Arbitration Commission regulations)

After the oral hearing:

1. the commission may record in writing what has been agreed if the party submitting the complaint and the financial service provider reach agreement during the oral hearing; or
2. the commission immediately issues an oral ruling (this will be confirmed in writing within two weeks); or
3. the commission may issue a ruling at a later date; or
4. the commission may not yet be able to issue a ruling, maybe because it requires some additional information.

Ruling (Question 46 Arbitration Commission Regulations)

Once a file is complete, the Arbitration Commission will issue its ruling within 90 days, as required by art. 8(e) of the EU ADR Directive. A file is regarded as complete once all the information that the Arbitration Commission needs to assess the complaint is available. This may be: (1) after the written procedure, (2) after the oral hearing, or (3) after receipt of any additional information requested by Kifid.

11.2.3 Admissible Complaints

As explained previously in Sect. 11.1.3 above, Kifid does not handle every complaint it receives. Various conditions must be met for a complaint to be admissible for handling by Kifid. As mentioned earlier, only the rules applying to complaints submitted by consumers are discussed below. Different rules apply to assess the admissibility of complaints by small businesses.

11.2.3.1 What Can Consumers Complain About and What Not? (Question 1 Arbitration Commission Regulations)

Kifid only handles complaints about financial services governed by Dutch law. Consumers must have accepted the financial service in their private capacity. Kifid also handles complaints about the processing of personal data within the meaning of the General Data Protection Regulation and complaints about a financial service provider's processing in the Central Credit Information System of the Credit Registration Office (BKR). There is no minimum amount for which claims can be referred to Kifid.

In line with question 2 in the Arbitration Commission regulations, Kifid does not handle questions about:

1. how a service pertaining to a benefits-in-kind policy has been provided, unless the complaint relates to the provision of legal assistance under a legal expenses insurance policy;
2. a financial service provider's actions or failure to act in a specific capacity relating to the issuing or re-issuing of securities; or
3. a financial service provider's refusal to enter into an agreement, or a refusal to extend services, unless the complaint is that the financial service provider has abused its freedom of contract or policy or has acted illegally.

11.2.3.2 When Does Kifid Not Handle a Complaint? (Question 3 Arbitration Commission Regulations)

In the following situations, Kifid does not handle a complaint:

1. Another organisation is authorised to handle the complaint;
2. The complaint is being or has already been handled by Kifid (or a predecessor of Kifid), an arbitrator or a binding adviser;
3. The complaint is already being handled by a court or other judicial body or a court judgment has already been issued;
4. The complaint has been submitted as part of a group or collective action;
5. The consumer has already reached agreement with the financial service provider on definitively resolving the complaint;
6. The complaint is clearly unfounded. This is the case if it is immediately clear from legislation or an earlier ruling that the complaint has no chance of succeeding;
7. The financial service provider against whom the complaint has been filed has been declared insolvent, has been granted suspension of payments or is subject to a debt management scheme or emergency regime;
8. The claim exceeds EUR 1,000,000 (excluding default interest and costs). In that case, Kifid will handle the complaint for only up to EUR 1,000,000; or

9. andling the complaint would seriously compromise the Arbitration Commission's work, such as where the research needed to handle the complaint would take too much time or be too complex.

11.2.3.3 Against Which Financial Service Providers Can a Complaint Be Submitted?

A complaint can only be submitted against a financial service provider affiliated to Kifid. A complaint can also be submitted against a financial service provider who was affiliated to Kifid up to three years previously, providing the complaint relates to something that happened when the financial service provider was still affiliated to Kifid. What if the financial services provider is not affiliated to Kifid? In that case, Kifid can only handle the complaint if the financial service provider signs a declaration to confirm that Kifid may handle it and that the provider will pay the costs of Kifid's handling of the complaint.

11.2.3.4 Which Consumers Can Submit a Complaint?

Not everyone can submit a complaint to Kifid. In Question 5 in the Arbitration Commission regulations, there is clarification about who is regarded as a consumer. See Sect. 11.1.3 above.

First complete the financial service provider's internal complaints procedure Under art. 4:17 of the Financial Supervision Act (Wft), a financial service provider must have an internal complaints procedure. The necessary elements of this procedure is detailed in the Decree on the Supervision of the Conduct of Financial Enterprises (arts. 39–44 BGfo).

The consumer must first have contacted the financial service provider before Kifid can agree to handle a complaint. In Question 6 of the Arbitration Commission Regulations, it is explained that Kifid will not take on a complaint until the financial service provider's internal complaints procedure has been completed and the financial service provider has rejected the complaint in writing or fails to issue a final decision within eight weeks.

11.2.3.5 Period for Submitting a Complaint (Question 7 Arbitration Commission Regulations)

If a complaint is to be submitted, it must be done so within three months after the financial service provider notifies the consumer of its final decision in writing. The financial service provider must inform the consumer of this avenue in the letter notifying its final decision. If the financial service provider does not notify a consumer of the option to submit a complaint within three months, the consumer may submit a complaint within a reasonable period after the consumer becomes or could reasonably have been expected to be aware of this opportunity. The period during which a complaint may be submitted can never be shorter than one year after the consumer first complained to the financial service provider. Under certain conditions, as set out in Question 7 of the Arbitration Commission regulations, a complaint submitted after the time limit may nevertheless be handled.

11.2.4 Obtaining Information and Collecting Evidence

11.2.4.1 Gathering Information and Evidence (Question 21 Arbitration Commission Regulations)

Wherever possible, Kifid has ensured that the rules governing the provision and assessment of evidence are in line with the rules applying to judicial procedures, i.e. arts. 149–162 of the Dutch Code of Civil Procedure.[25] This means that anyone making a claim must in principle be required to prove it. This applies unless a special rule or the requirements of reasonableness and fairness require the other party to provide evidence. The Arbitration Commission is only allowed to take a decision based on facts and rights established during the procedure. However, it may take account of facts and circumstances or empirical rules that are generally known at the time of the decision. Lastly, the Arbitration Commission is free to assess evidence for itself.

Parties must supply any information requested by the Arbitration Commission. Kifid may attach appropriate consequences if any party frustrates the establishing of facts.

The parties may first submit written evidence. Kifid can only use the written evidence submitted if the other party has had an opportunity to respond to it. Parties may also explain their positions orally if an oral hearing is scheduled. During an oral hearing the Arbitration Commission can also put questions to anyone present, including witnesses or experts engaged by the parties.

Lastly, the Arbitration Commission itself may decide to call a witness or engage an expert. The parties will be given the opportunity to attend any such hearing and to respond to any report compiled by an expert.

11.2.4.2 Sensitive Information (Question 27 Arbitration Commission Regulations)

A consumer will only be allowed to view the actuarial and business information of the financial service provider if the latter agrees to this. A party not wanting to share information with the other party can claim this information to be confidential. In

[25] *Wetboek van Burgerlijke Rechtsvordering*. For details, see Overheid.nl. Eenvoudig zoeken. https://wetten.overheid.nl. Accessed 16 Apr 2025.

such cases, the Chair of the Arbitration Commission will decide whether the claim of confidentiality is justified.

11.2.4.3 Consequences of Not Cooperating with the Handling of a Complaint

In Question 63 of the Arbitration Commission Regulation, it is specified that if a consumer does not cooperate with the handling of a complaint, Kifid may discontinue the procedure and close the file.

Question 64 deals with cases in which a financial service provider does not cooperate with the handling of a complaint. In such cases, the Chair of the Arbitration Commission may contact the financial service provider's board. If the financial service provider continues not to cooperate, the Chair of the Arbitration Commission may decide not to handle any new complaints against this provider and to discontinue its handling of any complaints currently active. The financial service provider must be notified of this and given the opportunity to respond. The consumer will also be asked to respond in the event of any intention to terminate the handling of a complaint. The Chair of the Arbitration Commission will notify the supervisory authorities if the decision to stop handling a complaint is enforced.[26]

11.2.5 Outcome of the Procedure

The procedure can end with a decision by Kifid that it cannot handle the complaint, in successful mediation or in a ruling by the Arbitration Commission. A consumer may also decide to withdraw a complaint during the procedure. This is possible at any time until the ruling is notified to the parties.

The Arbitration Commission views mediation as successful if the parties are able to agree on a solution during an oral hearing.

Any ruling by the Arbitration Commission will state: *(Question 47 Arbitration Commission regulations)*

1. the ruling on the complaint and why the Arbitration Commission arrived at this ruling;
2. the names of the members of the commission handling the complaint;
3. the secretary's name;
4. the consumer's name;
5. the name and registered office of the financial service provider;
6. the date of the ruling; and
7. the signatures of the commission chair and secretary.

[26] The Chair of the Appeals Board has the same powers.

In its ruling, the Arbitration Commission can:

1. decide that the complaint cannot be handled;
2. state that the consumer must receive compensation;
3. state that the financial service provider must comply with an obligation;
4. dissolve the contract to which the complaint relates or confirm that the contract has been voided or dissolved;
5. deny the financial service provider certain rights in the contract to which the complaint relates;
6. allow an appeal owing to the importance of the case;
7. state that the financial service provider must refund certain costs incurred by the consumer;
8. take any other decision that it considers to be reasonable and fair.

11.2.6 Kifid Decisions

11.2.6.1 Assessment Criteria

In line with its regulations, Kifid assesses complaints in accordance with Dutch law and taking account of any applicable codes of conduct and other rules that financial service providers have set for themselves, insofar as these rules apply to the relationship between the parties.

When assessing a complaint Kifid can actively look for relevant facts and circumstances, as well as supplementing the legal grounds. In the case of a consumer complaint, it can, at its own initiative, also check provisions in a contract to see whether these comply with European or other legislation and regulations designed to protect consumers. Pursuant to the case law established by the Court of Justice of the European Union (CJEU),[27] national courts are obliged by virtue of their office to establish whether the terms in a consumer contract are fair. In this way, courts provide for effective consumer protection. Although this obligation does not apply to ADR bodies such as Kifid, Kifid has opted to provide consumers with the same protection so as to compensate for a possible imbalance between financial service providers and consumers.

11.2.6.2 Binding and Non-binding Rulings

Kifid issues its decisions in the form of binding or non-binding rulings. A binding ruling has to be respected, whereas parties are not required to respect a non-binding ruling. Rulings are issued as binding if requested by both parties. A ruling is

[27] See Case C-243/08 *Pannon GSM Zrt. v Erzsébet Sustikné Győrfi.* [2009] ECLI:EU:C:2009:350. Accessed 23 May 2024.

non-binding if one of the parties did not want it to be binding or the consumer did not specify whether it should be binding or non-binding. This is because, under art. 9(2) of the Implementation Act, a ruling issued in an alternative dispute resolution procedure can only bind parties if both parties explicitly agree to this beforehand.

Most of the rulings issued by Kifid are binding. This is because most complaints submitted by consumers relate to banks or insurers that have opted for Kifid rulings to be binding. Sometimes, however, a non-binding ruling is issued, either because the consumer opted for this or because the financial service provider chose to affiliate to Kifid in this way. Details of financial service providers and how they are affiliated to Kifid can be found (in Dutch) in the register on the website.[28]

Just like decisions issued in the form of binding rulings, mediation results are also binding on the parties. Kifid records the outcome of the mediation in writing and the two parties then sign a document to confirm their agreement. This means that most of Kifid's work produces a result to which the parties can hold each other. Although compliance with binding rulings is admittedly voluntary, the vast majority of financial service providers do, in practice, comply with these rulings The same is also true of the outcomes of mediation.

11.2.6.3 Appeals

In certain cases, an appeal against a binding ruling can be submitted to Kifid's Appeals Board. The conditions under which parties can appeal a ruling is detailed in Rule 7 of the Appeals Board regulations. An appeal against a binding ruling is possible only if the amount on which the Arbitration Commission had to decide was at least EUR 25,000. Otherwise, an appeal is possible only if the Arbitration Commission itself or the Chair of the Appeals Board gives permission.

11.2.6.4 Consequences of Not Complying with A Binding Ruling

If a financial service provider does not comply with a binding ruling, Question 52 of the Arbitration Commission regulations provides that the Chair of the Arbitration Commission can call the provider to account. If this does not have the desired effect, the provider can be reported to the supervisory authorities. The Chair of the Arbitration Commission can also discontinue the financial service provider's affiliation to Kifid.

[28] For details, see Kifid. Dienstverlenersregister. https://www.kifid.nl/register. Accessed 16 Apr 2025.

11.2.6.5 Enforceability of Decisions

The Dutch Civil Code stipulates that a binding ruling must be complied with. However, there is no way Kifid can enforce a Kifid decision. If a financial service provider does not comply with the binding ruling, the consumer can use Kifid's decision in a civil law case and demand compliance.[29] The Chair of the Arbitration Commission and the Chair of the Appeals Board can inform the Dutch Authority for the Financial Markets (AFM) or Dutch Central Bank when a financial service provider fails to comply with a binding ruling (Question 52 Arbitration Commission regulations and Rule 48.2 of the Appels Board regulations). Fortunately, this hardly ever happens because binding rulings are actually always complied with.

11.2.6.6 Publication of Kifid Decisions

Kifid publishes both its binding and non-binding rulings on the website.[30] In the case of binding rulings, Kifid is required to publish details under the Decree on the Supervision of the Conduct of Financial Enterprises (art. 48e BGfo). The information published includes the name and registered office of the financial service provider, but not the name and other personal data of the consumer.

11.2.7 Oversight by Courts

Whether a decision can be submitted to a court for review depends on whether it is a binding or non-binding ruling. Parties cannot be bound by a non-binding ruling and can decide to submit the entire dispute to a civil court. In the case of a binding ruling, a civil court may, under art. 904, Book 7, Dutch Civil Code,[31] only order a change in the ruling if its contents are found to contain serious errors or the way in which it was arrived at is found to be seriously defective. Only rarely, therefore, is a binding ruling that has been issued by Kifid subsequently submitted to a civil court. In practice, non-binding rulings, too, are rarely submitted to a civil court. In other words, our decisions usually definitively resolve disputes between consumers and financial service providers.

---

[29] See Sect. 11.2.7.

[30] For details, see Kifid. Uitspraken. https://www.kifid.nl/uitspraken/. Accessed 16 Apr 2025.

[31] *Burgerlijk Wetboek*. For details, see Overheid.nl. Eenvoudig zoeken. https://wetten.overheid.nl. Accessed 3 May 2024.

11.3 Statistical Data

Around 7000 financial service providers are affiliated to Kifid. Each year, Kifid receives between 5000 and 5500 complaints. The numbers have been increasing since October 2021 because Kifid now also handles complaints about registrations at the Credit Registration Office. Not all of the complaints received by Kifid can be accepted. Consumers often contact Kifid too soon and before they have tried to resolve the problem through the financial service provider's internal complaints procedure. These procedures have to be completed before Kifid can start work. Sometimes, consumers also contact Kifid years after the event, by which time Kifid can no longer help them.

Each year, Kifid's staff members, most of whom are case officers, handle between 3000 and 3200 complaints.

In 2023, Kifid received 5616 new complaints and substantively handled 3201 complaints. Kifid achieved a successful outcome through mediation in 1664 of these cases (52%), while rulings were issued in 997 cases (31%). The other complaints were all withdrawn by the consumers, mainly after Kifid had discussed the complaint with them and explained that it was unlikely to succeed. Consumers are generally satisfied with the results of mediation. Taken together with the rulings issued during the year, this means that the outcome for consumers was positive in 60% of cases.

The average time taken to handle complaints in 2023 was less than seven months.[32]

The 2023 figures on complaints relating to insurance were as follows: the Arbitration Commission handled 362 complaints concerning life insurance and 909 concerning general insurance. These included complaints against insurers, insurance intermediaries, insurance advisers and pension advisers.

In the case of life insurance complaints, a total of 169 were settled through mediation. In 139 cases, a ruling was given, in 21 cases in favour of the consumer. A total of 40 complaints were withdrawn by consumers during the procedure.

In the case of general insurance complaints, a total of 565 were settled through mediation. In 179 cases, a ruling was given, in 34 cases in favour of the consumer. A total of 138 complaints were withdrawn by consumers during the procedure.

Any insurers that are members of the Dutch Association of Insurers have to be affiliated to Kifid. If the consumer then also opts for a binding ruling, the ruling will bind both parties. The results of mediation are also binding on both parties.

Kifid has arranged for an independent research bureau to monitor consumers' satisfaction with our services on an ongoing basis. The Decree on the Supervision of the Conduct of Financial Enterprises (art. 48f(7) BGfo) requires us to conduct periodic customer satisfaction surveys. Our average satisfaction score among consumers was 7.7 out of 10 in 2023. Each year, we also monitor financial service

[32] It should be taken into account that Kifid allows the option of submitting Response and Counterresponse (see Fig. 11.2 in Sect. 11.2.2.3).

providers' satisfaction with our services. Our average satisfaction score among financial service providers was 7.4 out of 10 in 2023.

11.4 Complaints About Insurance

11.4.1 Market Trends

Since July 2020, Kifid has published easy-to-understand knowledge documents on its website (under 'Kifid kennis').[33] These contain information on subjects relevant to its handling of complaints. For the past few years, our annual report has also included a section on 'Trends and developments in Kifid's day-to-day practice', based on our rulings in that year. In this section, we refer to the relevant rulings and knowledge documents. The annual report (in Dutch) is published on our website and so accessible for everyone. In this way, we provide wide-ranging information to the public on trends in our handling of complaints. These topics are also discussed at meetings with relevant stakeholders.[34] In our annual report of 2022, for instance, we published information concerning the trends discussed below.[35]

11.4.1.1 Failings in Legal Expenses Insurance

Although many complaints about legal expenses insurance prove to be unfounded, insurers' own performances can sometimes be less than optimal. In some cases, for example, legal expenses insurers have continued to fail to notify consumers of the other dispute resolution opportunities available, even though they have a duty to do so upon deciding not to continue handling a claim themselves. Sometimes a party providing legal assistance may also choose the wrong approach, as has happened in a case involving a dispute arising between a consumer and a contractor. In this case, the contractor failed to make sufficient progress on building work and also turned out not to be affiliated to an organisation offering insolvency insurance and quality assurance services for new homebuilders and buyers, with the result that the consumer would be left empty-handed if the contractor were to file for insolvency. The party providing legal assistance advised the consumer to continue the contract and to let the contractor finish the work. After completion, however, the consumer found numerous defects in the work but was no longer able to make a claim against the contractor, who had since become insolvent. The legal expenses insurer ultimately had to pay out EUR 38,000 to the consumer.

---

[33] For details, see Kifid Kennis. https://www.kifid.nl/kennis. Accessed 16 Apr 2025.

[34] See Sect. 11.1.7.2.

[35] For details, see Kifid. 2023. Jaarverslag 2023. https://jaarverslag.kifid.nl. Accessed 16 Apr 2025.

11.4.1.2 Recording Personal Data in Warning Registers

There are essentially two situations in which insurers record personal data in internal or external warning registers: when parties wishing to take out insurance intentionally breach their precontractual duty of disclosure (in other words, provide incorrect or incomplete information to an insurer when arranging a policy) or claim amounts in excess of loss or damage actually suffered (for example, by falsifying documents). Of the various opportunities available to insurers in such situations, the one with the greatest impact is to record the person's details in one or more warning registers. This can mean that consumers are unable to arrange insurance at normal rates for years. The Arbitration Commission has also seen that consumers are not always aware that insurers are then entitled to discontinue a relationship in its entirety. In the event, for example, of car insurance fraud, an insurer may also decide to cancel the policyholder's household contents insurance because the policyholder is no longer trusted at all. This risk must, however, be stated in the general conditions, and insurers obviously also have to prove the fraud. In one case, for example, a consumer who claimed for the loss of a suitcase after a trip to London was not initially believed because some of the information in his statement was ambiguous, including the fact that he could not remember the name of the hotel. The consumer was able, however, to establish the information required, and the Arbitration Commission subsequently ruled that no fraud had been committed. In other words, ambiguity does not in itself constitute sufficient grounds for assuming fraud.

11.4.1.3 Intermediaries' Discussion Reports

A few dozen complaints handled during the year related to financial advisers' duty of care. Intermediaries' recordings of discussions are an aspect requiring ongoing attention. In one case, for example, a consumer stated that, in a discussion with an adviser, she had indicated that she wanted additional cover, while a consumer in another case was prepared to pay up to a certain maximum, and another consumer stated that he had not been warned about certain risks. In each case, the intermediary had a different recollection of the discussions but was not able to prove this in the form of a discussion report (ideally approved by the consumer). This can have far-reaching consequences: in the absence of a record or notes of the discussions, the Arbitration Commission will in principle accept the consumer's version of events, given that the intermediary is a professional party and so has an enhanced duty to state reasons.

11.4.2 Effectiveness

Insurers generally accept the results when Kifid's complaints-handling procedure finds in favour of consumers. They respect Kifid's expertise in resolving disputes. Binding rulings have to be complied with. Monitoring of financial service providers' satisfaction has shown how insurers have changed their operating methods or conditions in response to Kifid's handling of complaints. This demonstrates that Kifid's procedures are effective.

In Kifid's handling of complaints, there are not any insurers that entirely disregard consumer protection or treat it too lightly. This is thanks to the strong regulatory framework in place in the Netherlands.

It is precisely because the Financial Supervision Act requires financial service providers to affiliate to Kifid that Kifid can operate so effectively. This is unfortunately not the case in many other European countries.

11.5 Other

11.5.1 Accessibility

Kifid is easy to contact. Under the Decree on the Supervision of the Conduct of Financial Enterprises (art. 42 BGfo), financial service providers rejecting a consumer's complaint, either in whole or part, have to inform the consumer of the option of submitting the complaint to Kifid. They also have to specify the applicable time limits.

Information about Kifid can also be found on the website, including information about the organisation and how Kifid operates, and some explanatory information in the form of animations. The website also provides a quick check for consumers wanting an indication of whether Kifid can take on their complaint, as well as information on how to submit a complaint. Kifid also publishes rulings, news items and knowledge documents on its website.

Kifid also posts information on news and developments on X (@Kifid_Den_Haag) and on Linkedin (https://www.linkedin.com/company/kifid).

Lastly, consumers are also referred to Kifid by the AFM and the Ministry of Finance.

11.5.2 Easy Access, Expertise and Impartiality

Kifid's strength is that it offers easy access, expertise and impartiality. It is this that makes us a valuable alternative to a civil court.

- Easy access because the Arbitration Commission procedure is free of charge for consumers. It is also easy to access because, unlike in most courts, consumers do not have to appoint a lawyer to represent them. Submitting a complaint is quick and easy and can be done digitally. In fact, more and more Kifid cases are now being handled entirely digitally as financial service providers are increasingly using the opportunity to upload documents to a designated portal;
- Expertise because Kifid's dispute resolution professionals are legal professionals, accountants, economists, actuaries, investment experts, doctors or occupational health specialists. This means Kifid can use the most suitable experts to assess each complaint. The chair of a Kifid commission is always a legal professional;
- Impartiality because Kifid does not allow dispute resolution professionals to work at or for financial service providers. Instead, they operate independently and as they consider best. They also do not accept instructions from anyone at all on how to perform their tasks.

11.5.3 Accountability

11.5.3.1 Annual Report[36]

Each year, Kifid accounts for its work in its annual report. This includes providing information on, for example:

- Kifid's organisation;
- the number of complaints submitted and the type of subjects to which they relate;
- the percentage of complaints that could not be handled and the reasons for this (as a percentage share);
- the percentage share of complaints that were discontinued and, where known, the reasons for this;
- trends and developments in Kifid's day-to-day practice;
- the results of Kifid's handling of complaints (for each service separately);
- the average time taken to handle complaints;
- the percentage of cases in which the outcomes were complied with, where known;
- information on collaboration with other alternative dispute resolution bodies.

The annual report also includes the budget and abbreviated financial statements. By publishing its annual report on the website, Kifid complies with art. 6(2) of the Implementation Act.

[36] For details, see https://jaarverslag.kifid.nl. Accessed 16 Apr 2025.

11.5.3.2 Budget

Under the Decree on the Supervision of the Conduct of Financial Enterprises (art. 48f BGfo), Kifid's budget has to be approved by the Minister of Finance. Each year, Kifid prepares its budget and submits it to the Minister of Finance for approval before 1 December of the year preceding the year for which the budget has been prepared.

11.5.3.3 Other Obligations

Under the Decree on the Supervision of the Conduct of Financial Enterprises (art. 48f BGfo), Kifid is subject to various other obligations with regard to accountability, including the obligation to provide any data and information requested by the Minister of Finance and to submit the annual financial statements and the Managing Board's report to the Minister of Finance for approval before 1 May of the next financial year.

11.5.3.4 Assessment Every Four Years

Under art. 18 of the Implementation Act, a body providing alternative dispute resolution has to be assessed for its procedural efficiency and for possible ways of improving its performance. This assessment report has to be submitted to the relevant minister. Pursuant to the Decree on the Supervision of the Conduct of Financial Enterprises (art. 48f(7) BGfo), this assessment must be performed by an independent research body every four years. The Minister of Finance presents the report of this assessment to the Dutch House of Representatives.

Legal Sources

Kifid. 2020. Statuten Stichting Kifid vanaf 14 augustus 2020. https://www.kifid.nl/wp-content/uploads/2020/08/Statuten-Kifid-Stichting-Klachtenintituut-Financiele-Dienstverlening-vanaf-14-augustus-2020.pdf. Accessed 3 May 2024

Kifid. 2024. Reglement Commissie van Beroep Kifid vanaf 1 april 2024. https://www.kifid.nl/wp-content/uploads/2024/05/Kifid_reglement-Commissie-van-Beroep-vanaf-1-april-2024.pdf. Accessed 23 May 2024

Kifid. 2024. Reglement Geschillencommissie Kifid vanaf 1 april 2024. https://www.kifid.nl/wp-content/uploads/2024/05/Kifid_Reglement-Geschillencommissie-vanaf-1-april-2024-1.pdf. Accessed 23 May 2024

Alternative Dispute Resolution for Consumer Disputes Implementation Act (Implementatiewet buitengerechtelijke geschillenbeslechting consumenten). https://wetten.overheid.nl/BWBR0036550/2018-09-19

Literature

Boomsma N, Knopper R, Van Lambalgen RE, Molkenboer GJP (eds) (2023) Kifid, toegankelijk recht doen in financiële geschillen, Financieel Juridische Reeks 23. Uitgeverij Paris, Zutphen

Hellegers DPCM & Nelemans MDH (2021) Kifid voor consumentengeschillen. In: Hellegers DPCM, Nelemans MDH, Van den Bos PJ, Gladdines G, Kleverlaan K, Rank WAK, Macpherson CR (eds) Alternatieve geschilbeslechting in de financiële sector (Preadvies voor de Vereniging voor Financieel Recht 2021) (serie vanwege het Van Der Heijden Instituut nr 173), Wolters Kluwer, Deventer, 1–47

Ruinaard E (2022) Kifid: Dutch institute for financial disputes. Droit du financement de l'entreprise 2022(12–13):27–30

Ruinaard EC (2019) Alternatieve geschilbeslechting als alternatief voor de civiele rechter. In: Groenewald T, De Bock RH, Du Perron CE, Timmerman L (eds) Naar vernieuwing van de (civiele) rechtspleging. Boom juridisch, Den Haag, pp 95–103

Chapter 12
Poland

Financial Ombudsman in Poland in Light of Insurance Schemes

Michał Ożóg, Paweł Rokosz, and Karolina Mendecka

12.1 Introduction

The institution of the ombudsman is an indispensable component of every modern democratic state, serving as one of the key pillars for safeguarding human rights and often representing the last recourse for individuals. The experiences of the Second World War underscored the necessity of establishing oversight institutions within democratic systems, while recent decades have emphasised the need for protecting the rights of individuals, especially those who are vulnerable or have been wronged by private or public entities.

At present, highly specialised bodies safeguarding the interests of financial market clients have become a standard in well-developed countries across Europe and around the world. Specialised institutions dedicated to the protection of the individual interests of consumers of financial services exist in countries such as Australia, Ireland, New Zealand, the United Kingdom, and Singapore. In Poland, the ombudsperson is responsible for protecting the rights of individuals in the

M. Ożóg (✉)
Department of Education and Communication, Office of the Financial Ombudsman, Department of Constitutional Law, Department of Comparative Constitutional Law, Faculty of Law, University of Bialystok, Białystok, Poland
e-mail: m.ozog@rf.gov.pl

P. Rokosz
Department of Extrajudicial Dispute Resolution, Office of the Financial Ombudsman, Warsaw, Poland
e-mail: p.rokosz@rf.gov.pl

K. Mendecka
Institute of Comparative and Interdisciplinary Research in Law, Faculty of Law, University of Łódź, Łódź, Poland
e-mail: karolina.mendecka@wpia.uni.lodz.pl

H. Heiss et al. (eds.), *Insurance Ombudsman Schemes*, AIDA Europe Research Series on Insurance Law and Regulation 15,
https://doi.org/10.1007/978-3-032-01500-6_12

financial and insurance markets, known as the Financial Ombudsman Service (*Rzecznik Finansowy*), has gained increasing recognition and appreciation over recent years.

The aim of this country report is to provide a historical overview of the Polish ombudsman institutions, including the Financial Ombudsman Scheme and its predecessor, the Insurance Ombudsman Scheme. Another aim of this chapter is to introduce the contemporary profile of this institution, with a focus on insurance schemes, and to delineate the role of the Financial Ombudsman Scheme within the Polish consumer protection framework on the financial market.

12.2 Historical Development

The ombudsman institution around the world takes on various forms. An ombudsperson can serve as a general advocate for human rights or specialise in overseeing compliance with specific areas of the law.[1] Oftentimes, the ombudsperson also acts as a dispute resolver.

One of the globally adopted models envisions the creation of several ombudspersons within a single country, each with distinct roles and jurisdiction. This model was also adopted in Poland. In addition to the establishment of the Commissioner for Civil Rights Protection in 1987 and the Commissioner for Children's Rights in 2000, the Commissioner for Patients' Rights was established in 2008 and the Insurance Ombudsman Service (*Rzecznik Ubezpieczonych*), the predecessor of the Financial Ombudsman Service (*Rzecznik Finansowy*), was established in 1995.

12.3 The Insurance Ombudsman in Poland

The 1990s in Poland ushered in numerous changes in the financial and insurance markets. The post-transitional period saw the emergence of many private banking and insurance institutions, as well as other financial entities. Clients gained widespread access to financial products and services, and it became feasible to earn returns through investments. However, it was also common to encounter complex and high-risk products and services at a time when the financial literacy of Poles was limited. Consequently, the rights of financial market customers and, more broadly, consumer rights were frequently violated. Abuses and even fraud became commonplace.[2] Furthermore, information asymmetry was widely exploited, and there was an underdeveloped system for representing consumers. Given the rapid social and economic transformations and the bankruptcies of insurance companies,

[1] See more e.g. Park (2008); Pickl (1987); Rosiak (2017).

[2] Orlicki (2020).

legislative actions were taken. The creation of regulations to protect the interests of the most vulnerable market participants while simultaneously respecting the principle of economic freedom proved to be a challenging task.[3]

The Office of the Insurance Ombudsman was established by the Act of 8 June 1995. The establishment of this specialised institution in the mid-1990s was inspired by the experiences of Western European countries (primarily Scandinavia) and the United States, where the operation of ombudsman offices in the insurance and banking sectors had become a permanent fixture.[4]

At the beginning of the functioning of the office, the most extensive area of activity was individual case proceedings. Requests for intervention in relation to institutions dealing with insurance matters were initially forwarded by the Insurance Department of the Ministry of Finance, where such correspondence had traditionally been directed. However, over time, these requests began to be submitted directly to the Insurance Ombudsman Service. In the first year of its operation, the Ombudsman Service received 1089 complaints and requests, with 40% of them relating to motor insurance. Since its inception, the Insurance Ombudsman Service has actively pursued its activities within the scope of its competence and has employed other forms of action. This has included providing opinions on legal acts, engaging in informational and educational activities, collaborating with the Insurance Ombudsman Council and other entities, and participating in meetings and conferences.[5]

In response to the influx of individual complaints and the need to further empower consumers in the field of insurance, it became necessary to strengthen the position of the Office of the Insurance Ombudsman through changes in the law. Legal provisions governing the activities of the Insurance Ombudsman Service underwent several revisions. The first significant changes to the law concerning the Insurance Ombudsman Service were introduced by the Act of 1 March 2002.[6] These amendments extended the scope of its activities to include the representation and protection of the interests of participants in employee pension programs and the protection of the interests of members of open pension funds.

The Act of 22 May 2003 on insurance and pension supervision and the Insurance Ombudsman[7] significantly extended the duties of the Insurance Ombudsman Service. Thereafter, the Ombudsman institution became the primary tool for assisting individual clients in the insurance market and complementing the Insurance and Pension Fund Supervisory Commission (later the Financial Supervision Authority) and the President of the Office for Competition and Consumer Protection. It is

---

[3] Budzianowski (2015), p. 2.

[4] Ibidem.

[5] *Sprawozdanie Rzecznika Ubezpieczonych za rok 1996 r.*, http://web.archive.org/web/20150101000000*/rf.gov.pl. Accessed 16 Apr 2025.

[6] Ustawa z dnia 1 marca 2002 r. o zmianach w organizacji i funkcjonowaniu centralnych organów administracji rządowej i jednostek im podporządkowanych oraz o zmianie niektórych ustaw.

[7] Ustawa z dnia 22 maja 2003 r. o nadzorze ubezpieczeniowym i emerytalnym oraz Rzeczniku Ubezpieczonych.

worth emphasising that this amendment enabled disputes between policyholders, insured persons, beneficiaries or those entitled under insurance contracts on the one hand and insurance companies on the other to be submitted to arbitration. Consequently, the legislature reaffirmed the position of the Insurance Ombudsman Service as a specialised and committed institution capable of meeting the challenges posed by the evolving insurance market landscape. By ensuring that the ombudsperson is supported by insurance experts, resolving disputes amicably has been made possible.[8]

Considering these newly conferred powers, the Insurance Ombudsman Service established an arbitration court by decree on 25 March 2004.[9] The most important aspects of the arbitration court under the ombudsperson were to ensure a short duration of proceedings, lower costs, and to foster a favourable image of insurance companies. However, insurance companies first had to agree to participate in arbitration proceedings, which significantly limited the ombudsperson's ability to act in this respect.

Over time, consideration was given to extending the scope of protection provided to individuals using financial services and, consequently, the ombudsperson's competence.[10]

12.4 The Polish Financial Ombudsman: A New Quality of Consumer Protection

Over time, there has been a growing interest in broadening the scope of the protection provided to individuals who use financial services—there was a pressing need for statutory regulations to define the procedure and time limits for handling complaints submitted to financial market entities by their customers.

Consequently, the decision was made to establish a highly specialised office to support customers of entities across all sectors of the financial market in Poland. A similar trend can be observed globally—as indicated by analyses, an institution such as the Financial Ombudsman Service currently exists in as many as 86 out of 124 countries surveyed worldwide.[11] The creation of the Financial Ombudsman institution filled a legal gap in the system: to protect customers of financial market entities.

By the Act of 5 August 2015 on the Handling of Complaints by Financial Market Entities and the Financial Ombudsman (hereinafter the RF Act),[12] it was established

---

[8] Daszewski (n.d.).

[9] Zarządzenie Rzecznika Ubezpieczonych z dnia 25 marca 2004 nr 4/SP/04.

[10] Kiziewicz (n.d.).

[11] Budzianowski (2015).

[12] Ustawa z dnia 5 sierpnia 2015 r. o rozpatrywaniu reklamacji przez podmioty rynku finansowego i o Rzeczniku Finansowym. Journal of Laws 2019, item 2279, as amended.

that the Insurance Ombudsman Service, would assume the position of the Financial Ombudsman upon the entry into force of the Act on 11 October 2015.

The jurisdiction of the Financial Ombudsman Service was extended to matters concerning customers of financial market entities. For the first time, a definition of "customer" was introduced into the Polish legal framework through the RF Act. This reflects the trend of moving away from the use of the term "consumer" in favour of the term "customer" of financial market entities, which is currently a common phenomenon—not only at the national level but also at the level of the European Union, as evidenced by directives that adopt an expanded scope of subjects compared to the concept of a consumer, especially in the context of banking and insurance services.[13]

The RF Act provides a precise definition of "customer" in art. 2(1). It states that the ombudsperson represents the interests of customers of financial market entities. These customers can be classified into several categories, including individuals who are insured, beneficiaries, or entitled under insurance agreements, individuals making claims under specific insurance laws, members of pension funds, participants in employee pension schemes, savers, recipients of capital pensions, bank customers, cooperative savings and credit union members, customers of payment institutions, electronic money institutions, credit institutions, financial institutions, investment funds, investment firms, and lending institutions. The Act clarifies that the ombudsperson's role is to advocate for these individuals in matters related to financial services.

The law is designed to protect individuals who typically have less power when dealing with financial institutions. This protection extends not only to consumers in the legal sense of the term but also to those making claims related to insurance contracts (including inheritors with a legal interest), farmers, and sole proprietors running small businesses. It is important to note that the law does not require individuals to meet specific criteria. It does not matter whether they are involved in business or are consumers when dealing with financial institutions.

Furthermore, the Financial Ombudsman Service's jurisdiction is limited to matters involving specific financial market entities. These entities are listed in art. 2(3) of the Financial Ombudsman Act and include payment institutions, banks, investment firms, insurance companies, and more.

Importantly, the ombudsperson can only act for individuals who are clients of these listed entities. This means that the ombudsperson cannot assist a complainant who is not a customer of one of these specific financial institutions. It is crucial to note that the law only applies to individual persons. It does not cover legal entities like companies, government bodies, non-incorporated organisations, foundations, associations, religious groups, or partnerships. However, it does apply to individual partners in partnerships, farmers, and lessees.[14]

[13] Jurkowska-Zeidler (2016), p. 194.

[14] Wyżykowski (2018a), p. 128.

12.5 Statutory Position of the Financial Ombudsman Service

In a modern democratic state, it is necessary to ensure adequate protection of the rights of the financial market customer. Undoubtedly, the implementation of this task requires the establishment by the legislature of a system of state bodies that will take measures to protect human rights in this area of social relations. In doing so, it is necessary to strive to compile an appropriate catalogue of tasks for these bodies and to determine their constitutional position in a manner that guarantees their capacity to act independently and effectively. In the following section, the constitutional position of the Financial Ombudsman Service in the Polish system of state bodies will be presented and the competences that are assigned this body will be outlined. It is in particular worth emphasising the distinctiveness and specificity of this Financial Ombudsman Service in the system of state bodies.

The Constitution of the Republic of Poland of 2 April 1997[15] contains provisions Law concerning the constitutional position of the Ombudsman (arts. 208–218) and the Ombudsman for Children's Rights (art. 72(4)). It does not contain any legal provisions concerning the Financial Ombudsman Service directly. This means that the establishment of the Financial Ombudsman Service and the definition of its powers are based on the regulatory discretion of the ordinary legislature. At the same time, it should be emphasised that the legislature does not have complete discretion in this respect. The establishment of this body and the definition of its competences require compliance with constitutional law in its entirety. The content of the statutory solutions relating to the Financial Ombudsman Service may be subject to judicial and constitutional control in relation to their conformity with the Constitution of the Republic of Poland. It is of utmost importance to ensure that this body is independent of state authorities and financial market entities, as well as to avoid a situation where powers are unnecessarily duplicated, i.e. entrusting the same areas of tasks to two or more bodies.

In terms of the issue of sources of law, it should be assumed that the question of the status of the Financial Ombudsman Service should be governed in a legal act due to the subject of legal regulation, i.e. the determination of competence and the shaping of the status of the financial market customer. This is undoubtedly the so-called statutory matter.[16] The competence of the Financial Ombudsman Service is defined in the Act of 5 August 2015 on the handling of complaints by financial market entities, the Financial Ombudsman and the Financial Education Fund.[17] The competences of this body have been extended significantly as a result of the 2022 amendment, which will be discussed in more detail later.

First, it is necessary to determine the status of the Financial Ombudsman Service in terms of the classification of state bodies. The legal provisions do not expressly deal with this issue. This is in contrast to, for example, the President of the Office of

[15] Journal of Laws. 1997 No. 78 item 483, hereinafter the Constitution.

[16] Wiącek (2016), pp. 74–75.

[17] Journal of Laws. 2015 item 1348, as amended.

Competition and Consumer Protection, who is referred to in art. 29(1) of the Act of 16 February 2007 on competition and consumer protection as a central body of government administration.[18] Given the presumption of rationality that is applied to the legislature, one would have to reject the assumption of such a classification of the Financial Ombudsman Service. It is worth pointing out that one of the elements shared by the President of the Office of Competition and Consumer Protection and the financial ombudsperson is the fact that persons are appointed to these positions by the Prime Minister and are subject to the supervision of this office. However, it seems that the Prime Minister's supervisory powers do not entitle the Financial Ombudsman Service to be considered a division of government administration bodies in the strict sense. Indeed, it is necessary to point to specific regulations that determine the unique status of the Financial Ombudsman Service.

According to the provisions of the Act, the Office of the Financial Ombudsman and the Ombudsman Service's activities are financed by the mandatory contributions made by financial market institutions.[19] These contributions are paid by, inter alia, banks, insurance companies and investment fund companies. Such a solution was not adopted in relation to the Office of Competition and Consumer Protection. The solution mentioned above should be evaluated as entirely positive, as it allows the Financial Ombudsman Service to remain a financially independent institution, since its activities are financed independently of the state budget. This enables the financial ombudsperson to take legal action without fear of pressure and the threat of a cut in subsidies for the next fiscal year.[20] If the amount of funding to be given to the Financial Ombudsman Office were dependent on the state authorities and set in the budget law, it could imply the risk of a reduction in funding. There is no such risk with the current funding model.

At the same time, it should be added that the funding mechanism adopted is also useful with regard to its potential impact on the image of the relationship between financial market customers and financial market entities, because—generally speaking—the better these institutions treat their customers, and thus the fewer the number of cases and possibly imposed fines, the lower the financial contributions to the activities of the Office of the Financial Ombudsman will be. Thus, the funding mechanism adopted not only contributes towards ensuring the independence of the Financial Ombudsman Service, but its significance extends far beyond its effects on the system of state bodies.

In light of the foregoing, it would appear that the Financial Ombudsman Service is an independent law enforcement body and this is an appropriate term to refer to the status of this body. This seems to be the term that best reflects the legal status of this body. The activities of this body are aimed at protecting the law and protecting the rights of the financial market customer.

---

[18] Journal of Laws. 2007 No. 50 item 331, as amended.

[19] See art. 20(1) and next of the Act of 5 August 2015 on the handling of complaints by financial market entities, the Financial Ombudsman and the Financial Education Fund.

[20] See the interview by Joanna Ojczyk with Aleksandra Wiktorow in Ojczyk (2023).

Pursuant to art. 11 of the Act, on the proposal of the minister responsible for financial institutions, the Prime Minister appoints the financial ombudsperson for a period of four years. Under the regulations, the same person cannot be the ombudsperson for more than "two consecutive terms." A literal interpretation would indicate that it would be possible for the same person to serve as financial ombudsperson for a third non-consecutive term. The addition of the phrase "consecutive terms" suggests that the legislature has allowed for this option. In doing so, however, there is a lack of consistency and axiological coherence in the duration of the terms of office and restrictions on the re-election of bodies with similar tasks, as Polish law provides for different solutions and lacks uniform systemic solutions.

The term of office of the financial ombudsperson is four years, which is different from the term of office for position with similar functions. For example, the term of office of the President of the Office of Competition and Consumer Protection is five years, limited to a maximum of two terms. On the other hand, the term of office of the ombudsperson for Small and Medium-sized Enterprises is longer at 6 years, but without an option for re-election.[21] The main purpose of the term of office is to prevent the perpetuation of ties through a change in personnel. This goal will be achieved and is unlikely to be hindered by the person's return to the position of financial ombudsperson.

The manner in which the financial ombudsperson is appointed differs from the model adopted for other bodies with similar tasks. The financial ombudsperson is appointed by the Prime Minister on the proposal of the minister responsible for financial institutions. The same mode of appointment has also been adopted for the ombudsperson for Small and Medium-sized Entrepreneurs. Consequently, there is no provision for a competitive mode, as in the case of the President of the Office of Competition and Consumer Protection. However, it seems that the key issue is the accurate definition and proper application of the statutory requirements that a candidate for financial ombudsperson must meet. In this context, the statutory mode of procedure remains a relatively secondary consideration.

Pursuant to art. 13 of the Act, the financial ombudsperson may only be a person who possesses:

1. a distinguished knowledge of the functioning of the financial market and the regulations that form its environment as well as at least seven years of professional experience in this area. It should be noted that it is not necessary to confirm this knowledge with a document or formal education, although the requirement of the first point will usually be correlated with the next premise;
2. a higher education. It is not stipulated that it must be higher education in a particular academic field. In Poland, the financial ombudsperson's duties are currently performed by the deputy financial ombudsperson, a lawyer by education. Previously, the position of financial ombudsperson was held by a practising lawyer. In the past, the function of the insurance ombudsperson has also been performed by a person with medical education, more specifically a doctor;

[21] Journal of Laws. 2023 item 1668, as amended.

3. full public rights;
4. Polish citizenship. There is no requirement in the provisions of Polish law a candidate for the office of financial ombudsperson to be a Polish citizen exclusively. Consequently, there is no formal obstacle to the appointment of an individual with dual citizenship, including Polish citizenship, to the position of financial ombudsperson; and
5. no final conviction for an intentional crime. It is worth noting that this provision excludes any individual with a final conviction for an intentional criminal offence, regardless of the nature of the crime. This exclusion is not limited to crimes against the security of financial transactions and economic crimes.

The financial ombudsperson's independence is guaranteed by the narrowly defined grounds for their dismissal. Under art. 15 of the Act, the ombudsperson may only be dismissed prior to the conclusion of the current term for the following reasons:

1. resignation;
2. failure to perform their duties for a period exceeding 6 months due to a prolonged illness, as evidenced by a medical certificate;
3. gross violation of the interests of customers of financial market entities;
4. gross violation of the provisions of the Constitution of the Republic of Poland or laws;
5. final conviction for an intentional crime.

The closed catalogue of grounds for dismissal of the financial ombudsperson means that these are the only reasons for removing a person from office. The grounds for dismissal set forth in art. 15(3)-(4) of the Act should be interpreted narrowly. A gross violation of the law should be understood as a violation of the law in a manner that does not raise any doubts on the basis of the application of methods of literal interpretation, or as repeated and persistent violations of legal norms.

12.6 Competences of the Financial Ombudsperson: General Remarks

An analysis of the competences envisaged for the Financial Ombudsman Service allows us to conclude that, although it is not the only body in Poland that deals with the protection of the rights of the individual customer, it can be considered the will of the legislature for it to be a body specialising mainly in this type of cases. This is fully justified given the complexity of the cases submitted to the financial ombudsperson and the need for highly specialised knowledge, if only in selected categories of insurance cases.

The financial ombudsperson's tasks are not limited to individual cases, as systemic actions are also taken. The ombudsperson has the authority to protect the rights of the financial market customer by intervening at the stage of judicial proceedings. This can be done by issuing a so-called "significant view", filing a lawsuit to stop an unfair market practice, filing an extraordinary complaint with the Supreme Court, and referring a request to the Supreme Court for a resolution to clarify discrepancies in judicial decisions. In comparison, the powers of the President of the Office of Competition and Consumer Protection are primarily intended to focus on protecting the public interest, rather than the interest of customer rights. The provisions of the Act of 16 February 2007 on the Protection of Competition and Consumers permits this body to undertake a very wide range of activities for the benefit of competition in various areas of the market, extending beyond the financial market.

Specifically, as stated in art. 1(2), the Act governs the principles and procedures employed to counteract practices that restrict competition, practices that violate the collective interests of consumers, including the use of prohibited contractual terms, and anti-competitive concentrations of entrepreneurs and their associations, provided that such practices, the use of prohibited provisions or concentrations, produce or may produce effects within the territory of the Republic of Poland. The emphasis of the activities of the Office of Competition and Consumer Protection is therefore on protecting the collective interest of consumers. It should be emphasised that the Act does not narrow the ambit of the authority's activity to a specific market segment or segments, which means its scope of jurisdiction is extremely broad. Cases concerning the protection of competition in the financial market constitute only a small segment of its activity. Essentially, these cases concern the protection of competition and the collective interests of consumers, the latter of which clearly also impinges to some extent on the rights of the individual. The legal actions taken to protect collective interests also require slightly different methods of action. In addition, it should once again be emphasised that the President of the Office of Competition and Consumer Protection does not have the authority to apply to the Supreme Court.

The competence of the Financial Ombudsman Service can most fully contribute to the protection of the rights of the individual, which is an important argument for maintaining this body in the Polish system of state bodies, despite recent attempts to transfer its tasks to the Office of Competition and Consumer Protection.[22] The latter body takes action primarily to counter practices that harm the collective interests of consumers, which of course also translates into the status of individuals, since it is impossible to completely separate these two aspects of competition and consumer protection.

It is important to note that the Financial Ombudsman Service operates from a specific standpoint, aiming to secure the rights of the individual customer, which, as already mentioned, distinguishes its activities from the tasks of the President of the Office of Competition and Consumer Protection, but also the Financial Supervision Commission.[23] The Commission undertakes systemic measures for the broadly

[22] See the draft of law at https://www.sejm.gov.pl/sejm9.nsf/PrzebiegProc.xsp?nr=834. Accessed 16 Apr 2025.

[23] Cyman (2017), pp. 332–333.

understood security of the financial sector and has appropriate supervisory powers. It is not a programmatically oriented body aimed at protecting one side of the financial market. Rather, its role is primarily to supervise compliance with sector regulations.

As mentioned, the protection of financial market customers is a matter of interest to numerous authorities, including the President of the Office of Competition and Consumer Protection. Nevertheless, it is evident that the protection of the rights of customers in this domain necessitates the establishment of an authority whose remit is exclusively focused on this particular area

Indeed, these cases are so complex and diverse that the office's staff require adequate and specialised training'. Hence, the Financial Ombudsman institution has legitimately been established in modern European countries. The scope of the jurisdiction of other authorities, including the Office of Competition and Consumer Protection, is so wide that it covers matters of various sectors, including, for example, the food market, automotive market, individual services, telecommunications, and matters pertaining to the financial market represent only a narrow slice of activity. Furthermore, as previously stated, the Office of Competition and Consumer Protection takes actions aimed at protecting collective interests.

Pursuant to art. 17(1) of the Act of 5 August 2015 on the handling of complaints by financial market entities, the Financial Ombudsman and the Financial Education Fund, the ombudsperson's tasks include taking action to protect the customers of financial market entities whose interests the ombudsperson represents, particularly in the following ways:

1. by processing complaints in individual cases that have been brought as a result of the failure of the financial market entity to consider the customer's claims under the established complaint procedure;
2. through consideration of complaints that have been submitted in relation to the failure to perform actions that have arisen out of a complaint that has been considered in accordance with the customer's wishes within the specified time limit as outlined in art. 9(4) of this Act.
3. by giving an opinion on drafts of legal acts concerning the organisation and functioning of financial market entities;
4. by making proposals to the competent authorities to take legislative initiative or to issue or amend other legal acts on matters relating to the organisation and functioning of the financial market;
5. by informing the relevant supervisory and control authorities of irregularities noticed;
6. through the provision of data to the Financial Supervision Commission concerning the number and nature of complaints indicating violations of the Payment Services Act of 19 August 2011, as of the end of each half-year, within a period of two months following the end of the respective half-year.

The financial ombudsperson's tasks also include:

1. initiating and organising educational and informational activities to increase the financial awareness of the public, especially in the field of financial market functioning, the use of innovative technologies and possible risks occurring in these areas;
2. cooperating with non-governmental, social and professional organisations whose statutory objectives include the protection of consumer rights, with associations, civic movements, other voluntary associations and foundations, as well as with foreign and international bodies and organisations in order to protect consumer rights.

It is important to note the expansion of the Financial Ombudsman Service's powers over the years. Significant changes in this regard were introduced with the Act on amending the Act on the handling of complaints by financial market entities and the Financial Ombudsman and certain other acts in order to increase the effectiveness and efficiency of the system of protecting customers of financial market entities and to promote the financial education of the Polish public.

It is worth emphasizing that on June 28, 2025, the Financial Ombudsman received supervisory powers for the first time and became a market supervisory authority within the meaning of the Polish Act of April 26, 2024, on ensuring compliance with accessibility requirements for certain products and services by business entities (Journal of Laws, item 731). This act is related to the implementation of Directive (EU) 2019/882 of the European Parliament and of the Council on the accessibility requirements for products and services (OJ L 151, 7.6.2019, pp. 70–115).

New educational and informational tasks of the Financial Ombudsman Service have been added by indicating in the Act that the initiation and organisation of such activities is aimed at increasing the financial awareness of the public. One of the most important projects remains the Financial Ombudsman Academy. This is a one-month internship programme for students at the Office of the Financial Ombudsman, which includes participation in lectures given by academics, NGO representatives and others, as well as a practical part in the' various departments of the Office. Students participate in the handling of authentic cases submitted to the Office.

It should be emphasised that this is a significant change, since under the previous law this duty had a narrower subjective scope and applied only to customers of financial market entities. At the same time, it has been pointed out that the scope of this part of the financial ombudsperson's activity concerns the functioning of the financial market, the use of innovative technologies and possible risks occurring in these areas. It is particularly positive that there is the addition to the Act of a legal position on the Financial Ombudsman Service's cooperation with non-governmental, social and professional organisations whose statutory objectives include the protection of consumer rights, with associations, civic movements, other voluntary associations and foundations, as well as with foreign and international bodies and organisations in order to protect consumer rights. Undoubtedly, the legal provision in question creates a legal framework for taking various measures to protect the rights of financial market customers in cooperation with other state bodies and social entities.

In terms of financial ombudsperson's substantive legal competence, there has been a significant strengthening of their procedural competence through the creation of an avenue for the financial ombudsperson to file lawsuits in civil cases on behalf of customers of financial market entities, or to join pending civil proceedings if, in the financial ombudsperson's assessment, this is required to protect the rights of customers of a financial market entity, with the exception of proceedings before the District Court in Warsaw, the Court of Competition and Consumer Protection. It is of particular importance that the financial ombudsperson may bring an action or participate in proceedings, with the consent of the complainant, only in cases involving unfair market practices, as defined in the Act of 23 August 2007 on counteracting unfair market practices.

Art. 26 has resulted in an expansion of the financial ombudsperson's authority to protect customers. This is because the ombudsperson can now participate in all civil proceedings important to customers of financial market entities, not just those relating to unfair market practices. Moreover, as a result of the amendment, it will be possible for the ombudsperson to participate in proceedings without having to obtain consent from the client. This is particularly important as obtaining such consent has often been problematic.

The financial ombudsperson also has the right to bring actions in class proceedings as a representative of the class with respect to claims by customers of a financial market entity or claims by individuals arising from a contract for the provision of services or performance of activities for the benefit of an individual with a financial institution within the meaning of art. 4(4) of the Act on Macroprudential Supervision of the Financial System and Crisis Management in the Financial System. At the time of submission of this country report, it is not possible to assess the impact of the implementation of this right due to the recency of the new legislation.

Significant changes have also been made to the rules governing the imposition of administrative fines by the financial ombudsperson, including an increase from PLN 100,000 to PLN 1,000,000 in the maximum amount of the financial penalty that can be imposed by the financial ombudsperson on financial market entities for their failure to fulfil certain obligations imposed on them by the RF Act vis-à-vis customers of financial market entities in connection with a pending complaint.[24]

Another change is that the financial ombudsperson may also impose a fine of up to PLN 1,000,000 on an entity that is not a financial market entity, from which the financial ombudsperson has requested certain information or documents, because the activities of this entity are related to the case under consideration by the ombudsperson; the fine may be imposed if the entity fails to take a position within the

[24] For general remarks on the financial penalty imposed by the Financial Ombudsman, see Wyżykowski (2018b), pp. 75–76.

statutory period or if it fails to provide the information and documents requested by the ombudsperson, i.e. for violating the obligation under art. 31 of the Act.

Furthermore, the financial ombudsperson now has the ability to impose a fine of up to PLN 100,000 on a financial market entity for violation of the obligation to participate in out-of-court dispute resolution proceedings. This is particularly important from the point of view of seeking to ensure the effectiveness of such dispute resolution methods.

Yet another novelty in the legal provisions governing the imposition of fines is the obligation to publish information on fines imposed on the basis of final decisions on the institution's website. The adopted solution should be evaluated positively, as it may have a preventive effect on actions taken by financial market entities.

The legislature has also taken steps to accelerate the course of out-of-court dispute resolution proceedings between a customer of a financial market entity and a financial market entity in the absence of an amicable conclusion. In accordance with the new legal solutions, the opinion of the financial ombudsperson, including an assessment of the subject matter of the dispute, will be drawn up at the request of the person interested in obtaining it within 14 days from the date of delivery of the record of the proceedings, rather than in every instance, as was previously the case.

The incorporation of the issue of fees comprising the financing of the activities of the financial ombudsperson and the Office into statutory law should be assessed with appreciation. This issue should be defined in detail in the Act due to the gravity of the subject matter governed. An annual fee declaration has been established (quarterly declarations are currently in force).

In doing so, the amount of fees paid by financial market entities was increased, and the method used to determine the amount was modified. The new financial management model has introduced a means of amending the financial plan of the Financial Ombudsman Office in the calendar year for which the it was drawn up. The Financial Ombudsman Service was previously also allowed to create its own funds - a basic fund and a reserve fund. However, the principle has been maintained that the activities of the ombudsperson and of the Office are financed by fees from financial market entities, and not from the state budget.

The amendment introduced a legal framework for a new organisation of the Financial Ombudsman Office. It enables the financial ombudsperson to appoint field lawyers from among the staff of the Office. The Financial Ombudsman Service is carrying out conceptual work on the appointment of representatives in specific regions of the country. Pursuant to the amendment, the work of the Financial Ombudsman Office is directed by the Director General.

The former Financial Education Fund (FEF), whose funds were at the disposal of the Financial Ombudsman Service, has been abolished, and in its place a state special-purpose fund under the same name has been created, with the minister responsible for financial institutions becoming its administrator. The titles from which the revenues of the FEF will come have been specified - these are primarily revenues from fines imposed by the Financial Supervision Commission, the President of the OCCP and the financial ombudsperson on financial market entities in cases determined in the Act. Tasks that can be financed from this fund have been defined. The Financial Ombudsman Service shall appoint a representative to participate in the work of the Financial Education Council. The newly created Council will carry out tasks in the field of financial education.

12.7 The Financial Ombudsman's Intervention Measures

The core function of this office is to protect the rights of individual clients, who may approach the Financial Ombudsman Service seeking what Paweł Rokosz describes as "first aid". The ombudsperson undertakes two types of actions: intervention measures and conciliation proceedings.

Firstly, through telephone conversations, email correspondence, or social media interactions, complainants may obtain basic information regarding their individual cases. Subsequently, a client of a financial market entity is entitled to pursue a claim through a pre-complaint intervention procedure. This signifies that if a financial market entity fails to redress a client's grievances within the confines of the complaint resolution process, clients will retain the prerogative to solicit an examination of their case by the financial ombudsperson. It is imperative to underscore that no fees will be levelled for the intervention procedure. It is noteworthy that financial market entities are subject to statutory deadlines for the provision of explanations, which consequently vests a degree of oversight over the intervention process in the Ombudsman institution. Pursuant to art. 32 of the Financial Ombudsman Act, the financial ombudsperson is empowered to impose financial penalties of up to PLN 1,000,000 on financial market entities that are found to have violated information obligations under the complaint resolution procedure or to have breached the statutory timelines for handling complaints as stipulated in the Act.

Furthermore, the financial ombudsperson can initiate legal action on behalf of clients of the financial market. The ombudsperson can also participate in ongoing legal proceedings.

Furthermore, the ombudsperson can present what is known as a "significant view" to the court in proceedings that are currently pending before it. A significant view is non-binding and does not constitute evidence. However, it is part of the evidentiary material in a broad sense. To illustrate, in one of the 2024 cases, the financial ombudsperson indicated in a significant view that there is an information obligation on the part of the bank when offering a customer a loan based on a variable interest rate. Despite the fact that the loan is based on such a rate, it is necessary in this case to specify precise rules for any rate changes, so that borrowers can foresee what consequences this change will have on their situation and obligations to the lender. The financial ombudsperson stated that: "The borrower must have an indication of the rules and circumstances under which interest rates will change." The ombudsperson emphasised that the loan interest rate clauses could not be formulated in a blanket, vague and imprecise manner, as this would leave borrowers unaware of their obligations. While the bank had the authority to make the interest rate binding, it failed to establish objective rules that allowed borrowers to verify how rate changes would be calculated.

Like the insurance ombudsperson, the financial ombudsperson is also actively involved in conducting educational initiatives with the objective of enhancing financial literacy and competence, particularly in the field of financial market operations, utilisation of innovative technologies, and potential threats present in these domains.[25]

In accordance with art. 83 § 2 of the Act of 8 December 2017 concerning the Supreme Court, the financial ombudsperson is permitted to file an application for an extraordinary complaint regarding judgments that conclude proceedings in cases finalised after 3 April 2018. It is crucial to underline that such an extraordinary complaint must be reserved for extraordinary circumstances, specifically when fundamental principles or the constitutionally protected freedoms and rights of individuals have been infringed upon. The Supreme Court has upheld the financial ombudsperson's extraordinary complaint regarding the settlement of early loan repayment. In order for the financial ombudsperson to prepare an extraordinary complaint, it is necessary to provide the ombudsperson with as complete a case file as possible. This means that it must include a description of the objections to the ruling, a presentation of the pleadings and the rulings of the courts of both instances with reasons and evidence. It is only on this basis that the financial ombudsperson can decide whether to apply to the Supreme Court.

For example, in 2018, the Supreme Court upheld the financial ombudsperson's extraordinary complaint regarding the settlement of early loan repayments. The District Court in Kielce, as the court of first instance, recognised the validity of the claimants' arguments and awarded the amount indicated in the lawsuit. Alior Bank filed an appeal, as a result of which the District Court in Kielce, acting as the court of second instance, amended the verdict and dismissed the claim, arguing that art. 49(1) of the Consumer Credit Act did not justify the clients' claim, and that the early repayment fee was not a cost related to the term of the loan.

It should be noted that, from the outset, the financial ombudsperson shared the position of the court of first instance, according to which the bank should reimburse borrowers for part of the fee charged in connection with early repayment of the loan. In the case of early repayment of a consumer loan, there is a proportional reduction in all the costs of taking out such a loan.

The financial ombudsperson did not share the view of the court of second instance, considering that the verdict violates the law in a gross manner, and since a review of the verdict could not be achieved by filing a cassation complaint, the ombudsperson decided to file an extraordinary complaint. The above-mentioned power to file an extraordinary complaint makes it possible to more fully realise the protection of customer rights of financial market entities.

Moreover, the ombudsperson is actively involved in the international arena, participating not only at the European level but also in international engagements. The

---

[25] Wyżykowski (2018b), p. 122.

Financial Ombudsman Service's international cooperation is conducted through membership and participation in events initiated by organisations such as FIN-NET, and the Organisation for Economic Cooperation and Development (OECD), of which the Ombudsman Service (formerly the Insurance Ombudsman Service) was a member until 2006.

Lastly, the financial ombudsperson resolves consumer complaints through mediation and conciliation.

One of the most popular ADR proceedings available to consumers on the financial market in Poland is the out-of-court procedure for the resolution of disputes between clients and financial market entities, conducted by the financial ombudsperson. This is a distinct procedure that features elements of both mediation and conciliation. This procedure is mandatory for financial market entities.

12.8 Complaints Handling Process and Requests for Out-of-Court Dispute Resolution

12.8.1 Complaints Handling Process

Firstly, the financial ombudsperson can act on the matter and examine whether, as a consequence of an action or omission on the part of the insurer (or other financial institution), there has been a breach of clients' rights (art. 24(2) in conjunction with art. 17(1)(1) and (2) of the Act). If so, the ombudsperson may undertake intervention activities, which is a complaints procedure. It should be noted that the procedure is free of charge.

Under this procedure, the ombudsperson may, in particular, intervene on behalf of a client, as well as delineate their rights and available courses of action. In addition, if the case has already been brought to court, the ombudsperson may submit to the court, at the client's request, the so-called "significant view" on the case. This is defined as the position of the ombudsperson on the issue that is the subject of court proceedings. It should be noted, however, that presenting such a position is not the responsibility of the financial ombudsperson, and when deciding to present it, the ombudsperson takes into account the welfare of the client.

An application for intervention proceedings can be submitted by the traditional means of post or electronically to a dedicated email address.

The financial ombudsperson may only take action after a consumer has submitted a complaint to a financial market entity, and it has been rejected or the consumer's claims have not been fully upheld.

The financial ombudsperson will also consider a complaint when a financial market entity:

1. has failed to respond to the complaint within the applicable deadline
2. has not performed the activities resulting from the complaint accepted in accordance with the customer's will

3. has failed to fulfil other obligations set out in the RF Act (e.g. has not included information in the contract regarding the procedure for submitting and considering complaints or has not provided the required information in response to the complaint).

In this procedure, the financial ombudsperson has the right to request documents from the financial market entity based on which a decision to dismiss the consumer's claims in whole or in part was made. The ombudsperson cannot compel a financial institution to change its position; rather, its role is limited to engaging in legal discourse with a financial market entity. The intervention procedure ends with a final letter addressed to the customer in which the ombudsperson informs the customer of the result of the intervention undertaken. In the event that the intervention is ineffective, the consumer will be presented with the legal provisions applicable to the case and a legal assessment of the consumer's legal situation.

12.8.2 Out-of-Court Dispute Resolution Handling Process

The second avenue available to the financial ombudsperson is that of conducting an out-of-court (amicable) resolution of a dispute between a client and a financial market entity (art. 35 of the Act).

A request to initiate extrajudicial proceedings may be submitted by a consumer in one of four ways:

1. by using the form on the Financial Ombudsman Service's website (in order to use this form of submitting an application, the consumer must have a qualified electronic signature)
2. by post with relevant enclosures to the address of the Financial Ombudsman Office
3. by using the ePUAP platform[26]
4. by submitting the application with the relevant enclosures in person at the headquarters or the local branch of the Office of the Financial Ombudsman.

The proceedings in question are characterised by the fact that the procedure governing them is set out in a number of legal acts:

- the Act of 5 August 2015 on the consideration of complaints by financial market entities, on the Financial Ombudsman and on the Financial Education Fund - in particular Chapter 4 (Financial Ombudsman Act);[27]
- Regulation of the Minister of Development and Finance of 15 February 2017 on out-of-court proceedings before the Financial Ombudsman,[28] constituting

[26] This is a nationwide platform through which citizens in Poland can communicate with public administration bodies.

[27] Journal of Laws 2023, item 1809.

[28] Journal of Laws of 2017, item 313.

implementing provisions issued on the basis of the delegation concluded in art. 43 of the Act on the Financial Ombudsman; and
- the Act of 23 September 2016 on out-of-court resolution of consumer disputes (hereinafter the "ADR Act")[29] - to the extent that the procedure is not governed by Chapter 4 of the Act on the Financial Ombudsman (specifically art. 35a(1)) and the EU ODR Regulation.[30]

Another distinctive feature of the aforementioned procedure is its unique type. Even though the authors of the draft of the proceedings in question defined it as a mediation procedure, an analysis of the relevant provisions indicates that it is a kind of hybrid procedure, trying to combine the best features of mediation and conciliation. The fact that this does not strictly constitute mediation proceedings is evident in the fact that it is not conducted by a mediator, but by the financial ombudsperson with the help of authorised persons who meet specific requirements in terms of professional experience, seniority and education. Another argument for not recognising the out-of-court proceedings conducted at the Financial Ombudsman Service as purely mediation proceedings is that a party cannot enforce the settlement agreement by initiating enforcement proceedings. Finally, the main principle of mediation proceedings is the voluntary participation of the parties to the proceedings. However, in accordance with art. 37 of the Financial Ombudsman Act, the participation of a financial market entity in the proceedings is mandatory. The proceedings discussed in this chapter also feature elements taken directly from classic conciliation proceedings. As a dispute resolution method, conciliation is characterised by the fact that a dispute between the parties is resolved by a third party in a manner that is not binding on the party.[31] The introduction of a conciliatory element into the proceedings emphasises its advantages, such as professionalism, handling of the subject of the dispute by a specialist and the informal nature of the proceedings.[32] The proceedings are conducted in an independent, impartial and confidential manner.

The financial market is a specific one associated with complex processes and products, and also with information asymmetry occurring between the parties to contracts, especially between financial market entities and non-professional clients (so-called retail clients).[33] The financial market is a very sensitive one, prone to crises potentially resulting in serious economic consequences for its participants. Therefore, it is necessary for the financial market to have mechanisms that ensure it can operate in a stable manner.[34] In order for the market to function in a stable man-

[29] Journal of Laws 2016, item 1823.

[30] Regulation (EU) No. 524/2013 of the European Parliament and of the Council of 21 May 2013 on online consumer dispute resolution and amending Regulation (EC) No. 2006/2004 and Directive 2009 /22/EC (Regulation on consumer ODR) [2013] OJ L165/1.

[31] Cf. Herrmann (1983), p. 145; Fischer-Zernin and Junker, (1988), p. 25; Hoellering (1987), pp. 526–527; Fox (1990), pp. 154–159.

[32] Szumański (1997).

[33] Cyman (2019), p. 105.

[34] Cyman (2019), p. 101.

ner and to be resistant to crises, it should be designed in such a way as to ensure the highest standards of professionalism in virtually every aspect of its trading. Therefore, the architecture of amicable dispute resolution methods available on this market must be of high quality and professionalism. In light of the aforementioned considerations, specific requirements have been established for individuals conducting out-of-court proceedings at the Financial Ombudsman Service. Thus, a person conducting out-of-court proceedings at the Financial Ombudsman Service must have outstanding knowledge of the functioning of the financial market and the legal framework that shapes it, as well as a minimum of five years of work experience, including a minimum of three years in this specific domain. The person conducting the proceedings should also have a higher education in law or economics, along with comprehensive understanding of the field of judicial or out-of-court dispute resolution. Additionally, they must have outstanding knowledge in the type of contracts concluded between the client and a financial market entity. The introduction into the Act of such requirements for persons conducting proceedings should be assessed as positively as possible, considering the level of complexity of products offered to clients on the financial market, the information asymmetry between the parties and the unequal economic opportunities available to the parties. A person who meets the criteria set forth in the regulations governing the proceedings in question, due to their appropriate education and knowledge of the principles and mechanisms governing the financial market, is capable of impartially, independently and effectively supporting the parties to reach an agreement and concluding settlements, despite not having authority. The legislature's guarantee that the persons conducting the proceedings are practitioners with appropriate knowledge supported by appropriate education, as well as appropriate procedural and mediation experience, allows for amicable resolution to even the most complex disputes arising from contracts concluded on the financial market in such proceedings. Furthermore, the advantages of the aforementioned criteria include the fact that ensuring that proceedings are handled by well-prepared professionals increases the parties' chances of finding a reasonable way to resolve the dispute and allows them to diagnose and become aware of the risks for each party related to further conduct of the dispute. Individuals with theoretical and practical knowledge of the use of products offered on the financial market also serve as "translators" in the aforementioned proceedings, who understand the complicated language used by financial market entities, which very often contains specialist terms and concepts in the field of law and economics. These individuals are capable of translating such specialised language into one comprehensible to clients engaged in dispute resolution. The above skill enables the conductor of the proceedings to show the parties the essence of the dispute, thereby facilitating a concentrated effort towards the formation of a constructive agreement. Possessing the competencies required by the legislature also allows them to fully focus on helping the parties resolve their dispute as well as to present proposals to that end to the participants in the proceedings, taking into account the interests of the parties, legal provisions governing the subject of the dispute, and allowing for maintaining good relations in the future.

Provisions regulating out-of-court proceedings at the Financial Ombudsman Service do not specify precisely what may be the subject of the dispute. The request may concern disputes concerning property or non-property matters.

12.8.2.1 Procedure

As mentioned at the beginning, the extrajudicial proceedings before the ombudsperson are unique on the Polish market. The aspects pertaining to the formal assessment of the complaint and the preparation of a report concluding the proceedings bear resemblance to classic administrative proceedings.[35]

When analysing the provisions governing out-of-court proceedings at the Financial Ombudsman Service, it can be concluded that the proceedings consist of three stages: the first is the preliminary examination of the complaint, the second is the actual out-of-court proceedings and the third is the completion of the proceedings.

12.8.2.2 Initial Examination of the Complaint

The preliminary examination of complaints can be described as a type of formal assessment. The preliminary examination of the complaint is not carried out by the person conducting the proceedings, but by a person in the extrajudicial proceedings team. In the course of the inspection activities, the complaint is assessed for its compliance with the requirements specified in art. 33(2) ADR Act, art. 36(2) of the Act on the Financial Ombudsman, as well as § 6 of the Regulation. In accordance with the aforementioned provisions, the complaint should at least contain the names of the parties to the proceedings, a precise description of the request, an indication of the type of proceedings and the complainant's signature. By marking the pages, in accordance with the Regulation, it is understood to provide the name or company name of the financial market entity along with the address details of its registered office, as well as the complainant's data, including at least the name and surname, residential address and correspondence address, if different from the residential address, as well as the telephone number or e-mail address, if the complainant has them.[36] The complaint should also include a precise description of the request. This request should be expressed in monetary terms or contain a clearly defined expectation of the complainant towards the financial market entity as to how to resolve the dispute arising from the legal relationship between them. The complaint submitted by the client is checked at this stage to ensure that the complainant has indicated the type (mode) of proceedings in which the extrajudicial proceedings pertaining to the

---

[35] Chołodecki and Strzelbicki (2017), p. 77.

[36] § 6 of the Regulation of the Minister of Development and Finance of 15 February 2017 (Journal of Laws of 2017, item 313 of 21 February 2017).

dispute is to be conducted. The legislature has permitted the client to select from the types of procedures offered by the Financial Ombudsman Service. In accordance with the regulations, the client may choose a procedure that involves approximating the positions of the parties' in order to resolve the dispute or one that presents the parties with a proposal for an amicable resolution to the dispute. The structure of the provisions also permits the complainant to use both modes of procedure in the proceedings at the same time. Those seeking to utilize the out-of-court procedure at the Financial Ombudsman Service are required to attach to or enclose with the complaint a description of the circumstances of the case, information on the course of the dispute thus far and a copy of the documents held by the complainant confirming the information contained in the complaint. The description of the circumstances of the case should contain concise information focusing on the subject of the dispute, i.e. reflecting its essence as precisely as possible, why the dispute occurred, what its background was and in what circumstances the dispute arose. The documents attached or enclosed by the complainant should confirm the facts of the case as set forth in the complainant's description thereof.

If it is not possible to present such documents, the complainant should indicate this in the complaint. The documents attached to or enclosed with the complaint should also confirm the completion of the complaint procedure or indicate the circumstances that prevent the attachment or enclosure of such documents.

For out-of-court proceedings at the Financial Ombudsman Service, a fee is charged. Pursuant to Art. 38 of the Act on the Financial Ombudsman, a fee of PLN 50 must be paid by the client to the Financial Ombudsman Service's account when submitting an complaint. The complainant must attach to or enclose with the complaint proof of payment of the fee or an application for exemption from the obligation to pay it. An application for fee exemption should include a description of the factual circumstances justifying the application, as well as documents confirming the circumstances cited by the client in the application for exemption from the fee (e.g. bank statement confirming low income, documents confirming a difficult life situation).

In the event that any formal flaws are found in the complaint submitted, the financial ombudsperson will notify the complainant in writing, requesting the completion of the complaint within 14 days from the date of delivery of the request. If there is no response to this request, the ombudsperson may complete the activities and leave the client's complaint without consideration. The client will be duly informed in writing.

This stage of formal assessment ends with the provision of written confirmation to the parties, confirming the submission of the complaint by the client and the initiation of proceedings. Alternatively, written notification is provided to the complainant, informing them of the refusal to initiate proceedings.

The provision in § 10 imposes an obligation on the financial ombudsperson to notify the parties about the initiation of proceedings within seven days. This deadline is calculated from the date of commencement of the proceedings, i.e. from date of receipt of the client's complaint, which must contain the client's name and the name of the financial market entity, a detailed description of the request and the type of proceedings selected by the complainant from those referenced in art. 36(2) of the Act on the Financial Ombudsman, along with the signature of the complainant or their representative.

It is also noteworthy that the financial ombudsperson is permitted to refuse to initiate proceedings in only a limited number of exceptional cases, as specified in the Act. This catalogue is a closed catalogue covering the following conditions: the subject of the dispute goes beyond the categories of disputes covered by the ombudsperson's jurisdiction, the client has not exhausted the complaint procedure outlined in Chapter 2 of the Act on the Financial Ombudsman, the request to initiate proceedings will cause inconvenience to a financial market entity, a case involving the same claim between the same parties is pending or has already been considered by the ombudsperson in proceedings, by an arbitration court, by another competent entity or by a state court, consideration of the dispute would seriously disrupt the ombudsperson's activities, the client has not paid the fee referred to in art. 38(1), and the client was not exempted from paying it. The financial ombudsperson is bound by the aforementioned conditions in their entirety.

12.8.2.3 The Stage of Proper Out-of-Court Proceedings

Once the complaint to initiate proceedings has been positively verified, it is assigned to an employee of the Financial Ombudsman Office who is authorised to conduct extrajudicial proceedings. First, upon receipt of the case files, the individual responsible for conducting the proceedings is obliged to determine whether there are any circumstances that preclude proceeding with the case. In the event that there are indications of a conflict of interests, the individual is required to notify the Director of the Department of Extrajudicial Dispute Resolution. In the absence of any circumstances indicating the necessity of excluding the person conducting the proceedings, the latter is required to notify the parties in writing of the appointment of a person to conduct the proceedings. This document also contains information regarding the impartiality and independence of the appointed individual, as well as a reminder of the necessity for confidentiality throughout the proceedings. Furthermore, the parties are furnished with the contact details of the person conducting the proceedings.

In the course of the proceedings, the person conducting the proceedings acquaints the financial market entity with the client's claim, presents the legal provisions applicable to the case to the parties to the proceedings and takes steps to enable the parties' positions to be approximated in order to resolve the dispute by the parties, or presents the parties with a proposal to that end.

In the course of activities aimed at approximating the parties' positions, the person conducting the proceedings should, in accordance with Art. 39 of the Financial Ombudsman Act, present to the parties the legal provisions applicable to the case. The provisions of generally applicable law presented to the parties in the course of the proceedings should be significantly related to the subject matter of the dispute. Other actions taken with the intention of approximating the parties' positions are understood as forms of conciliatory activity. These activities must be conducted by the person responsible for the proceedings with the goal of eliminating the differences in interest between the parties involved. These include the initiation of settlement negotiations between the parties. Settlement negotiations between the parties in out-of-court proceedings at the Financial Ombudsman Service may end with the parties signing a settlement agreement. In the phase of settlement negotiations between the parties, the role of the conductor of the proceedings is essentially to provide the parties with a platform on which they can freely negotiate disputed issues among themselves. Negotiations give the parties the greatest freedom in resolving the dispute between them.[37] As part of other conciliation activities, the person conducting the proceedings should, in accordance with the principles of evaluative mediation, actively seek to determine the facts, try to assess the credibility of the facts by posing well-crafted questions, indicate for the parties' consideration the legal provisions that may apply to a given fact, or signal areas of risk to the parties and express their opinions about them.[38]

In the event that conciliation activities aimed at reconciling the parties' positions have been exhausted and proven unsuccessful, and if the complainant has indicated in the request to conduct the proceedings that they are requesting the proceedings to be conducted with a conciliatory element, the person conducting the proceedings presents the parties with a proposal for an amicable solution to the dispute. The legal basis for presenting the proposal is art. 39 of the Financial Ombudsman Act.

Furthermore, in § 12 of the Regulation it is stipulated that the person conducting the proceedings is required to submit a proposal to resolve the dispute regarding the demands outlined in the complaint, provided that the circumstances of the case allow for such a proposal to be formulated. The deadline for the parties to respond to the proposal should not be shorter than 7 days. This stipulation allows the person conducting the proceedings the option to refrain from submitting proposals for an amicable settlement of the dispute in the event that they determine that the discrepancies between the parties' positions and legal assessments of the facts are too significant, or that the factual circumstances of the case necessitate the undertaking of complicated and costly evidentiary proceedings. The proposal is not binding on any of the parties.

In practice, proposals for resolving the dispute, especially in matters related to the insurance market, focus on the performance by the parties of additional activities aimed at establishing the facts of the case. These activities may include calling for an additional expert opinion, performing additional inspections, or conducting an eye-witness medical examination aimed at determining the actual damage to the complainant's health. Alternatively, the financial entity may recognise the customer's claim based on the legal analysis carried out by the person conducting the proceedings and pay benefits to the customer. The financial ombudsperson's proposals for resolving the dispute also encourage the parties to re-examine their positions

[37] Dębska (2021), p. 63.

[38] Brown (2004), p. 279.

(including taking into account the image and business aspects of the case) and requests, if possible, for an exceptional payment by the financial market entity to the client.

The rule is that any proceedings and individual activities undertaken therein must be conducted in writing or via electronic means of communication. This should be assessed positively, as it undoubtedly contributes to reducing the costs of proceedings for all participants in the process. However, should the nature of the dispute require it, the ombudsperson may schedule a meeting with the relevant party or parties to the proceedings. Such a meeting may take place via means of distance communication (teleconference, video call) or at the headquarters of the Financial Ombudsman Service.

The person conducting the proceedings is also obliged to ensure the time discipline of the process. The provision in § 11 indicates that the result of the proceedings should be presented to the parties within 90 days from the date of receipt of a complaint that meets the formal requirements. In instances of particularly complex cases, the person conducting the proceedings may extend the duration of the proceedings. The legislature has not stipulate a maximum time frame for the duration of the proceedings or the maximum number of extensions of the proceedings in statutory law. Instead, they imposed an obligation on the individual conducting the proceedings to inform the parties of the extension of the proceedings.

12.8.2.4 The Stage of Termination of Out-of-Court Proceedings

Out-of-court proceedings at the Financial Ombudsman Service end when the parties reach an agreement, fail to reach an agreement or for other reasons.

The parties may reach an agreement in the proceedings by concluding or determining the terms of the settlement, redefining mutual rights or obligations within the scope of the legal relationship between the parties to the proceedings, or by direct performance by one of the parties (or mutual performance by both parties to the dispute) in full or in part, without the need to prepare and sign any documents. The settlement agreement developed by the parties with the help of the financial ombudsperson has a conciliatory function. It enables the parties to choose how to resolve the dispute in a way acceptable to the parties. Furthermore, it helps to end the existing dispute and helps to prevent the dispute from escalating or arising in the future. Additionally, it contributes to the preservation and the development of positive, long-term future relationships between the parties. Such an agreement also serves a stabilising function, which helps to establish certainty the parties' regarding their legal situation. This function is also expressed in the fact that, as a result of a settlement reached through out-of-court proceedings, the parties are afforded the opportunity to change the content of the uncertain obligation. The stabilisation of relations is also facilitated by the option available to the parties to waive any objections they may have. In terms of enforcement, a settlement agreement concluded with the financial ombudsperson does not have the same effect as a court settlement.

This is an out-of-court settlement and does not, in principle, constitute an enforcement order.

If the parties reach an agreement during the process, the person conducting the proceedings prepares a report that contains the information outlined in art. 41 of the RF Act. The minutes of the proceedings should include the following details: the time and place of the proceedings, the name, surname and addresses of the parties, an indication of the subject of the dispute and information on how the dispute was resolved.

Out-of-court proceedings may also end when the parties are unable to reach an agreement. In such an instance, the person conducting the proceedings is obliged to prepare a report on the proceedings if they determine that further mediation activities will not result in an amicable resolution to the dispute. Following the delivery of the report to the parties, each of them may, within 14 days, request the financial ombudsperson to prepare an opinion containing a legal assessment of the facts established during the proceedings. The opinion is advisory in nature, has no binding force, and is therefore not subject to any appeal. At the end of the conciliation and mediation proceedings, the ombudsperson does not decide on the client's claims; rather, the ombudsperson presents their own position, which must contain a legal assessment of the factual situation as confirmed by the participants in the proceedings.

12.8.2.5 Other Forms of Ending Out-of-Court Proceedings at the Financial Ombudsman Service

In accordance with the provisions set out in § 15, the financial ombudsperson is vested with the authority to end the proceedings, in the event that the client withdraws the complaint during the proceedings or in the event that the proceedings become impossible for other reasons. In such instances, the ombudsperson ends the proceedings and immediately notifies the parties.

If the person conducting the proceedings is made aware of the client's intention to withdraw the complaint, they will promptly end the proceedings and duly inform all of the parties involved. In such an instance, the proceedings are not documented in the form of minutes and no opinion is prepared. Furthermore, the financial ombudsperson may terminate the proceedings if there are other reasons that make it impossible to continue to conduct them. The catalogue of such cases includes situations in which the complainant does not actively participate in the process (for example by failing to respond to letters or telephone calls) or the complainant may have died or may meet the grounds for refusing to initiate proceedings as specified in art. 36(4) of the RF Act. In the aforementioned cases, no report with an opinion is drawn up; instead the parties are only notified of the completion of the proceedings.

12.8.3 *Out-of-Court Proceedings at the Financial Ombudsman Service in the Insurance Sector: Product Problems*

As mentioned in the introduction, out-of-court proceedings at the Financial Ombudsman Service are the most frequently utilised method among consumers seeking assistance from a public institution for the amicable resolution to a dispute with insurance companies.

From the practice of conducted cases, it is possible to identify recurring problems that were the subject of the complaints. The product groups discussed below have been identified as the subject of ongoing proceedings in 2023.

In the case of motor insurance, as was the case in previous years, the implementation of compulsory civil liability insurance contracts for motor vehicle owners (third party liability insurance) and auto insurance contracts continued to generate the largest number of disputes within this segment in 2023. The financial ombudsperson observed that in the implementation of compulsory civil liability insurance contracts for motor vehicle owners, the so-called "discount depreciation" used by insurance companies in the process of settling claims with regard to vehicles is still the dominant problem. The disputes in this case focus on the practice of insurance companies in the compensation due to customers is automatically reduced by applying discounts and allowances for parts and materials for vehicle repair. These reductions are the result of individual contracts concluded between insurance companies and specific repair workshops. This practice effectively prevents the injured party from repairing the damaged vehicle unless it is repaired in one of the workshops indicated by the insurance company because it has a signed cooperation agreement.

In the field of voluntary motor insurance, such as car insurance, the majority of disputes pertain to the determination of compensation in the event of a total loss. The crux of the dispute is typically the question of correctly determining the value of the vehicle on the date of the damage. In complaints submitted to the Financial Ombudsman Service, clients also point out large discrepancies in the determination of compensation by insurance companies using expert programmes and car auctions.

The Financial Ombudsman Service continues to record disputes that arise from the implementation of voluntary life insurance contracts. As in previous years, as part of the proceedings conducted by the financial ombudsperson, the issues of proceedings conducted in this insurance segment have focused on the interpretation by the parties to the dispute of the provisions of general insurance conditions. This has included the definition of terms such as accident, heart attack, serious illness, or specialised surgery (for example, the definition of an ablation procedure). An important issue that has been raised in the proceedings conducted by the ombudsperson is the estimation of health damage by insurance companies that their clients suffer as a result of accidents. In this instance, clients have also accused insurers of incorrectly assessing the damage to their health as a result of the absence of visual medical examinations and the inaccurate analysis of the medical documentation.

Where disputes related to the implementation of insurance contracts with an insurance capital fund are concerned, the financial ombudsperson has observed that there has been a change in customer sentiment, with an increasing number of customers expressing discontent over a lower profit from the product than expected and assured in the sales process. In previous years, disputes of this nature were predominantly related to issues pertaining to the redemption amount in the event of an early termination of the contract or misselling. Disputes in this product segment increasingly focus on the issue of the amount of the survivorship benefit.

As in previous years, a large number of out-of-court proceedings were concerned with voluntary civil liability insurance. The most important issues in this insurance group were problems with the implementation of civil liability insurance contracts for road managers and real estate managers. In particular, in this second line of insurance, the financial ombudsperson observed a disturbing practice among insurers of transferring liquidation obligations to the injured parties (e.g., the obligation to determine the potential repair costs, the scope of repairs, or to obtain confirmation of the circumstances causing the damage from the entity responsible for the damage). Complainants still report problems for people injured as a result of inadequate winter maintenance or the technical condition of pedestrian routes for which property managers are responsible.

In the field of travel insurance, the issue of trip cancellation insurance (in particular in relation to illnesses caused by COVID-19) has become a prominent topic of discussion. These disputes often concern the provisions of general insurance terms and conditions, which remained unaltered during the pandemic despite the prevailing quarantine regulations in force at that time. The inability to contact doctors, which obviously made it impossible to submit the documentation required by insurance companies regarding a medical' diagnosis of the illness or a referral for a test, also contributed to these disputes.[39]

12.9 Summary

The aim of this critical examination of Poland's Financial Ombudsman institution was to demonstrate its pivotal role in balancing consumer protection with financial market stability. The evolution of the institution from the Insurance Ombudsman to the Financial Ombudsman reflects Poland's growing recognition of the need for specialised oversight in an increasingly complex financial landscape. The institution's unique hybrid model, combining elements of mediation and conciliation, offers a nuanced approach to dispute resolution that addresses the power imbalance between consumers and financial institutions. Its expanding competences, including the ability to file extraordinary complaints to the Supreme Court, demonstrate its growing influence in shaping financial jurisprudence. However, this country report also highlights ongoing challenges, such as the persistent issues in insurance claim

[39] Report of the Financial Ombudsman on the activities and comments on the state of compliance with the law and the interests of clients of financial market entities for 2023. https://rf.gov.pl/o-nas/sprawozdania/. Accessed 16 Apr 2025.

settlements, suggesting that despite progress, there remains room for improvement in consumer financial protection. The Financial Ombudsman Service's dual focus on individual case resolution and systemic reform positions it as a key player in enhancing financial literacy and market fairness in Poland.

References

Brown CJ (2004) Facilitative mediation: the classic approach retains its appeal. Pepp Disp Resol Law J 4(2) https://digitalcommons.pepperdine.edu/drlj/vol4/iss2/9

Budzianowski P (2015) Od Rzecznika Ubezpieczonych do Rzecznika Finansowego. Monitor Ubezpieczeniowy 63. https://mu.rf.gov.pl/63/pdf/art-2.pdf

Chołodecki M, Strzelbicki M (2017) Act on the consideration of complaints by financial market entities and on the Financial Ombudsman. Insytut Wydawniczy EuroPrawo, Warsaw

Cyman D (2017) Zarys sytemu instytucjonalnej ochrony praw konsumentów na rynku finansowym. Gdańskie Studia Prawnicze 38:332–333

Cyman D (2019) Customer protection system as a condition for maintaining the stability of the financial system. In: Rutkowska-Tomaszewska E, Monkiewicz J (eds) Consumer protection on the Polish and international financial market. Wolters Kluwer, Warsaw

Daszewski A (n.d.) Geneza powstania Urzędu Rzecznika Ubezpieczonych w Polsce. http://web.archive.org/web/20150101000000*/rf.gov.pl

Dębska J (2021) Types of alternative dispute resolution methods. In: Rogula C, Zemke-Górecka A (eds) Mediation in the practice of mediator and attorney. Warsaw

Fischer-Zernin V, Junker A (1988) Arbitration and mediation: synthesis or antithesis? J Int Arbitr 5(1)

Fox WF Jr (1990) International commercial agreements. Kluwer/Deventer

Herrmann G (1983) Conciliation as new method of dispute settlement. In: Sanders P (ed) New trends in the development of International Commercial Arbitration and the role of arbitral and other institutions. Kluwer/Deventer

Hoellering MF (1987) Emerging techniques of private dispute in long - term contracts. In: Nicklisch F (ed) Der komplexe Langzeitvertrag. Strukturen und Internationale Schiedsgerichtbarkeit, Heidelberg

Jurkowska-Zeidler A (2016) Konsekwencje zmian w systemie ochrony konsumenta usług finansowych. Gdańskie Studia Prawnicze, XXXVI

Kiziewicz E (n.d.) Rok działalności Sądu Polubownego przy Rzeczniku Ubezpieczonych. http://web.archive.org/web/20150101000000*/rf.gov.pl

Ojczyk J (2023) Interview with Aleksandra Wiktorow: Rzecznik Finansowy bardzo potrzebny. https://www.prawo.pl/biznes/liwkidacja-rzecznika-finansowego-argumenty-przeciw-aleksandry,502908.html

Orlicki M (2020) Raport i opinia prawna. In: Rzecznik Finansowy jako niezbędny element systemu ochrony konsument w usług finansowych w Polsce. Biała Księga Rzecznika Finansowego. Warsaw

Park S (2008) Korean preaching, Han, and narrative. American University Studies, Theology and Religion, series 7

Pickl V (1987) Islamic Roots of Ombudsman Systems. The Ombudsman Journal

Rosiak J (2017) Porównanie instytucji ombudsmana w Polsce i Argentynie. Repozytorium Uniwersytetu Wrocławskiego

Szumański A (1997) Conciliation as a form of resolving economic disputes. Legal Monitor 2
Wiącek M (2016) Commentary on art. 87. In: Safjan M, Bosek L (eds.), Konstytucja RP. Tom II. Komentarz art. 87–243. Warsaw
Wyżykowski B (2018a) Istotny pogląd Rzecznika Finansowego jako instrument ochrony klientów podmiotów rynku finansowego. Studia Prawa Publicznego 1(21)
Wyżykowski B (2018b) Kompetencja Rzecznika Finansowego do nakładania kar pieniężnych na podmioty rynku finansowego. Studia Prawa Publicznego 3

Chapter 13
Spanish System

Juan Bataller Grau

13.1 Introduction

The writing of this chapter on the Spanish insurance market introduces two additional difficulties to the already complex task of tackling the problems of this book. On the one hand, the Spanish system presents divergences from the approximations made by other legal systems within the European Union. On the other hand, at the time of writing this country report, we are awaiting the approval of a reform of the system that Spain is obliged to undertake, as the current system is deemed to be in non-compliance with the mandates contained in the EU ADR Directive.[1]

Hence, we believe that the most logical structure is to briefly analyse the legal framework. We will then look at the current system, giving as exhaustive an overview as possible of the system of the two bodies that make it up. Finally, we will

[1] Directive 2013/11/EU of the European Parliament and of the Council of 21 May 2013 on alternative dispute resolution for consumer disputes and amending Regulation (EC) No 2006/2004 and Directive 2009/22/EC (Directive on consumer ADR) [2013] OJ L165/63. About Spanish System see Aguilar Olivares (2015), Albanés (1988), Almarcha Jaime (2015), Badillo Arias (2011), Bataller Grau (1997), Bataller Grau (2002), Bataller Grau (2005), Bataller Grau (2013), Bataller Grau (2018), Bataller Grau & Seguí-Mas (2013), Bataller Grau & Veiga Copo (2014), Campuzano Laguillo et al. (2013), De Angulo Rodríguez (1998), Gómez Urquijo & Tomás Martínez (2012), Pérez-Serrabona González (2010), Quintáns Eiras (2005), Quintáns Eiras (2016), Rivera (2018), Rodríguez Ponga (1997), Sagrera Rull (2017), Sánchez Calero (2010), Sánchez Hernández (2018), Sucunza Totoricagüena (2015), Vercher Moll (2014)

J. B. Grau (✉)
Universitat de València, Valencia, Spain
e-mail: juan.bataller@uv.es

H. Heiss et al. (eds.), *Insurance Ombudsman Schemes*, AIDA Europe Research Series on Insurance Law and Regulation 15,
https://doi.org/10.1007/978-3-032-01500-6_13

deal with the reform, as it currently stands, since the final text will probably not entail a substantial alteration of its last wording.

13.2 Legal System

The legal regime in force in Spain has been articulated around two regulatory areas: the first regulates the relationship between the customer and the insurers; the second is limited to the specialties of insurance distributors.

13.2.1 Insurance Companies

13.2.1.1 Law 30/1995 on the Regulation and Supervision of Private Insurance

Without going back to the origins of the institution,[2] we can affirm that Law 30/1995 on the Regulation and Supervision of Private Insurance (hereinafter Law 30/1995 OSSP),[3] since its first draft in 1995, any violation of arts. 3, 5, 8, 10, 12, 15, 18, 19, 20, 22, 76, 88, 94, 95, 96, 97 and 99 of the Insurance Contract Law (hereinafter LCS) is considered to be an administrative infraction (art. 40(5)(b) of Law 30/1995 OSSP). Consequently, the decision-making sphere of the Administration supervising insurance companies, the General Directorate of Insurance and Pension Funds (*Dirección General de Seguros y Fondos de Pensiones*, hereinafter DGSFP), has been extended beyond mere administrative regulations, to encompass fundamental aspects of. of insurance as a contract. This is shown by a reading of the matters that have been resolved by the claims service of the DGSFP in the years in which its report has been published. For example, an insured person who considered that their rights had been violated was able to undertake, with the exception of the expert procedure set out in art. 38 LCS, two perfectly compatible avenues: on the one hand, they could file a lawsuit before the competent court and, on the other hand, they were able to seek administrative protection. This is because if the DGSFP recognised their right, the insurance company, faced with the threat of a possible sanction, might ultimately satisfy the insured's claim.

Next, it should be expressly stated that the right to effective judicial protection is enshrined in the Spanish legal system, namely art. 24 of the Spanish Constitution. Consequently, the competence to judge and enforce what has been judged is reserved exclusively to the courts, whereas the DGSFP is a public administration governed by administrative law.

---

[2] See Bataller Grau (1999).

[3] Ley 30/1995, de 8 de noviembre, de Ordenación y Supervisión de los Seguros Privados.

It should also be noted that in Spain the supervision of distributors and insurers is not the responsibility of an independent authority, as is the case in other EU insurance markets, but is assigned to a DGSFP currently under the administration of Ministry of Economy, Trade and Entrepreneurship (in the past to the successive denominations of the ministry, depending on the government).[4] There is thus a significant distinction between the insurance market supervisor and the rest of the financial market supervisors in Spain, which have independent administrations. Indeed, the Bank of Spain and the Securities Market Commission are autonomous entities, not attached to any ministry; as a result, their respective bodies are fully independent.

Likewise, without prejudice to a later development of this issue, it should be made clear at this point that compliance with the decisions of the DGSFP resulting from the claims made by policyholders can only be achieved indirectly through the imposition of an administrative sanction.

The consequence of the DGSFP undertaking the determination of policyholders' claims led to the collapse of the service responsible for resolving them. For this reason, the next step in the regulatory evolution was Law 14/2000, of 28 December, on Fiscal, Administrative and Social Order Measures.[5] This made the admission and processing of the claim conditional on the need to justify that it had been previously formulated and submitted in writing to the insured person's Ombudsman Scheme or, in the event that this did not exist, to the complaints service of the insurer or to the head office of the insurance company. Access to administrative protection was thus subject to prior recourse to the system provided - and organised - by the insurer.

13.2.1.2 Law 44/2002 of 22 November on Measures to Reform the Financial System

A new milestone in this regulatory development was the introduction of the Commissioner for Customer Protection by Law 44/2002 of 22 November on measures to reform the financial system (hereinafter Law 44/2002 MRSF).[6] As in the current reform, the law envisaged the creation of an independent administrative body that would integrate the claims services of the three supervisors. Likewise, and despite the criticism of this statute, its function as a method of resolving disputes was strengthened by establishing the incompatibility between administrative and judicial channels enshrined in art. 7(3)(c) of Royal Decree 303/2004 of 20 February (hereinafter Royal Decree 303/2004),[7] which approved the Regulations of the

[4] This is without prejudice to the competences of the Autonomous Regions, which is beyond the scope of this country report.

[5] Ley 14/2000, de 28 de diciembre, de Medidas Fiscales, Administrativas y del Orden Social.

[6] Ley 44/2002, de 22 noviembre, de Medidas de Reforma del Sistema Financiero (Ley 44/2002, de 22 noviembre, de Medidas de Reforma del Sistema Financiero.

[7] Real Decreto 303/2004, de 20 de febrero, por el que se aprueba el Reglamento de los comisionados para la defensa del cliente de servicios financieros.

Commissioners for the protection of customers. This rule required a reduction in the rights of the insured, since users who considered their rights to have been violated, but who, because of the high amount of the claim, considered it appropriate to file a lawsuit as the most appropriate means of satisfying their claim, namely for compensation, ended up abandoning the administrative channels. Despite these criticisms, the dispute resolution function of the law prevailed, precluding recourse to other procedures.

In our opinion, even in the hypothetical case of a resolution by the Commissioner that favoured an insured, the disadvantages suffered by the insured were not offset. Firstly, its resolutions were not enforceable (arts. 5.1 and 12.6 of Royal Decree 303/2004 of 20 February approving the Regulations of the Commissioners), meaning that the insurer could simply not comply with them. The resolution was not an enforceable title, as Royal Decree 303/2004 was careful to make clear. Secondly, we believe that the Commissioner's decisions would not have been systematically supported by the case law, as our experience with the decisions of the claims services shows. Therefore, not only would it have been theoretically possible for the courts to issue a judgment contradicting the Commissioner's favourable decision, but it would also probably have happened, and in either direction—both in favour of and against the customer.[8] Finally, under the Law 44/2002 MRSF, the question is left open as to whether or not a complaint made to the Commissioner interrupts the statute of limitations for civil action, while it is clear, on the other hand, that the commencement of possible legal proceedings must be postponed until the Commissioner's decision has been obtained. In short, this regulation has led to the most important matters being ignored by the Supervisory Authority, whose intervention was reduced to small claims and always after the mandatory filtering by the Commissioner.

13.2.1.3 The Current System

A subsequent stage in this regulatory evolution can be found in art. 31 of Law 2/2011 of 4 March on Sustainable Economy,[9] in which the legislature enshrined the practice developed by our regulatory institutions. Indeed, this Law establishes that the competences assigned to the Commissioners are exercised by the claims services, in our case, by the DGSFP. Likewise, the 11th Additional Provision to the Law 2/2011 lays the foundations for subsequent regulatory developments, declaring arts. 7 to 15 of Royal Decree 303/2004 to be applicable in the meantime (Fifth Transitional Provision).

The guidelines for the procedure do not offer any substantial novelties either: the initiation of the procedure is conditioned upon a prior complaint to the insurer's complaints service or ombudsperson; its operation as a unique window is

[8] See Marimón Durá (2005).

[9] Ley 2/2011, de 4 de marzo, de Economía Sostenible.

proclaimed; the process will end with the provision of a reasoned decision that cannot be appealed against; in the event of an unfavourable decision, the insurer is obliged to inform the claims service if it has proceeded with the voluntary rectification within one month; finally, a review will be published annually containing the criteria used to resolve the cases.

Finally, the current regulation of the system of claims to the Supervisory Authorities (in our case the DGSFP) is currently contained in Order ECC/2502/2012 of 16 November (hereinafter Order ECC/2502/2012),[10] which governs the procedure for submitting complaints to the Claims Services of the Bank of Spain, the National Securities Market Commission and the DGSFP, a statute which will be dealt with under the corresponding heading below.

The latest milestone in this legislative evolution is represented by art. 97 of Law 20/2015 of 14 July on the Regulation, Supervision and Solvency of Insurance and Reinsurance Entities (hereinafter Law 20/2015 OSSEAR),[11] which addresses the methods of resolving dispute between insurers and clients. A catalogue of different options is provided in the legislative act. Its text can be described as a compilation, but not as a regulation, since its contribution is limited to systematising the different modes of dispute resolution. Moreover, it does not go to any great lengths in this attempt to systematise.

Firstly, recourse to the courts is included, which is superfluous in Spain. Depriving the courts of their jurisdiction over disputes in the insurance sector would violate art. 24 of the Spanish Constitution. We fail to see the usefulness of the legislative act, beyond being a simple reminder that, if the other methods fail, the parties will have to resort to the courts as a way of closing the system provided for in the rest of art. 97 of Law 20/2015 OSSEAR.

Nor is its reference to the common and consumer arbitration regime particularly clarifying. Its wording simply recognises that these are methods applicable in the insurance market that have not been questioned in the legal literature or case law.

A reference to mediation has also been introduced, which in our opinion is a mere consequence of the fact that the matter is already expressly governed in Spanish legislation.

Finally, the last paragraph includes an express reference to the duty of insurers to handle and resolve the complaints and claims that policyholders, insured persons, beneficiaries, injured third parties or successors in title to any of them may present in regard to their legally recognised interests and rights. To this end, the regulation requires insurance companies to have a complaints service in charge of attending to and resolving complaints and claims.

The main criticism to be made of the legislative act, given its already limited approach, is that it does not include all of the methods of dispute resolution

[10] Orden ECC/2502/2012, de 16 de noviembre, por la que se regula el procedimiento de presentación de reclamaciones ante los servicios de reclamaciones del Banco de España, la Comisión Nacional del Mercado de Valores y la Dirección General de Seguros y Fondos de Pensiones.

[11] Ley 20/2015, de 14 de julio, de Ordenación Supervisión y Solvencia de Entidades Aseguradoras y Reaseguradoras.

available. If its purpose was simply to offer an exhaustive catalogue of methods of conflict resolution, it certainly did not achieve this by omitting two methods whose practical application in the Spanish insurance market stands out: the expert procedure of art. 38 LCS, which governs the procedure for the settlement of claims typically made in damage insurance, and the conciliation procedure included in the Voluntary Jurisdiction Law.

13.2.2 Regulation of Private Insurance and Reinsurance Distribution

The abrogated Law 26/2006 on Private Insurance and Reinsurance Mediation,[12] Section 2 of Chapter V, was entitled "Protection of the Client of Insurance Intermediation Services". This section contained three provisions: art. 44 on the obligation to handle and resolve complaints and claims, art. 45 on the ombudsperson and, finally, art. 46 on the administrative protection of financial services customers.

In short, it was stipulated in art. 44 of Law 26/2006 that insurance intermediaries, as well as insurance companies on behalf of their agents, were obliged to handle complaints and claims submitted by their customers.

In terms of the organisation of the claims system, Law 26/2006 distinguished between insurance agents and brokers, a logical consequence of their different relationships with the insurers. To avoid a duplication of services, complaints against insurance agents, would be taken on by the complaints service and, where appropriate, the Ombudsman Scheme, under whose jurisdiction insurers fell in accordance with the legal provisions governing customer protection, which also applied to them.

Insurance brokerage (legal entities), but also brokers (physical persons), should have a customer service department. However, the same regulation allowed for the complaints service to be replaced by an ombudsperson for the customer, provided that all claims are assigned to the ombudsperson. The aim was to facilitate in this way the externalisation of a need that in small brokerage firms or for individual brokers is difficult to assume in-house.

The current Royal Decree-Law 3/2020 of 4 February on urgent measures transposing into Spanish law various European Union directives in the field of public procurement in certain sectors, private insurance, pension plans and funds, taxation and tax litigation (hereinafter Royal Decree-Law 3/2020 Distribution)[13] reproduces the previous regime, but introduces two new features that are worthy of note.

---

[12] Ley 26/2006 de Mediación en Seguro y Reaseguros Privados.

[13] Real Decreto-ley 3/2020, de 4 de febrero, de medidas urgentes por el que se incorporan al ordenamiento jurídico español diversas directivas de la Unión Europea en el ámbito de la contratación pública en determinados sectores; de seguros privados; de planes y fondos de pensiones; del ámbito tributario y de litigios fiscales.

The first of these features is the extension of the regime's application to all distributors, rather than restricting it to intermediaries only. This is in line with the principles inspiring the Directive, whose transposition triggered the need for the reform, particularly the principle of establishing equitable conditions for all distributors. It should be noted that insurance companies were already subject to a similar discipline set forth in the aforementioned art. 97 of Law 20/2015 OSSEAR. However, the introduction of the Royal Decree-Law 3/2020 Distribution has made clear that insurance companies are also subject to this regime as regards distribution regulations, thus ending any debate as to whether their private insurance distribution activity falls within the scope of application of art. 97 of Law 20/2015 OSSEAR.

The second notable aspect pertains to the heading of the section undergoing modification. Its title has been altered from "Protection of the Client of Insurance Intermediation Services" to "Dispute Resolution Mechanisms". It is noteworthy that the provisions concern administrative supervision. This foresees the existing conception in the draft law relating to the Independent Authority, which we will deal with at the end of this chapter.

13.2.3 A Preliminary Conclusion

It can be stated that the legal regime in force in the Spanish legal system is the result of an ongoing search for a dispute resolution system that would allow the insurance market to resolve disputes out of court. However, this objective has not been achieved. Furthermore, it would be unfair to overlook the achievements made in the field of automobile insurance. These include amicable settlement agreements, the construction of a personal injury scale and the latest reform which gives forensic doctors[14] a leading role in the quantification of personal injury. However, in the other branches, the evolution has not resulted in the desired reduction in the number of lawsuits.

As far as we are concerned, the system of complaints and claims has evolved towards a two-step process. The first step is to lodge a complaint with the complaints service of insurer and/or the ombudsperson attached to the insurance company or distributor. In the event that there is dissatisfaction with the handling of the claim before these bodies, access will be granted to the Claims Service of the DGSFP.

[14] In Spain, forensic doctors are a corps of civil servants with relevant functions within the judicial institutions.

13.3 The Insurer's Complaints Service and Ombudsperson

Law 20/2015 OSSEAR and Royal Decree-Law 3/2020 Distribution impose the duty to attend to complaints and claims. This implies the creation of two distinct entities: the complaints service of insurer and ombudsperson. Despite their distinctive features, these two entities should be studied together, as they have the same origin, the same function and sometimes even form part of the same procedure.

The regulatory development of the complaints service of insurer and the ombudsperson is still to be found today in Order ECO/734/2004 of 11 March 2004 on complaints services and ombudsperson (hereinafter Order ECO/734/2004).[15] As a consequence of the obligation imposed on insurers to handle and resolve complaints, this Order has established the duty of all insurance companies to provide complaints services, while the ombudsperson is conceived as an optional body.

13.3.1 The Insurer's Complaints Service

The heads of the complaints service of the insurer (hereinafter "SAC") must be persons of commercial and professional integrity, with suitable knowledge and experience to perform their functions. Commercial and professional integrity, as established in Order ECO/734/2004, is found in those who have displayed a personal commitment to the mercantile laws or others that regulate the economic activity and the operations of businesses, as well as good commercial and financial practices. Similarly, it is clear that those who have carried out functions related to the financial activity of the entity or entities in question are also deemed to have the knowledge and experience necessary for the purposes set out in this Order (art. 4 of Order ECO/734/2004).

Art. 5 of Order ECO/734/2004 establishes minimum—and insufficient—measures to guarantee the desired independence and efficiency:

1. The entities shall adopt the necessary measures to separate the SAC from the remaining commercial or operational services of the organization.
2. The entities shall adopt the appropriate measures to guarantee that the procedures foreseen for the transmission of the information required by the SAC to the rest of the organisation's services comply with the principles of timeliness, safety, efficacy and coordination.
3. The entities shall ensure that their SAC are equipped with the appropriate human, material, technical and organisational resources required for the performance of their functions. In particular, they must take the necessary steps to guarantee that the personnel employed in the service of these departments have adequate

[15] Orden ECO/734/2004, de 11 de marzo, sobre departamentos y servicios de atención al cliente y el defensor del cliente. See Gisbert (2007).

knowledge of on transparency and protection regulations for financial services clients.

In conclusion, the SAC is conceived as a second instance within the same entity. Its aim is to provide a minimum of rigour and efficiency, but not independence. The rule imposes no other requirement, allowing the entity complete freedom in the organisation of the service and the appointment of its personnel.

13.3.2 The Ombudsperson

The Spanish legal system includes Ombudsman Scheme. However, it should be expressly stated that the main distinction between the Spanish system and those of other European countries lies in the lack of effective guarantees of independence and impartiality. Despite the proclamation in art. 7.1 of Order ECO/734/2004 to the effect that the ombudsperson will act independently of the entity and with total autonomy in respect of the criteria and guidelines to be applied in the exercise of their functions, the only measure adopted to guarantee such autonomy is the requirement that the person appointed has a recognised standing, in addition to having commercial and professional integrity. This statement is not unjustified, as each insurance company carrying on business on the Spanish market has its own ombudsperson. While the regulations permit and even encourage this, the market reality is that the office of ombudsperson is not unique, nor is it only organised by branch or geographical proximity, as expressly provided for in art. 29 of Law 44/2002 MRSF. The option chosen by the insurance companies has been to individually designate their ombudsperson, whose authority is confined to a single entity.

This diminution of independence is mitigated by the force of their decisions, which bind only the entity in question. Furthermore, this binding nature must not be an obstacle to full judicial protection, to the recourse to other conflict resolution mechanisms, nor to administrative protection (art. 7.3 of Order of ECO/734/2004).

The cornerstone of the system resides in the operating regulations that each entity has to approve (art. 8 of Order ECO/734/2004). These regulations determine the organisational structure and the procedural framework to be followed. The regulations must be made available to the client, accompanied by a document referring to: the existence of the SAC and, if applicable, the ombudsperson; to the Claims Service of the DGSFP with a reference to its duty to resolve complaints and claims; and to the regulations in force for the protection of the policyholder (art. 9 of Order ECO/734/2004).

13.3.3 Procedure

It should first be pointed out that despite the great flexibility that exists, there are certain minimum requirements set out in arts. 10–16 of Order ECO/734/2004 that any regulation must respect.

We shall begin by highlighting that following the submission of a complaint or claim, the obligation to issue a decision within a period of two months—or one month in the case of a consumer–, from which point onwards, access to the Claims Service of the DGSFP will be granted, in instances where the complaint or claim has not been dealt with to the customer's satisfaction or when no ruling has been made. Notwithstanding the regulation, the sector's employers' association, UNESPA,[16] has promoted a code of good practice that requires insurers to resolve complaints and claims within a period of one month in all cases.

The procedure shall be initiated through the submission of a document, either in paper form or electronically, which shall contain a minimum number of requirements (art. 11 of Order ECO/734/2004).

The complaint or claim must then be analysed to determine whether it is to be admitted or rejected. This determination can only be made on the basis of one of the reasons exhaustively provided for in the regulation (art. 12 Order of ECO/734/2004).

In the course of the processing of the files, the SAC and the ombudspersons may request from the complainant and from the different departments and services of the institution concerned, any data, clarifications, reports or evidence they consider relevant to adopt their decision (art. 13 of Order ECO/734/2004).

In the event that the case is heard by the ombudsperson, a specific period of time, the duration of which will be established in the operating regulations, will be set for the entity concerned to present its allegations (art. 13 of Order ECO/734/2004).

The procedure may be terminated by acceptance or withdrawal (art. 14 of Order ECO/734/2004) or upon the issuance of a decision (art. 15 of Order ECO/734/2004). The decision must always be reasoned and must comprise clear conclusions pertaining to the request made in each complaint or claim. These conclusions will be based on the contractual clauses, the applicable rules on transparency and customer protection, as well as good financial practices and usages. The decision shall be communicated to the relevant parties in writing or via electronic means within ten calendar days of its date.

13.3.4 The Particularities in Private Insurance Distribution

The most noteworthy provision within the field of insurance distribution is contained in art. 166.3 of Royal Decree-Law 3/2020 Distribution, under which in the case of insurance brokers, both for natural and legal persons, the establishment of

[16] Unión Española de Entidades Aseguradoras y Reaseguradoras.

the SAC may be forgone provided that its functions are entrusted to an ombudsperson. Consequently, brokers or brokerage firms have three options with regard to the organisation of their complaints and claims resolution systems:

1. The establishment of an internal SAC for the handling and resolution of complaints and claims.
2. The engagement of an ombudsperson who will necessarily be external.
3. The design of a double instance procedure whereby, following recourse to the SAC, the user is permitted to turn to an external ombudsperson.

The majority of brokers have selected the ombudsperson option, which is typically organised by Bar Associations. It should be borne in mind that given the requirements set forth in Order ECO/734/2004, the size of most brokerage firms does not allow them to take on the functions of SAC internally. For this reason, Bar Associations have responded to this necessity and now offer their members the option of joining the Ombudsman Scheme's office, which is organised by the association. This approach results in greater efficiency in terms of costs, and more importantly it ensures greater independence. Basically, the preferred option for insurers is to have their own Ombudsman Scheme, whereas brokers can present themselves to their clients with a truly independent arbiter in the event of a dispute who is often more qualified than the person appointed by an insurance, who occasionally recruits the ombudsperson from among its own staff.

On the other hand, agents are subject to the same system as the insurer. Any complaints or claims are handled through the system used by the insurance companies with which they are affiliated through the agency contract.

13.4 Claims Before the Claims Service of the DGSFP

The second stage of this procedure is the submission of the matter to the Claims Service of the DGSFP. The pertinent regulation is found in Order ECC/2502/2012, which we will analyse below.

13.4.1 Institutional Framework

The DGSFP is an administrative body that is part of the State Secretariat for the Economy and Business Support (*Secretaría de Estado de Economía y Apoyo a la Empresa*), which is attached to the Ministry of Economic Affairs and Digital Transformation (*Ministerio de Asuntos Económicos y Transformación Digital*), in accordance with Royal Decree 403/2020, of 25 February, which develops the basic organisational structure of the Ministry of Economic Affairs and Digital Transformation.[17]

The Claims Service of the DGSFP is currently responsible for dealing with complaints and claims from customers in the insurance market. Until the provisions of the first additional provision of Law 7/2017 of 2 November,[18] transposing into Spanish law the EU ADR Directive, are developed, the Claims Service will report to the head of the DGSFP, with the structure determined in its list of work posts.

This body is a part of the General State Administration, made up of civil servants and financed using public funds. Insurance companies, distributors and consumer associations have absolutely no say in its composition. It is a public administration body that is part of a ministry.

Similarly, as has already been pointed out, the assignment to the Claims Service is imposed by the legislation in force, so that there is no need for any declaration or agreement on the part of the insurance companies or distributors.

13.4.2 Scope

Any natural or legal person, Spanish or foreign, who is duly identified as a user of financial services provided by one of the entities supervised by the DGSFP has the right to file complaints and claims where their legally recognised interests and rights are concerned. The interests of consumer associations are also recognised as having broad legal standing (art. 3 of Order ECC/2502/2012).

The provisions in Order ECC/2502/2012 define complaints and claims. The former are those submitted by users of financial services due to delays, inattention or any other type of inadequate behaviour observed in the operation of the financial institutions against which the complaint is made. The latter, claims, are submitted by customers of financial services who, with the aim of asserting their interests or rights, submit specific facts relating to actions or omissions of the financial institutions addressed that are detrimental to their interests or rights and that result from alleged breaches by the institutions addressed of the provisions on transparency and customer protection or of good financial practice and use (art. 3 of Order ECC/2502/2012).

Finally, the regulations do not establish restrictive criteria in terms of scope. Thus, the Claims Service must deal with any complaints and claims submitted by users of financial services that relate to their legally recognised interests and rights and that arise due to alleged breaches by the entities concerned of the regulations on transparency and customer protection or of good financial practice and usages.

[17] Real Decreto 403/2020, de 25 de febrero, por el que se desarrolla la estructura orgánica básica del Ministerio de Asuntos Económicos y Transformación Digital.

[18] Ley 7/2017, de 2 de noviembre, por la que se incorpora al ordenamiento jurídico español la Directiva 2013/11/UE, del Parlamento Europeo y del Consejo, de 21 de mayo de 2013, relativa a la resolución alternativa de litigios en materia de consumo.

Furthermore, a division of competences among the different claims services of the three supervisory authorities is provided for in art. 4 of Order ECC/2502/2012 in an attempt to preserve the unique office of the system.

13.4.3 Procedure

Complaints or claims may be submitted on paper or electronically on a form drafted by the Claims Service (art. 5 of Order ECC/2502/2012). However, the acceptance and processing of claims or complaints by the Claims Service of the DGSFP requires proof that they have previously been submitted to the SAC or, where applicable, to the Ombudsman of the entity against which the claim is made. Therefore, the customer must provide proof that the claim has been rejected or that the time limit has expired without receipt of a resolution (art. 7 of Order ECC/2502/2012).

The claim or complaint must contain a minimum number of details and may be accompanied by any documentation that the customer considers relevant (art. 6 of Order ECC/2502/2012). Once the claims or complaints have been received by the Claims Service of the DGSFP, it will verify whether the requirements have been met and, if so, a file will be opened. Otherwise, the claimant will be required to complete the information within ten working days from the date on which the claimant receives such notification, clearly indicating the information is required to complete the claim or complaint, with a warning that failure to complete the information will be considered as a withdrawal of the claim or complaint (art. 7 of Order ECC/2502/2012).

Once the procedure has been opened, the claimant will be informed, within a period of ten working days, that the procedure is without prejudice to the actions that they may take to assert their rights and the deadlines and channels for exercising them, that it does not affect the decision and the processing of the corresponding procedures and that its conclusion in the final decision of the Claims Service of the DGSFP is not binding and is not considered an administrative act against which an appeal may be lodged.

Within this period, a copy of the claims and the documents provided will also be sent to the entity against which the claim is made, so that it may present the Claims Service of the DGSFP with the allegations and documentation it deems appropriate within fifteen working days, without prejudice to the possibility of obtaining directly from the entities against which the claim is made the information necessary for an adequate understanding of the claim presented. The Claims Service of the DGSFP will send the claimant a copy of the aforementioned allegations and documentation. The claimants will have the opportunity to express their opinion on the allegations made by the entity within a period of fifteen working days. Any requests made to the entity must be complied with within fifteen working days, after which time any reply shall be deemed to be void for the purposes of continuing the processing of the procedure (art. 11 of Order ECC/2502/2012).

The procedure must be concluded with the issuance of a decision within a maximum period of four months from the date of submission of the claim to the Claims Service of the DGSFP, although in practice this period is not always respected. Furthermore, failure to issue a decision within this period does not imply acceptance of the basis for the claim (art. 12 of Order ECC/2502/2012).

The procedure shall conclude with a decision, which shall be reasoned and contain clear conclusions as to whether or not there has been a breach of the rules governing transparency and protection and whether or not the entity has followed good financial practice and usages. In any case, the final decision in the final report must address all the issues raised in the claims. The report shall be notified to the parties concerned and to the institution against which the claim was made within ten working days from the date of issue. The final decision of the Claims Service of the DGSFP is not binding and is not considered an administrative act subject to appeal (art. 12 of Order ECC/2502/2012).[19]

Finally, in the event that the processing of claims or complaints files reveals data that may constitute evidence of punishable conduct, in particular if it is concluded that there has been a serious or repeated breach of transparency or customer protection rules, or if evidence is detected of criminal conduct or of tax, consumer, competition or other infringements, the Claims Service of the DGSFP will report the facts to the department or institution responsible for the matter for the appropriate purposes (art. 18 of Order ECC/2502/2012).

13.4.4 Statistical Data

According to the latest published annual report of the Claims Service of the DGSFP for the financial year 2022, the number of resolved cases amounted to 9969.

To provide a general sense of the outcome of the reports closing the complaint files, 35.4% ended with a decision in favour of the claimant, 29.8% ended with a decision in favour of the entity, and in the remaining 34.8% the Claims Service was unable, given the circumstances, to issue an explicit statement upholding or rejecting the claim of the party concerned. Looking only at those cases in respect to which the Claims Service issued a decision, approximately 54.3% were resolved in favour of the claimant and the remaining 45.7% were resolved in favour of the insurer or distributor.

[19] Art. 13 of Order ECC/2502/2012 establishes the specialities in the field of complaints, which take the form of a shorter time limit.

13.5 The Proposed Independent Authority

On 16 December 2022, a draft law was published in the Congress of Deputies at the proposal of the Spanish Government, which aims to create the Independent Administrative Authority for the Protection of Financial Customers (hereinafter the "Independent Authority") to facilitate the out-of-court resolution of conflicts between financial institutions and their customers.[20] However, the dissolution of the Spanish Parliament due to the convocation of elections coincidentally took place in the same week that the bill was due to be voted on, so that the draft law lapsed.

Following the constitution of the current Parliament on 5 April 2024, a new draft law was published in the Congress of Deputies. The draft replicates the previous text, albeit with the introduction of some modifications.

At the heart of the draft is the establishment of the Independent Administrative Authority for the Protection of Financial Customers. From its very name, we can deduce its three defining features: it is an independent public administration body; its scope extends to the whole financial system (i.e. across the three branches that make it up: banking, stock exchange and insurance); and its function is to establish a mechanism for resolving disputes between financial institutions and their clients.

The draft law is divided into eight titles, the headings of which show not only its structure but also its main regulatory focus: general provisions; out-of-court dispute resolution system; the Independent Administrative Authority for the Protection of Financial Customers; the processing of claims; information and parliamentary control; cooperation with other bodies; the promotion of financial education; sanctions regime.

13.5.1 Institutional Framework

The future Independent Authority is referred to in the draft law as the Independent Administrative Authority, which means that it is part of the public sector. Within its sphere of competence, it is assigned the administrative powers necessary for the fulfilment of its purposes. As a consequence of this classification and this attribution of administrative powers, its internal legal regime is subject to administrative law.

The Independent Authority shall be governed by a Governing Council composed of a Chairperson, a Vice-Chairperson, representatives of the Supervisory Authority,

[20] In respect of the bill, see Bataller Grau (2022); Blanco Sánchez (2023); Rabanete Martínez (2023); Ríos Árbol (2022); Zunzunegui (2023).

and other administrations, and two elected members. The Authority shall be organised into General Directorates,[21] Sections[22] and Members' Offices.[23]

One of the most controversial issues during the legislative process of the bill was the financing of the Independent Authority. The final wording provides for a fee to be paid by the financial institutions to cover all costs generated by the activity of the Authority, although it is envisaged that this could be allocated to the general state budget.

13.5.2 Scope

Financial institutions will be subject to the supervision of the Independent Authority if the institutions fall within its jurisdiction. We are therefore not dealing with a voluntary system, but with a competent administration acting within its scope of action.

The purpose of the Independent Authority will be to increase the level of protection afforded to the customers of financial institutions and the degree of legal certainty concerning the rules of conduct and good financial practices and usage established by the supervisory authorities, which must be observed by financial institutions through the independent and impartial determination of their customers' claims and the promotion of financial education.

The Independent Authority must attend to customer claims. The draft law defines a claim as any action brought by one or more customers against one or more financial institutions with the aim of restoring or repairing their interests or rights on the grounds that these have been violated in the contracting or provision of a financial service, as a result of non-compliance with rules of conduct, the abusive nature of contractual clauses, or non-compliance with good financial practices and usages as defined by the supervisory authorities, even if such claim has no financial content.

Its role is to be the cornerstone of the claims system. First, it is necessary to submit a claim to the SAC and/or Ombudsman, which we have already analysed and which would remain unchanged, with the Independent Authority taking the place of the second instance within this channel. Furthermore, it is specified in the draft law

[21] Each Director General shall be appointed by the Governing Council, at the proposal of the person holding the Presidency, in accordance with the principles of merit, capacity and publicity, from among those with at least ten years' of experience in matters pertaining to the corresponding Directorate.

[22] Sections are the collegiate bodies competent to resolve the claims, with pronouncements in accordance with the law and the good financial practices and uses defined by the supervisory authority, once the procedures have been investigated by the Member of Directors' Offices.

[23] Members' Offices will investigate the files of the claims assigned to them in accordance with the rules of distribution and will submit the file together with a proposal for resolution of the respective claim.

that this system is an alternative to the other methods of dispute resolution, including recourse to the courts.

13.5.3 Procedure

The draft law governs the procedure applicable to claims in a manner consistent with their nature. Complaints before the Independent Authority are governed by Law 44/2002 MRSF, the application of which is expressly referred to in. Furthermore, Law 7/2017 of 2 November, which transposes into Spanish law the EU ADR Directive, and, in its absence, the provisions of Law 39/2015 of 1 October on the Common Administrative Procedure of Public Administrations[24] and Law 40/2015 of 1 October on the Legal Regime of the Public Sector[25] will also be applied. The result is a complex set of rules governing the claims procedure.

The principles that guide the procedure are equality, equity, impartiality, independence, transparency, contradiction, legality, freedom of proof, efficiency and promptness.

Perhaps the most novel aspect is that the Independent Authority may issue two types of decisions as a result of the aforementioned procedure:

1. Binding: those concerning breaches of conduct regulations and abusive clauses when the amount claimed is less than EUR 20,000
2. Non-binding: amounts equal to or greater than EUR 20,000 and those issued on good financial practices and uses.

Under the draft law there is reliance on the system of sanctions to be a sufficient mechanism to ensure compliance with decisions. In other words, given that it is not possible for the Independent Authority to enforce such decisions, it subjects the entities to a disciplinary regime as an indirect way of ensuring the enforcement of its decisions. Furthermore, it should be noted that an administrative decision may also impose a sanction on the claimant, although this is limited to cases in which the claim is fundamentally rejected and there is evidence of fraud or fault on the part of the claimant.

Binding decisions issued by the Authority shall be final and not subject to appeal proceedings before the Authority. Either party may bring an action against such binding decisions before the civil courts.

Finally, a decision, even one issued by the Independent Authority, does not adequately fulfil its function of dispute resolution. The decision, even if it is in favour of the client's claims, cannot be enforced against the financial institution.

[24] Ley 39/2015, de 1 de octubre, del Procedimiento Administrativo Común de las Administraciones Públicas.

[25] Ley 40/2015, de 1 de octubre, de Régimen Jurídico del Sector Público.

13.6 Conclusion: A Critique of the Spanish System

Overall, we can assert that both the current system and the proposal of the Independent Authority have diluted the role of the administrative sanctioning channel. Indeed, customers' access to this channel has been restricted: not only are they required to submit a prior complaint or claim, but the procedures are stringent and claims are only passed on to the supervisory authorities when there are indications of serious or repeated breaches of the rules of transparency and customer protection or of good financial practices and uses by the same entity.

In our opinion, the problem lies in the distortions caused by the duplication of competences presented by the Claims Service of the DGSFP. A clear distinction should be made between the determination of claims or complaints—a competence which has finally been acquired as a consequence of the evolution of the system of regulation—and purely administrative grievances which will end with the imposition of an administrative sanction if it is considered pertinent and after conducting the corresponding administrative procedure. A similar conclusion can be drawn from looking at the status of the draft Independent Authority.

Insurance companies have the right to disagree with the criteria and principles issued by the DGSFP, and therefore the appeal procedure must be guaranteed. The administrative sanctions procedure is a key element in the supervision of insurance companies and must guarantee compliance with the principles inherent in any procedure that may result in a sanction.

Furthermore, a decision will not adequately fulfil its function, even if it has been issued by the supervisory authority with its standing. Even if a determination is favourable to the client's claims, it cannot be enforced against the insurance company, so it carries no exceptional weight in any subsequent ordinary proceedings where it will have the same value as any other evidence. It therefore represents an ineffectual means.

However, the most questionable point, in our opinion, lies in the fact that such decisions hinder purely administrative protection, which only seeks to ensure compliance with the intervention regulations, and subordinates such protection to the prior function of resolving complaints and claims. This presents serious limitations in relation to conflicts involving most relevant amounts, where it is essential that the decision be enforceable, a quality that cannot be attributed to the decisions of the Claims Service of the DGSF. It is not advisable to mix institutions - a dispute concerning a premium of EUR 50 should not be equated with a claim in which the damages awarded are much higher. We sincerely do not believe that the only reason that has induced insurers to comply with the decisions of the Claims Service of the DGSFP is the *autoritas* (authority) of the body, i.e. the result of the insurance industry's recognition of its extensive legal knowledge, but rather the *potestas* (power) that the imposition of sanctions has to affect insurance market players.

In addition, we would like to defend the stance in the sanctions procedure that arises *a posteriori*, namely that the client should not be denied the status of an interested party when a lawsuit has been submitted due to an infringement by the insurer, or distributor, of some right, as is currently the practice.[26]

For this reason, a clear distinction must be made between the two competences: administrative proceedings and dispute resolution. In the first case, the DGSFP should maintain full powers to assess infringements and impose the corresponding sanctions. Furthermore, an insurer has the right to appeal against sanctions. In the second case, it is necessary to introduce a dispute resolution scheme that complies with the requirements of independence, impartiality, transparency, effectiveness, promptness and fairness. So, my proposal requires that claimants can find an extra-judicial procedure that enables them to pursue their claims and obtain satisfactory outcomes. It is only through the inadequacy of the successive claims systems that we can understand the extension of the competences of the DGSFP or the creation of an Independent Authority. This is a way forward that could be considered in the not-too-distant future to permit direct access to administrative proceedings before the DGSFP.

References

Aguilar Olivares Y (2015) Un paso más hacia el consumidor europeo: la nueva regulación de los ADR de consumo. Revista CESCO de Derecho de Consumo 14:36–37

Albanés A (1988) El arbitraje y el contrato de seguro. Revista Española de Seguros 55:64–65

Almarcha Jaime J (2015) Los nuevos deberes de información al tomador del seguro, los mecanismos de solución de conflictos y el régimen de cantidades adelantadas a cuenta del precio durante la construcción en la compra de viviendas tras la Ley 20/2015, de 14 de julio, de ordenación, supervisión y solvencia de las entidades aseguradoras y reaseguradoras (LOSSEAR). Revista CESCO de Derecho de Consumo 15:152–153

Badillo Arias JA (2011) (ed) Ley de contrato de seguro. Jurisprudencia comentada. Thomson Reuters Aranzadi, Cizur Menor

Bataller Grau J (1997) La liquidación del siniestro en los seguros de daños. Tirant lo Blanch, Valencia

Bataller Grau J (1999) La desregulación de los seguros privados. Revista Española de Seguros 97:37–63

Bataller Grau J (2002) La resolución extrajudicial de conflictos surgidos de un contrato de seguro. Revista vasca de derecho procesal y arbitraje = Zuzenbide prozesala ta arbitraia euskal aldizkaria 14(1):23–24

Bataller Grau J (2005) La protección del asegurado en el Ordenamiento Jurídico Español. Revista Aranzadi de Derecho Patrimonial 14:87–88

Bataller Grau J (2013) Las reclamaciones en el mercado asegurador: bases para su reconfiguración. In: Cuñat Edo V, Bataller Grau J (eds) Supervisión en seguros privados: Hacia Solvencia II. Tirant lo Blanch, Valencia, p 621

Bataller Grau J (2018) Una mejor protección del asegurado es posible. In: Girgado Perandones P (ed) El contrato de seguro y su distribución en la encrucijada. Thomson Reuters Aranzadi, Pamplona, p 347

[26] Taking a position against the acknowledging the locus standi of an interested party in the sanctions procedure before the supervisory authority in the credit market, but with arguments that can be applied to insurance, Ruiz López (2003); same opinion Marimón Durá (2005).

Bataller Grau J (2022) La autoridad administrativa independiente española de defensa del cliente financiero: los mecanismos de resolución de conflictos en los seguros privados a debate. In: Jaramillo CI (ed) Liber Amicorum en homenaje al maestro J. Efrén Ossa, Bogotá
Bataller Grau J, Seguí-Mas E (2013) La distribución como factor determinante en la protección del asegurado. In: Quintans Eiras MR (ed) Estudios sobre mediación de seguros privados. Thomson Reuters Aranzadi, Pamplona, p 119
Bataller Grau J, Veiga Copo A (eds) (2014) La protección del cliente en el mercado asegurador. Thomson Reuters Civitas, Madrid
Blanco Sánchez MJ (2023) Proyecto de Ley de creación de la Autoridad Administrativa Independiente de Defensa del Cliente Financiero. Actualidad civil, 9
Campuzano Laguillo AB, Conlledo Lantero F, Palomo Zurdo RJ (eds) (2013) La protección del cliente en los mercados financieros. Tirant Lo Blanch, Valencia
De Angulo Rodríguez L (1998) El arbitraje en las vigentes leyes de contrato de seguro y de ordenación y supervisión de los seguros privados. Revista Española de Seguros 93:20–21
Gisbert M (2007) La protección de los clientes de los servicios de mediación de seguros. In: Cuñat Edo V, Bataller Grau J (eds) Comentarios a la Ley de mediación de seguros y reaseguros privados. Thomson Civitas, Madrid, p 237
Gómez Urquijo L, Tomás Martínez G (2012) La Orden Ministerial de transparencia y protección del cliente de servicios bancarios: un ejemplo del nuevo marco de confianza en el sistema financiero europeo. In: Gómez Isa F, Herrán A, Atxabal Rada A (eds) Retos del derecho ante una economía sin fronteras. Universidad de Deusto, Bilbao, p 65
Marimón Durá R (2005) La nueva regulación de los órganos de defensa del cliente bancario. La experiencia del Servicio de Reclamaciones del Banco de España. In: Cuñat Edo V (ed) Protección de particulares frente a malas prácticas bancarias. Cuadernos de Derecho Judicial, Madrid, p 215
Pérez-Serrabona González FJ (2010) La resolución de conflictos de consumo: la adaptación del derecho español al marco europeo de resolución alternativa (ADR) y en línea (ODR). In: A propósito de la ley 7/2017, de noviembre: nuevas perspectivas para los métodos de reclamación de consumo en el ámbito de los seguros. Thomson Reuters Aranzadi, Pamplona, p 189
Quintáns Eiras MR (2005) Protección a los asegurados en contratos intermediados por mediador de seguros. Revista española de seguros: Publicación doctrinal de Derecho y Economía de los Seguros privados 23–124:445446
Quintáns Eiras MR (2016) De la mediación a la distribución de seguros: la nueva directiva 2016/1997. Revista general de derecho europeo 39
Rabanete Martínez I (2023) Comentario al Anteproyecto de Ley de creación de la autoridad administrativa independiente de defensa del cliente financiero: posibles problemas jurídicos y de aplicación de la norma. Revista de Derecho del Sistema Financiero 5:201–222
Ríos Árbol JE (2022) El largo camino hacia la creación de una autoridad independiente para la protección del cliente financiero: necesidad, funciones y cuestiones controvertidas. Revista de derecho del mercado de valores 30
Rivera J (2018) Las ODR en el ámbito de los seguros. In: Barrals Viñals I (ed) La resolución de conflictos con consumidores: de la mediación a las ODR. Editorial Reus, Reus, p 273
Rodríguez Ponga MF (1997) La Administración pública y la protección del asegurado in: Estudios y comentarios sobre la Ley de ordenación y supervisión de los seguros privados. Fundación MAPFRE, Madrid, p 349
Ruiz López EJ (2003) La defensa del consumidor de servicios bancarios. In: Sánchez Calero F, Sánchez-Calero Guilarte J (eds) Comentario a la Ley 44/2002, de 22 de noviembre, de medidas de reforma del sistema financiero. Thomson Aranzadi, Pamplona, p 770
Sagrera Rull J (2017) Mecanismos de solución de conflictos derivados de contratos de seguro. Revista española de seguros: publicación doctrinal de derecho y economía de los seguros privados 170:191–192
Sánchez Calero F (ed) (2010) Ley de contrato de seguro. Comentarios a la Ley 50/1980, de 8 de octubre y sus modificaciones, 4th edn. Thomson Reuters Aranzadi, Cizur Menor

Sánchez Hernández C (2018) La resolución alternativa de los conflictos de consumo en la ley 7/2017: entre la dispersión normativa y la seguridad jurídica. CEFlegal: Revista práctica de derecho. Comentarios y casos prácticos 215
Sucunza Totoricagüena S (2015) Los métodos alternativos de resolución de conflictos en el ámbito de la responsabilidad civil y seguro. Revista de la asociación española de abogados especializados en responsabilidad civil y seguro 55:9–10
Vercher Moll J (2014) La protección del cliente en el mercado asegurador. Thomson Reuters Aranzadi, Cizur Menor
Zunzunegui F (2023) Autoridad de Defensa del Cliente Financiero: la pieza que falta para completar el sistema. Revista de Derecho del Sistema Financiero 6

Chapter 14
Switzerland

The Swiss Insurance Ombudsman Scheme

Martin Lorenzon and Ann-Catherine Nabholz

14.1 Institutional Framework

14.1.1 Establishment

The Swiss Insurance Ombudsman Scheme was established in 1972. It was one of the first private sector ombudsman schemes to be created in Europe. At a time when public sector ombudsman schemes scarcely existed in Switzerland—the first one being the Municipal Ombudsman of Zurich, which was established in 1971—Swiss consumers were given the opportunity to resolve their complaints about the insurance sector at a relatively early stage.

One might go so far as to say that the political debate about the role of ombudsman institutions in the early 1970s led to the almost simultaneous creation of the public sector ombudsman scheme mentioned above and the Insurance Ombudsman Scheme. In 1970, a postulate mandated the Federal Council to establish a national ombudsman scheme.[1] It is under the impact of this discussion that the first media

[1] Otto Fischer submitted a postulate (10513) demanding the establishment of a national ombudsman on 14 December 1970. This resulted in a preliminary draft for an act of parliament. Following a temporary suspension by the Federal Council, the parliament has made several attempts to establish a national ombudsman. Whereas various cantons have established public ombudsman institutions,

M. Lorenzon
Ombudsman of Private Insurance and of Suva, Zürich, Switzerland
e-mail: lorenzon@versicherungsombudsman.ch

A.-C. Nabholz (✉)
Head of Process Management, Ombudsman of Private Insurance and of Suva, Zürich, Switzerland
e-mail: nabholz@versicherungsombudsman.ch

H. Heiss et al. (eds.), *Insurance Ombudsman Schemes*, AIDA Europe Research Series on Insurance Law and Regulation 15,
https://doi.org/10.1007/978-3-032-01500-6_14

release was distributed, announcing the creation of the Insurance Ombudsman Scheme on 2 June 1972, followed by one designating the first ombudsperson.[2]

Before looking more closely at the creation of the Insurance Ombudsman Scheme, some consideration will first be given to Switzerland's regulatory framework. As pointed out by Lili Nabholz Haidegger,[3] it is specified in the Federal Insurance Supervision Act (hereinafter VAG)[4] that all insurance companies are obliged to obtain a licence for their business activities from the supervisory authority. The supervisory authority ensures that insured persons are protected from abuse by and insolvency risks of insurance companies. However, the supervisory authority is not competent to decide disputes related to private insurance claims. Disputes arising between an insured person and an insurance business are heard by civil courts (art. 85(a) VAG). In other words, the individual relationships between an insurer and its customers are not subject to federal supervision.[5]

Considering the fact that conflictual situations could occur in the contractual relationship between the insured and the insurer and that they could only be settled at court, the Swiss Association of Accident and Liability Insurers appointed a commission to submit recommendations for an impartial dispute resolution body in 1970. The commission's proposal to establish an "Ombudsman of Private Insurance" was adopted by the Swiss Insurance Association.[6]

In addition to the increased public interest in the ombudsman concept in the early 1970s, a further motivation behind the creation of an ombudsman scheme was that the insurance industry had observed a change in consumer perceptions. In a media release, it was stated that while a vast majority of insurance matters were handled to the satisfaction of customers, a small number of negative cases received disproportionate media coverage and public attention. It was assumed that a lack of knowledge may have raised false expectations, or that a feeling of powerlessness in the face of formalised procedures and the technical language used by the industry for risk evaluation may have had a negative impact on customer relations. As a result, dissatisfied customers seldomly directed their complaints to the involved insurers, which in turn did not have an opportunity to clarify a misunderstanding or to correct

---

a national ombudsman institution still does not exist in Switzerland. For a survey of the political debate, see the statement of the Federal Council of 5 September 2007 with regard to a motion proposed by Luc Barthassat, submitted on 22 June 2007, Die Bundesversammlung – Das Schweizer Parlament (2007). https://www.parlament.ch/en/ratsbetrieb/suche-curia-vista/geschaeft?AffairId=20073541. Accessed 16 Apr 2025.

[2] von Moos, Stiftung Ombudsman der Privatversicherung, Fondation Ombudsman de l'assurance privée, press conference of 23 August 1972, and Broger, Raymond, Stiftung Ombudsman der Privatversicherung, Fondation Ombudsman de l'assurance privée, press conference of 31 August 1972.

[3] Lili Nabholz Haidegger was the Ombudsperson for the Insurance Ombudsman Scheme from 1992 until 2010.

[4] *Versicherungsaufsichtsgesetz*. For details, see Fedlex, Die Publikationsplattform des Bundesrechts (2023). https://www.fedlex.admin.ch/eli/cc/2005/734/de. Accessed 16 Apr 2025.

[5] See Nabholz Haidegger (2000), pp. 121–122.

[6] See Nabholz Haidegger (2000), pp. 119–128.

a possibly wrong decision. Finally, it was noted that dissatisfied customers mainly had low-value claims and were reluctant to take costly legal action.[7]

According to the initiators, the resulting discontent benefited nobody. Hence, it seemed promising to establish an ombudsman scheme to offer a new path for insured persons to resolve their disputes. Although the initiators emphasised that the creation of an ombudsman scheme should not be regarded as an attempt to control insurance businesses, they hoped that an independent ombudsman scheme might provide an outlet for dissatisfied customers to have their justified or unjustified complaints heard.[8]

The impartiality of the ombudsperson was all the more crucial as the idea of an ombudsman scheme was initiated by the Swiss Insurance Association itself. The goal was to create an independent ombudsman scheme that investigates complaints from customers against the association's member companies. In their opinion, the best legal structure for implementing this intention was a foundation. The choice of this specific legal form—i.e. an independent legal entity which acts through the intermediary of a managing body (the foundation board), subject to supervision by a state authority, which ensures that the foundation carries out its activities in accordance with its purpose—enabled the Insurance Ombudsman Scheme to comply with the principles of independence, clarity of scope and accountability.[9]

In Swiss law, a distinction is drawn between three forms of foundations.[10] The "Ombudsman of Private Insurance and of Suva" Foundation is a classic foundation, which is governed primarily by the provisions in arts. 80–89 of the Swiss Civil Code (hereinafter ZGB).[11] The basic principle of a foundation is that it "is established by the endowment of assets for a particular purpose" (art. 80 ZGB). A foundation must be entered in the commercial register based on its charter. Entry into the register must be in accordance with any directions issued by the supervisory authority. The entry must also indicate the members of the board of trustees (art. 81(2) ZGB).[12]

A foundation's governing bodies and its method of administration are set out in the Foundation Charter (art. 83 ZGB). As the activities of a foundation are based on the founder's intention, the foundation's governing bodies (i.e. foundation board)

---

[7] Stiftung Ombudsman der Privatversicherung, Fondation Ombudsman de l'assurance privée (1972).

[8] At a press conference on 31 August 1972, Ludwig von Moos, the first president of the Ombudsman of Private Insurance Foundation, drew an explicit distinction between the existing supervisory authorities, whose purpose it is to ensure the insured persons' greatest possible security by controlling the soundness of companies operating in the insurance sector, and any ADR methods aimed at restoring the imbalance between the customer and the insurance business.

[9] It is noteworthy in this context that the Federal Council's proposal to govern the Insurance Ombudsman as an element of the revised Insurance Supervision Act (VAG) was dismissed by the Swiss Parliament on 18 March 2022.

[10] The three types of foundations are the classic or charitable foundation, family and ecclesiastical foundations, and foundations consisting of retirement schemes for employees. The latter are regulated under special legal regimes.

[11] Zivilgesetzbuch.

[12] Upon registration with the commercial register, the foundation acquires legal personality (art. 52(1) ZGB).

have a duty to pursue this intention.[13] On the basis of the foundation charter, foundation regulations are issued. They allow for flexibility and enable the foundation to adapt to new circumstances.[14] The regulations are enacted by the foundation board and reported to the supervisory authority. For the purpose of transparency, the regulations governing the "Ombudsman of Private Insurance and of Suva" Foundation have been made available on the organisation's website.[15]

Financial accounting standards obviously also apply to foundations. This means that they must undergo a normal audit. Under art. 83b ZGB, the board is mandated to appoint external auditors. The external auditors must provide the supervisory authority with a copy of the audit report and important communications with the foundation (art. 83c ZGB). The Federal Supervisory Authority for Foundations (*Eidgenössische Stiftungsaufsicht*, hereinafter ESA) must, pursuant to art. 84(2) ZGB, ensure that the foundation's assets are used for their declared purpose. The "Ombudsman of Private Insurance and of Suva" Foundation is thus required to submit an annual report with a comprehensive description of its activities, annual financial statements, the auditors' report, minutes of the foundation board meeting concerning approval of the revised annual accounts and the annual report. Finally, the minutes must include the full name of foundation board members and their function.

14.1.2 Governance Model

As mentioned above, the "Ombudsman of Private Insurance and of Suva" Foundation is governed by the Foundation Board. The work undertaken by foundations in practice is not governed by the Swiss Civil Code. Neither the founder nor the regulatory authorities are responsible for a foundation. Rather it is in the foundation board's sole responsibility to ensure good governance.[16] In other words, the board members are responsible for the overall supervision of the foundation's activities.

As the Scheme's strategic management body, the Foundation Board and its members must meet high standards to ensure independent decision-making. Six out of eight members of the Board are impartial Swiss public personalities—i.e. current or former Members of Parliament from different political parties. Two members are representatives of the insurance industry. The Board assumes collective responsibility. Decisions are made by majority vote. Last but not least, the Foundation Board constitutes itself and appoints its own members.

[13] Sprecher et al. (2021), p. 20.

[14] Sprecher et al. (2021), pp. 49–52.

[15] Stiftung Ombudsman der Privatversicherung und der Suva (2017). https://versicherungsombudsman.ch/ueber-uns/. Accessed 16 Apr 2025.

[16] Sprecher et al. (2021), p. 56.

14.1.3 Coverage

The Insurance Ombudsman Service provides consumers with recourse to dispute resolution for insurance complaints only. To be more precise, our Service deals with complaints, disputes and claims with or arising out of private insurance contracts pursuant to the Swiss Insurance Contract Act (hereinafter VVG),[17] as well as complaints against accident insurers pursuant to the Accident Insurance Act (hereinafter UVG)[18] and insurance companies offering affiliation to collective foundations for occupational pension schemes pursuant to the Occupational Pension Schemes Act (hereinafter BVG).[19]

14.1.4 Insurance Businesses Covered

The Insurance Ombudsman Service can only handle complaints against insurance businesses which are affiliated to the Foundation. While the ambit of the Ombudsman Scheme covers the activities of a vast majority of Swiss retail insurance providers, there is no obligation to participate in it. Despite the fact that there is no obligation to participate, new members are continuously added to the list of affiliated insurers.

14.1.5 Appointment of the Ombudsperson

The most important asset of an ombudsperson is the trust and reputation they enjoy with consumers and insurance companies alike. This is especially true when an ombudsman scheme does not exercise the powers of a public authority.[20] Since trust is so important for any mediation activity, the ombudsperson must be independent and impartial. It is thus crucial that only a person with a good reputation and integrity is appointed as ombudsperson.

The ombudsperson must be willing to investigate complaints efficiently and take an active part in addressing problems. It is important that the appointed person possesses the necessary knowledge and skills to form an independent opinion.

[17] *Bundesgesetz über den Versicherungsvertrag*. For details, see Fedlex, Die Publikationsplattform des Bundesrechts (2023). https://www.fedlex.admin.ch/eli/cc/24/719_735_717/de. Accessed 16 Apr 2025.

[18] *Bundesgesetz über die Unfallversicherung*. For details see Fedlex, Die Publikationsplattform des Bundesrechts (2023). https://www.fedlex.admin.ch/eli/cc/1982/1676_1676_1676/de. Accessed 16 Apr 2025.

[19] *Bundesgesetz über die berufliche Alters-, Hinterlassenen- und Invalidenvorsorge.* For details, see Fedlex, Die Publikationsplattform des Bundesrechts (2023). https://www.fedlex.admin.ch/eli/cc/1983/797_797_797/de. Accessed 16 Apr 2025.

[20] See Nabholz Haidegger (2000), p. 124.

Moreover, they must have good communication skills and credibility. This becomes increasingly clear when we consider that the ombudsperson must communicate in a way that is not only legally proper but also comprehensible for consumers without any legal knowledge. At the same time, the ombudsperson must be able to negotiate on equal terms with insurance businesses. Consequently, the office holder should not only possess knowledge about the insurance market, they should also have a degree in Law. The ombudsperson should ideally have the qualification to be a judge and also be fluent in a second official language.[21] Finally, to be considered for the position as the managing director of the "Ombudsman of Private Insurance and of Suva" Foundation, candidates must display leadership qualities and the capacity to oversee the Foundation's personnel.

It is in the exclusive competence of the Foundation Board to appoint the ombudsperson. Following an overall evaluation of applications, the Foundation Board appoints the selected person by majority decision. While the remuneration is determined according to the office holder's function and skill set; it is not linked to the outcome of the mediation procedure.

There is no term of office. Nevertheless, the independence of the office holder is ensured insofar as their professional activity is incompatible with other economic activities for or against insurance businesses. Still, the Foundation Board may deem permissible a secondary employment under the condition that it allows the office holder to carry out their duties with complete impartiality and without any conflict of interest.

Finally, it is in the exclusive competence of the Foundation Board to prematurely terminate the ombudsperson's appointment. The grounds on which dismissal can be made include severe breach of duty or inability to perform the duties properly.

14.1.6 Funding

The Insurance Ombudsman Scheme's budgeting process can be described as follows: the ombudsperson, in consultation with the president of the Foundation Board, first prepares a draft budget for the year ahead. The annual budget must cover the Ombudsman Service's activities and be approved by the Foundation Board. On final approval of the budget by the Foundation Board, the affiliated insurance businesses are requested to pay their contributions. The total contribution payments correspond to the approved annual budget.

The pro rata contribution is composed of a per capita contribution per insurer of CHF 1000 as well as a proportional contribution. After deduction of the per capita contribution from the annual budget, the remainder of the annual budget is distributed in the ratio of the gross premium income of the respective insurer to the total gross premium income of all affiliated insurance companies. Phrased differently,

[21] Switzerland has four national languages: German, French, Italian and Romansh.

the Ombudsman Scheme is financed through a solidarity-based system of contribution.

From the outset, it was clear that the objective of the Insurance Ombudsman Scheme to offer consumers an efficient and more accessible way to present their complaints would not be fulfilled if case fees were levied. Hence, the Ombudsman Scheme has been offering its services free of charge for more than fifty years.

In summary, the "Ombudsman of Private Insurance and Suva" Foundation is an industry-funded scheme. Its services, which are provided free of charge, are entirely funded by the insurers through a levy system that varies in accordance with the size of the individual insurance business, but it does not take into account the respective number of cases involving the individual insurer that the Insurance Ombudsman Service has had to handle.

14.1.7 Insurance Ombudsman Functions

Consumers seeking to use the assistance provided by the Insurance Ombudsman Service have wide-ranging needs and varying levels of knowledge with regard to insurance matters. Accordingly, on a conceptual level, the Ombudsman Service has to fulfil a wide array of functions. Providing impartial resolution of individual disputes in connection with and arising out of private insurance contracts is obviously the primary duty of the Insurance Ombudsman Service. However, dealing with complaints and enquiries also entails giving dispute-related advice to consumers. Managing the consumers' expectations and helping them understand the reasons why their complaint might not be valid, is a further crucial function of this Ombudsman Scheme and its staff.

Through the handling of complaints, insights into where things can go wrong are gained, too. Such insights can be of significant importance to insurance businesses. This is the reason why the ombudsperson is committed to sharing relevant information, thereby helping insurers to prevent future problems. When meeting members of the executive management or other direct contacts in the insurance businesses, the office holder shares anonymised data that shows the number of cases the Scheme has handled in the various insurance fields and the key trends in complaints. In addition, the ombudsperson provides advice on how to improve customer relationships and insurance claims management procedures.

According to the Foundation's regulations, the Insurance Ombudsman Service does not have a duty to impart knowledge to consumers. This does not mean that the staff members of this Ombudsman Service will not provide advice to consumers in relation to the specific handling of their disputes. However, it is important to mention that the provision of insurance consulting services is expressly precluded under the Foundation's regulations.

Although it is not the Insurance Ombudsman Service's role to educate consumers, the office holder may indirectly help consumers to become more financially literate. For example, in media appearances and in the annual report, the ombudsperson regularly raises important questions and provides recommendations that they deem useful for consumers. This includes things such as what to consider before concluding a life insurance contract.

The Insurance Ombudsman Service also tries to encourage early resolution. To support consumers who are uncertain about how to complain about an insurance business, the Ombudsman Service has set up a customer helpline. This helpline is primarily used to assess whether a complaint falls within the Ombudsman Service's remit or to explain the procedure. However, the Ombudsman Service's early assistance team are often also able to give advice on how consumers can get their complaints resolved before they escalate further.

Moreover, efforts have been made to publish concise case studies on the organisation's website and in the annual reports.[22] The latter also include recommendations with regard to the chosen case studies. Some of the published examples and recommendations contain business-relevant information about how to prevent specific disputes, others have an informative and educative character. We assume that such information can help interested consumers and insurance representatives to resolve disputes at an early stage.

As mentioned earlier, training consumers and financial service providers is not included within the Insurance Ombudsman Service's scope of responsibility. The ombudsperson is nevertheless occasionally invited by academic institutions to give a guest lecture on alternative dispute resolution or on issues in insurance law and to provide practical advice.

14.1.8 Insurance Ombudsman Office

The ombudsperson is the managing director of the "Ombudsman of Private Insurance and of Suva" Foundation. They manage the head office in the German-speaking part of Switzerland. The representatives of the two regional offices—in the French and Italian-speaking parts of Switzerland—report to the ombudsperson. The representatives of the regional offices ensure that all linguistic groups are able to access the Scheme's services.

The ombudsperson has the primary responsibility for the Insurance Ombudsman Service's mediation activities. The process by which the Service deals with complaints is based on the so-called "four-eyes principle" (dual control). This means that the ombudsperson approves correspondence with the customer or the insurer, which ensures that a fair complaints management process as well as high-quality service is provided.

In addition to the ombudsperson, three experienced lawyers (3.3 full time equivalents, hereinafter FTE) handle complaints raised by German-speaking, and where

[22] Stiftung Ombudsman der Privatversicherung und der Suva. For details, see https://insuranceombudsman.ch/case-studies/. Accessed 16 Apr 2025; for annual reports in German or French, see https://versicherungsombudsman.ch/ueber-uns/. Accessed 16 Apr 2025.

necessary, English-speaking consumers at the head office. The head office's intake and early assistance team consists of two non-lawyers (1.4 FTE). They are the first point of contact for consumers who wish to refer their complaint to the Ombudsman Service. They determine whether complaints fall within the Insurance Ombudsman Scheme's jurisdiction. In addition to gathering complaint data and setting up cases, they look after customer communication standards, projects to raise public awareness of the Service's activities, data and statistics as well as the day-to-day running of the office.

In summary, the "Ombudsman of Private Insurance and Suva" Foundation employs 6 (4 FTE) legal case analysts, including the ombudsperson and the two regional representatives. The Ombudsman Service's case analysts all have a legal education and have additionally passed the bar examination.

Furthermore, the Foundation's training budget ensures that the Ombudsman Service's employees can develop their skill sets. The case analysts, for instance, regularly attend conferences on insurance law and other expert meetings.

14.2 Insurance Ombudsman Jurisdiction

14.2.1 Substantive Scope

The regulations of the "Ombudsman of Private Insurance and of Suva" Foundation lay down the jurisdiction of the Insurance Ombudsman Scheme. The Scheme has (voluntary) jurisdiction over the activities of affiliated insurance businesses. In other words: it covers complaints about the activities of insurance businesses that are domiciled in Switzerland and subject to Swiss law.

More specifically, the Insurance Ombudsman Service can consider a complaint if it relates to the Insurance Contract Act (VVG), the Accident Insurance Act (UVG) or to pension schemes. The latter includes both pension plans in the form of life insurance policies (VVG) or affiliation to collective foundations offered by insurance companies for occupational benefits plans (BVG). Finally, the Service can consider a complaint if it relates to a mortgage loan contract with an insurance business for owner-occupied residential property.

According to the regulations of the Foundation,[23] the Service is authorised to:

- obtain relevant information from the involved insurer.
- obtain documentation from the insurer on condition that the customer is unable to do so.
- request a written statement by the involved insurer.
- make mediation proposals.

[23] See Stiftung Ombudsman der Privatversicherung und der Suva (2022), p. 1. https://versicherungsombudsman.ch/wp-content/uploads/2021/06/OM-reglement-de.pdf. Accessed 16 Apr 2025.

- seek an expert's opinion in cases that are of considerable importance and affect large numbers of insured people.
- inform the complainant about the insurer's position. If the Service's intervention proves unsuccessful, it may confirm, where necessary, their opposite point of view and advise the complainant to contact a lawyer and take legal action. The insurer will be informed about the recommendation.

In contrast, the Ombudsman Service does not have jurisdiction to consider certain complaints, such as disputes currently pending before court or those that have already been dealt with by a court. To understand the substantive scope of the Service's jurisdiction, it also seems worth mentioning the areas over which the Service lacks jurisdiction. Pursuant to the regulations of the Foundation,[24] the following types of complaints fall outside the Service's jurisdiction:

- Matters concerning the insurance companies' business policies.
- Complaints for which the supervisory authorities are responsible.
- When court action is already ongoing or when an accident insurer has issued a formal decision (*Verfügung*) pursuant to the Accident Insurance Act (UVG).

The Foundation's regulations do not define the activities covered by the Insurance Ombudsman Service. At the risk of oversimplification, we may distinguish three categories of activities addressed by the Service. First, claims handling and resulting disagreements about the extent of cover, the amount of a claim, appropriate handling of third-party claims and so on. Second, information provided during contract negotiations and resulting disagreements about underinsurance, policy term and so on. Third, administration and resulting complaints about processing time, billing and so on.

Generally speaking, our Ombudsman Service deals with complaints in relation to and arising out of existing insurance contracts. However, there is one exception: if the ombudsperson deems that a recently concluded insurance contract does not meet the conditions to be considered legally valid, they may intervene with the insurance business. Despite this, it is important to stress that it is not the task of the Ombudsman Service to support consumers in contract negotiations.

Freedom of contract is rather extensive under Swiss law. As a result, an insurer cannot be compelled to conclude a contract. Questions of discrimination are occasionally raised by people seeking to utilise the Service. They are mainly raised in the context of premium pricing. This is the reason why consumers who feel they have been wronged are advised to contact the supervisory authority (*Eidgenössische Finanzmarktaufsicht* (FINMA)). It is the task of the supervisory authority to protect policyholders from malpractice by their insurance providers.[25]

---

[24] Stiftung Ombudsman der Privatversicherung und der Suva (2022), p. 2. https://versicherungsombudsman.ch/wp-content/uploads/2021/06/OM-reglement-de.pdf. Accessed 16 Apr 2025.

[25] Further complaints that are examined by the supervisory authority and, therefore, fall outside the Ombudsman's jurisdiction concern questions regarding the calculation of surrender values of life insurance policies.

The final aspects of the Insurance Ombudsman Service's substantive scope to be discussed here are the handling of enquiries and claim limits. Our Service primarily deals with disputes and strives to provide a fair and effective treatment of complaints. Even though dispute resolution is a key function of the Service, it also handles enquiries made by consumers who wish to obtain an independent second opinion. Typically, such enquiries focus on questions as to whether the insurer has acted correctly.

As we noted earlier, the Foundation's goal is to provide an easily accessible platform for consumers. As a consequence, the amount of a claim is not a jurisdictional criterion. The Insurance Ombudsman Service handles both low-value complaints and disputes involving high-cost claims as long as the complaint is considered to be appropriate for the Service's complaints handling process. While the disputed amount of a claim is irrelevant, the question of whether the dispute can be resolved effectively within the Ombudsman Scheme's framework for the assessment of a complaint is crucial. If the ombudsperson is of the opinion that the subject matter of the complaint should better be dealt with by a lawyer or by a court, the complaint will not be considered. A victim of a car accident whose injuries may have long-lasting effects and whose complaint addresses, on the one hand, issues involving several insurers—such as third-party liability insurance, invalidity insurance, accident insurance, occupational pension scheme etc.—and, on the other, questions regarding compensation for pain and suffering is a typical example. This demonstrates that our swift dispute resolution methods are inadequate for addressing the complexity and multifaceted nature of such complaints, which require sustained case monitoring.

14.2.2 *Personal Scope*

As discussed above, accessibility for consumers plays a central role. An attempt to define eligible complainants is therefore necessary. Basically, any directly affected private individual or small business may submit a complaint to the Insurance Ombudsman Service. However, under the Foundation's regulations, the Service may not deal with a case if a specialist (i.e. lawyer, legal protection insurance or insurance consultant) is involved.[26] Moreover, the Service cannot handle complaints submitted by a rival insurance business or the media, rather than by the claimant personally. Finally, a third restriction concerns businesses and institutions that possess a legal service. The impetus for the creation of this Service was a yearning to assist lay persons. By implication, the Insurance Ombudsman Service was never intended to provide free support to remunerated providers of legal aid.

[26] Stiftung Ombudsman der Privatversicherung und der Suva (2022), p. 2. https://versicherungsombudsman.ch/wp-content/uploads/2021/06/OM-reglement-de.pdf. Accessed 16 Apr 2025.

On the other hand, the Ombudsman Scheme only covers insurance businesses which are affiliated with the "Ombudsman of Private Insurance and of Suva" Foundation. More specifically, the Scheme has jurisdiction over activities performed by insurance companies and their insurance agents. By contrast, the Scheme does not cover issues arising from the work of insurance brokers (i.e. non-tied insurance intermediaries).

14.2.3 Territorial Scope

The territorial scope of the Insurance Ombudsman Scheme's jurisdiction covers complaints about activities of insurance companies domiciled in Switzerland. The respective insurance contracts governing the activities must be subject to Swiss law. There are no jurisdictional restrictions with regard to the residence of a complainant. The Ombudsman Service is open to anyone living in Switzerland or abroad.

14.2.4 Time Limits

The regulations of the Foundation do not specify a time limit for referring a complaint to the Insurance Ombudsman Service. However, it should be pointed out that limitation periods under Swiss law determine the extent of the Service's involvement. The Ombudsman Service staff are trained to identify risks pertaining to the limitation or prescription periods, ensuring that these do not expire during the ombudsman procedure.

14.3 Procedure

14.3.1 Regulatory Framework

The regulations of the "Ombudsman or Private Insurance and of Suva" Foundation set out the purpose of the scheme and define both the extent of its jurisdiction and the procedural rules. The Foundation Board issues, and where necessary, amends the regulations and reports them to the supervisory authority of foundations (ESA).

Hence, the procedural rules are set by the Board of the Foundation. This is set out succinctly in the Swiss Foundation Code: "The foundation board is a foundation's ultimate governing body. It is responsible for the foundation's activities, and acts under its own responsibility. It does not administer the foundation, it governs it."[27]

---

[27] Sprecher et al. (2021), p. 59.

By specifying the organisational structures and the procedural rules of the Insurance Ombudsman Scheme, the Foundation Board ensures that the Foundation's purpose is implemented effectively. A corollary of this is that the ombudsperson cannot replace or change the procedural rules.[28]

Although it is worth underlining the role of the Foundation Board, it is equally important to note that the regulations ensure transparency with regard to the Ombudsman Service's procedure. It is for this reason that the regulations are available on the organisation's website.[29]

14.3.2 Complaint and Enquiry Handling Process

14.3.2.1 Complaints Handling Process

The Ombudsman Service's complaints handling process entails a number of organised steps. These include the assessment and review of complaints, the provision of advice and mediation. The three stages of the Ombudsman Service's complaints handling process will be described in general terms below. In order not to complicate matters, we will focus on the handling of written complaints. Although consumers may call our office to understand, for example, the scope of our service or our complaint handling procedures, they cannot submit their complaint by telephone or in person. In other words, the complaints handling process described below begins once the Service receives a complaint either by mail or via the electronic form on our website.

Preliminary Steps or Initial Assessment

The Insurance Ombudsman Service takes seriously all of the complaints and enquiries that are submitted. It uses an electronic end-to-end case management system. This digital case management system assigns individual complaint reference numbers and keeps all of the correspondence and related documents in an individual file. The advantages of such case management systems are that every step and decision in the complaints handling process is recorded. In addition, its deadline management supports the Ombudsman Service's goal of resolving complaints efficiently and effectively, of keeping complainants regularly updated and of ensuring that complaint resolution is not delayed by any staff absences. Finally, the software produces data for analysing complaint trends.

Upon receipt of a written complaint, the first task is to determine whether the complaint falls within the Ombudsman Scheme's jurisdiction. Hence, the intake

[28] However, the ombudsperson may submit a proposal to modify the regulations to the Foundation Board.

[29] For more information see https://insuranceombudsman.ch/about-us/. Accessed 16 Apr 2025.

team examine the complaint and any supporting information and documents that were sent with it in order to decide whether there is jurisdiction to consider the complaint. Even though complaints are initially assessed by the intake team, it should be noted that it is the ombudsperson's responsibility to determine that a complaint cannot be considered either because it falls outside the Scheme's jurisdiction or—in rare cases—because it is no longer suitable for mediation due to an advanced stage of conflict escalation, i.e. when both parties have hardened their positions.

When the complaint cannot be considered because it does not fall within the Scheme's jurisdiction, the complainant is promptly informed about the reasons for the rejection. Where appropriate, we try to offer advice regarding other ADR schemes, legal aid offices or any other alternative means to resolve the complaint.

Some complaints are not considered because they are premature. Consumers whose complaints are premature, are asked to contact the insurance company in a first instance so that it has an opportunity to respond to the complaint before our Ombudsman Service reviews the case.

Further Assessment and Mediation

Once it has been determined that a complaint falls within our jurisdiction, the Ombudsman Service's case analysts move on to the next stage. The first priority at this fact-finding stage is to discern whether further documents or information are required to examine the complaint. As the quality of complaint files varies greatly, the initial stages of our Service's complaints handling process often involve writing to the complainant in order to request further documents or general information on the case. It is only in exceptional cases that the Service contacts the involved insurer to receive missing documents. This is done to give practical assistance to complainants who face severe challenges with communication.

After the fact-finding phase has been completed, the legal case analysts are required to consider insurance law and case law when assessing the complaint. Depending on the circumstances of the complaint, other fields of law (e.g. road traffic law), and reflections on what might seem fair and reasonable, may also have to be taken into account. This stage of the complaints handling process is designed to evaluate the facts and decide whether the complaint has merit. Consideration is also given to the outcome that may be achieved through a mediation process. Once this assessment has been completed, two options are available. At this stage, the case analyst may either decide that it is not appropriate to continue to consider the complaint or to move on to a voluntary dispute resolution process, i.e. mediation. In conformance with the dual control mentioned previously, the case analyst's decision has to be approved by the ombudsperson.

When deciding not to consider the complaint any further, the case analyst informs the consumer in writing and sets out the grounds for the decision. Care is taken to provide detailed information to the complainant about the reasons for why there is no prospect of a successful mediation process. Reasons for refusing to continue to consider a complaint may include that the complaint has no merit (e.g. the insurer has acted correctly, or the consumer has unreasonable expectations respectively), or that it is unfounded (e.g. the complainant does not have evidence to support his or her version of the facts).

It should be emphasised that the insurance company involved is not notified that the Ombudsman Service has received a complaint which was not given further consideration. Confidentiality plays an important role in our conflict resolution process. The corollary of this is that the complaint is only brought to the knowledge of the insurer when the case analyst decides to initiate a mediation procedure. The complainant's agreement to take part in such a procedure is of course required. Therefore, the electronic form provided by the Service to consumers who wish to submit a complaint, contains a consent form. In other words, the Ombudsman Service never acts without the complainant's permission.

If the case analyst identifies a problem or a service failure, we will begin a mediation process. The term used for this process is "intervention". The modalities of an intervention may be described as follows. First and foremost, an intervention is an informal and voluntary dispute resolution method. In this process, it is crucial that the Ombudsman Service does not represent either side. Rather, the Service explores solutions impartially. The outcome of this mediation process is not binding nor can it be appealed. A mediation strategy premised on impartiality, fairness and equality must also be applied to verify that individual cases are handled according to the same method. For this reason, all interventions, including those which are written by the representatives of the two regional offices, have to be approved by the ombudsperson.

When the Ombudsman Service decides to intervene, we notify our contact partner of the insurance business concerned in writing. The Service's contact partners mostly fulfil a management function that enables them to make decisions and to solve problems. An intervention by the Service contains an assessment of the complaint along with reasons warranting the intervention. In addition, the documents that were provided by the complainant will be transferred to the insurer. Once notified, the Service expects a written reply from the insurer within four to six weeks.

Conclusion of Mediation

Many complaints are resolved as a result of the Insurance Ombudsman Service's intervention. Our Ombudsman Service's intervention success rate is approximately 65 percent. The vast majority of cases (85 percent) can be closed after one intervention. Should the insurer's response not be satisfactory, the Service may decide to intervene a second time, and in very rare cases a third time.

Upon completion of the aforementioned intervention process, the complainant is informed of its outcome. If the complaint can be resolved either fully or partially and the proposed solution is deemed acceptable by the complainant, the Service will inform both parties that a mediated settlement has been reached and that the case will be closed.

If the Ombudsman Service's intervention fails to resolve the complaint, both parties will be notified. It goes without saying that in such cases the complainant expects a comprehensive account, including the reasons for why the complaint could not be resolved.

The reasons for unsuccessful interventions are manifold. In some cases, mediation fails because the documents or information provided by the complainant prove to be incomplete or inaccurate. In other cases, the insurer concerned does not share the ombudsperson's legal interpretation. Due to the Insurance Ombudsman Scheme's informal mediation strategy, the Ombudsman Service can only strive for solutions which are mutually acceptable to both parties. As a consequence, if despite several interventions the involved insurer does not share the ombudsperson's legal interpretation, we sometimes advise the complainant to take further legal action and notify the insurer of this recommendation.

One final point in our intervention process needs further clarification. Namely that even if the matter cannot be resolved through mediation, it is generally accepted that a complaint to the Insurance Ombudsman Service should never result in a deterioration of the complainant's position, unless the re-examination of the case reveals fraudulent behaviour on the part of the consumer.

14.3.2.2 Form

As indicated above, the Insurance Ombudsman Service's interventions consist of informal mediation procedures. Despite this, there are some key elements in our complaints handling process, which formalise the mediation process to a certain extent.

In accordance with the established procedure, insurance companies affiliated with the Foundation are required to designate a contact person. The ombudsperson expects this individual to undertake managerial responsibilities. One immediate implication of this precondition is that the contact person's function in itself entails that they were in all likelihood not involved in any of the procedures that have given rise to the complaint. Another advantage is that the involvement of a contact person with sufficient decision-making capacity renders the mediation process more efficient. Furthermore, the ombudsperson expects to receive a written reply to an intervention within four to six weeks. Finally, the insurer's written statement is expected to adhere to high standards of quality, including the incorporation of an assessment of the complaint and substantiated arguments.

14.3.2.3 Ex officio Proceedings

The Insurance Ombudsman Service acts on request of a consumer and initiates an intervention only upon the receipt of individual complaints filed by natural persons or legal entities. Hence, at the centre of any mediation effort is a specific and well-documented complaint. Nevertheless, it is precisely the informal character of the

Ombudsman Scheme's mediation procedure that allows the ombudsperson to draw an insurance company's attention to general issues, thereby contributing to the improvement of the services it provides.

14.3.2.4 Collective Proceedings

As pointed out earlier in this chapter, the Insurance Ombudsman Service's task is to resolve specific conflicts between individuals and insurance companies. Yet, on the other hand, we have also suggested that our Service's informal dispute resolution system enables us to adapt to particular circumstances. A good example to illustrate this point is that of the collective interventions taken during the COVID-19 pandemic. They paved the way for amicable solutions for thousands of businesses in the restaurant industry which, despite holding epidemic insurance, had not received compensation from their insurers for the losses incurred during the closure of business imposed by the government.[30]

The aforementioned example allows us to briefly summarise the general requirements for collective interventions. The type of conflict and the questions they raise should be of considerable importance and significantly affect many people. Although our Ombudsman Service can resort to collective interventions as a dispute-handling method, it should be stressed that it is only chosen in exceptional circumstances.

14.3.2.5 Complaint Intake

As the preceding description of the Insurance Ombudsman Service's complaints handling process shows, interventions cannot be carried out unless the Ombudsman's office receives a written complaint and supporting documents. Nevertheless, easy access to our Service is provided by offering an electronic form for complaint submissions on our website. Alternatively, consumers can download a complaint form, which can be used to submit a complaint by regular post. The benefits of providing an electronic point of access are that it helps consumers to structure their complaints, to submit sufficient documentation and to consent to the mediation procedure.[31]

Even though the Ombudsman Service can only intervene upon request from a consumer who submits a complaint in writing, the importance of telephone calls should not be minimised. The first point of contact that customers have with the Ombudsman's office is still by telephone. While many customers call our office to understand the nature of the services we provide, the majority obviously also wish to obtain a preliminary assessment of their complaints. If the staff members can give

---

[30] Stiftung Ombudsman der Privatversicherung und Suva (2021), pp. 8–9. https://versicherungsombudsman.ch/wp-content/uploads/2021/07/OM-Jahresbericht_2020.pdf. Accessed 16 Apr 2025.

[31] Complainants lacking basic digital skills may send their complaints by regular post.

advice to solve the issues the complaint raises without paperwork, they try to help customers to resolve their complaints on their own. The advantage of this facilitative approach is that it allows for an efficient complaints handling process. The disadvantage is that we cannot determine the success rate of this early settlement stage. Naturally, a customer whose complaint cannot be resolved by telephone may still approach the Ombudsman Service in writing and apply for a standard intervention process.

14.3.2.6 Limitation Periods

Submitting a complaint to the Insurance Ombudsman Service does not interrupt or suspend any legal time limits. Complainants whose claims raise questions with regard to statutory limitations are advised to take the necessary steps. If the limitation period for a claim is near its expiry, we advise the complainant to immediately obtain a waiver of the limitation period from the insurer or to initiate legal action. It hardly needs mentioning that disputes relating to time-barred claims cannot be considered by the Ombudsman Service.

14.3.2.7 Enquiry Handling Process

Our understanding of an enquiry is that it is a situation in which the consumer asks the Insurance Ombudsman Service for a second opinion. In contrast to a complaint against an insurer, an enquiry simply prompts the Ombudsman Service to examine whether an insurer's decision was correct. Our Service handles enquiries and complaints in like manner. Should our case analysts come to a different conclusion, we will intervene and attempt to resolve the issue by presenting our own point of view to the insurance business involved.

In spite of this, it should be emphasised that for enquires and complaints alike, the Ombudsman Service can only conduct an examination based on the facts provided by the complainant on the one hand and on the legal situation on the other. As a consequence, the Ombudsman Service staff cannot seek, for instance, medical expert advice to determine whether a complainant's incapacity to work was correctly contested by a daily sickness insurance. Additionally, they are not in a position to assist the complainant in gathering further evidence.

14.3.3 Admissible Complaints

The Foundation's regulations do not include a definition of a complaint. However, taking as a starting point the Oxford English Dictionary's definition of a complaint as a "statement that somebody makes saying that they are not satisfied",[32] one might describe the complaints addressed to the Insurance Ombudsman Service as a consumer's expression of dissatisfaction with the quality of service provided by an insurance business. Looking at the complaints handling procedure from this perspective, it becomes clear that eligible complainants are individual people or small businesses who are directly affected by an insurance business's actions. Accordingly, we can only consider complaints submitted by insured persons, policyholders, beneficiaries or injured third parties. As mentioned earlier, mandated specialists such as lawyers, legal-protection insurers or insurance consultants are excluded from the definition of eligible complainant.

In order to be considered admissible, a complaint must be lodged in writing and based on documented evidence. It is needless to say that the complaint must fall within the remit of the Insurance Ombudsman Scheme. As pointed out earlier, the amount of a claim is not an admissibility criterion.

It is important to note, though, that consumers are required to first try to resolve their complaints with the insurer on their own. The first step, therefore, is to contact the insurance business in writing. If the issues remain unresolved, the complaint can be taken further to the Ombudsman Service, on condition that the business has provided a written explanation.

There is no institutionalised process defining the rules or time limits to consider during this stage of complaints handling by insurance businesses. Nevertheless, the Ombudsman Service may intervene without proceeding through the standard mediation process if the insurance business involved appears to delay the procedure unnecessarily. Moreover, if a dispute must be resolved quickly due to time limits or certain circumstances, the Service may also choose a more flexible approach to resolve the complaint.

Finally, the Ombudsman Service may dismiss a complaint without considering its merits if the dispute is pending before a court, if a legal deadline has begun to run, if the complainant has given an explicit mandate to a lawyer or insurance specialist, or if the complainant does not comply with our request to send us further information or documents.

[32] Oxford Advanced Learner's Dictionary (2005).

14.3.4 Obtaining Information and Collecting Evidence

In order to conduct an independent review of the complaint, the consumer is asked to submit the evidence and information we deem necessary to form our own opinion. The burden of proof falls on the complainant. When the effort demanded seems to be unreasonable, the Ombudsman Service may also contact the insurer involved to obtain documents.

Access to documents is an area that is particularly important for the independence of the Insurance Ombudsman Scheme's mediation procedure. While the complaint form mentioned above authorises us to contact the involved insurer and request copies of case files, access to sensitive documents is only demanded if the complainant expressly authorises us to do so.

Despite the fact that it is of vital importance that we have access to all of the information relating to a complaint, our Ombudsman Service does not have any powers of investigation. In other words, the Service cannot ask a third party to supply evidence.

As pointed out in Sect. 14.2.1, under the regulations of the Foundation, the Insurance Ombudsman Service may request access to documents from the insurer. This means that requests for access to documents are part and parcel of the mediation process. To date, insurance businesses have never refused access to documents despite the informal character of the Ombudsman Service's mediation procedure.

Moreover, the processing of personal data carried out by, amongst others, legal entities and private individuals is governed by the Swiss Data Protection Act (*Datenschutzgesetz*, hereinafter DSG).[33] Pursuant to art. 25 DSG, the data subject has a right to information. In addition, the affected person has a right to have their personal data transferred to another data controller under art. 28(2) DSG. As indicated earlier, written consent by complainants is a prerequisite for the Insurance Ombudsman Service to obtain any personal data.

14.3.5 Outcome of the Process

Given the informal mediation process described above, the ombudsperson can only express an opinion. When a mediated settlement can be reached, the ombudsperson provides a legal assessment of the proposed solution. It is then up to the complainant to accept or reject the solution offered. In the latter case, the complainant may continue to pursue the complaint through other avenues.

If the complaint cannot be resolved because the insurance business involved does not share our view, the ombudsperson may advise the complainant to take further

[33] For details, see Fedlex, Die Publikationsplattform des Bundesrechts (2023). https://www.fedlex.admin.ch/eli/cc/2022/491/de. Accessed 16 Apr 2025.

legal steps. The insurance business will be informed about the recommendation given to the consumer.

If the insurance company's reply to the Insurance Ombudsman Service's intervention reveals evidence which raises questions as to the merits of the complaint, we will notify the complainant in writing that the outcome they were seeking does not seem justified or legally enforceable and that, as a result, the mediation procedure will be discontinued.

14.3.6 Insurance Ombudsman Decision

The ombudsperson does not have any executive powers. This absence of decision-making capacities restricts the Ombudsman Service's interventions to the presentation of its legal assessment of the complaint, or the elaboration of a recommendation.

Phrased differently, the opinions and recommendations expressed in the Ombudsman Service's interventions do not have a binding character and cannot be appealed. Yet, it bears repeating that our Service enjoys a high level of acceptance among insurance businesses and consumers.

Regardless of the Ombudsman Scheme's informal mediation procedure, our Ombudsman Service has to meet certain complaints handling standards. Apart from considering insurance law and jurisprudence, the Ombudsman Service should, for instance, strive for a fair and just outcome for both sides. As there is often an imbalance of power and knowledge between the two parties, our Ombudsman Service is also committed to transparency and to informing consumers about their rights. Finally, we firmly believe that good complaints handling procedures must ensure that all complaints are dealt with in a fair and unbiased manner.

The Ombudsman Service is competent to address issues that arise from the activities of insurance businesses that are subject to Swiss law. However, complaints that are subject to foreign law do not fall within the remit of the Ombudsman Scheme. Having said that, some complaints may arise as a result of, for instance, a Swiss driver's problems with a foreign motor third party liability insurance. In such cases, our Ombudsman Service can try to accelerate the procedure under the condition that the competent claims handler is a Swiss insurance business. Another example is that of complaints that arise in connection with agreements between Switzerland and neighbouring countries for cross-border workers.

To recapitulate, due to the informal mediation procedure, the ombudsperson does not have any decision-making authority or individual redress powers. Hence, the ombudsperson's opinions and recommendations are not enforceable by the courts. Moreover, our Ombudsman Service's activities are not overseen by the courts.

14.4 Statistical Data

The Swiss Insurance Ombudsman Service receives an average of 3,000 complaints and enquiries per year. The number of enquiries received via telephone calls is approximately 1800. The yearly average of complaints received via completed web-forms and letters is 1200.

Out of these 1200 written complaints, around 200 have to be declined because they are outside the Ombudsman Scheme's jurisdiction. This leaves us with a total of 1000 complaints that are covered by the Scheme. An average of 150 complaints are immediately discontinued because they are manifestly unfounded. An additional 50 cases are discontinued because the complainant does not wish to pursue the complaint, or because the complainant fails to provide the required information within a reasonable period of time.

The initial stages of the Ombudsman Service's complaints handling procedure bring the total to 800 complaints requiring an in-depth examination. Following a detailed assessment of complaints, an average of 500 complaints are considered to have no merit and will, thus, not be given further consideration. Approximately 300 complaints result in interventions with the relevant insurance business.

The average processing time of an intervention is between four and six weeks. It should be noted though that the average time to resolve disputes varies greatly depending on the type of complaint. One of the principal reasons for lengthy processing times is the limited capacity of the involved insurance company's medical officers to provide opinions on medical questions that certain complaints raise.

When reporting on the number of complaints that are resolved per year, it is important to interrogate what is meant. As mentioned earlier, in 300 cases the Ombudsman Service seeks to resolve the complaint through an intervention. This number does not take into account the complaints that are resolved at an early stage. The Ombudsman Service does not collect statistical data on the number of complaints which may have been resolved as a result of the Service's initial assessment of the complaint. Furthermore, complainants rarely inform the Service of a positive outcome they may have achieved subsequently.

The Ombudsman Service records successful mediations in its statistics. On average the Service's interventions result in the satisfactory resolution of 65 percent of complaints. The outcome of a small number of complaints (around 5 percent) is recorded as "neutral". The Service considers the outcome to be neutral if the intervention merely consisted of demanding access to information, if the complaint was withdrawn and so on. In approximately 25 percent of cases, either the insurance business involved does not agree with the ombudsperson's opinion, or the insurance company's response to an intervention reveals no error in how they handled the complainant's matter.

Although it is difficult to effectively measure the success of our Ombudsman Service, we believe that the considerable intervention success rate (65 percent) reveals a high degree of willingness on the part of insurance companies to resolve complaints amicably, provided that the legal situation and the particular circumstances of the case permit a mediated settlement.

Last but not least, a large majority of complaints are resolved with the agreement of the complainant. Notwithstanding the fact that the Ombudsman Service collects and analyses data pertaining to the cases and complaints that it handles, the percentage of positive responses to the total number of proposals made to consumers is not recorded.

14.5 Insurance Ombudsman Practice

14.5.1 Market Trends

Over the last few years, the Ombudsman Service's activities have primarily focused on personal insurance, which accounts for around 50 percent of the caseload. The largest number of complaints received by the Ombudsman Service concern compulsory accident insurance pursuant to the Accident Insurance Act (UVG) and daily sickness insurance pursuant to the Insurance Contract Act (VVG). This is mainly due to the fact that a suspension of daily allowance benefits can quickly bring about financial distress. Our services are particularly well suited for such complaints as they allow for a faster settlement and involve lower costs than court-based dispute resolution processes.

A high-risk area for consumers is that of unit-linked life insurance contracts. Policyholders of such contracts in particular can suffer losses. Unless their contract guarantees a minimum return on premiums paid, or a guaranteed survival benefit, the consumers bear all the investment risks.

When it comes to the approach taken by insurance businesses towards the Ombudsman Scheme, it can be said that insurers are aware that by providing a strict alternative to the use of courts, our Ombudsman Service has helped them avoid a number of expensive and time-consuming legal procedures. There is also recognition that the Ombudsman Scheme's informal and swift conflict-resolution methods tend to enhance consumer confidence and maintain consumer trust. Consequently, the insurers cooperate well. Their responses to interventions generally fulfil the quality standards expected by the ombudsperson.

14.5.2 Limitations

Since its creation in 1972, the "Ombudsman of Private Insurance and of Suva" Foundation has encountered a wide variety of needs on the part of complainants and has been able to adjust its complaints handling procedure accordingly. The regulations of the Foundation as well as the ombudsperson's right to request a modification of the regulations from the Foundation Board ensure that the Ombudsman Service can adapt to changing circumstances. In other words, the effective functioning of the Service within the framework of the purposes of the Foundation is not hindered.

Over the years, the Ombudsman Service staff have also developed a greater awareness of the complainants' individual needs. It is in the nature of things that the quality of complaints submitted can vary enormously. When assessing a complaint, our case analysts also take into account the complainant's financial literacy and their understanding of key financial concepts. It is, therefore, important that the Service's communicative efforts are designed to meet the complainants' needs. Notwithstanding its commitment to recognise and respond to such individual needs, the Service does not undertake statistical surveys of the consumers' financial awareness and literacy.

In the context of consumer literacy, it is important to note that the partial revision of the Insurance Contract Act (VVG), which entered into force on 1 January 2022, and the revised Insurance Supervision Act (VAG), which entered into force on 1 January 2024, contain some changes which are intended to cover the information requirements imposed on insurers and insurance intermediaries. These modifications are likely to improve financial literacy as the new duties to supply information to consumers should enhance their capabilities to understand financial information and ultimately enable them to make better decisions.

The Insurance Ombudsman Service is committed to efficiency and effectiveness. Being able to adapt to new circumstances is therefore very important. Currently, the Ombudsman Service faces many challenges connected to electronic methods of communication. The proliferation of information and communication technologies has transformed both customer expectations and the customer service provided by many insurance businesses. While these technologies have facilitated interaction between the insurer and the customer, a complaint submitted to the Service still must meet various criteria which ensure that it can be assessed effectively. As a result, some consumers find it difficult to gather the information required to lodge a complaint concerning an insurance product which they had purchased online, or to document text messages they had exchanged with the insurance business.

As a general rule, the ombudsperson tries to make informed decisions about adaption measures which also take into account cost benefits considerations.

14.6 Accessibility and Accountability

14.6.1 Accessibility

It is generally believed that the effectiveness of an Ombudsman Service can be measured by its accessibility.[34] Making our services accessible goes beyond offering them free of charge to consumers, including vulnerable customers. It also requires raising awareness and understanding of the Insurance Ombudsman Service's role in general. To ensure that consumers know that our Ombudsman Service exists and what to expect of it, we have taken various measures to raise awareness, such as improving the organisation's web presence, distributing leaflets in four languages to various organisations that offer legal aid, social counselling, or consumer advice.

Furthermore, we believe that accessibility is improved when our Ombudsman Scheme is well known to insurance businesses. The Insurance Ombudsman Service not only tries to raise awareness by distributing the annual report and other information materials such as leaflets, insurers are also encouraged to mention the Service in their general terms and conditions of insurance. Yet, for all that, insurers are not obliged to inform consumers about the option of complaining to the Ombudsman Service. Insurers voluntarily refer potential complainants to our Ombudsman Service.

When trying to offer a fair complaints handling service, it is also vital to accommodate the specific needs of different groups. Hence, the Insurance Ombudsman office offers its services in four languages and uses, where appropriate, jargon-free language to communicate with complainants. Consumers who are vulnerable because of issues relating to literacy, language or disability are advised to ask a relative or a carer to submit the complaint on their behalf.

Another method of ensuring accessibility is a strong online presence. While our website is user-friendly and uses language that is simple to understand, it is not entirely barrier-free. The multilingual website (www.insuranceombudsman.ch) provides comprehensive information about the role of the Insurance Ombudsman, about the service offered and about the complaints handling procedures. In contrast, our Ombudsman Service does not utilise social medial platforms for the dissemination of information regarding our services.

---

[34] The International Network of Financial Services Ombudsman Schemes (2014), p. 7 or the British and Irish Ombudsman Association (2007), p. 9; both consider accessibility to be one of the fundamental principles for an ombudsman scheme.

14.6.2 Accountability

The ombudsperson's annual report provides the Foundation Board, the insurance businesses, the media, and the interested public with an overview of the Ombudsman Service's activities. The Foundation is obliged to submit the annual report to the Federal Supervisory Authority for Foundations (ESA).

The annual report includes statistics on the number of complaints received and reviews the complaint trends. It contains a documentation of the Ombudsman Service's activities and reports on the cooperation with insurers in general. Moreover, it contains various case studies which provide insights into relevant issues as well as recommendations for insurers and consumers. The identities of the parties are not revealed.

The Insurance Ombudsman Scheme's budget is not published in the annual report. The budgeting process described in Sect. 14.1.6 has made clear that it is the Foundation Board which is responsible for the Scheme's financial management.

References

British and Irish Ombudsman Association (2007) Guide to Principles of Good Complaint Handling. https://www.ombudsmanassociation.org/sites/default/files/2021-03/BIOAGoodComplaintHandling.pdf

Broger R, Stiftung Ombudsman der Privatversicherung, Fondation Ombudsman de l'assurance privée (1972) Geschäftsstelle der Stiftung Ombudsmann der Privatversicherung (31 August 1972)

International Network of Financial Services Ombudsman Schemes INFO Network (2014) Effective Approaches to Fundamental Principles https://www.networkfso.org/resources/INFO-Network_Effective-approaches-to-fundamental-principles_September2014.pdf Accessed 22 Sep 2023

Nabholz Haidegger L (2000) Ombudsstellen von Anbieterorganisationen unter Berücksichtigung der Versicherungsbranche. In: Brunner A, Rehbinder M, Stauder B (eds) Jahrbuch des Konsumentenrechts 1999. Stämpfli Verlag AG, Bern, pp 119–128

Oxford Advanced Learner's Dictionary (2005) Oxford University Press, Oxford

Sprecher T, Egger P, von Schnurbein G (eds) (2021) Swiss foundation code principles and recommendations for the establishment and management of grant-making foundations. Stämpfli Verlag AG, Bern

Stiftung Ombudsman der Privatversicherung und der Suva (2021) Jahresbericht 2020. https://versicherungsombudsman.ch/wp-content/uploads/2021/07/OM-Jahresbericht_2020.pdf

Stiftung Ombudsman der Privatversicherung und der Suva (2022) Reglement für die Ombudsstelle. https://versicherungsombudsman.ch/wp-content/uploads/2021/06/OM-reglement-de.pdf

Von Moos L, Stiftung Ombudsman der Privatversicherung, Fondation Ombudsman de l'assurance privée (1972) Der Ombudsmann der Privatversicherer – Warum ein Ombudsmann? (23 August 1972)

MIX
Papier aus verantwortungsvollen Quellen
Paper from responsible sources
FSC® C105338

If you have any concerns about our products,
you can contact us on
ProductSafety@springernature.com

In case Publisher is established outside the EU,
the EU authorized representative is:
Springer Nature Customer Service Center GmbH
Europaplatz 3, 69115 Heidelberg, Germany

Printed by Libri Plureos GmbH
in Hamburg, Germany